The Arts of the North American Indian

ESSAYS BY

Marvin Cohodas

Norman Feder

Christian Feest

Wolfgang Haberland

Jamake Highwater

Gerhard Hoffman

Bill Holm

J. C. H. King

Evan M. Maurer

Rennard Strickland

William C. Sturtevant

Edwin L. Wade

John Anson Warner

Gloria A. Young

The Arts of the North American Indian

Native Traditions in Evolution

Edited by Edwin L. Wade

Carol Haralson
COORDINATING EDITOR

Hudson Hills Press, New York

IN ASSOCIATION WITH PHILBROOK ART CENTER, TULSA

First Edition

© 1986 by Philbrook Art Center.
All rights reserved under International
and Pan-American Copyright Conventions.

Published in the United States by Hudson Hills Press, Inc.,
Suite 1308, 230 Fifth Avenue, New York, NY 10001-7704.

Distributed in Canada by Irwin Publishing Inc.
Distributed in the United Kingdom, Eire, Europe, Israel,
and the Middle East by Phaidon Press Limited.
Distributed in Japan by Yohan
(Western Publications Distribution Agency).

Editor and Publisher: Paul Anbinder
Copy Editor: Eve Sinaiko
Designer: Christopher Holme
Index: Gisela S. Knight
Composition: U.S. Lithograph Inc.
Manufactured in Japan by Toppan Printing Company

Library of Congress Cataloguing-in-Publication Data
Main entry under title:

The Arts of the North American Indian.

    "Published in association with Philbrook Art Center,
Tulsa."
    Bibliography: p.
    Includes index.
    1. Indians of North America—Art—Addresses, essays, lectures.
I. Wade, Edwin L.
E98.A7A78   1986   704'.0397   85-21932
ISBN 0-933920-55-5 (alk. paper)

Contents

List of Illustrations   7

Foreword   10
The Honorable George Patterson Nigh
Governor of Oklahoma

William C. Douce
Chairman of the Board of Directors and Chief Executive Officer, Retired,
Phillips Petroleum Company

Fred Myers
Director, Thomas Gilcrease Institute of American History and Art, Tulsa, Oklahoma

Preface   11
Marcia Y. Manhart
Executive Director, Philbrook Art Center, Tulsa, Oklahoma

Acknowledgments   13

Introduction: What Is Native American Art?   15

I. MEANING   21
The Meanings of Native American Art   23
William C. Sturtevant
Department of Anthropology, National Museum of Natural History, Smithsonian Institution,
Washington, D.C.

Aesthetic Archives: The Visual Language of Plains Ledger Art   45
Gloria A. Young
Coordinator of Research and Special Projects, Philbrook Art Center, Tulsa, Oklahoma

II. TRADITION   63
Tradition in Native American Art   65
J. C. H. King
Curator, Museum of Mankind, The British Museum, London

European Influences on Plains Indian Art   93
Norman Feder
Consultant Editor, American Indian Art Magazine, Sidney, British Columbia

III. AESTHETICS   105
Aesthetics in Native American Art   107
Wolfgang Haberland
Curator, Museum für Völkerkunde, Hamburg

The Dancing Headdress Frontlet:
Aesthetic Context on the Northwest Coast   133
Bill Holm
Curator, Thomas Burke Museum, University of Washington, Seattle

IV. QUALITY   141

Determining Quality in Native American Art   143
Evan M. Maurer
Director, University of Michigan Art Museum, Ann Arbor

Sculptural Arts of Native America   157
Christian Feest
Curator, Museum für Völkerkunde, Vienna

V. INDIVIDUALITY   169

The Individual in Native American Art: A Sociological View   171
John Anson Warner
Professor, University of Regina, Saskatchewan

Washoe Innovators and Their Patrons   203
Marvin Cohodas
Professor, University of British Columbia, Vancouver

VI. CONTROVERSY   221

Controversy in Native American Art   223
Jamake Highwater
New York

Straddling the Cultural Fence:
The Conflict for Ethnic Artists within Pueblo Societies   243
Edwin L. Wade
Curator, Non-European Art, Philbrook Art Center, Tulsa, Oklahoma

VII. THE FUTURE   255

Frames of Reference:
Native American Art in the Context of Modern and Postmodern Art   257
Gerhard Hoffman
Professor of American Studies, University of Würzburg, Würzburg

Tall Visitor at the Indian Gallery;
or, The Future of Native American Art   283
Rennard Strickland
Dean and Professor of Law, Southern Illinois University, Carbondale

Glossary   308

Bibliography   313

Index   318

Photographic and Illustration Credits   324

List of Illustrations

Colorplates are preceded by an asterisk (*)

CHAPTER I. MEANING

1. Bowl. Shinnecock   22
2. Peregrine falcon plate with man's head. Mississippian (Spiro Mounds)   24
3. Ceremonial wand. Mississippian   24
4. Ceremonial effigy axe. Mississippian (Spiro Mounds)   24
5. Ceremonial axe. Mississippian (Spiro Mounds)   24
6. Spiro mace. Mississippian (Spiro Mounds)   25
7. Ceremonial flint mace. Mississippian (Duck River)   25
8. Spatulate form. Mississippian (Spiro Mounds)   25
9. Buffalo effigy. Sioux or Cheyenne   26
10. Buffalo effigy. Sioux or Cheyenne   26
*11. Fetish and fetish bundle. Crow   27
12. Horse stick. Plains   28
13. Necklace. Cheyenne   29
*14. Cosmic Mobile. Rio Grande Puebloan   30
*15. Speaker's staff. Tlingit (Frog Clan)   31
16. Dance wands. Hopi   32
17. Dance sash. Hopi   32
18. Fan. Kiowa   34
*19. Peyote fan. Southern Plains   35
*20. Peyote fan. Southern Plains   35
21. Shell gorget. Mississippian (Spiro Mounds)   36
22. *Pipesmoker* pipe bowl. Mississippian (Spiro Mounds)   36
23. Effigy pipe. Mississippian (Spiro Mounds)   36
24. Painted shield. Arapaho   37
25. *War Dance Gathering Scene.* Earnest Spybuck, Shawnee   39
26. Untitled. Andrew Standing-Soldier, Sioux   39
27. *Zacharie Vincent, Huron of Lorette, with His Son Cyprien.* Zacharie Vincent, Huron   40
28. *Scene in a Yard of the Huron Village, Lorette, Quebec.* Zacharie Vincent, Huron   41
29. *Indian New Year, Fourth Day on Jan. 25th, 1901. Cattaraugus Reservation.* Jesse J. Cornplanter, Seneca   42
*30. *Mohawk Headdress.* Richard Glazer Danay, Mohawk   43
31. Hat. Iroquois   44
32. Sun Boy, a Kiowa Chief   47
*33. *The Exploits of Sun Boy.* Silverhorn (Haungooah), Kiowa   49
34. Diagram of *The Exploits of Sun Boy*   50
35. Pictographic images: Hopi, Eskimo, Japanese, Colorado River, Utah, and Ojibwa   54
36. Pictographic images: Cree, Mandan, Oto, Pawnee, Kiowa, and Comanche-drawn figures   55
37. Pictographic images: Mandan, Crow, and Cheyenne   55
38. Iroquois pictographic images   55
39. Comanche pictographic image   56
40. Sioux pictographic images   58
41. Pictographic images: Kiowa and Dakota Sioux calendar glyphs   58
42. *The Exploits of Sun Boy* (detail). Silverhorn (Haungooah), Kiowa   61

CHAPTER II. TRADITION

*43. Container, front and back views. Huron   64, 65
*44. Sword and case. Crow   66
*45. Mirror and case. Crow   66
46. Knife case and belt. Cree   68

47. Bonnet. Santee Sioux   69
48. Chilkat blanket. Tlingit   70
49. Basket, Wikchumni Yokuts   71
50. *Lucifer* pipe. Mississippian (Spiro Mounds)   72
51. Pipe bowl. Ojibwa (Chippewa)   72
52. Pipe bowl. Southern Great Lakes/Ohio River   73
53. Pipe bowl. Micmac   73
*54. Jar. Zia   75
55. Headstall. Crow   77
56. Horse breast ornament. Crow   77
*57. Saddle blanket. Sioux   78
*58. Necklace. Rio Grande, probably Santo Domingo   79
59. Cross. Robert Cruickshank, Canadian   80
60. Cross with crescent. Southern Plains, possibly Kiowa   80
61. Cross. Kiowa   80
62. Bandolier and bag. Delaware   81
63. Coat. Oto   81
*64. Saddle. Cree   83
65. McCartys polychrome jar. Acoma   85
66. Seed jar. Lucy Lewis, Acoma   85
67. Jar. B. J. Cerno, Acoma   85
68. Basket. Sarah Hunter, Panamint   86
69. Basket with lid. Nootka   86
70. Pipe, front and back views. Inuit (Eskimo)   88, 89
71. Knife. Inuit (Eskimo)   89
72. Tusk, front and back views. Inuit (Eskimo)   90, 91
*73. Painted hide. Kill Eagle, Cheyenne/Sioux   91
74. Sash. Osage   94
*75. Sash. Osage   95
*76. Sash. Southeastern Woodlands   95
77. Cradle. Kiowa   96
78. Moccasin pattern. Omaha/Ponca-style   97
79. Moccasins. Ponca(?)   97
80. Moccasins. Ponca   98
81. Moccasins. Ponca   98
82. Moccasins. Ponca   98
83. Pipe stem. Western Great Lakes   99
84. Necklace. Central Plains/Ohio Valley   99
85. Shield. Comanche   101
86. Roach and spreader. Osage   101
*87. Roach and spreader. Plains   102
*88. Painted hide. Washakie or Katsikodi, Shoshone   103

CHAPTER III. AESTHETICS

*89. Child's blanket. Navajo   106
90. First Phase blanket. Navajo   110
*91. Wedgeweave blanket. Navajo   111
92. Second Phase blanket. Navajo   112
93. Moki blanket. Hopi   112
*94. Saddle blanket. Navajo   113
95. Chilkat blanket. Tlingit   114
96. Button blanket. Kaigani Haida   115
*97. Dance apron. Kwakiutl   116
*98. Leggings. Tlingit   117
99. Pictorial blanket. Navajo   119
100. Blanket. Navajo   119
*101. Chilkat tunic. Tlingit   120
*102. Horse breast decoration. Crow   121
103. Basket. Evelyn Lake Potter, Pomo   122
104. Basket. Pomo   122

105. *Beaver* monitor pipe. Hopewellian   123
106. *Raccoon Priests* gorget. Mississippian (Spiro Mounds)   123
107. Jar. Tonita and Juan Cruz Roybal, San Ildefonso   125
108. Jar. Zia   126
109. Jar. Gila   127
110. Whale mask. Kwakiutl   128
*111. Bear mask. Attributed to Charley George, Sr., Kwakiutl
       (Nakwakhdakw tribe)   129
*112. Raven mask. Kwakiutl   129
113. Bear mask. Eastern Cherokee   130
114. Buffalo mask. Eastern Cherokee   130
*115. Frontlet. Bella Coola   132
*116. Mask. Bella Coola   134
117. Feast dish. Tlingit   135
118. Oil bowl. Haida   135
119. Amulet. Tsimshian   136
120. Platter. Charles Edenshaw, Haida   137

CHAPTER IV. QUALITY

121. Bella Coola dancers performing in Berlin,
       January, 1886   138
122. Bag. Apache   139
*123. Dress. Sioux   142
124. Ramos polychrome effigy jar. Casas Grandes   144
*125. Dagger. Tlingit   146
126. Slaver killer or dagger. Nootka   147
127. Mask. Nootka   147
128. Bowl. Haida   149
*129. Serape. Navajo   150
*130. Child's blanket. Navajo   151
131. Basket. Louisa Keyser (Dat So La Lee), Washoe   152
132. Basket. Maggie James, Washoe   152
133. Olla. Tularosa   153
134. Jar. Nampeyo, Hopi   154
*135. *Red Totem*. George Morrison, Chippewa   155
136. Smithport plain jar. Caddoan   156
137. Dog effigy vessel. Mississippian   158
138. *Polikmana* Katcina. Hopi   160
139. Mask. Key Marco   161
140. Ocelot effigy pipe bowl. Mississippian   162
141. Human effigy pipe. Ohio, Adena Mound   163
142. Club. Oto   164
143. Ladle. Mohawk   165
144. False-face mask. Seneca   167

CHAPTER V. INDIVIDUALITY

*145. Ceremonial shawl. Hopi   170
146. Basket. Minnie Lacy, Yavapai Apache   176
147. Basket. Pima   176
148. Basket. Paiute   176
*149. Baskets. Mrs. Cruz I. Billy, Pomo   177
150. Jar. Nampeyo, Hopi   180
151. Jar. Nampeyo, Hopi   180
152. Jar. Nampeyo, Hopi   181
153. Seed Jar. Nampeyo, Hopi   182
154. Jar. Nampeyo, Hopi   182
155. Jar. Nampeyo, Hopi   183
156. Jar. Nampeyo, Hopi   183
157. Jar. Maria and Julian Martinez, San Ildefonso   184
158. Plate. Maria and Santana Martinez, San Ildefonso   185

159. Jar. Maria Martinez, San Ildefonso   186
160. Plate. Maria Martinez and Popovi Da, San Ildefonso   186
161. Jar. Maria Martinez and Popovi Da, San Ildefonso   186
162. *Self-Portrait*. Buffalo Meat, Cheyenne   187
163. *Two Young Cheyenne Warriors*. Making Medicine,
       Cheyenne   188
*164. *Buffalo Hunt*. Making Medicine, Cheyenne   188
165. *U.S. Cavalry*. Making Medicine, Cheyenne   189
*166. *Train to Fort Marion*. Making Medicine, Cheyenne   189
167. *Indians Shingling Their Barracks*. Making Medicine,
       Cheyenne   189
168. *Kiowa Scalp Dance*. Stephen Mopope, Kiowa   190
169. *Eagle Dance* (mural). Tonita Pena (Quah Ah),
       San Ildefonso   191
170. *Basket Dance* (mural). Romando Vigil (Tse-Ye-Mu),
       San Ildefonso   191
*171. *Pollination of the Corn*. Waldo Mootzka, Hopi   192
*172. *Koshares of Taos*. Pablita Velarde, Santa Clara   192
*173. *Night Chant Ceremonial Hunt*. Harrison Begay, Navajo   193
*174. *Navajo Woman on Horseback*. Gerald Nailor, Navajo   193
175. *In the Days of Plenty*. Quincy Tahoma, Navajo   194
176. *Navajo Woman Weaver*. Andrew Tsinahjinnie,
       Navajo   194
177. *Cheyenne Sun Dance, First Painting of the Third Day*,
       Richard West, Cheyenne   195
*178. *Prairie Fire*. Blackbear Bosin, Kiowa/Comanche   196
*179. *Victory Dance*. Oscar Howe, Yanktonai Sioux   197
180. *Symbols of the Southwest*. Tony Da, San Ildefonso   199
*181. *His Hair Flows like a River*. T. C. Cannon, Caddo   201
182. Louisa Keyser, 1921–1922   204
183. Abe Cohn, 1924   204
184. The Cohn Emporium basketry display, ca. 1900   205
185. A Washoe woman   206
186. A Washoe basket   206
187. The Washoe weaver Sarah Jim Mayo with basket finished in
       1913 for presentation to President Woodrow Wilson   211
188. Basket. Sarah Mayo, Washoe   213
189. Maggie Mayo James at Lake Tahoe, ca. 1913   214
190. A group of *degikup* by Tootsie Dick, 1925   215
191. Lena Frank Dick, ca. 1943   218
192. Basket. Lena Dick, Washoe   218
193. Fred Settelmeyer on horseback, 1935   219

CHAPTER VI. CONTROVERSY

194. *The Blind*. Oscar Howe, Yanktonai Sioux   222
195. Effigy. Cochiti   224
196. Effigy. Tesuque   224
197. *White Man's Bad Medicine*. Jerome Tiger,
       Creek-Seminole   226
198. *Indian Prisoners in Costume*. Buffalo Meat, Cheyenne   227
199. *Custer's Last Stand Revised*. Randy Lee White, Sioux   228
200. *Buffalo Dance*. Crescencio Martinez, San Ildefonso   229
*201. *Hopi Ceremonial Dance*. Fred Kabotie, Hopi   230
*202. *Land of Enchantment*. Woodrow Crumbo,
       Creek-Potawatomi   231
203. *Making Wild Rice*. Patrick Desjarlait, Ojibwa
       (Chippewa)   232
204. *Maple Sugar Time*. Patrick Desjarlait, Ojibwa
       (Chippewa)   232
205. *Pueblo Green Corn Dance*. Fred Kabotie, Hopi   233

*206. *View of Taos*. Albert Looking Elk, Taos   234
207. *Woman and Animals*. Wa Wa Chaw, Mission   235
208. *Woman*. Wa Wa Chaw, Mission   235
209. *Woman and Children*. Wa Wa Chaw, Mission   235
210. *Polar Bears and Seal*. Kivetoruk Moses, Inuit (Eskimo)   236
211. *Neophyte Cowboy*. Bob Haozous, Chiricahua
    Apache/Navajo   237
*212. *Laughing Indian*. Fritz Scholder, Mission (Luiseno)   239
213. Four Yei masks. Navajo   244
214. Jar. Lois Gutierrez, Santa Clara   245
215. Ceremonial bowl. Zuñi   245
216. Julian Martinez, Velino Herrera, and Alfonso Roybal   248
217. Crescencio Martinez and Anna Montoya Martinez,
    ca. 1915   248
218. Juan Cruz and Tonita Roybal, ca. 1935   249
219. San Ildefonso women making pottery, ca. 1919   250
220. Rose Gonzales selling pottery, ca. 1935   252
221. Julian Martinez firing pottery, ca. 1940   253

CHAPTER VII. THE FUTURE

*222. *Peyote Road Man*. Carl Sweezy, Arapaho   256
223. *Number 1, 1948*. Jackson Pollock, American   260
224. Puberty robe. Apache   261
225. *Mesa*. Dan Namingha, Hopi   262
226. *Plaza Indian*. Bob Haozous, Chiricahua
    Apache/Navajo   263
227. *Seated Figure*. Henry Moore, British   263
*228. *Spirit Guide/Healer*. George C. Longfish,
    Seneca/Tuscarora   264
*229. *Revenge in Trade for a Wife*. Randy Lee White, Sioux   265
*230. *Shoots the Soldier*. Randy Lee White, Sioux   265
231. *Crow*. Kevin Red Star, Crow   266
232. *Collector #5 or Osage with Van Gogh*. T. C. Cannon,
    Caddo   267
*233. *Koshares with Cotton Candy*. Harry Fonseca, Maidu   269
*234. *Koshares with Watermelons*. Harry Fonseca, Maidu   269
235. *Strawberry Dance*, Paper Bag series. G. Peter Jemison,
    Seneca   270
236. *Goldfish and Sculpture*. Henri Matisse, French   270
237. Untitled Hopi design. Millard Dawa Lomakema, Hopi   271
*238. *Stillwater #2*. James G. Schoppert, Tlingit   272
*239. *Migrations*. James G. Schoppert, Tlingit   272
*240. *Eagle Egg*. James Havard, Choctaw/Chippewa   273

241. *Black Lines*. Vasily Kandinsky, Russian   274
242. *Landscape #2*. Emmi Whitehorse, Navajo   274
*243. *American Landscape #3*. George Morrison, Chippewa   277
*244. Untitled, Camus series. Jaune Quick-to-See Smith,
    Cree/Shoshone   277
245. *Cold Snap on the Prairie II*. Earl Biss, Crow   279
246. *Kickapoos Have More Fun*. Richard Glazer Danay,
    Mohawk   279
*247. *Georgia O'Keeffe*. David Bradley, Ojibwa   280
248. Bag. Nez Percé   284
249. *Rose and the Res Sisters*. Harry Fonseca, Maidu   285
250. Bowl. Effie Garcia, Santa Clara   286
251. Bowl. Jody Folwell, San Ildefonso   287
*252. Jar. Iris Nampeyo, Hopi   288
*253. Jar. Stella Huma, Hopi   289
254. *Seal Hunter*. Inuit   289
255. Bracelet. Charles Loloma, Hopi   290
256. Bracelet. Lloyd Wadhams, Haida   290
257. *The Shaman Restores a Dead Soul to Life*. Lyle Wilson,
    Haisla/Kwakiutl   291
258. Sculptural hat. Lelooska, Cherokee   291
*259. Design. Julian Martinez, San Ildefonso   292
*260. *The Deer Spirit*. Acee Blue Eagle, Creek/Pawnee   293
261. *Deer Rattle/Deer Dancer*. Frank LaPena, Wintu   293
262. *Deer at Laguna*. Fritz Scholder, Mission (Luiseno)   293
263. *Taos Lady*. Bob Haozous, Chiricahua Apache/Navajo   295
264. *Sensuous Cowgirl*. Bob Haozous, Chiricahua Apache/
    Navajo   295
*265. *You Can't Rollerskate in a Buffalo Herd Even if
    You Have All the Medicine*. George C. Longfish,
    Seneca/Tuscarora   297
266. Indian document protesting railroads. Osage   298
267. *Tocito Waits for Boarding School Bus*. Grey Cohoe,
    Navajo   299
268. *Tall Visitor at Tocito*. Grey Cohoe, Navajo   299
269. *Winter Loon Dance*. John Hoover, Aleut   300
270. *Ooger Uk Inua (Walrus Spirit)*. Larry Beck,
    Chnagmiut Eskimo   300
271. *Wooden Pole Construction*. Truman Lowe,
    Winnebago   301
272. *Car Scaffold Burial*. Ron Anderson, Comanche   302
273. *Nahookoos Fetish Pot*. Conrad House, Navajo   303
*274. *The Four Worlds*. Joe Herrera, Cochiti   304

Foreword

The cultural heritage of our country is rich with Native American traditions. In our state, Plains Indians, as well as members of the Five Civilized Tribes, fostered a vast wealth of creative and functional art that reflects a proud history and progressive future.

Museums and private collectors throughout our state have spearheaded the effort to preserve the art and artifacts of America's native cultures. We salute the organizations that worked together in the exhibition and publication of *The Arts of the North American Indian: Native Traditions in Evolution*. This project, supported financially by corporations, individuals, the State Arts Council of Oklahoma, the National Endowment for the Arts, and the National Endowment for the Humanities, is a splendid example of private and public partnership, which has provided a valuable historical resource for present and future generations.

THE HONORABLE GEORGE PATTERSON NIGH
Governor of Oklahoma

One hundred fifty years ago, the federal government set Oklahoma aside as Indian Territory. There, Native American culture developed in relative isolation until 1889, when the territory was opened to homestead settlement. Since statehood in 1907, Indians, white settlers, industrial pioneers, and welcome arrivals from throughout the nation have worked together to make Oklahoma prosper. As a young but flourishing state, we now wish to share our unique cultural wealth with the world community.

Phillips Petroleum Company is honored to have played a role in bringing greater public attention to the wisdom and beauty of this Native American art.

WILLIAM C. DOUCE
*Chairman of the Board of Directors and
Chief Executive Officer, Retired
Phillips Petroleum Company*

Tulsa is extraordinarily fortunate to have two strong cultural institutions whose supporting publics have mandated the interpretation and presentation of their superb Native American collections. Philbrook Art Center and the Thomas Gilcrease Institute of American History and Art, along with private collections and our sister institutions throughout the state, hold collectively a resource of enormous depth and beauty, mirroring the life and dreams of a great people.

This book and the exhibition of the treasures it contains are an unprecedented example of what can happen when those who have a commitment to share the art they hold in trust join strength together. The Gilcrease Institute is extremely pleased to have been part of that fruitful collaboration.

FRED MYERS
*Director, Thomas Gilcrease Institute
of American History and Art*

Preface

The idea for this publication and the accompanying exhibition was born in 1981. The first step, taken in 1981 and 1982, was a comprehensive search throughout the state for Oklahoma's most telling and significant American Indian masterworks. Dr. Edwin L. Wade, Curator of Non-European Art at Philbrook Art Center, canvassed over sixty public and private collections, finding a breadth and richness in the state's holdings that were even greater than we had believed, and the project gathered momentum. The second major step was an international colloquium, sponsored by Philbrook, with invaluable assistance from Phillips Petroleum Company, at which American Indian artists and consultants from throughout the United States met with scholars from five nations. The text of the present volume arose from this convocation of those whose lives have been devoted to the practice and study of native arts. We are deeply grateful to the participants for sharing their vision with one another and with Philbrook.

Our sincere gratitude goes to Phillips Petroleum Company, whose support and encouragement have been integral to the project since its inception, and to the lenders to the exhibition, with whom we are honored to act in collaboration. Without their willingness to share their cultural treasures, our goal of making our collective holdings available to a broader national audience would never have been realized. We are also indebted to the State Arts Council of Oklahoma, the National Endowment for the Arts, and the National Endowment for the Humanities for partial support. Each agency, institution, individual, and our patron corporation for this project have again demonstrated that most heartening of truths: that through creative partnership, a dream can become a reality.

Marcia Y. Manhart
Executive Director, Philbrook Art Center

Acknowledgments

The formal acknowledgments are typically the last portion of a book to be written. This is understandable in that those people whose energies fuse in the final product continue to populate the creative landscape of the work throughout its evolution. Contributions vary, but each, whether of criticism, praise, information, or moral support, is essential to the process that results in a unique joint creation.

This book is part of a larger vision that has inspired an intensive four-year exploration of the humanistic foundations of aesthetic endeavor. We have asked how a body of artworks, the product of the human hand, eye, and spirit, came to exist and what further developments it is likely to inspire in the future. Foremost in this quest have been staff members, past and present, of Philbrook Art Center. To those present at the beginning of this pursuit, Jesse G. Wright, Jr., John A. Mahey, and Marcia Manhart, I acknowledge my deepest appreciation. Thanks to Carol Haralson for her hard work and clarity of purpose during this complex and sometimes confused journey. To my staff, both past and current, including Steven Domjanovich, Isabel McIntosh, Jan Fleming, Charles Taylor, and especially Gloria Young, who has excelled throughout under difficult conditions, go my sincere affection and personal regard.

In addition to the dedicated scholars who have contributed their knowledge to this work, I would like to thank Arthur and Shifra Silberman, directors of the Native American Painting Reference Library, Oklahoma City, Oklahoma, who have been of inestimable value to the project. Their passionate concern for the art of Native Americans and their deep historical understanding have been appreciated by all of us. Equally important has been the unstinting generosity of the American Indian artists, both in works of art loaned and in their perceptive critiques of our written interpretations. Often their comments were blunt, demanding our reappraisal of cherished opinions, yet the changes were always for the better. Special thanks are due George C. Longfish, Richard Glazer Danay, Bob Haozous, and G. Peter Jemison. Captions for the many illustrations shown are very important to us, functioning as a subtext throughout the book, and I am grateful to Carol Haralson for assistance in their preparation. Special aid in the writing of captions was provided by Bill Holm, Rennard Strickland, Norman Feder, and William C. Sturtevant. Captions not written by me are signed with the initials of their authors. The efforts of many people have gone into gathering the most complete data possible, but the birth and death dates of some artists were not available and therefore are not given.

The program of which this book is a part would have been impossible without the assistance of Oklahoma's public and private collections. Unless otherwise stated, all artworks illustrated here are from Oklahoma collections, which have proven to be a profoundly rich source. The other critical element is the generosity of the various foundations, corporations, and individuals who have funded this vision. Without the commitment of Phillips Petroleum Corporation and the particular support of William C. Douce, the program could never have begun. The enthusiastic cooperation of Phillips, characterized by a dedication to excellence, was fundamental to our motivation to achieve the highest standards. Also instrumental in the funding of this program were National Endowment for the Humanities Grant RD 20263-82, National Endowment for the Arts Grant 42-4422-0330, the Oklahoma Foundation for the Humanities, in cooperation with the National Endowment for the Humanities, the State Arts Council of Oklahoma, and our exhibition cosponsor, the Thomas Gilcrease Institute of American History and Art. Of the many people who worked diligently within these organizations to make this vision a possibility, I would like especially to thank Scott Carlberg, Anita May, Betty Price, Peter Caldwell, and Fred Myers.

Thanks go also to Michael Sudbury, who was involved in the initial conference that brought together the writers of this book, and to her husband, Graham; to E. G. Schempf, whose skills as a photographer are apparent in a number of the images reproduced here; to Richard Bigda, who has worked hard in the interest of American Indian art in Tulsa, Oklahoma; and to Addis Osborn and Doug Phillips, whose ideas fueled the project in its initial stages. We are grateful to our publisher, Paul Anbinder, for his thoroughness and professionalism, and to Eve Sinaiko for her editorial skills. And to J. Patrick Manhart, a superb mentor whose contributions to many of our projects have been fundamental to their success, go my sincere and lasting thanks.

EDWIN L. WADE
December 8, 1985

Introduction:
What Is Native American Art?

EDWIN L. WADE

Primitive art, embracing all the diverse traditions of native North America, remains mysterious to the contemporary Western mind, and in its mystery, its "otherness," has lain much of its superficial allure. But the observer who looks beyond the exotic surface of so-called "primitive art" to the aesthetic complexity and the alternative philosophies underlying it sees a new potential, a vast store of untapped creative vision. Such art can have vital significance for our beleaguered civilization and frighteningly depersonalized world, offering hope and an expressive alternative.

The acknowledgment of these latent riches, however, has not come easily to our technologically arrogant civilization. Euro-American cultures, in spite of their genius for innovation, have shown a philosophic and fundamental wariness of new or differing beliefs. Two common reactions to the unfamiliar have been a condescending curiosity and the fear of potential danger. Seldom have other world views been seen as viable alternatives to our accustomed way of seeing.

In light of the fact that flexibility has been the major tool for securing and ensuring human survival, our rejection of the gifts of strangers is ironic. While other species have wedged themselves tightly into a given niche or life-sustaining strategy, man has ranged widely. His mental and physical adaptability has allowed for the extreme variety that characterizes the cultures of mankind. The twentieth century, however, has witnessed a new and alarming development in the evolution of human society. We are becoming more and more alike. Mass communication increasingly erodes the ethnicity of formerly isolated cultural enclaves. Distinctive social behavior that had survived for millennia is dissolving in the melting pot of a nondescript world. The signs of pan-global uniformity are everywhere.

The descendants of once-proud Navajo horsemen who roamed the vast deserts of northern Arizona now traverse their canyon lands in pickups, listening to Indian radio stations and worrying about tribal bond issues, mineral contracts, and reservation energy development. Obscured by the social glitter of Santa Fe and scenic New Mexico are pockets of ancient Puebloans still secluded in the shadowy valleys of the Rio Grande, where they attempt to preserve the passing lifeway of an egalitarian society. Yet each year the dissenting voices that argue against a tribal craft cooperative, cameras in the villages, tourist parking behind the adobe homes, or public bus tours of the sacred dances, become fewer and fainter. Occasionally there is a brief reappraisal and an attempt to revitalize waning ideals. But the dependence of the contemporary Native American upon the Western economy has stripped him of cultural self-sufficiency and ensured his inevitable assimilation into our world. Such a view might appear to contradict the much-publicized resurgence of Indian powwows, ceremonies, and political militancy; however, recovering a few shards does not restore the pot. Cultures are not viable as amputated parts or as associations of convenience. Elements of Indian visual expression and social activity abound, yet living societies, with communally acknowledged values, roles, and identities, are almost extinct.

Mine is not a joyful proclamation. The extinction of small-scale societies throughout the world represents a fundamental human loss of unparalleled proportion. Paradoxically, it occurs at a time of indulgent intellectual escapism, when the literary and artistic talents of Western society have turned to fantasy and speculation about alien worlds. Real, meaningful, alternative worlds already exist, encapsulated in the traditional thoughts and behavior of hundreds of ancient societies. But these other worlds are now being extinguished by the onslaught of technological modernization. The ancient America of sucking doctors, transformational tricksters, shape-shifters, and contrary warriors is already gone. The transitional America of Cheyenne, Seneca, Cayuse, Walla Walla, Delaware, Oto, and Comanche is rapidly waning. And with it goes a set of unique solutions for survival, the values that justified and enriched human lives, and directed a quest for meaning and beauty.

It is too late—and perhaps not even desirable—to reverse the momentum of modernization. Both technological societies and developing nations want change even at the expense of their ancient traditions. Yet the specter of a world devoid of tribal cultures and of their rich aesthetic expression is desolate. Posterity deserves at least an accurate record of the brilliance of native traditions, for we, the "civilized," have yet to surpass them in either conviction or vision. Aesthetics, which x-rays the creative thinking of a society, is a logical starting point for this record. Two hundred years of anthropological research, charting cultural behavior and the structure of non-European thinking, makes the task possible. It is a task well worth accomplishing, for the visual arts are the Rosetta Stone of aesthetic language. These creations of the mind and hand speak of religious feeling, social beliefs, the fear of the unknown, and the dignity of a purposeful life. They are the physical clothing of a society's imagination; they embody its sense of awe and its love of beauty. The tribal artist speaks in a language of socially preferred colors, shapes, textures, designs, and techniques of construction. As with written and oral language, the symbols are communally understood, though the degree and sophistication of communication ultimately depend upon the eloquence of the speaker. This evolved language defines innovation by providing a stable framework within which change can occur.

Imagination is not tied to place or time. The most ancient recognizable arts of man, the twenty-five-thousand-year-old Cro-Magnon cave paintings and sculpture, display remarkable sophistication. The abstraction of the Willendorf figures contrasts with the realism of the animal renderings. Time and mortality are expressed by the creatures adorning the walls of La Chapelle. Like cicadas, they shed their earlier forms for mature shapes, then dissolve into frailty and age.

The sculptor-dramatists of the American Northwest Coast made kinetic art centuries before its emergence in twentieth-century Europe. Sculptural minimalism is at least three thousand years old in the New World. Communal murals, such as the sacred paintings of subterranean Pueblo kivas are evident by the fifteenth century in northern Arizona. Ojibwa tooth-impressed birchbark patterns and northeastern anthropomorphic love charms dispel the idea that art for art's sake began in the civilized world.

The art of those displaced times, when boys wore on their shields the marks of their vision-bestowed supernatural guardians, and chieftains raised great sculpted houses and danced on the prows of sixty-foot war canoes, is different from the art of today. But the difference between the art of primitive societies and that of civilized cultures is less important than the commonality of their impulse, which ultimately makes visible both the quests and the revelations of man.

It will be a tragedy if we forget—or worse, never experience—the fragile brilliance of past visions, the great inspirations of a truly new world. As a beginning, then, the intention of this book is to explore the aesthetic phenomena of American Indian art, not as anthropologists compiling trait lists, nor as art historians laboriously charting design elements, but as humanists concerned with aesthetic experience and human expressive potential.

We start by asking, What is Native American art? The question is vast, involving whole societies as well as individual people, their values and beliefs, their imaginations, and their personal talents; and we do not suggest that it has a single, definitive answer. This book will examine objects made by members of over sixty tribes, representing all the major Native American culture areas, Alaskan, Eskimo, Subarctic, Northwest Coast, Plateau, Plains, Great Basin, Southwest, Eastern Woodlands, and Southeast, and spanning a period of three thousand years. The authors have taken a variety of approaches, some primarily scientific and others humanistic, and one writer has even employed the form of dramatic dialogue. But ultimately, whether the focus is on historical reconstruction, aesthetics from the native point of view, or insight into individual personalities, we share a profound concern for the future of this art and its makers. We look both forward and back, seeking the fundamental principles underlying the vast sweep of American Indian art, but at the same time we realize that our desire to define it in this way is peculiar to us as Western viewers of a broad and complex art tradition; to the artists who made and continue to make these artworks, creation itself is justification. We will divide the issue into seven major constituents, asking the questions: What are the messages or symbolic contents of American Indian art? What does tradition mean in the context of Native American artworks? What did, or do, they mean to their makers? What is the aesthetics of native art? How do we establish criteria for degrees of quality in native work? What is the place of creative individuality in native traditions? How has American Indian art generated controversy in our century? And finally, we will ask: What are some possible scenarios for the future of Native American art? Is its tribal, ethnic, or individual aesthetics still viable? Indeed, is the concept "ethnic" any longer an acceptable social identifier in the twentieth century?

Meaning in American Indian art is discussed by William Sturtevant and Gloria Young. Sturtevant starts from the premise that meanings implicit in contemporary Indian art differ widely from those of earlier traditional art. In fact, the very division of "art" from "artifact" is problematic in older traditional art, since it is likely that the originating societies did not separate art objects from nonart objects. In distinguishing between art and artifact, Sturtevant suggests that all objects have stylistic characteristics and that style carries associations with time, place, function, and value: these are the meanings inherent in objects. "Art" objects might be those which engendered a strong emotional reaction in the societies of their origin. Sturtevant goes on to discuss Indian art history in terms of cultural areas and Indian art in terms of its symbolism, ultimately providing a road map of the aesthetic sensibilities of ancient North America.

Gloria Young's essay on a recently reinterpreted Kiowa muslin painting focuses on the symbolic content of a particular historic North American artwork. The painting, newly attributed to Silverhorn, shows the Kiowa warrior Sun Boy engaged in battle with other Indian tribes and with U.S. and Mexican cavalrymen, in a style that descends from the Plains pictographic tradition, providing a rarely seen, intimate example of secular meaning in North American art.

Jonathan King and Norman Feder address the issue of tradition, dispelling the common stereotype of a changeless, unidimensional Indian cultural expression, of a "good old days" when native art was traditional, and therefore legitimate, or "truly Indian." In its place, they paint a picture of an "infinite number of art traditions, many of which overlap and interplay to form a highly complex mosaic." King explores some problems arising from oversimplified use of the basic concept "tradition." He shows how what we think of as "traditional" and "nontraditional" in American Indian art have been profoundly influenced by trade, exchange, and war; by early contact with Euro-American culture; by adaptation of European designs and materials; by colonization, commercialization, and the influence of white institutions. He makes the point that those who study American Indian art have had to draw their conclusions about what is traditional on the basis of what has been collected and preserved. Besides being necessarily arbitrary and incomplete, most such collections available for study were formed between 1860 and 1930, a period of enormous upheaval for North American Indians. Yet, King argues, even if one could have a full panoramic view of Indian artifacts from prehistory onward, one would not see smooth transitions within single traditions. Rather, one would see a panoply of change in which raw materials and finished objects, and even whole ceremonial complexes, were transformed completely in nature or context. As King says, "The use of the words 'traditional' and 'nontraditional' suggests a black-and-white situation, when reality is much subtler."

Norman Feder underscores these points in an essay that focuses on the Plains Indians and the alteration of their art by internal and external forces. He discusses the effects on North American art of European raw materials and European-made versions of Indian objects, such as wampum beads; of trade among tribes and with white men; of forced migrations and warfare; of the extinction of certain plants and animals; of the tourist trade; and of the horse, the gun, and Christianity.

Though North American art is reforged on the anvil of time, as King and Feder point out, Native American objects, especially those in the sacred domain, continue to be charged with philosophical and symbolic content. They are points at which the real and the supernatural merge. Yet, though symbolic content is found throughout the universe of Indian art, there is no simple, universal symbolism that applies to all native visual expression. Rather, there is a great diversity and complexity of meaning in the aesthetic products of American Indian tribes.

The investment of meaning in objects, the conscious perfection of individual style within an evolving tradition, and the artist's own self-critical appraisal of his or her work, all are elements in tribal aesthetics. Wolfgang Haberland undertakes the question of native North American aesthetics, starting from the idea that although appreciation of the beautiful is universal, the definition of beauty differs in space and time. A given culture's idea of beauty is seen as the "group aesthetics," as opposed to the "universal aesthetics," which embraces the general human ability to create and appreciate beauty. A group aesthetics can only be fully understood by members of the group that evolved it, a predicament that has led to frequent misinterpretations and underestimations of "primitive" art by Euro-Americans. An examination of Navajo and Northwest Coast blanket designs provides Haberland with a framework for tracing changes in group aesthetics as a result of internal and external forces. The utilitarian nature of the blankets also encourages an interesting discussion of the question, Are such objects "art"? Questions concerning the differences between art and craft, the existence of art for art's sake, and professionalism among tribal artists are considered.

Bill Holm adds to the chapter on aesthetics a vivid and poetic picture of ceremonial masked dancing on the Northwest Coast, showing how a tribal aesthetics has been expressed as a fusion of sound, sight, and motion, a creative complex arising from tribal history, individual genius, and group aesthetics. Holm reveals the existence among the Northwest Coast cultures of a meticulously choreographed celebration of group consciousness and aesthetic exuberance, a sensory collage of living arts.

Central to any system of aesthetics is the question of quality. How is a masterwork recognized? Can such a judgment be made cross-culturally? Evan Maurer points out that in North American cultures judgments concerning the quality of an object were usually based on its technical perfection. Since most objects we now refer to as "artworks" were primarily functional, the emphasis on fine technique is understandable; a well-executed pot, for example, was one which would not break easily in use. Maurer contends that our modern willingness to consider aesthetic quality separately from technical mastery is "one symptom of the separation of art from life that exists in our culture, a separation that has...led to the estrangement of the artist from his own society."

In his related essay, Christian Feest focuses upon the question of quality with regard to the sculptural arts of native North America. In a provocative discussion of how excellence is measured, Feest views art as a communicative process between the maker and the user or viewer, with excellence resulting from the closest approximation of product to cultural ideal, or artwork to group expectation. The rules governing this process are based upon aesthetics, are continually in flux, and are culture-specific. The fact that they are not transferred from society to society has limited the Western understanding of excellence as perceived by Native American societies. Feest goes on to present a thorough overview of the sculptural traditions of the Southwest, the Eastern Woodlands, the North, and the Northwest Coast.

Whatever the group aesthetics may be, whatever the unspoken tribal agreement about the nature of excellence, it is ultimately the single human hand, eye, and mind that create a work of art. John Warner and Marvin Cohodas present a pair of essays dealing with the place of the individual in Native American art. What were his or her obligations to the communal group, and how far did personal freedom extend? Contrary to the stereotype of a faceless, nameless, homogeneous tribal society, we will see that the flares of private genius burned brightly within even the most conservative tribal traditions.

John Warner discusses individuality among the collectivistic Plains cultures, and on the postcontact reservations. The effect of white patronage on recognition of individual artists, the role of the Santa Fe Studio, and the new attitudes toward individuality in modernist, post-World War II traditions are analyzed.

Marvin Cohodas, in a humane and thoughtful essay, paints a portrait of five basket-weavers who stand out as true innovators in the history of Washoe fancy basketry. Louisa Keyser, Sarah Mayo, Maggie James, and Lena and Tootsie Dick guided the development of Washoe basket weaving from 1895 to 1935. Their life stories, particularly the effect on them of white patronage, provide a vivid account of the nature of individuality in one tribal tradition.

The upwelling of individuality within the context of rule-governed and collectivistic societies, though natural to the fertile evolution of art traditions, has not been without friction: Jamake Highwater and I discuss the controversy that has surrounded contemporary Native American art and artists.

Highwater probes the nature of controversy in Native American art from several angles. He discusses the conflict between personal and cultural identity among today's increasingly individualistic artists. Central to this issue is the question of who has the right to define "Indianness" in artistic imagery and style. He describes the important, but subtle, dispute concerning historical pictographic Indian artworks, seen by some as "precious reservoirs of an alternative history." He discusses the painful social repercussions of individuation among conservative tribal cultures, such as those of the Southwest. The advent of modernism among native artists and the great controversy it has provoked, particularly among more traditional Indian art institutions, is put into perspective, along with the effects of international renown on some provocative contemporary Indian artists. Ultimately, he creates a picture of Indian individualists not as heretics but as highly traditional people, whose inspiration often still comes from "visions, revelations, and the cumulative heritage of their people," but who at the same time inhabit the "global village" of today.

My case study of individuality among Puebloan pottery-makers highlights the effects of the arts and crafts market on native artists, their families and communities. Individual artistic success runs counter both to Southwestern attitudes concerning man's relation to the supernatural and to the egalitarian idea of what constitutes a "good" man or woman; the result can be bitterness and disruption. I focus on the controversy surrounding the merchandising of sacred Indian icons such as Katcinas and Yeis, and on the conflict between the Puebloan world view and the role of the contemporary artist, with all the psychological trappings the term implies in Westernized thought. Particularly revealing is the career of the famous potter Maria Martinez. Maria's brilliance extended even beyond her consummate artistic skill, for in addition to world acclaim as the "greatest" Native American artist, she also carefully and quietly altered the very fabric of ancient Puebloan life. Maria's efforts as a culture broker, a social mechanic, cautiously retuning Pueblo beliefs and values to better survive in the non-Indian world, proved successful, though they were theoretically impossible. Through strength, conviction, and innovation, she welded a viable future society for the pueblo of San Ildefonso, and refuted the axiom that one person cannot change the system.

In the concluding chapter, we look both forward and back. Gerhard Hoffman takes an incisive look at American Indian art in the context of Euro-American modernist and postmodernist art movements. Contemporary American Indian painters have clearly been influenced by modern styles: Oscar Howe by Cubism; T. C. Cannon by Matisse's decorative aesthetic; Grey Cohoe by Surrealism; Fritz Scholder by Expressionism; George C. Longfish by Abstract Expressionism; Harry Fonseca by Pop art; and Ben Buffalo by Photorealism. But Hoffman argues that the nature of modernist expression is subtly and profoundly altered in its transfer from the originating Euro-American culture to the artists of the "Fourth World," those "native peoples whose lands fall within the national boundaries...of the countries of the First, Second and Third Worlds." Fourth World artists, who have the full range of evolved modernist styles available for their creative expression, must approach the use of those styles differently than did the representatives of the cultures that developed them, in part as a response to the painful existential upheavals of our century.

Hoffman discusses the primal aspect of traditional Indian art and its relationship to modernism; the trivialization of the traditional into tourist art; and regionalism in Indian art. After an enlightening analysis of the foundations of modernism and its impact on contemporary Native American art, he goes farther, to trace the postmodernist trends of the 1960s and 1970s and their relation to Indian art, and to pose some questions about future aesthetic developments.

In a final essay that provides a delightful counterpoint in texture and voice to much of what precedes it, Rennard Strickland sets the stage of "memory and imagination" and peoples it with characters based upon stereotypes from the world of contemporary Indian art. Among those we meet are the elderly owner of a trading post on a Navajo reservation, a dealer in Indian art who specializes in tax-shelter schemes, a young Puebloan potter, an abstract painter of Indian blood, an anthropologist, an art critic, and two traditional Indian painters. In the rousing debate that ensues, each argues his or her passionately held viewpoint about the nature of American Indian art, its past, present, and future. The narrator—and referee—drops the curtain with a summation that is an expression of hope for the continued "mature flowering of a truly American art form" which has many futures and whose real power will be recognized in centuries to come.

I

MEANING

1. Bowl. Shinnecock. 1700–1770, carved wood, 6 × 20 × 14 inches. Philbrook Art Center, Tulsa, Elizabeth Cole Butler Collection, L82.1.400.

The significance of eighteenth-century European-influenced utilitarian objects to the native artists who produced them is speculative. This transitional burled-wood bowl is in the form of a precontact handmade wooden vessel of the Atlantic Coast but has unusual European innovations, including a columnar spout, fantailed handle, and curving rim, suggesting a lathe-turned object. Its teapot form, unique among eighteenth-century Woodlands containers, intimates an equally unusual inspiration, but one that is lost to time.

The Meanings of Native American Art

WILLIAM C. STURTEVANT

The meanings of Indian art are quite different for the old or "traditional" objects and the new or "contemporary" works. The old art is the product of exotic societies, now extinct or so changed as to be difficult to understand on the basis of their modern representatives. The new art is made by artists who belong to an ethnic minority but share most cultural forms and understandings with the non-Indian members of the larger society they participate in. Exploring problems of the definition and meanings of traditional art is a necessary background for discussion of the history and current state of contemporary art and its contexts and meanings.

INDIAN ART ?

An important problem with traditional art is whether art may be distinguished from other artifacts, and if so, on what basis. We do not know whether most historic and present Indian cultures had or have any native category that can be translated as "art." Anthropologists usually hold that Indian societies, like nearly all others, lacked the modern, Western notion that some objects qualify as art while others do not. To say that Indians lacked art in this special modern sense is not to assert that they lacked aesthetic standards, nor, conversely, that all their artifacts are art. European and Euro-American artifacts recognized as art also have other identifiable functions—the phrase "art for art's sake" is not a definition—and these other functions are more obvious for the period before the rise of specialized museums and displays, over the last two centuries or so.

If we cannot appeal directly to Indian classifications, terminology, and understandings to identify traditional Indian art, it might nevertheless be possible to formulate a definition of art that would permit assigning objects to this category either on the basis of their inherent characteristics, or according to their functions and meanings within their society of origin.

Our concern is with artifacts—with tangible, plastic, and (usually) durable objects—not with the arts of music, dance, or literature. Any artifact has recognizable characteristics of form or shape, texture or surface character, scale or absolute size, and color. These are stylistic characteristics. No object can be made that lacks them, and furthermore, they cannot be completely determined by the intended uses and the constituent materials of the artifact. Whatever the function and materials, there are at least several (and usually very many) possible variants that would serve equally well. The maker selects among them, unthinkingly following the models customary in that place and time, but also often consciously innovating. The result is an object that has a recognizable style. If we have enough examples, we can identify its provenience, usually to a specific society at a specific time, and sometimes to a specific maker (who may be known only from his or her surviving works).

The style of an artifact implies both contextual and semantic associations: with the times, places, and social occasions when objects of the type were or are used, and with its associated functions or uses, iconography, and value. These associations may be called its meanings. They vary with the sensitivity, experience, and knowledge of the observer; and ours cannot be the same as those of the original makers and users.

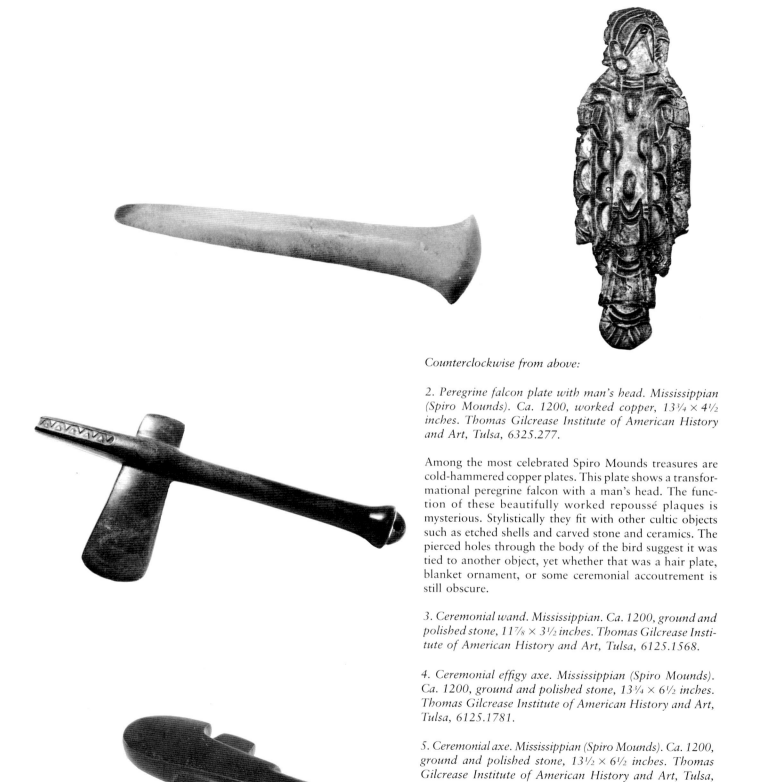

Counterclockwise from above:

2. *Peregrine falcon plate with man's head. Mississippian (Spiro Mounds). Ca. 1200, worked copper, 13¾ × 4½ inches. Thomas Gilcrease Institute of American History and Art, Tulsa, 6325.277.*

Among the most celebrated Spiro Mounds treasures are cold-hammered copper plates. This plate shows a transformational peregrine falcon with a man's head. The function of these beautifully worked repoussé plaques is mysterious. Stylistically they fit with other cultic objects such as etched shells and carved stone and ceramics. The pierced holes through the body of the bird suggest it was tied to another object, yet whether that was a hair plate, blanket ornament, or some ceremonial accoutrement is still obscure.

3. *Ceremonial wand. Mississippian. Ca. 1200, ground and polished stone, 11⅞ × 3½ inches. Thomas Gilcrease Institute of American History and Art, Tulsa, 6125.1568.*

4. *Ceremonial effigy axe. Mississippian (Spiro Mounds). Ca. 1200, ground and polished stone, 13¾ × 6½ inches. Thomas Gilcrease Institute of American History and Art, Tulsa, 6125.1781.*

5. *Ceremonial axe. Mississippian (Spiro Mounds). Ca. 1200, ground and polished stone, 13½ × 6½ inches. Thomas Gilcrease Institute of American History and Art, Tulsa, 6125.18910.*

6. *Spiro mace. Mississippian (Spiro Mounds). Ca. 1200, ground and polished novaculite, 1⅜ × 5⅛ inches. Thomas Gilcrease Institute of American History and Art, Tulsa, 6125.194.*

7. *Ceremonial flint mace. Mississippian (Duck River). Ca. 1200, flaked chert, 12¼ × 3½ inches. Thomas Gilcrease Institute of American History and Art, Tulsa, 6125.1565.*

8. *Spatulate form. Mississippian (Spiro Mounds). Ca. 1200, ground and polished greenstone, 16½ × 3¾ inches. Thomas Gilcrease Institute of American History and Art, Tulsa, 6125.4290.*

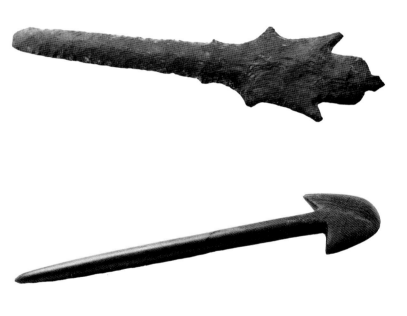

Little is known of the ancient high cultures of prehistoric North America that produced the objects shown in figures 3–8 and 21–23. Unfortunately, the elaborate ceremonialism, hierarchical social order, and complex cosmology of the Mississippian, and especially of the Spiro Mounds people has been lost. The complex shell-etched friezes of men, supernaturals, and symbolic ideograms interconnected in what clearly suggests components of a visual narrative provide our only glimpse into the sophistication of those ancient times. From an analysis of such scenes, it would appear that honorific badges and batons of status were significant among these people. We can discern classes of ground-stone spatulated forms, distinct from chipped flint and polished novaculite corona-topped wands. What appear to be ceremonial effigy axes, depicting various animals and curvilinear motifs, comprise yet another class.

We might label "art" those artifacts that engender a strong emotional effect in members of their society of origin. Such objects have a symbolic content, and in addition, the reaction to their meanings or significance must somehow be pleasurable, or at least engaging. To apply this definition cross-culturally, it is necessary to identify the aesthetic component in the evaluations and choices people make, beyond the practical or intellectual reasons they have. That, then, is an ethnographic fact to be determined. It probably cannot be deduced for objects known only archaeologically. Furthermore, not enough is known about most historical Indian societies to allow the identification of what was to them art in this sense. It is not safe to read modern attitudes back into the past, even if they are known, because such evaluations often change over time. It is sometimes assumed that aesthetic standards are universal, that a well-informed collector or scholar finds better or more beautiful the same pieces as would members of their society of origin, and presumably for the same reasons—that is, applying the same standards to judging style or form. But there is very little evidence to justify such an assumption, and it is one not normally made by relativistic anthropologists. Ethnographers have usually found it difficult to disentangle people's purely aesthetic standards from evaluations based on judgments of other kinds, especially those of familiarity or strangeness, of practicality or appropriateness, of the technical skill of the maker, of age or rarity, of meaning or function.

One can attempt a universally applicable definition of art along the lines just suggested, but it is extremely difficult to apply this and other definitions to individual cases, even when one can interview the artists and other members of their societies. It is usually impossible to make such distinctions among the products of past societies, even if they have modern descendants or are well known to anthropology or history. A universalistic definition of art is not operationally useful. This and similar definitions do not permit us to recognize art as opposed to non-art among the artifacts available for our study and appreciation.

There is another way to identify art (Alsop 1978; 1982; and, to a lesser extent, Thompson 1979). If we apply in our definition the historical and socioeconomic determinants of fine art as it exists in Europe and Euro-America, the category delimited in this way is far from universal in human cultures. In fact, it is a relatively rare phenomenon. It is defined by the existence of art collecting, art history, and an art market. Objects that are otherwise produced for consumption, with the expectation that they will eventually wear out or be destroyed, are converted by collectors into durable goods with a potentially indefinite life span and a constantly escalating value. Art history is necessary to validate the objects, to establish their authenticity and value, and to determine attributions. When collectors turn to a new category of objects, scholarship certifies it and establishes its merit, distinguishing better from worse examples on aesthetic and other grounds. A special-

9. Buffalo effigy. Sioux or Cheyenne. Ca. 1860–1880, carved wood, tufted fiber tail, 8³⁄₄ × 7 × 2⁷⁄₈ inches. Philbrook Art Center, Tulsa, Roberta Campbell Lawson Collection, MI 2277.

Wooden male and female buffalo effigies like those here and in figure 10 were placed at the base of the sacred Sun Dance pole in the ceremonial brush arbor. They petitioned for fecundity of the buffalo, upon whose survival the equestrian hunters of the Plains depended.

10. Buffalo effigy. Sioux or Cheyenne. Ca. 1860–1880, carved wood, hide, hair, feathers, 8¹⁄₄ × 6¹⁄₂ × 2³⁄₄ inches. Philbrook Art Center, Tulsa, Roberta Campbell Lawson Collection, MI 2278.

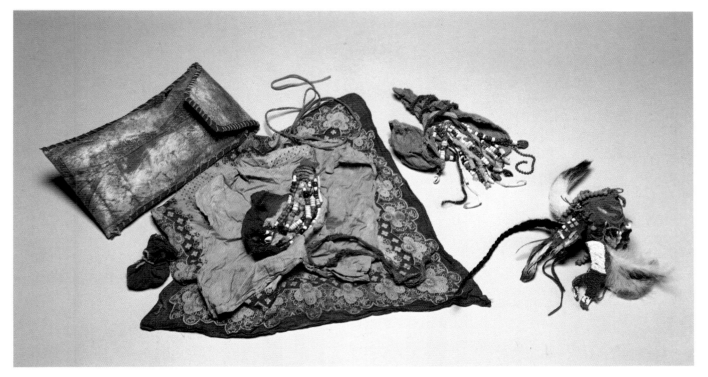

11. *Fetish. Crow. Ca. 1860, rock, hide, beads, scalplock, 17 × 12½ inches. Woolaroc Museum, Bartlesville, Philip R. Phillips Collection, IND 1274.*

Far right: Fetish bundle. Crow. 1850–1900, medicine objects, cloth, rawhide case, 14 × 17 inches. Philbrook Art Center, Tulsa, Elizabeth Cole Butler Collection, 82.1.96.

Personal visionary experiences were extremely important in the personality development and socialization of many Native American peoples. Although this was particularly true among hunters and gatherers, even agricultural people such as the Puebloans of the Southwest and the fisherfolk of the Northwest Coast relied upon individual supernatural encounters, which brought them power, knowledge, and often wealth. The aesthetics of visionary arts, with the exception of painted Plains shields, are alien to non-Indians, springing as they do from the animistic, shamanistic belief that all elements of the cosmos, both animate and inanimate, possess vitality and consciousness and can reveal themselves to those attuned to the ethereal powers. To honor such a revelation and to cement future contacts with the guardian forces, mortals made personal fetishes, medicine bundles, and protective symbolic designs like those pictured here.

ized art market promotes and serves the competition and demand of collectors for a necessarily limited supply of art objects of varying value. These are Alsop's (1982:16) "primary phenomena": the "irreducible triad" of art collecting, art history, and an art market. There was no art in this sense in traditional Indian societies. But many of their artifacts have now been defined as art within our own cultural categories. Indian artifacts have been the subject of collecting, scholarship, and commerce for perhaps two hundred years in Europe and America. However, until recently, Indian art was collected, studied, and sold in contexts quite distinct from those of fine art. In recent decades, this separate status has decreased.

Now the "secondary phenomena" that Alsop identifies as frequent but not necessary concomitants of fine art are also involved with Indian art: art museums, art faking, art historical reevaluations of previous styles, antique collecting, and high prices. To these should be added theft and looting, and museum deaccessioning scandals—and the curious economic and prestige dependencies among collectors, dealers, museum curators and trustees, scholars and teachers, tax

12. Horse stick. Plains. 1880–1890, carved wood, horse-hair, rawhide, beads, satin ribbon, 79 inches. Philbrook Art Center, Tulsa, Ellis Soper Collection, 31–958.

A common misconception about horse effigy staffs, one even perpetuated by twentieth-century Indian paintings, is that they were children's toys and hobby horses. Actually, they were the most important element of a Plains horse medicine bundle, owned by a man who had successfully amassed a substantial herd through raiding, trading, and dowry. It was also thought to assist him magically in acquiring additional horses, which were wealth objects.

lawyers and accountants, "philanthropoids" in foundations and government, art critics and writers, and artists, who are sometimes in opposition, usually in cooperation, and frequently the same individuals simultaneously or at different times in their careers.

ART HISTORIES OF NORTH AMERICA

Europeans began collecting Indian artifacts in the earliest period of exploration. However, no items known to have been collected in North America in the sixteenth century survive. Those few from the seventeenth and early eighteenth centuries that we have are, with only a handful of exceptions, without precise provenience information. But with the rise of museums in the late eighteenth century in Europe and in the mid-nineteenth century in North America, very large collections were preserved. The information accompanying the pieces improved in precision and in quality. From about 1880 until the 1930s, anthropologists gathered large numbers of objects directly from Indians, and devoted increasing attention to recording Indian knowledge of their production, uses, meanings, and, to some extent, histories. It is these collections, and the monographs about them, that form the basis for art histories of Indian societies. Our collections and museums now include tens of thousands of Indian artifacts that are not accompanied by adequate information, but most of these can ultimately be at least partly understood when they have been compared with properly documented pieces—that is to say, through art historical (or anthropological) research. Since the 1930s, the field collecting of "traditional" Indian art has gradually declined, as less was made and many of the surviving heirlooms were recycled, sold, stolen, buried, or destroyed. The focus of anthropological research also shifted. But beginning in the mid-1950s, a renewed interest in Indian art arose among some anthropologists, and, somewhat later, art historians and art museums expanded their attention to include these materials. Early precursors of this enlarged interest were the Exposition of Indian Tribal Arts in 1931, and the exhibition "Indian Art of the United States" in 1941, both in New York City.

The history of Indian art is a composite of many separate art traditions that have influenced one another. For the last 450 years, they have also been increasingly affected by the arts and technologies of Europe and of Europeans settled in America. Over the last century, these distinct Indian traditions

13. Necklace. Cheyenne. Ca. 1860, nuts, hide, cowrie shell, chipped stone, brass clamp, hide ring, green string, 24 inches. State Museum, Oklahoma Historical Society, Oklahoma City, OHS 113.

Personal adornment, including medicine pouches, amulets, and necklaces, was often protective as well as decorative. Just as with painted shields and medicine bundles, fetish necklaces were created from visionary spiritual experiences. In the supernatural encounter, which bestowed power and protection on a mortal, he was instructed how to fabricate an object combining particular symbolic elements. The meaning of the three medicine pouches, decorative rawhide tab, arrowpoint, miniature netted shield, and brass whisker-pullers was known only to the maker/wearer.

have become more similar, due to shared outside pressures and models and because of increasing contact among Indian societies at greater and greater distances from each other. Part of the rise of a pan-Indian ethnic identity is the rise of pan-Indian art styles.

Yet even contemporary Indian art is not homogeneous across the continent, and certainly "traditional" Indian art was less so. Tribal differences are known and often well recognized. Generalizations about these differences, and about similarities, nearly always involve the use of the culture area concept of anthropologists. This is a reasonable approach, for these areas were first defined as a method for classifying Indian artifacts for exhibits in museums (Brown 1980). Such an arrangement was evidently first developed by Otis T. Mason, William Henry Holmes, and Franz Boas for the 1893 World's Columbian Exposition in Chicago, as a better alternative to the then customary scheme based on functional types of artifacts, where each type was arranged in a pseudodevelopmental evolutionary series. Soon after, culture-area arrangements were introduced in the U.S. National Museum, the American Museum of Natural History, and elsewhere, for storage and research collections and their catalogues, as well as for organizing public exhibition halls. Aboriginal North America was divided into some four to twelve culture areas, which remain the conventional means for organizing knowledge about Indian cultures and history. The essential arbitrariness of most culture-area boundaries has long been recognized, but a scheme of this sort serves better for Indian art than it does for many other purposes. The areas were worked out in order to display similar artifacts together, and they have been defined primarily on the basis of environmental differences; they are based on the raw materials used in Indian subsistence and technology, which are fairly well correlated with the techniques and styles of art and artifacts.

The Southeast culture area could almost be defined and mapped as the region in which split cane, sometimes dyed red and black, was used in a limited set of twilling techniques to make certain types of basketry containers, trays, and mats. Similarly, the Northwest Coast area is nearly congruent with the distribution of certain types of twined basketry, while the Plains could be defined on the basis of women's clothing (before the mid-nineteenth century), and the Arctic, more than most areas, can be mapped from the coincident distributions of many types of clothing, tools, weapons, and boats. Many other examples could be cited. There are other styles of artifacts that are typical of one culture

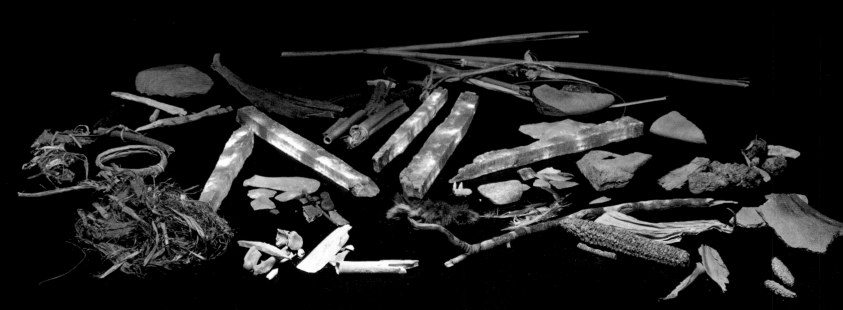

area but do not occur throughout it; for example, in the Southwest, pottery and weaving among the Pueblo; in the Northeast, wooden and cornhusk masks among the Iroquois.

However, culture areas are not entirely suitable as a framework for Indian art histories, for two reasons: the distributions of different styles do not necessarily coincide even at one time period, and the boundaries of style areas usually do not persist over long periods (Feest 1980:16–18; Douglas 1934). Archaeologists, whose fundamental evidence is artifactual, have rarely attempted to map the continent or any major part of it, even for one prehistoric period, since the artifact types and styles they recognize have different distributions; and within one medium, such as pottery or chipped stone, the differences between types are of different degrees and the distinctive attributes are incompatible. In addition, the pattern of distributions changes markedly over time. The same difficulties exist with Indian artifacts of the historic period. Thus, for example, similar coiled basketry occurred in the Southwest, California, and part of the Great Basin; snowshoe types crosscut the Subarctic and Northeast; patterns of women's facial tattooing were spread over most of western North America and also the Arctic; there was a very distinctive type of male chest tattooing found in the eighteenth-century Northeast (Iroquois) and Southeast (Creek), and also in the nineteenth century on the southern Plains; the style of geometric painting on hide clothing that is recognized for the late-nineteenth- and early-twentieth-century Naskapi in the eastern Subarctic is also documented for painted robes of the eighteenth-century Northeast (Iroquois) and Southeast (Creek, Louisiana) and of the eighteenth- and nineteenth-century Plains, and for garments in the central Subarctic of the nineteenth century. Culture areas can only serve as very approximate sorting devices, and the temptation to reify them must be resisted.

Indian artists must always have been experimenters and innovators—trying new materials, new forms and designs, new functions—and also learners, not only from their elders and contemporaries, but also from neighboring societies whose styles they knew from observation and from acquisitions by gift, trade, or capture. This is not merely a logical assumption —there is much archaeological, historical, and ethnographic evidence for innovation and diffusion. But influence may be negative as well as positive; there is sometimes an effort to

14. Cosmic Mobile. Rio Grande Puebloan. Ca. 1740–1780, painted hide, rabbit fur, rock, crystals, potsherds, painted sticks, fiber hoops, tree bark, reeds, and miscellaneous ceremonial objects. Philbrook Art Center, Tulsa, anonymous loan.

This enigmatic object was recovered from a cave in the Gobernador territory of New Mexico. Following the successful revolt of the combined Puebloan and Navajo peoples against the Spanish colonists in 1680, many Puebloans of the Rio Grande area fled to the hills and isolated regions for refuge from the feared Spanish military reprisals. This important religious object, which may have been a central altar to one of the pueblo's religious societies, was probably removed from its original location at that time. The work may symbolize the holistic cosmic view of the Pueblo Indians. The interdependent dualities of night and day, the gods and man, are depicted with fertility symbols and celestial lights.

15. Speaker's staff. Tlingit (Frog Clan). Ca. 1890, carved and painted cedar, abalone shell, 35 × 5 × 4½ inches. Philbrook Art Center, Tulsa, Elizabeth Cole Butler Collection, 82.1.63.

Among the aristocratic high cultures of the Northwest Coast, rank (ranging from slaves to hereditary nobles) was all-important. Various family lineages formed components of a larger village which in turn comprised a subdivision of what could loosely be called a tribe. Among the Tlingit, as with other Northern Coastal people, each political and economic unit had a hereditary head and political spokesman. This speaker for the people possessed a speaker's staff, painted and carved with the supernatural patrons and guardians of his family. Thus, when he spoke formally, the emblem of power indicated that his proclamations were sanctioned not only by his lineage but also by its supernatural allies.

16. Dance wands. Hopi. 1910–1920, painted wood, 22 × 5 inches; 21¼ × 5 inches. Philbrook Art Center, Tulsa, anonymous loan.

Painted cottonwood plaques with handles were used in a variety of ways in Hopi ceremonialism. In certain public dance performances, women held the objects, fanning blessings toward the crowd in an alternating dipping motion. Occasionally, they were also erected amid altars. The importance is not in the form of the object but in its germination and fertility images. The crosshatched figure at the bottom of each paddle represents a germinating ear of corn. Above it float three stacked rain clouds with vertically falling raindrops, and surmounting the topmost cloud is the two-horned fertility god.

17. Dance sash. Hopi. Ca. 1900, homespun cotton, commercial yarns, 84 × 11 inches; fringe: 7 inches. Museum of the Red River, Idabel, 01.

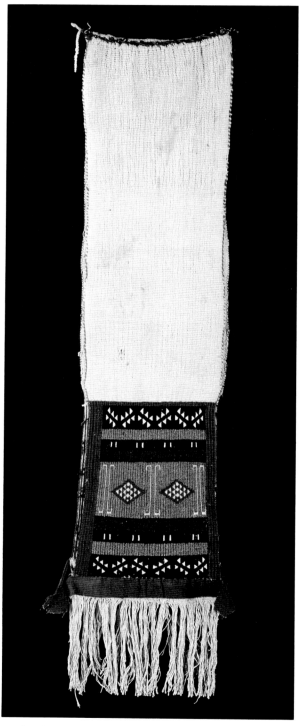

An agricultural people's predominant concern is understandably fertility, as their survival is inexorably linked with the earth's bounty. Therefore it is not surprising that, even in abstract compositions, the sacred Puebloan arts focus on fertility symbolism. The Katcina sash represents an inverted step pyramid whose bottommost level of red crosshatched lozenges stands for the cultivated, planted earth. The blue bands stand for sky, the black bands with white vertical marks for falling rain, and the serrated, zigzagged bands for lightning and rain clouds on a distant horizon. The field of the sash stands for the germinative summer cycle and the plain white cotton portion for the winter cycle.

do something different from one's neighbors, for example by reversing their forms or meanings. Art is both a result and a medium of communication.

In the 1960s archaeologists attempted to identify prehistoric residence patterns by combining the meticulous recording of the find-spots of artifacts within a single site with analyses of microstylistic differences. The hypothesis was that stylistic similarities identify learning groups, who lived together and thus taught and learned from one another and whose products ended up together. The effort was not very successful, because the learning patterns of artists and the movements of artifacts before their ultimate disposition were more varied and complex than was at first assumed. But less fine-grained studies, based on similar assumptions (not very different, after all, from those of art historians), should reveal details of the learning, transmission, and change of styles.

A good deal is known about the creative Native American adaptation of motifs and materials of European origin, and their spread over the past two to three hundred years. The most obvious example is the use of small colored glass beads for embroidery and some weaving, all across the continent but especially in those regions where embroidery with dyed porcupine quills served as a model. Designs themselves spread: floral motifs, probably learned initially from the French in Canada, replaced earlier designs (mainly geometric ones) as they spread first over the Northeast, then the Southeast, and finally the Plains and Subarctic, reaching the Northwest Coast in the mid- to late nineteenth century. Also in the Northeast, basketry made from thin wooden splints—learned from Europeans, probably Swedish immigrants—replaced the aboriginal techniques so early that it is not clear what the original forms, materials, and techniques were (Brasser 1975). Silver jewelry was first made by Euro-American silversmiths for the Indian trade, but soon there were Indian smiths in both the Northeast and Southeast, usually using silver coins as their raw material, but changing, reinterpreting, and elaborating the introduced forms. The techniques and the styles spread, developing in the process, through the Plains to the Northwest Coast and the Southwest, merging in the latter area with another stream of influence from Mexico, this one ultimately Spanish and Moorish as the other was British, Scandinavian, and French in origin. In Indian Territory in the late nineteenth century, the industry was adapted to work in German silver, especially for ornaments, such as water-bird brooches associated with the Native American Church. The spread of the Peyote religion over much of the central and western part of the country during the past hundred years has carried with it a special iconography and particular artifact forms, for example the beadwork and feather Peyote fan (figs. 18–20) and the Peyote waterdrum. The history of weaving in the Southwest, both Pueblo and Navajo, is fairly well known, including how European sheep's wool was added to the native cotton, and how Navajo wearing blankets evolved into rugs made for sale to non-Indians, at first as floor covers and later as art collectibles, with concomitant changes in patterns. But little is known of the complexities, especially in the Northeast and Southeast, of the stylistic history of clothing made of trade cloth by Indian women, who at first copied non-Indian garment forms but soon, in several areas, developed fashions that evolved in ways largely unrelated to clothing style changes among neighboring non-Indians. Such fashions could be traced into the 1960s in Indian-made garments worn every day by most Florida Seminole women and some men. A related modern art form, also poorly studied, is the elaborate, exuberant, rapidly changing costuming for powwows, especially in the Midwest.

MEANINGS IN TRADITIONAL INDIAN ART

What might be called the external meanings of Indian art are qualities recognized in it by the society that has classified it as art. There are also internal meanings, the messages intentionally or unintentionally conveyed by the artist. Some of these may be the same as the external meanings, especially when the artist and observer share cultural understandings. But for ancient objects, the two kinds of meanings must be very different, since the culture of the artists and the audience they worked for was unlike our own.

We cannot recover the original meanings for archaeological objects in any detail, although hypothetical meanings can be proposed on the basis of parallels with better-known, later societies. For historic cultures, we are dependent on the quality of the contemporary records and on the similarity of those cultures to better-known related ones (including better-understood descendants).

Postcards sold in Indian country display "Indian symbols and their meanings." One explains that "the earliest writings of the American Indian were those of signs and symbols. These symbols are always apparent in their handicrafts and jewelry." This represents a common view of art—especially Indian art—as a system of communication. Around the turn of the century, Boas and his students investigated the topic in some detail. At that time, a contrast was sometimes drawn between "realistic" or "representative" art and "(purely) geometric" art. The latter was often seen as derived from the former, by the process of "stylization" or "conventionalization." Or, as Kroeber (1900:69) explained, a tendency toward greater "fidelity to nature," toward making ornament "more realistic, more

18. Fan. Kiowa. Ca. 1900, eagle feathers, beadwork, 7½ inches. Philbrook Art Center, Tulsa, Bright Roddy Collection, 31–66.

19. *Peyote fan. Southern Plains. 1910–1930, beadwork, feathers of scissortail, military parrot, macaw, hide fringe, 18½ inches. Thomas Gilcrease Institute of American History and Art, Tulsa, 8427.217.*

This "peyote fan" and the one in figure 20 are twentieth-century adaptations of the earlier nineteenth-century Plains eagle-wing fan (fig. 18). Both objects have social and religious associations, and are also honorific badges. They are not simply decorative, but are used to move power or

blessing toward participants engaged in ritual. Such fans are consummate examples of the many layers of meaning that can be inherent in a single object. Ideally, each feather was collected and bundled and fastened to the fan's handle by its owner, who blessed it as he did so.

20. *Peyote fan. Southern Plains. 1910–1930, German silver, scissortail and macaw feathers, beadwork, hide fringe, 23 inches. Thomas Gilcrease Institute of American History and Art, Tulsa, 8427.218.*

imitative," leads to the development of "art as we know it"; whereas a tendency to "emphasize and exaggerate the salient features; that is, to think the object, instead of see it . . . will cause the art to be more symbolic" and leads "ultimately into writing." These ideas now seem dated, in view of what was beginning to happen in European art even as Kroeber wrote. But the old-fashioned theoretical

21. Shell gorget. Mississippian (Spiro Mounds). Ca. 1200, carved shell, 7½ inches maximum diameter. Stovall Museum of Science and History, University of Oklahoma, Norman, LF CRi B108–9.

22. Pipesmoker *pipe bowl. Mississippian (Spiro Mounds). Ca. 1200, carved stone, 8⅛ × 5¼ × 10⅛ inches. Stovall Museum of Science and History, University of Oklahoma, Norman, LF CRi B99 2.*

23. Effigy pipe. Mississippian (Spiro Mounds). Ca. 1200, carved stone, 8½ × 3⅝ × 8¾ inches. Stovall Museum of Science and History, University of Oklahoma, Norman, CRi I A9–1.

24. Painted shield. Arapaho. Ca. 1890, hide, pigments, feathers, bells, 15¼ inches in diameter. Philbrook Art Center, Tulsa, Elizabeth Cole Butler Collection, L82.1.103.

The 1890s witnessed a series of desperate revitalization movements among Native Americans which were directed toward reconstituting their rapidly disintegrating world. Most widely known of these was the so-called Ghost Dance, in which corrupt white ways were put aside and ancient ways readopted in the hope that they would displace the destructive influence of white civilization. Though armed conflict had virtually ceased between Indians and whites by this time, the old warrior gear was nevertheless introduced into these peaceful ceremonies as a traditional protective device. This painted hide dance shield decorated with Ghost Dance symbols of antelopes, turtles, moons, and suns, was not a device of war but a symbol of protection.

interest led Kroeber and others to make some useful ethnographic inquiries regarding the meanings of "decorative" designs in several North American Indian societies far more "traditional" than any of today.

Investigating symbolism among the Arapaho, especially in beadwork, quillwork, and painting, Kroeber tabulated a large number of design elements with specific meanings: "The number of symbols is considerable; several of them express abstract ideas; connection between the symbols is usual, and they may even tell a story. All this suggests picture-writing. At the same time there is no real pictography. The symbols described cannot be read. One man may guess the meaning of another's design; but he may also fail to understand it, or may even misinterpret it" (Kroeber 1900:84).

Inquiring of makers and, where different, also of the owners of objects about the significance of the designs on them, Kroeber (1902) found much variation among individuals in the meanings ascribed to specific designs. Boas (1903) pointed out that the same or similar designs also were given quite different meanings in different Plains tribes. Some but by no means all of this variation among the Arapaho was accounted for by the larger context. For example, a thin vertical rectangle might represent a trail when associated with other symbols that refer to landscape features, but a bow in the context of a buffalo hunt. Among other possible meanings of this same design element are river, rope, worm, sunray, smoke, tent pole, and sky. Quite similar structures of meaning were found by Speck (1927) in inquiries among the Penobscot, and by Bunzel (1929) in interviews with Zuñi potters: minimal meaningful design units, whose significance varies depending on the larger contexts in which they appear. Reichard's (1930:461) comment about these and other investigations can still stand as a summary of the North American situation: they "have shown that 'naming' of designs and 'reading-in' of meaning is very common, but that true symbolism, symbolism which is understood by many members of a group, is rare."

INDIAN ART IN THE EUROPEAN TRADITION

From the sixteenth century on, Indians made maps for Europeans in the early stages of exploration all across the continent. Although these must often have been ephemeral, even traced on the ground, still, a few early examples by Indian and Eskimo hands do survive, and others are known because their influence is recognizable in maps drawn by non-Indians (Vollmar 1981). Also in early eastern North America are pictographic signatures by Indians on Euro-American land conveyances, treaties, and an occasional letter. In the Northeast, they are usually representational, often depicting clan totems and perhaps sometimes alluding to the meaning of the name, and evidently derived from a native tradition of pictographs used for other purposes. In the Southeast, such marks on European documents are usually abstract geometric designs, which may have originated in the marks and rubrics used by European signers (although here, too, there are hints of aboriginal systems of marks to identify individuals). Perhaps only in the eighteenth century, when paper became more readily available, did other work in this medium develop. Mandan drawings on paper from the early nineteenth century show European stylistic influences, as does a self-portrait done in 1815 by Josiah Francis, the Muskogee prophet. These, like most others that survive, were done to meet European and Euro-American interests. Yet it is possible that drawings·on paper were quite common everywhere for internal consumption. Examples known from the twentieth-century Iroquois could probably have been matched in these and other Indian communities of the nineteenth century: sketches of masks done by carvers as trial designs; depictions of religious themes made and kept by followers of the Longhouse religion; portraits; and erotic drawings by an artist so skilled that other members of his community were willing to pay some two dollars apiece for them during the Depression.

Contrastive European influences can be seen in early-twentieth-century Eskimo carving, drawing, and painting. A comparison of modern Canadian and Alaskan Inuit art with recent Greenlandic art (e.g., in Kaalund 1979) and modern Siberian Eskimo art (e.g., in Antropova 1953; Efimova and Klitina 1981) quite clearly shows the effects of the rather different North American, Danish, and Soviet national styles.

The origins of contemporary Indian easel painting have been traced to Plains ledger drawings (fig. 163) mostly done for Army officer collectors, and to Southwestern drawings and paintings encouraged by anthropologists and school art teachers (fig. 197). The themes of these were greatly influenced by the interests of those for whom they were drawn. Aside from the themes, there are unresolved problems over the sources of the styles: how much they are "native," "aboriginal," "traditional," or even, according to some naïve commentators (including some teachers and some of their Indian students), innate. How much is style influenced by art teachers and other non-Indian consumers and the models they provided (including reproductions of Chinese and Japanese paintings and prints, and of older Indian materials in museums, as well as of European "modern" art said to exemplify the sort of abstraction or treatments of form and color proper for Indian art)? How much is it influenced by the popular art of the larger society (perhaps especially comic strips, particularly for Disneyesque animals)? The work of the Indian painters of the first half of this century in the Southwest and in Oklahoma is well known because it was collected, exhibited, studied, and published, and because these artists worked in a readily recognizable style. They participated in a school of painting that changed and developed (and ultimately stultified) through formal teaching and by informal imitation, reacting to the standards of a body of consumers that included teachers, jurors of shows, curators, collectors—and other Indian artists, but rarely or never other non-artist members of Indian communities (although there are some well-known instances of negative sanctions applied to artists by Pueblo communities).

However, there were many other Indian painters outside the Santa Fe–Oklahoma orbit, in addition to those in the unrelated, clearly marked, viable traditions on the modern Northwest Coast,

25. War Dance Gathering Scene. *Earnest Spybuck (1883–1949), Shawnee. Ca. 1910, watercolor on paper, 17¼ × 24¾ inches. Museum of the American Indian, Heye Foundation, New York, 2/5614.*

This scene, typical of the time, depicts a Shawnee ceremony in Oklahoma. The artist himself may be shown in the center foreground, perhaps shaking hands with the ethnologist M. R. Harrington (holding bridle), for whom this painting was done (Callander and Slivka 1984:21). —W. C. S.

26. Untitled. *Andrew Standing-Soldier (1917–1967), Sioux. Ca. 1948, oil on circular fiberboard, 16⅛ inches in diameter. William C. Sturtevant Collection, Washington, D.C.*

This is a very close copy, laterally reversed, of a fine color lithograph reproduction (Alexander 1938: pl. 9) of a painting on canvas entitled *An Indian Horse Dance* by the Oglala Sioux artist Kills Two (Nupa Kte), born in 1869 and died in 1927. The original was in the collection of H. B. Alexander. The style is a development from that of classic Sioux hide painting. According to R. J. DeMallie (personal communication, 1984), there is no other evidence for the use of buffalo masks and buffalo-skin horse leggings in the Horse Dance. The painting was purchased in 1948 for $3.00 in the crafts shop on the Pine Ridge Reservation, South Dakota.—W. C. S.

27. Zacharie Vincent, Huron of Lorette, with His Son Cyprien. *Zacharie Vincent (1815–1886), Huron. 1845, oil on canvas, 19 × 16¼ inches. Musée du Québec.*

Zacharie Vincent had some formal training in art, as is evident from this self-portrait, one of many similar ones he painted. He depicted himself in formal dress, including explicit symbols of his Indian and Huron identity: wampum sash, pipe-tomahawk, and silver brooch, arm band, and medal, and his son with silver brooch and bow and arrows.—W. C. S.

among the Ojibwa and Odawa of Ontario, and in the Canadian Arctic. Artists whose names and some of whose works are known—but who rarely, if ever, appear in surveys of Indian painting —include in the early twentieth century the Shawnee Earnest Spybuck (fig. 25) and the Winnebago Angel Decora. A much earlier example is the West Greenlander Aron of Kangeq (Meldgaard 1982). Working into the 1940s (when he also did some paintings in the "traditional" Plains style) was Andrew Standing-Soldier (fig. 26), a Dakota. The career of the Lorette Huron painter Zacharie Vincent (1815–1886; figs. 27, 28) is instructive (Labelle and Thivierge 1981; Sioui 1981). There were several established Iroquois (especially Tuscarora) artists of the early nineteenth century, the best known being David Cusick, author of a volume (Cusick 1826) that was illustrated with crude woodcuts after his own drawings; no originals of his work are definitely known, but several survive by Dennis Cusick, who was evidently his brother. An especially interesting and well-documented Iroquois artist is Jesse J. Cornplanter (1889–1957), who began drawing at the age of eleven or twelve and continued all his life, with no formal training and no known informal artistic influences, but with great and widely recognized talent. His earliest known drawings are lively and accurate depictions of scenes of reservation life, especially ritual subjects (fig. 29). Quite soon, he introduced reconstructions—the poses and activities being ones he had observed, but the clothing and architecture those of an earlier day. Later, he drew illustrations of myths (examples of his work can be seen in Starr 1903; Parker 1913; Trigger 1978:307, 446, 456, 458, 461, 462; and Cornplanter 1938; a biographical sketch is Fenton 1978).

Cornplanter and the other artists just mentioned share several characteristics. They are isolated individuals, each with his own style, but without influence or followers; the naïve styles are not recognizably affected by older, traditional Indian art; the themes are self-consciously Indian, and often with some reconstruction (they are usually illustrations of aspects of Indian life, and often display the effects of research in books or museums on local traditions); their markets, as far as is known, were non-Indian, and the economic rewards were very small. Probably the most significant of these characteristics, by comparison with the Indian art of the pan-Indian or Santa Fe–Oklahoma style and of the modern Northwest Coast, Ojibwa-Odawa, and Inuit schools, is the lack of evidence for the adaptation of Indian stylistic features: only the iconography, the subject matter, is "traditional" or recognizably Indian, not the style. This surely limited the market and the influence of these artists.

There are similarities, especially in their iconographic themes, between the work of these isolated artists and products of the Plains and Southwestern schools of "contemporary" Indian painting, both in the early stages and in the florescent and decadent periods of these later schools, and with many works of modern Indian painters and sculptors as well. The themes tend to be genre topics, here ethnographic illustrations of aspects of daily life and appearances foreign to the viewers. These may include self-portraits of the artists displaying signs of their Indianness. Later there sometimes appear depictions of supernatural beings, mythological themes and incidents, and more or less secret or rare ceremonies. Especially in regions where the externals of Indian life as experienced by the

28. Scene in a Yard of the Huron Village, Lorette, Quebec. *Zacharie Vincent, Huron. Ca. 1870s, charcoal on paper, 11¼ × 15½ inches. Chateau de Ramezay, Montreal.*

Here Vincent provided an ethnographic document on contemporary Huron life, of interest chiefly to the non-Indian purchasers of his work.—W. C. S.

artists are like those of their audience, artists reconstruct earlier appearances and earlier activities now lost—exposing the works to anthropologists' criticism of their accuracy. Indian artists have often internalized the exoticism, the interest in "tradition" so strongly manifested by their non-Indian contacts. After all, this antiquarian, sentimental interest in obsolete customs, ancient objects, and surviving fragments of old systems of belief and behavior is an important aspect of Indian identity as seen by the larger society and thus, inevitably, as seen by many Indians.

INDIAN ART?

What has happened in so-called contemporary Indian art over the last ten years or so should be seen against this background. The self-consciously Indian stylistic features that characterized it are disappearing, and the label "traditional Indian painting" is more frequently applied to these styles as they become outmoded. But because the ethnicity of Indian artists remains important to many of them and to their audience, it continues to be signalled in their works. Representational paintings and sculpture nearly always include recognizable Indian themes, while nonrepresentational works often include obvious references to stereotypic Indian abstract designs (such as those on much

29. Indian New Year; Fourth Day on Jan. 25th. 1901. Cattaraugus Reservation. *Jesse J. Cornplanter (1889–1957), Seneca. 1901, watercolor on paper, 7 × 10 inches. New York State Library, Albany, Cornplanter Collection.* The False Face Dance in the Longhouse during the Midwinter Ceremony was observed and recorded with great accuracy by the Seneca artist Jesse Cornplanter, when he was twelve years old.—W. C. S.

30. Mohawk Headdress. *Richard Glazer Danay (1942–   ),*
Mohawk. 1982, acrylic on hard hat, 6½ × 9⅛ × 11⅝
inches. Seneca-Iroquois Nation Museum, Salamanca, New
York.

This "headdress" by Richard Glazer Danay is a painted
hard hat of the type worn by the Mohawk artist when he
worked, like many other Mohawk, as a structural high
steel worker. The garish colors refer to the surroundings
in Coney Island, where he was raised. The female figure
on each side alludes to the ogling of passersby by high
steel workers, a practice recognized to represent a risk to
life and limb of the workers and their fellows, who depend for safety on concentration and attention to the tasks
of their job. The falling worker is part of this scene and

probably refers to the death of a friend of the artist, which
precipitated his abandonment of the profession. The spot-
ted orange circle is said by Danay to represent the jigsaw-
puzzle fragmentation of modern life. On the front of the
headdress is a face representing the wooden masks used in
the traditional Iroquois religion. The crest on top is interpreted as representing the old, stereotypic Mohawk hair-
cut. Thus the whole work has clear allusions to Indian
ethnicity and particularly to Mohawk identity (cf. Mitchell 1960, Freilich 1958, 1977), as well as carrying more
personal meanings. It was painted in part for a high steel
worker uncle of the artist who had told him he did not
understand his art; unfortunately, he did not appreciate
this work either.—W. C. S.

Southwestern pottery or Plains beadwork) and are nearly always given titles that allude to Indianness.
The ethnicity of the artist is made even more explicit by the use of identifying tribal designations and
by the adoption of clearly Indian personal names by some artists who lack them.

The Indian artist faces an ambivalence between, on the one hand, being allowed and able to
compete on an equal basis in contemporary cultural movements of the larger society, gaining recognition as an artist *tout court* rather than as a special, separate "Indian artist" (discriminated against or
in favor of), and on the other, being able and allowed to maintain and express in art his special
Indian or even tribal identity, and to have that special status recognized and valued by the rest of the
society, not just by tourists and anthropologists. It is, once again, the strain between the melting pot
and pluralist ideals.

To fragment individual artists in analysis helps to clarify the tensions that exist in interethnic
relations in the modern world, and sheds some light on the meanings of the art that bears the ethnic

31. Hat. Iroquois. Late 1800s, beadwork on fabric, 5½ × 9½ × 8 inches. Woolaroc Museum, Bartlesville, IND 433.

This is an unusual variant of a type of cap common among the Iroquois for a brief period in the mid-nineteenth century. Beautifully made, the form is influenced by Scottish Glengarry bonnets, while the floral motifs are ultimately of French origin.—W. C. S.

label "Indian." However, it is surely more significant for comprehending the observers and consumers of Indian art and the art world than it is for understanding the motivations and sensibilities of working artists.

There are several markets for Indian art, both "traditional" and "contemporary." One, the older and in some ways less sophisticated, favors recognizably realistic and representational work. This bias is reflected in price differentials at auctions of "ethnographic art" and in the emphases of many exhibitions and publications of contemporary as well as traditional Indian art. Another, more sophisticated (but not necessarily wealthier) audience values abstract, largely nonrepresentational work by artists who are not ethnically categorized, and is sometimes willing to apply similar standards to work that is identified as Indian. Other Indian artists follow current realist styles of non-Indian art. Their work is sometimes said (by those who dislike such styles) to convey a "message" or a "protest" or to be "controversial"—as though it needed to be more meaningful than more familiar styles.

There are many meanings of Indian art. For old or traditional Indian art, the meanings that artifacts carried for their original makers and users can be understood—and that only very incompletely—if we suspend the ethnocentrism involved in classifying them as fine art, and if we pay serious attention to the findings of ethnographers over the past century or so. For new or contemporary Indian art, one must remember that the artists and their works belong to a larger society. The nature of Indian ethnicity within that larger society affects the meanings of identifiable Indian art. And for both old and new Indian works of art, it may be that semantic ambiguity is an inherent and necessary characteristic, as it perhaps is for all art.

Aesthetic Archives:
The Visual Language of Plains Ledger Art

GLORIA A. YOUNG

H istoric Native Americans were a visually oriented people. They developed not one, but several systems of visual, nonverbal communication. This is not surprising since north of Mexico some three hundred languages from more than fifty different language families were spoken, making intertribal communication difficult. One of the best-known means of visual communication between tribes was the hand-sign language of the Plains, but this was only one of the most overt systems.

Many kinds of meaning, at many levels of interpretation, were embedded in historical Native American art. Personal shields and regalia often bore designs whose significance was known only to their owners, having been obtained through private visions. Many sacred objects were ornamented with esoteric symbols known only to special religious practitioners. The decoration on clothing and horse regalia carried information about the wearer's identity, which was easily interpreted by members of his tribe and those who interacted with them, both friends and foes.

But even more widely understood was a type of art, figurative drawing, which carried meaning so overtly that it was almost a universal language. On the Plains, this pictorial imagery that recorded the exploits of tribes and individuals came to be called ledger drawing. Originally made on hides, by the mid-1800s these records began to be drawn on the blank pages of ledger books obtained by Indians from military posts and traders. In art, Native Americans recorded their history.

Historic Europeans were a verbally oriented people. The nineteenth-century Europeans and Americans who came to the Plains relied almost exclusively on words for communication—and to an astonishing extent on the written word. The verbal descriptions in their letters, journals, and official documents comprise the natural and social histories of their times. Along with census reports, records of business transactions, and Bureau of Indian Affairs correspondence, they are preserved, catalogued, and microfilmed in today's archives. They are written history and, as such, are believed. Perhaps it was because of the Euro-American faith in the written word that these plainsmen took such pains to write down even simple messages. They knew that what is written is official, and becomes history. And they had a fine sense of themselves as makers of history as they pushed civilization westward.

Such men were the special agents sent from the Kiowa, Comanche, and Wichita Agency at Anadarko, Indian Territory, out to the Kiowa camp one hundred miles away to be present as the Indians gathered for the Kiowa Sun Dance of 1881. The agents took paper, pens, and ink with them and, probably at some inconvenience, communicated by letter with Colonel P. B. Hunt back at the Agency. These letters, excerpts of which follow, tell a story and make the events surrounding the Sun Dance official in Indian Service history.

Letter to Col. P. B. Hunt, United States Indian Service, Kiowa, Comanche, and Wichita Agency, Anadarko, Indian Territory, from E. L. Clark, Special Agent:

> July 14, 1881
> Camp, North Fork of the Red River

Sir:

I have the honor to report that I reached the Kiowa camp at this place with Lieut. Eggleston's command on the evening of the 12th inst., finding the Indians all together. Heap O'Bears is moving this morning up this stream a distance of 15 or 20 miles where he proposes to make the "Medicine House" which will be about 85 or 90 miles from the agency. . . .

The Indians all claim to be without rations, though I think most of them have a little flour. They depend on deer and antelope for their meat. Herds of cattle are still passing over the Cattle trail 5 miles east of us. Many of the Indians go and meet the herds, and beg for, or try to trade for cattle, but I think with little success. I have so far heard of no trouble of any kind between the Indians and white men. . . .

There are a few Cheyennes and Arapahoes here moving with the Kiowas—numbering about 160 Cheyennes, men, women and children, and 44 Arapahoes under "Powder Face" and "Black Coyote." These all claim to be without rations and express themselves as very hungry. . . .

None of the Indians have expressed or shown any hostile feeling towards anyone and so far as I can learn they intend nothing wrong. . . .

After the dance is over, the man will make his attempt to create buffalo and failing in this will of course cause disappointment and it would be mere conjecture to say what may be the result or effect of the failure, a short time, however, will disclose it, and I think Lieut. Eggleston's idea a good one, in asking for a few more men, as his force is now too small to be of any service in case of any emergency requiring the use of troops.

If you can send immediately to the cattle herd and order beef and start party with the cattle as soon as possible in charge of some careful white man and make arrangements with someone to haul flour, to be paid from beef hides, I am sure it would give great relief and satisfaction to these Indians (Clark 1881a).

Letter to Col. P. B. Hunt from Lieut. M. C. Eggleston, Tenth Cavalry:

> July 19, 1881
> Medicine Lodge Camp, North Fork, Red River

Sir:

I have the honor to acknowledge receipt of your letter of instructions of the 18 inst. and to inform you that the Indians have finally established their Medicine Circle at a point on the North Fork of the Red River about one hundred miles distant from the Agency. Your prompt and judicious action in forwarding supplies and the arrival today of beef cattle almost entirely removes all apprehension of mischief likely to be caused by hungry Indians so far from their agency . . . (Eggleston 1881).

Letter to Col. P. B. Hunt from E. L. Clark:

> July 20, 1881
> Camp on the North Fork of Red River

. . . The pipe was loaded by Heap O'Bears and tendered to *Bau-tigh*, also one to *Sit-bo-haunt*, by Woman Heart's son, the Buffalo Medicine Man, by which they were authorized

32. Sun Boy, a Kiowa Chief.

Sun Boy was a Kiowa warrior born to a noble clan. He lived to see Kiowa domination in the Black Hills of South Dakota, the final days of glory for the raiding masters of the Southern Plains, and a life of tribal peace and diplomacy on the Kiowa reservation in Indian Territory. With the passing of men like Sun Boy, the prerogative of owning and displaying pictographic records of personal war deeds ended. Though Plains pictography as a communicative language died, it provided the foundation for an artistic tradition which would become the Oklahoma Indian art movement of the twentieth century.

to hunt a Buffalo Bull for the Medicine dance. They both started this morning before day and had not returned when I was at their camp this evening... (Clark 1881b).

Letter to Col. P. B. Hunt from E. L. Clark:

July 26, 1881

... The Kiowas succeeded in killing 2 Buffalo, 1 Bull & 1 Cow. Just the thing they were so anxious for. They cut the sacred Cottonwood fork yesterday and hoisted the Bull Scalp without its decorations as offerings on yesterday evening. They will complete their arbor in 3 or 4 days, then the 4 day dance takes place. I think there [are] about 50 Cheyennes and 40 Arapahoes here yet who will probably remain till dance is over. I issued them flour, coffee and tobacco... (Clark 1881c).

The U.S. Indian Service's fears of warfare after the Kiowa Sun Dance of 1881 were unfounded, even though the attempt to return the vanishing buffalo herds to the Southern Plains through the Buffalo Medicine Man's rites failed. Yet these letters remain historical documents, carefully stored by the Service for many years and then preserved and catalogued in historical archives. They are deemed military notes of some importance, worthy of care and preservation because they document the relationship of the military and the Indian Service to the Kiowa tribe in a turbulent period of history. Hunt, Clark, and Eggleston were wise to be on the lookout for warlike actions after the Sun Dance and to keep the large gathering of Indians well fed and pacified. For the elder Kiowa chiefs gathered on the North Fork of the Red River that summer were heroic warriors who had once lived in freedom, wreaking havoc among their foes on the Plains before reluctantly settling down near Fort Sill and the newly created Anadarko Agency in the late 1870s. Peace was still an uncertain phenomenon in 1881.

Had there been a newspaper reporter, a historian, or a journalist with an anthropological bent accompanying the cavalry that summer, he might have interviewed some of the old warriors about the battles they had fought in their long and colorful lives. Had he committed the interviews to paper, they might have been stored, preserved, and catalogued like the letters to the Agency. For example, had he entered in a journal the military exploits of one Kiowa chief of fifty-odd years of age, Sun Boy (fig. 32), a chief who was skeptical of the Buffalo Medicine Man's efforts at the Sun Dance that year, we might have available today a document which would read like this:

1833. Sun Boy, as a young man, fought in a battle between the Kiowa and Osage warriors who attacked the Kiowa camp at Cutthroat Gap.

1843. Sun Boy went on a raiding party to Tamaulipas, Mexico, and was fallen upon by Mexicans while recrossing the Rio Grande.

1844. Sun Boy was once again involved in battles in Mexico.

1849. Sun Boy fought against Pawnee warriors in Nebraska.

1851. Sun Boy, with Dohasan's party, attacked and killed Pawnee warriors who had taken offerings attached to the cottonwood pole of the recently abandoned Kiowa Sun Dance lodge.

1852. Sun Boy, with a party of Kiowa, Kiowa-Apache, Apache, Cheyenne, Arapaho, and Dakota, fought the Pawnee.

1854. Sun Boy fought in a skirmish near the Smoky Hill River in Kansas, in which a war party of fifteen hundred warriors from seven tribes—the Kiowa, Kiowa-Apache, Comanche, Cheyenne, Arapaho, Osage, and Crow—were defeated by approximately one hundred Sac and Fox warriors and a small number of Potawatomi armed with American long-range rifles.

1854. Sun Boy fought in a battle in which the Kiowa killed 113 Pawnee.

1860. Sun Boy fought with Kiowa and Comanche against U.S. soldiers under the command of Captain S. D. Sturgis on Republican Fork of the Kansas River.

1864. Sun Boy fought with Kiowa and Comanche against Kit Carson's troops at Adobe Walls.

1869. Sun Boy, with Kicking Bird's party, robbed a mail coach at Rock Station, Jack County, Texas, then fought against troops of the Sixth Cavalry from Fort Richardson under Captain Curwen McClellan at Seymour, Texas.

1871. Sun Boy and the rest of Dohate's war party of Kiowa allowed General Sherman's ambulance, escorted by fifteen cavalrymen, to pass their ambush unharmed, following Dohate's prophecy, and then attacked the second party of travelers, a wagon train hauling corn, capturing forty-one mules.

1872. Sun Boy visited Washington, D.C., with a six-man delegation of Kiowa, Kiowa-Apache, and Comanche chiefs.

33. The Exploits of Sun Boy. *Silverhorn (Haungooah, 1861 –ca. 1941), Kiowa. 1885–1890, pencil, colored pencil, ink, and commercial paint on muslin, 86 × 75 inches. Philbrook Art Center, Tulsa, 82.6, gift of Muskogee Public Library.*

In Plains society, autobiographical robes and calendars preserved the significant events in the history of the tribe. Certain men were granted the privilege of also chronicling their own lives, as these were indelibly meshed with the ebb and flow of the life of their people. A work such as this life history of the Kiowa warrior chief Sun Boy would once have been painted on a bison hide, but as this transitional work was probably intended for white rather than Indian use, it freely incorporated the alien materials of muslin and commercial pigments along with the owner's penciled script.

34. Diagram of The Exploits of Sun Boy.

The Expoits of Sun Boy depicts the Kiowa warrior in battle with an Osage warrior (1), with Pawnee warriors (5–8), Mexican soldiers (2–4), U.S. Army troops (10,11), and civilians (12), some of whom were probably Texas Rangers. The vignettes are not arranged chronologically but rather in an aesthetically pleasing manner.

1873. Sun Boy fought Mexican soldiers again.

1874. Sun Boy fought against Texas Rangers under Major John B. Jones in the Lost Valley Fight.

1876. Sun Boy's horses were stolen by Mexicans during the Sun Dance and he pursued the Mexicans but was unable to catch them.

1878. Sun Boy's band was attacked by Texas Rangers while hunting buffalo under a reservation escort of black troopers, led by Captain Nicholas Nolan. Sun Boy's brother, Ato-t'ain, was killed.

1879. Sun Boy led a raid into Texas and killed a white man named Earle to avenge the death of his brother, Ato-t'ain, killed by Texans.[2]

This is a fictitious journal. None of the white men present at the Sun Dance of 1881 felt that the military history of one Kiowa warrior was important enough to document for posterity. Yet we know that *someone* did because, within seven years of the Sun Dance, a document recounting the exploits of Sun Boy had been created. It was carefully stored by one or more individuals for decades before being given to the Muskogee, Oklahoma, Public Library in 1934. There it was stored in the Grant Foreman Room until 1982, when it was transferred to Philbrook Art Center. It now resides in a climate- and security-controlled environment, carefully preserved and catalogued. It has taken its place among the documents important to a history-conscious nation. This "journal" is a section of unbleached muslin eighty-six inches by seventy-five inches, embellished with pictographic renderings in graphite, colored pencils, inks, and some commercial paints (which may have been a later addition). The artist who painted the muslin and the warrior whose exploits it portrays also had a sense of making history. For pictorial documents such as this had perhaps more historical validity to the Kiowa than did the letters to the Indian Service. Only those individuals whose lives best exemplified the Kiowa ideals of leader and warrior were privileged to display their personal histories in pictures. It was the visual image of human behavior that carried historical significance for the Kiowa, not what was said or written. These biographies were painted on hide wearing robes, on tipi sides and liners, and on muslin cloth like that of *The Exploits of Sunboy.* Because its meaning is communicated in pictures, this document is considered art. And art it is. It conforms to the recognized Native American artistic style called ledger drawing and it conforms clearly enough to an individual artistic style to be attributed to the Kiowa artist and historian Silverhorn. Furthermore, it has a value in the art marketplace.

"READING" HISTORY

To those who read the language of ledger art, *The Exploits of Sun Boy* is a significant historical document. This is true even though the stories of warfare are told in pictorial vignettes with no apparent chronology. They are not arranged by year in a spiral as are Kiowa pictorial calendars, nor do they read from right to left, top to bottom, as in old painted hides. They are arranged, rather, in an aesthetically balanced composition. The vignettes are mnemonic devices, each intended to bring to mind well-known events—stories of strategies, battles, massacres, and narrow escapes. Characters are defined with stylized visual traits such as shields, warrior attire, uniforms, and weapons. The scenes on the muslin are not all of fighting. The most important aspects of the incidents served as the best reminders: counting coup, lying in ambush, and being pursued, as well as skirmishing and close fighting.

Someone has interpreted parts of *The Exploits of Sun Boy* and has penciled in captions to identify the scenes. Warfare against several different types of foes by a figure carrying the same shield, and thus identified as Sun Boy, are depicted: Sun Boy in battle with Mexican soldiers, Sun Boy fighting Osage warriors, Sun Boy skirmishing with U.S. Army troops, Sun Boy fighting Pawnee warriors, Sun Boy pursued by the Sac and Fox, and Sun Boy pursuing or counting coup on a white civilian.

Many of the scenes can be documented historically. Although in only a few instances can the actual presence of Sun Boy be verified, as a prominent warrior he would have accompanied many war parties. My historical reading of this record on muslin is as follows (see fig. 34).

Scene 1. Sun Boy is depicted killing an Osage warrior. Sun Boy was old enough to have taken part in an 1833 clash between Kiowa and Osage in which so many Kiowa were killed that it was called a massacre. Disturbed by this large-scale intertribal warfare on the Plains, the U.S. Army launched an expedition of dragoons late in 1833 to invite tribes of the Southern Plains to a peace conference, which was held the following summer. Peace was made between the Kiowa and Osage less than a year after the massacre, and they never fought another full-scale battle. Unless this vignette refers to an incident between individuals, it must depict the 1833 event. The Osage warrior is identifiable by his roached hair and black moccasins with upturned flaring cuffs (see Feder, chapter II, this volume).

Scenes 2, 3, and 4. These scenes depict Sun Boy in battle with Mexican soldiers, according to the descriptive caption to one of the vignettes. The Mexican soldiers wear coats and brimmed hats. Sun Boy could have fought Mexican soldiers in 1843, 1844, and 1873 in skirmishes which occurred on Kiowa raids into Mexico. The Kiowa calendars record a definite incident in 1878 in which Sun Boy's horses were stolen by Mexicans, and although he pursued them, his horse gave out and he was unable to overtake them.

Scenes 5, 6, 7, and 8. These scenes depict Sun Boy fighting Pawnee warriors. The Pawnee are identifiable by roached hair, black moccasins with upturned flaring cuffs, brightly colored shirts, and jaguar-skin accoutrements. The Kiowa and Pawnee did not make peace until 1872, just prior to the Pawnee removal from Nebraska to Indian Territory. Sun Boy had several opportunities to encounter Pawnee warriors. In 1849 and 1852, Kiowa fought the Pawnee with the help of other traditional enemies of the Pawnee tribe, and, in 1854, the Kiowa killed 113 Pawnee in a particularly fierce incident. In three of the vignettes, Sun Boy wears a military coat and carries a lance with a flag attached to it. These must depict the incident of 1851. That summer, just after the Kiowa had left the site of their Sun Dance on the North Canadian River, Pawnee warriors came and took the offerings that had been hung upon the Medicine Lodge as a sacrifice. Among the offerings was a flag that had been given to the Kiowa by the Osage when the two tribes made peace in 1834. Later, Dohasan's band of Kiowa met the Pawnee, learned of their thievery, and attacked and defeated them (Mooney 1898).

Scene 9. This scene, the only one in which Sun Boy is not the victor, is easily identified. Sun Boy is pursued by Sac and Fox warriors who, as the victors, are pictured on the right of the vignette. In 1854, a large party of some fifteen hundred Kiowa, Kiowa-Apache, Comanche, Cheyenne, Arapaho, Osage, and Crow warriors went to eastern Kansas to attack the Sac, Fox, and Potawatomi tribesmen who had been relocated west of the Mississippi River. The buffalo herds were decreasing and the Plains tribes hoped to cut off the competition in their hunting ground, just as the Osage had tried to cut off the Kiowa in 1833. Around one hundred Sac and Fox warriors, armed with American long-range rifles, met their attackers near the Smoky Hill River. The fight was disastrous to the Kiowa and their allies. About twenty of the bow-and-arrow-wielding warriors were killed, including twelve Kiowa. The remainder fled in haste and concentrated their hunting in areas of the Southern Plains from then on.

Scenes 10 and 11. These scenes depict incidents involving the U.S. Army. Scene 10 shows soldiers in formation firing rifles while Sun Boy, oblivious to the bullets, creeps along with bow and arrow. The soldiers wear caps with plumes attached, the pictographic symbol for U.S. troops. This scene might depict a battle between troops under the command of Captain S. D. Sturgis and Kiowa and Comanche warriors on the Republican Fork of the Kansas River in 1860, the battle of Adobe Walls, in which buffalo hunters and Kit Carson's troops fought Kiowa and Comanche in 1864, or a skirmish in 1869 with troops under Captain Curwen B. McClellan from Fort Richardson, after a party of

Kiowa under Kicking Bird had robbed a mail coach at Rock Station, Texas. Sun Boy could have been with the Kiowa warriors in any of these incidents. Scene 11 is easier to place. It depicts Sun Boy, his horse tied to a tree rather than at hand, counting coup with his bow on a vehicle with a U.S. Army officer inside. In 1871, General W. T. Sherman made a visit to the Southern Plains to investigate reports of Indian depredations. He rode in an ambulance, the only military vehicle of the time with springs, and thus often used by important persons for overland travel. He was accompanied by a guard of fifteen cavalrymen. On May 18, the party traveled from Fort Belknap to Fort Richardson through the rocky Texas terrain, seeing no Indians. There were, however, over one hundred Kiowa and Kiowa-Apache and at least one Comanche warrior watching them from behind a small rocky hill as they crossed Salt Creek Prairie. The Indians were ready to attack, having been waiting all night and most of the day. They allowed this party to pass, however, because the leader of the war party, Dohate, a powerful medicine man, had instructed them to let the first party they should see pass and attack only the second group of travelers. Thus, General Sherman was saved from almost certain death and the attack was made on a train of corn wagons pulled by mules that came by afterward. Most of the wagon drivers were killed and the Kiowa captured forty-one mules. Scene 11 must refer to Sun Boy's participation in that war party's sparing of General Sherman. Counting coup rather than attacking was an important deed in the process of becoming a respected warrior of the Plains. Also perhaps a part of scene 11 is a warrior attacking an individual in buckskin clothing, perhaps a scout or wagoneer.

Scene 12. In this scene, an individual in civilian clothes is pursued by Sun Boy, or Sun Boy counts coup on him with a rifle. Sun Boy was involved in several incidents with Texans, both civilians and Texas Rangers (who did not wear uniforms at the time). Although the Kiowa observed treaties signed with the United States in the 1870s, they seldom considered Texans to be covered by these treaties. More than likely, they had been encouraged in this belief during the Civil War by Union soldiers who considered the Kiowa their allies against the Confederate armies (Mayhall 1962:234). Since Sun Boy was apparently with Dohate's party when it spared General Sherman, he also might have participated in the Lost Valley Fight in 1874 between Kiowa warriors under Dohate and Texas Rangers accompanying Major John B. Jones, commander of the Texas Frontier Battalion. This was a fight to avenge the death of Lone Wolf's son at the hand of a Texan. Two other incidents involving Texans are better documented historically. In 1878, Sun Boy's band was attacked by Texas Rangers while hunting buffalo in Texas under a reservation escort. In 1879, just two years before Lieutenant Eggleston's caution at the Kiowa Sun Dance, Sun Boy had led a raiding party into Texas. Because his brother, Ato-t'ain, had been killed by Texans, Sun Boy killed a Texan named Earle to avenge his brother's death.

The muslin painting that bears these vignettes commemorates the accomplishments of a great Kiowa chief of the warpath and buffalo-hunt days who survived into the reservation period. Sun Boy would have known the north country of Nebraska and the Yellowstone as well as the Kiowa's later home in the South. He was present at many pivotal tribal events. Thus, his personal history is also, in part, a tribal history of the Kiowa in the nineteenth century.

Because the year of Sun Boy's death, 1888, marks the last year of the Kiowa Sun Dance, his passing serves as the chronological marker for that year on the Kiowa calendars. In the calendar pictograph recording the event, the concentric circles of Sun Boy's shield are drawn over a figure in a coffin, recalling poignantly that this chief walked away from the warpath to follow the white man's road to a white man's burial. Sun Boy, whose life paralleled so closely the life of his people, is fittingly remembered through pictography, the medium of his tribe's historical records.

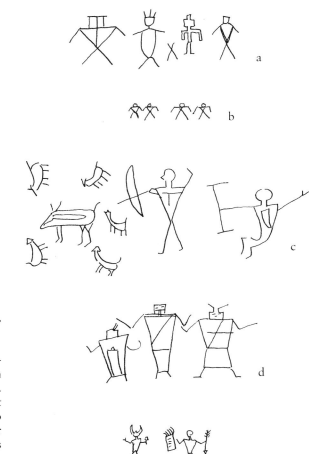

35. Pictographic images. a. *Hopi,* b. *Eskimo,* c. *Japanese,*
d. *Colorado River, Utah,* e. *Ojibwa.*

In petroglyphs throughout the northern hemisphere, animals were drawn from the side with stick legs and with
identifying features such as horns, antlers, humps, or tails.
Humans and mythic humanoids are depicted from the front
with geometric bodies, the sides of which are extended to
form legs. This style of drawing forms the basis for later
Native American pictography, drawn on planed tree trunks
and logs, hides, birchbark, and tipis.

"READING" ART

The origin of pictographs as visual language is ancient. It dates back to the earliest rock carvings,
bone etchings, and less lasting marks that indicated territory, served as memory aids, and recorded
important events. This ancient form of human communication is also one of the most widespread,
found virtually everywhere humans have lived. Pictorial representation is linked with the concept of
self. The development of self-awareness and awareness of others as separate entities led naturally to
the need for a way to transmit ideas. Pictographic representation arose as a form of abstract communication analogous to verbal language and is as old as the spoken word. However, unlike human
speech, the pictographic embodiment of an idea could stand when there was no speaker.

The oldest examples of pictorial imagery that may still be seen in the United States are petroglyphs,
usually carved on rock faces near reliable sources of water where people often camped. There,
stories of hunts, battles, alliances, and visions may be read among the more prosaic "Kilroy was
here"-style signatures. Images of animals and humans are recognizable. In the majority of petroglyphs around the world, people are depicted "face-on," from the front, while animals are drawn
in profile. There are many styles of drawing petroglyphs, but the style widespread in northern
latitudes, which was the prototype for later Plains pictography, incorporates a geometric shape for
the body of the animal or person. Legs are portrayed by extending the outlines of the body shape.
Examples of this style of drawing are shown in figure 35: *a.* petroglyphs by Hopi artists; *b.* Eskimo
human figures; *c.* Japanese people and animals; *d.* petroglyphs on the Colorado River in Utah; and
e. Ojibwa figures.

By the time of the arrival of the Europeans on the Plains, more rectangular bodies were favored,
resulting in pictographs like those in figure 36: *a.* human figures by Cree; *b.* Mandan, and *c.* Oto

36. Pictographic images. a. Cree, b. Mandan, c. Oto, d. Pawnee, e. Kiowa, f. Comanche-drawn figures.

Early Native American pictographic images of humans were "walking playing-cards": legs with slightly bent knees, a symbol of action, were attached to flat rectangular bodies. Heads were open or colored circles without features, identity being indicated by weapons or other objects held in the hand and by costume. The men in image *f*—in trousers and hats—are white men.

37. Pictographic images. a. Mandan, b. Crow, c. Cheyenne.

Horses and humans are the images most often portrayed in Plains pictography, since most scenes depict hunting or warfare. Early styles of the Central Plains used a stylized "hoofprint" to identify the animals portrayed as horses. Isolated lines of hoofprints conveyed the passage of time, and multiple lines of hoofprints indicated a large party of mounted men.

38. Iroquois pictographic images.

An Iroquois war record shows the captives of battle, including one woman, and victims of war, symbolized by the decapitated figure. Records such as these, surmounted by the pictographic signature of the victorious warrior, were engraved on trees, logs, and rock faces along well-traveled trails, or drawn on birchbark so that all who passed might read them.

artists; *d.* a Pawnee person; *e.* a Kiowa Sun Dance figure; and *f.* white men who are veritable "walking playing-cards," drawn by a Comanche artist. All depict the humans from the front or just slightly to the side. Horses were drawn in profile and had stick legs with stylized hooves like those in figure 37 by *a.* Mandan, *b.* Crow, and *c.* Cheyenne artists.

Pictographic images had long been drawn on more perishable substances than rock faces by artists in all tribes of North America. The Comanche depiction of white men (fig. 36*f*), for example, was drawn on a buffalo shoulder blade. Birchbark in the Northeast and woven cotton blankets in the Southwest were ideal surfaces for painting and drawing upon. And wherever there were trees, flat surfaces were planed on the trunks or on fallen logs and pictographs drawn on them. In 1724, Father LaFitau described pictographs made by the Iroquois and northeastern Algonquian:

> When an Indian returns from war and wishes to make his victory known to the neighboring nations through whose country he passes . . . he supplies the lack of an alphabet by those characteristic symbols which distinguish him personally; he paints on a piece of bark, which is raised on a pole by a place of passage [trail], or he cuts away some pieces from a tree trunk with his hatchet, and after having made a smooth surface, traces his portrait and adds other characters, which give all the information he desires to convey (Mallery 1893:554, brackets his).

Figure 38 shows an Iroquois battle record, enumerating male and female captives and a decapitated victim of the warrior-artist's escapade.

For the nomadic people of the Plains, the most portable objects were preferred for painting and

39. Comanche pictographic image.

When early Plains pictographers first began to portray riders on horses, they simply superimposed a standing man on a horse. The resulting X-ray image may have been the desired effect. Later, riders were often drawn with no legs at all, thus circumventing the dual problems of drawing a human in profile and placing the visible leg in the correct position. It was only after visits to the Plains by European and American artists such as Karl Bodmer and George Catlin in the mid-1800s that Plains Indian artists changed from the age-old style of depicting humans from the front and drew realistic mounted horsemen in profile.

the best of these were hides—dressed deer or antelope hides or the inner surfaces of buffalo-hide robes.[3] The information Plains men "desired to convey" were the records of their personal feats.

> In the old days the surest way for a Plains Indian to win the admiration and respect of his fellows was by the performance of brave deeds in war. The successful warrior was rewarded for his bravery, not with medals, but with the right to wear certain kinds of ornaments, to recount his deeds on special occasions, and to picture on his buffalo robe or teepee his outstanding achievements, so that all who saw him might know he was a brave and important man (Ewers 1939:17).

Painted tipis and buffalo robes were reported on the Plains by the earliest European explorers. Coronado found the Zuñi in possession of painted buffalo robes in 1540 and, sending one from the pueblo to his superior, Mendoza, he explained its origin.

> They inhabit some plains eight day's journey towards the north. They have some of their skins here very well dressed, and they prepare and paint them where they kill the cows, according to what they tell me (Winship 1896:560).

One year later, members of De Soto's expedition into what is now Arkansas actually observed a painted tipi.

> The house of the Cacique [chief] was canopied with colored deer-skins, having designs drawn on them, and the ground was likewise covered in the same manner as if with carpets (Bourne 1922:134, my brackets).

The first pictorial painted hide actually collected on the Plains was a Mandan buffalo-hide robe sent by Lewis and Clark to President Jefferson in 1805. The drawing depicts a battle fought about 1797, so the hide must have been painted between 1797 and 1805. The figures are drawn in dark brown outline and some are filled in with colors—dark brown, blue green, reddish brown, and yellow. Quivers are painted solid red or yellow (Ewers 1939:26, pl. 22). The painting conforms to early Plains style in that horses with stick legs are shown in profile and "walking playing-card" men from the front. This last poses a problem in depicting men on horseback. They look as though both human legs are on the same side of the horse. This is also illustrated in a figure of a mounted Indian with the white men on the Comanche buffalo shoulder bone, which was collected in the 1830s by Schoolcraft (fig. 39). The human figure is simply a standing man superimposed on a horse. The round object, probably a shield, identifies him as a warrior. The pictographs on the Mandan robe collected by Lewis and Clark also distinguish some individuals by shields, weapons, or buffalo-horn headdresses, the identification badges of Plains warriors. This early example of Plains pictography is now preserved in the Peabody Museum at Harvard University.

Another early hide, presented by the Pawnee to Major O'Fallon of the Long Expedition of 1819–1820, depicts a battle between mounted Pawnee and Kansas warriors on foot (Ewers 1939: pl. 23). The Kansas warriors are in the same stance as those illustrated in figure 36, with knees slightly bent in an unrealistic position symbolic of action. Many of the horses have elongated necks, a stylization that was becoming a common trait of Plains drawing, with their legs squarely under them like those of the Lewis and Clark Mandan robe. But here the horses' legs appear fuller and more realistic; they are no longer sticks. The mounted Pawnee warriors, however, are the most interesting. Each is fully identified by weapons, headdress, or a shield, which also help solve the difficult problem of portraying mounted men. Each shield is carried so that it conceals the body and the men simply have no legs. On each horse is a saddle blanket, above which is a shield, above which is a head, usually facing the viewer (i.e., at a right angle to the direction in which the profiled horse travels). Facial features are shown by dots on only two of the circular heads. The bodies of those men depicted without a shield simply end at the horses' backs.

The Mandan artist Four Bears (Mato-tope) was painting in a very refined version of this style when he was visited in the summer of 1832 by the American artist George Catlin, and a few months later by Maximilian, Prince of Wied Neuwied, and the Swiss artist Karl Bodmer. A buffalo-hide robe depicting the exploits of Mato-tope, collected in 1838 by Maximilian and now in the museum at Bern, Switzerland, was presumably painted by Mato-tope himself in this style. The human figures, though in lifelike positions, are still of the "walking playing-card," two-dimensional style, and the body of a rider ends at the horse's back. Mato-tope's people look as though their feet are planted firmly on the ground, not hanging in the air with slightly bent knees as in the earlier pictographs, but his stylistic innovations up to this date had not been great. But with the visits of Catlin and Bodmer, Mato-tope's art and the subsequent art of the Plains were destined to change.

Both Catlin and Bodmer painted illustrations of Mato-tope's robes—and both, rather than copying his figures faithfully, drew figures more acceptable to American and European viewers. The male figures they drew looked very much like the figures on Greek vases—apparently their concept of "primitive" painted figures. Although Bodmer kept closer to Mato-tope's style, he, like Catlin, drew rounded, muscular mounted figures, some in full profile, and all with one leg visible against the horse's flank. Both artists depicted running horses with both forelegs extended somewhat forward and both hindlegs extending backward, a position never actually taken by a running horse, but often used to indicate movement in European painting (see the painting of mounted German knights, Mallery 1893: pl. LIII). It would have taken only one look over Bodmer's or Catlin's shoulder for a talented artist like Mato-tope to adopt some elements of European style. The style of drawing pictographic horses changed very quickly after the visits of American and European artists on the Plains.

John Ewers (1981) has suggested that Maximilian (who was an artist himself), Bodmer, Catlin, and other American and European artists collected and publicized the works of those Indian artists who best exemplified artistic ability according to European aesthetics. For example, Mato-tope's human figures were well-proportioned, rounded, and had feet planted firmly on the ground, despite their slightly bent knees (see Ewers 1981: fig. 1). Yellow Feather, another Mandan artist whose work was collected, drew detailed human portraits that were not as realistically proportioned, but he mastered the knack of drawing the rider astride the horse with head and leg in profile, shield covering the body (Ewers 1981: fig. 4). Both Mandan artists were given paper, pencils, and watercolors. Using these media, they were more prone to copy the style of the foreign artists. In the works that resulted, figures are not outlined in black or brown as in a pictograph, a departure that was even more radical than the rounding out of flat pictographic figures had been. Neither of these Mandan

40. Sioux pictographic images.

By the mid-1800s a recognizable Sioux style of pictography had developed. A horse had a bobbed tail, stylized phallus, and definite point on the back, behind which the rump sloped to the tail. Humans were depicted with torsos facing the viewer. Direction of movement was indicated by the feet and head. Cheyenne styles developed along much the same line. Under the influence of non-Indians and artists from other tribes, capable Sioux pictographers used a minimum of stylized traits to carry the meaning of their work. Unusual creative individuality produced artistic works like the Kill Eagle buffalo hide shown in figure 73.

41. Pictographic images. a. *Kiowa calendar glyph,* b. *Dakota Sioux calendar glyph.*

Kiowa calendrical pictographs differed from those of the Sioux winter counts in one fundamental way. Kiowa human figures resembled the figures of Mexican codices, always shown in full profile, while Sioux figures adhered to the old style reminiscent of Egyptian wall murals.

artists had long to influence their fellow Plains artists, however. Within three years both were dead, victims of a smallpox epidemic that virtually wiped out the Mandan tribe in 1837, leaving the Sioux as the master artists of the Northern Plains.

Another example of the influence of traveling artists, including John Mix Stanley as well as Catlin and Bodmer, on Plains pictography is seen in the work of an artist identified by Norman Feder (1980) as belonging to the Gros Ventre tribe. Several hide paintings thought to be by this artist were collected and are now in widely scattered museums, often attributed to other tribes. One hide painting of this group, now in the Linden Museum in Stuttgart, is known to have been collected by Maximilian. The artist who produced this work remained true to Plains pictographic style, drawing stick legs, horses with stylized hoofprint hoofs (as in figure 37), and playing-card humans with slightly bent knees. However, the addition of stick feet and the positioning of the figures in many action poses, well-balanced over their stick legs, gives a feeling of reality to the fighting and dancing figures. Most importantly, mounted figures are portrayed in realistic poses. Some have their legs akimbo, unbalanced on their mounts by the vicissitudes of mounted warfare but, though the upper torso faces the viewer at a right angle to the profiled horse and the head is a solid blob of color, the figure sits squarely on his horse. In one instance, the human is astride normally, with the visible human leg in exactly the right position for the rider of a rearing horse (Feder 1980: fig. 3). These pictographs were probably collected because of their aesthetic appeal to the traveling European and American artists. Identified as Gros Ventre by Feder because of the quilled rosettes attached, these hide paintings may be the earliest examples of a style that became the classic of the Central Plains, and that is usually known as the Sioux style because of the prolific artistic production of the Sioux.

By the second half of the nineteenth century, the classic Sioux style could be identified by the presence of running horses with well-drawn extended legs and stylized, elongated necks. Human figures were also more rounded, but for many years the upper torsos remained depicted from the front, although head and legs were drawn in profile, like Egyptian mural figures (fig. 40).

It was among the Kiowa on the southern Plains that full-profile depictions of humans first became a stylistic trait. Early Kiowa-style figures are best seen in the Kiowa calendars. Of all the Plains tribes, only the Kiowa and Sioux kept calendars, spiraling lines of mnemonic pictographs marking the years by winters in the Sioux "winter counts," and by both winters and summers, and sometimes by months, in the Kiowa calendars. Sioux calendars are known to have been kept since the eighteenth century, although the Kiowa calendars collected in the late nineteenth century dated only from 1833. Most, however, were on paper and were said to be a continuation of earlier calendars on hide (Mooney 1898:143). Though alike in form, Kiowa calendars differed from some Sioux calendars in one important respect: the style of depicting human figures. This is obvious in Mooney's (1898:284–285) comparison of two glyphs: the initiation of Hornlessbull (Kiowa marker for the summer of 1846) and the initiation of a member of the dog soldier society from the Sioux calendars (fig. 41). Whereas the dog soldier is the expected walking playing-card of the buffalo-robe style, the Kiowa man stands in full profile in front of the Sun Dance lodge with offerings on the cottonwood fork, the glyph for summer. Almost all the human figures on Kiowa calendars are in profile from the waist up, and many are portrayed only to the waist, looking—right down to the almond-shaped eyes—like crude northern examples of Mexican calendrical glyphs. Whether the Kiowa style of drawing humans in profile was a result of the artistic abilities of the many Mexican captives who were a part of the tribe or of the influence of Catlin or other artists on the Southern Plains, it was evidently a distinctive Kiowa trait before 1880. It was only very late in the century that artists from other tribes began to adopt the profile form of pictographic human depiction and regularly draw eyes of almond shape.

Many examples of Plains pictography from the last half of the nineteenth century are extant, the earliest painted (and sometimes incised) on buffalo, deer, elk, and antelope hides. Pictographic painting flourished among the Sioux, Crow, Cheyenne, Arapaho, Comanche, and Kiowa tribes. Mastery of the horse had led to greater leisure for war-making, war cults and societies, ceremonial life, and the art production concomitant with these activities. Most spectacular were the autobiographically painted tipis. These were limited in number, as only one was allowed per band among the Sioux, while among the Kiowa and other tribes, only families with a hereditary right established through civil, military, or religious leadership could thus embellish their dwellings. Painted tipis recorded the history not only of an individual but also of the tribe.

Increased contact with non-Indian settlers and soldiers brought new media and materials to Plains artists. New colors obtained in trade reduced the search for natural vegetal and mineral pigments so that more time could be spent in painting and a greater number of works produced. By the middle of the nineteenth century, much of the painting once reserved for hides alone was being applied to other surfaces. Bolts of muslin cloth and sheets of paper, often in the form of blank ledger and account books, were easily acquired by Indian artists. Once again, the most portable surfaces were the best. In the turbulent years of the 1860s and 1870s many villages were burned and warfare and hasty flight were the order of the day. "War books" were more portable and therefore easier to save than bulky hides or tipis. This new form of pictographic record became known to non-Indians as "ledger-book drawings." Graphite, colored pencils and inks, and commercial paints and dyes began to be used regularly.

Along with new materials, a new market also grew up for Plains pictography. Soldiers and civilian employees at military posts, and their wives and friends back home, began to commission Plains painting. Throughout all the change, however, pictographic themes remained constant, consisting of personal and group exploits in war and hunting and the Kiowa and Sioux chronological records. Native Americans of the Plains continued to use the language of pictography to write their own histories and the histories of their tribes.

In 1875, seventy-one Kiowa, Comanche, Cheyenne, and Arapaho, and one Caddo were taken from their tribes and confined at Fort Marion, Florida, in hopes of discouraging the remaining tribesmen from straying outside their reservation boundaries. Among the prisoners were twenty-six younger men of warrior age, whose prerogative it was to depict their exploits. They began to draw pictographs and pictures in the ledger style. A new interest in Indian painting was spurred when some of the Fort Marion paintings were published on the East Coast. Partly as a result of this interest, the collection of pictography for scientific purposes began.

But the early buffalo-robe style of pictography was not dead, even at Fort Marion, as evidenced by two drawings done by a Cheyenne, Making Medicine, in August 1875. In one (see Petersen 1971: pl. 16), the mounted warrior is drawn without legs, with upper torso facing the viewer but the head in profile, and with no facial features indicated except the profiled nose. Another drawing, *On the War Path* (Petersen 1971: color pl. 1), depicts riders with visible legs, but they are very much the old "playing-card" people. By 1877, however, Making Medicine was drawing his humans more rounded, in profile, and with almond-shaped eyes. These are some of the stylistic traits that define the classic Kiowa style in which the muslin painting *The Exploits of Sun Boy* is painted. Making Medicine was apparently copying the Kiowa. At least six of the Kiowa prisoners at Fort Marion—Zotom, Koba, Etahdleuh Doanmoe, Tonkeuh, and Tsadeltah—drew in this style while incarcerated. Another prisoner, Ohettoint, certainly painted in this style later in life, when he re-created his father's tipi with battle pictures.

The main characteristics of the classic Kiowa style are as follows:

1. Horses have long legs, elongated necks, small heads, and straight or slightly curved backs, with the tail emanating from the body very high on the rump. This is an anatomical characteristic of mares. Perhaps the horses drawn in this style are mares; it was noted by early writers that Kiowa horses are not drawn with a stylized phallus as are those by the artists of some other tribes. The characteristic backs of Kiowa-drawn horses differ from those of other tribes, which come to a very stylized point just behind the saddle and then slope off to a point where the tail is attached much lower on the rump (see fig. 37).

2. Human figures are shown in profile or partial profile. Faces are always in full profile with almond-shaped eyes and, often, line-drawn mouths. Many figures are depicted with bare legs and feet or bare arms. The limbs are molded but not muscled, very reminiscent of the Mexican style of codices or petroglyphs. Many human figures are depicted in poses which look to the non-Indian eye as if the person were kicking forward or backward—as if he were performing a European folk dance. These poses are very different from the poses of Native American dancers, and are meant to indicate motion, running, or violent action.

3. Clothing, headdresses, and accoutrements of both men and horses are accurately detailed, identifying both Indian and non-Indian individuals.

4. Animals such as buffalo, cattle, antelope, bear, and puma are depicted, like horses, with the tail attached to the highest point on the rump.

5. Paintings are made up of two-dimensional vignettes with no background except the pictographic representation of trees, hills, tipis, or other objects which carry explicit meanings. Tipis are drawn very tall and narrow.

6. A sureness of line, careful application of color, and balance of proportions are apparent in work by the better painters, which have the authoritative look of a classic style.

Of the six Fort Marion prisoners who painted in this style, Tsadeltah died in Massachusetts in 1879 and Koba within three months of his return to the Kiowa reservation in 1880. Etahdleuh Doanmoe returned to the reservation from 1882 until 1884 and then went east again. Zotom returned to the reservation in June 1881 and remained there until his death in 1913 (see Petersen 1971). In 1897, Zotom painted model tipis at the request of the ethnologist James Mooney, for exhibit at the Trans-Mississippi and International Exposition in Omaha the following year. According to Petersen (1971:190), this is Zotom's only known artistic endeavor after his incarceration at

42. The Exploits of Sun Boy *(detail). Silverhorn (Haungooah, 1861–ca. 1941), Kiowa. 1885–1890, pencil, colored pencil, ink, and commercial paint on muslin, 86 × 75 inches. Philbrook Art Center, Tulsa, 82.6, gift of Muskogee Public Library.*

The episodic vignettes of the muslin painting of Sun Boy's life reveal more than the warrior's history. They also illustrate the artistic versatility and meticulous detailing that were hallmarks of the artist Silverhorn, the last master of the Kiowa ledger style.

Fort Marion. In 1880, Tonkeuh returned to the reservation, where he remained until he died sometime between 1889 and 1912, producing only two known artworks. Ohettoint returned to the reservation in June 1880 and remained there until his death in 1934.

Ohettoint was a highly respected member of the Kiowa tribe and served as a reservation policeman, agency timekeeper, and carpenter, and as an artist and informant for James Mooney. He continued his painting and is credited with 142 known artworks. He was joined in his work for Mooney, and perhaps in some of his other artwork, by his younger brother Silverhorn. Their artistic styles are almost indistinguishable. Mooney called Silverhorn "my Kiowa artist" and collected not only model tipis and shields from him but also a series of painted buckskins depicting Sun Dance scenes (Ewers 1983:44, fig. 1). Without a doubt, one of these men executed the painting *The Exploits of Sun Boy.* Both, in fact, may have worked on it. Slight variations in the treatment of horses' heads and hoofs suggest that there were two hands, or possibly three, at work on the piece. Zotom or Tonkeuh might have helped, or there might have been student artists involved. Comparison of this piece with other works attributed to Silverhorn show that he probably had the largest part in its production. The muslin was probably painted between Sun Boy's last act of war, the raid into Texas to avenge his brother in 1879, and his death in 1888. Silverhorn would have been between eighteen and twenty-seven years of age. Already he was very proficient in the art of pictography.

Silverhorn and his brother were sons of Dohasan III, members of a prominent family of the largest and most important division of the Kiowa tribe. Their father, nephew of the famous Kiowa chief Dohasan, called Little Bluff, had the right to live in a heraldic tipi. He also had kept a pictographic calendar since his youth, which he gave to General Hugh Scott of Fort Sill in 1892. Because of their family prerogative, both Silverhorn and Ohettoint probably learned pictography when very young. When Mooney asked for model tipis in 1897, Ohettoint made a model of a famous tipi his father had owned. Called *Dogiagyaguat*, "Tipi with battle pictures," it had been a gift from a Cheyenne chief to Chief Dohasan in 1845. It was restored many times when it was in use (until 1892), each time with slightly different scenes painted by great warriors, or by artists in their stead. After making the model of it, Ohettoint, probably aided by Silverhorn, reproduced a full seven-and-a-half-foot-tall replica of the tipi between 1916 and 1918. He painted it with battle scenes and had the last of the ancient warriors of the Kiowa tribe record some of their heroic deeds. When these warriors died, the art of pictography among the Kiowa died with them. There was no longer any need to paint men's personal military histories. Young warriors who went away to fight in the First World War were mainstream soldiers. Their rewards were the ribbons, medals, and commendations that are the symbolic recording of participation in military actions of the United States.

Silverhorn did not stop painting, however. He continued to produce many works until his death in 1941, but not in the pictographic style. His later work lacked the authoritative line and sureness that had made his earlier pictography pleasing to European and American mainstream viewers.

Because *The Exploits of Sun Boy* is a fine example of the culmination of an art style, done by possibly the last and best Kiowa pictographer, it is a classic work of art. Plains pictography had progressed from crudely pecked and carved lines on rock to intricately drawn figures in pencil and ink. The style had coalesced, and with that coalescence the meaning had become so universal that the prisoners at Fort Marion wrote home and received letters regularly in pictography. To the astonishment of their captors, they read the messages easily. The successful blending of stylization and reality which was essential to the meaning of pictography is also what makes non-Indians appreciate it aesthetically.

Furthermore, *The Exploits of Sun Boy* is classic because it depicts scenes from the culmination of a life-style. Plains culture had progressed from a society with a tenuous hold on the land in the fourteenth century, maintained by small fields in the river bottoms and communal hunts of big game on foot, to a swashbuckling mounted hunting and raiding society at its culmination in the nineteenth century. The Kiowa and their allies were lords of the Southern Plains, ranging a thousand miles from Nebraska to Mexico. They remembered their glorious defeats at the hands of Osage or Sac and Fox warriors with as much ceremonialism as they did their glorious victories. Sun Boy was one of the last of those warriors who merited a pictographic biography. *The Exploits of Sun Boy* is, then, doubly a classic work of history and art.

Notes

1. Two colleagues at Philbrook played an important part in the writing of this case study. M. S. Domjanovich, former assistant curator of Native American art, carried out the initial research on the lives of Sun Boy and Silverhorn. From his notes, Carol Haralson, chief of publications, produced text utilized in this article and the drawing that schematizes the Sun Boy painting. My thanks to both of them.

2. The details of these military encounters may be gleaned from Mayhall 1962, Mooney 1898, and Nye 1937.

3. For a full description of the techniques of painting on hides, see the quote from Haberland 1964 in Warner, chapter v, this volume.

II

TRADITION

Tradition in Native American Art

J. C. H. KING

CHANGE AS INNATE TO ALL CULTURAL SYSTEMS

All cultural systems exist in a constant state of change, brought about both by internal and external forces.[1] If societies change continually, often as a result of foreign influence, then the concept of tradition in culture and art cannot be viewed as absolute. Instead, it must be seen as a relative term, used, for instance, to compare one situation or object with another, or to describe an art object with respect to a given corpus of related material. As such, it is a heuristic device, inseparable from the equal but opposing idea of nontraditional art. Tradition, which the *Oxford English Dictionary* defines as "something that has prevailed from generation to generation," is also a highly emotive term, used in many contexts to validate not only art objects but also political and cultural ideas. Used in this way, it is not an objective idea, and therefore is not necessarily useful in scientific investigation. However, because it appears such a simple and clear-cut term, suited to an infinite number of situations, it has become a "semantic booby trap" (Brody 1971:59).

43. *Container, front and back views. Huron. Mid-1800s, birchbark, dyed moosehair embroidery; container: 4⅞ × 3 × 1¼ inches; lid: 2¼ × 3 × 1¼ inches. Philbrook Art Center, Tulsa, Elizabeth Cole Butler Collection, L 82.1.- 383a & b.*

European influence is evident in the form, function, and design of this birchbark container. The object served as a cigar or cigarette case, clearly a nonindigenous function, and was intended for the tourist trade of the mid-nineteenth century in New York and Canada. The stylized birds suggest the flamboyant designs of French crewel embroidery and the frock coat of the pipe-smoking, moosehair-embroidered Indian is modeled after continental clothing styles.

LIMITATIONS IN USE OF THE CONCEPT "TRADITION"

Everybody has an idea of what "tradition" means. However, few address the limitations of this concept, whose general use often raises more problems than it solves. While the various uses of the concept may be defined either explicitly or implicitly through context, they cannot be applied rigorously as art historical tools any more than they can be employed as instruments for scientific analysis.

USE OF THE CONCEPT OF TRADITION IN ARCHAEOLOGY

In discussing well-known categories of Indian art, we see the problematical phrase "traditional Indian art" constantly in use but constantly eluding definition. We also see that native North America possesses an infinite number of art traditions, many of which overlap and interplay to form a highly complex mosaic. There is, however, one important area in which the concept of tradition has had a scientific application: American archaeology. In order to break away from theoretical foundations based on discussion and description of material finds, more general concepts were introduced in the 1940s and 1950s. These concepts, which included ideas such as "cultural tradition" and "horizon style," were employed in order to create more inclusive cultural descriptions, and to introduce spatial-temporal properties into archaeology. They were used particularly to help articulate and define chronological sequences and culture-area boundaries.

"Tradition" has, however, no single definition, even in archaeology. Some writers have employed the term to refer to specific groups of objects, and others have applied similar concepts to refer to whole cultural phenomena. An example is J. R. Caldwell's (1964) description of the Hopewellian "interaction sphere," in which a series of regional cultures share some traits (such as form of mortuary ritual and types of ceremonial artifacts), but not necessarily all traits. These ideas provided a basis for renewed emphasis on the concept of cultural evolution, which in part enabled fuller explanations of archaeological phenomena to replace more limited factual statements (Willey and Sabloff 1974:174–177).

The archaeological use of the concept "tradition" is, therefore, radically different from that found in American Indian art. For archaeologists, the term is not a heuristic device with an opposing counterpart, but rather a unifying idea, designed to bring together common elements of a material culture. As a concept it is extremely useful, enabling artifacts and ideas possessing clusters of shared traits to be identified and discussed. In any particular tradition, individual traits may be introduced

44. Sword and case. Crow. Ca. 1880, painted hide, cloth, beadwork, metal; sword: 34 × 4½ inches; case: 47 × 5½ inches. Philbrook Art Center, Tulsa, Elizabeth Cole Butler Collection, 82.1.91a & b.

Metalwork was known sporadically throughout ancient North America, particularly in the Southeast, the middle Mississippi, and the Northwest Coast. In regions other than the Northwest Coast, indigenous swords were unknown, especially those which incorporated the elongated handle of the European saber. Southern and Central Plains tribes did adopt the European sword as an offensive weapon during the nineteenth century, but this richly embellished Crow sword and scabbard were probably intended not as an actual weapon but as a presentation object for use during tribal celebrations.

45. Mirror and case. Crow. Ca. 1880, hide, quillwork, beadwork, wood, cotton cord, 26 × 5 inches. Philbrook Art Center, Tulsa, gift of Mrs. Mark Dunlop, 78.8.

This glass mirror was undoubtedly acquired through trade and then mounted by its native owner in a wooden protective frame and encased in a bag of native-tanned skin, richly embellished with trade beads and yarn. Mirrors served an entirely different purpose among Native Americans than they did among Europeans. For Native Americans, mirrors were symbols of wealth and prestige. They were commonly mounted in dance batons or other objects of ceremonial regalia, since it was their light-reflective property, not their ability to reflect images, that was considered important. This Crow mirror is an example of a European object thoroughly incorporated into a Native American aesthetic context.

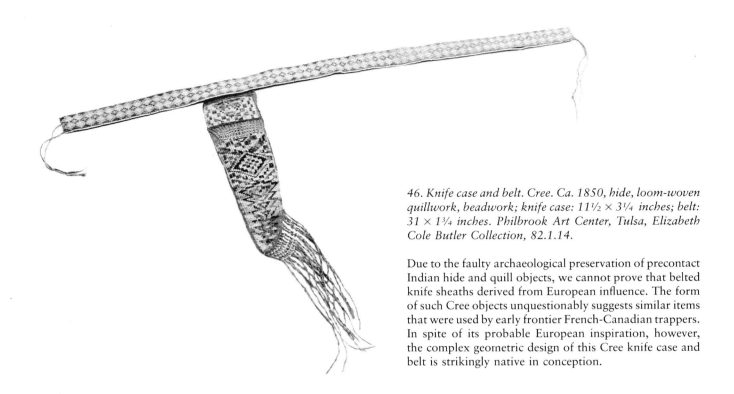

46. *Knife case and belt. Cree. Ca. 1850, hide, loom-woven quillwork, beadwork; knife case: 11½ × 3¼ inches; belt: 31 × 1¾ inches. Philbrook Art Center, Tulsa, Elizabeth Cole Butler Collection, 82.1.14.*

Due to the faulty archaeological preservation of precontact Indian hide and quill objects, we cannot prove that belted knife sheaths derived from European influence. The form of such Cree objects unquestionably suggests similar items that were used by early frontier French-Canadian trappers. In spite of its probable European inspiration, however, the complex geometric design of this Cree knife case and belt is strikingly native in conception.

and ancient traits may disappear. In this way specific attributes of artifacts may or may not be thought of as traditional; yet, the material culture as a whole continues to be referred to as a single tradition.

THE CONCEPT OF TRADITION AS BASED ON TECHNIQUE AND MATERIALS, FORM AND FUNCTION, SYMBOL AND MEANING

Traditionalism within a material culture complex can arise through a variety of different means, all of which are dependent on time-persistent elements within each tradition. Traditionalism can be based on technique and materials, and identification by these two criteria is relatively straightforward. Pottery, carving techniques, and embroidery, to take three separate areas, are easily defined, and can be related to the vast body of materials in museum collections. Technology varies within traditions. The use of metal tools and metal needles, for example, altered Woodlands carving, quillwork, and moosehair embroidery (figs. 43–47). However, the techniques themselves need not alter, so that the coiled and twined basketry traditions in the Southwest, California, and the Northwest Coast survive, using the same techniques found in the most ancient examples of basketry. The persistence of materials is more complex, in part because Euro-American trade goods came to be substituted for their aboriginal American counterparts, such as wool yarn for goat wool on the Northwest Coast (fig. 48), beads for porcupine quills, and wool cloth for skin. However, as in all the elements that go to make up any particular material culture tradition, the change in technique or tools and the substitution or addition of foreign materials do not necessarily alter the total traditional aspect of an object.

Traditionalism can also be evaluated (inevitably with some subjectivity or ethnocentrism) through discussion of changes of form and function and through alterations in the symbolic value, either of the object itself or of the symbols with which it is decorated. The study of traditionalism in motifs and realistic symbols is a very complex subject, to a large extent because of our inadequate historical knowledge.

Certain basic ideas about the origin of conventionalized designs should be mentioned because

47. Bonnet. Santee Sioux. Ca. 1890, quillwork on hide, plaid fabric lining, ribbon, 16 × 10 × 8½ inches. Philbrook Art Center, Tulsa, Elizabeth Cole Butler Collection, 82.1.38.

This hide woman's bonnet is a direct translation of the nineteenth-century headgear worn by American frontier women. The designs, however, show a more circuitous influence. The distinctive angular floral motifs favored by the Santee are their interpretation of the more fluid curvilinear designs and embroidery compositions found among the natives of the Great Lakes region, who in turn had absorbed these influences from the French-Canadian métis trappers.

they underscore the paucity of our understanding of traditionalism in symbol and meaning. Although not always appreciated by contemporary students of Native American art, this traditionalism and Indianism were and are perhaps the most important aspects of art for its makers. Conventional designs arise in three ways. They can derive from or relate to the technical basis of the artifact. Northwest Coast carving (figs. 110–112), coiled and twined basketry (fig. 131), and southwestern weaving (fig. 17) all utilize the qualities of the materials and techniques for aesthetic purposes. The simple introduction of lines of even adze work on Northwest totem poles, and the alternation of different materials in single stitches and blocks of color, enable basket weavers and carvers to build up designs without symbolic intent (fig. 49). Similarly, Navajo textiles, through the use of different weft colors, can effect striking designs without suggesting any specific symbolic intention (fig. 90). The data for the meaning of much conventional design is absent today and may also have been absent for the Native American; in these cases, we are predisposed to look for meanings where no meaning may actually exist. Second, and related to this, is the possibility that conventional designs were provided with meanings after their creation by the Native American artist (see Cohodas, chapter v, this volume). This makes it very hard to define what is traditional and what is not traditional in Indian art, even in a vulgar, day-to-day manner. Third, conventionalized design may originate in the deliberate attempt by an artist to associate a realistic form, whether sculptural or two-dimensional, with another aesthetic tradition, and then reproduce the design in the new technique. In this case, the reproduced motif or realistic subject matter frequently becomes less realistic or more conventionalized in the second tradition. The transference of design may occur with a change in traditionalism, or may not. Two examples of the former are the translation of sacred Navajo Yei designs from sand paintings used for healing to secular rugs woven for sale, and the reproduction of shamans in wood and argillite by Haida carvers of the Northwest Coast.

THE NECESSITY FOR BASING IDEAS ABOUT TRADITION ON AVAILABLE COLLECTIONS AND INFORMATION

The appreciation of Indian art and the understanding of traditionalism in Indian art depend on the

48. Chilkat blanket. Tlingit. 1800s, cedar bark, wool, cotton yarn, 26 × 64 inches; fringe: 13 inches. Thomas Gilcrease Institute of American History and Art, Tulsa, 9936.47.

Chilkat blankets are the best known of Northwest Coast textiles, representing an extremely complex form of tapestry twining in which highly intricate designs symbolizing conventionalized crest animals are woven in imitation of painting. The blankets are considered the prestigious regalia of noble people. They are worn on ceremonial occasions and used especially in dancing, where their bold designs and heavy fringe contribute to the dramatic effect.

collections available for study. Most of the principal North American collections of Indian artifacts were created between 1860 and 1930, in large museums in eastern and central North America. It is inevitable, therefore, that most of the standards by which traditionalism in Indian art is judged depend upon these collections for purposes of definition and comparison. The late nineteenth and early twentieth centuries, however, saw enormous upheaval in Indian North America. During this period, formerly independent tribes were confined to reservations. The Dawes Act of 1887 proposed converting Indians into American citizens by allotting 160 acres to each head of household. The final military battles between Plains Indians and the United States Government were fought. In Canada the potlatch—the important Northwest Coast Indian feast at which goods and money were distributed—was banned by an 1884 law. And ironically, this was the peak period of collecting. As a result, the most traumatic period in Native American history has provided the material basis for the definition of what is traditional and what is not. Basketry, bead costume, and carving from this time exist in such large quantities that they are used as a general, though often unstated, yardstick by which the unconscious standards of traditionalism are set.

49. Basket. Wikchumni Yokuts. Ca. 1900, grass bundle warp; marsh grass root and willow weft, 7 × 10¾ inches. Philbrook Art Center, Tulsa, Elizabeth Cole Butler Collection, L82.1.529.

The unusual slip-stitch, wrapped-coil construction of this basket is unique to the Wikchumni, a subtribe of the Yokuts of California. Oddly, the style of weaving is more typically associated with Mexican, Algerian, and African tourist baskets of cheap raffia than with Native American basketry. Yet the delicate craftsmanship of this willow-weft container is perfectly complemented by its meticulously executed and ancient step-fret design. The rarity of this basket's style might preclude its inclusion in a typical California basket collection, but such rarity should not cloud the integrity of its origin.

Similar problems occur in the examination of art traditions within an archaeological context. Archaeological collections are characterized by the sparseness of prehistoric remains and the fact that most artifacts come from burial or ceremonial sites. When collections of objects from the distant past are suddenly fleshed out, it is due to the addition of artifacts preserved under either the most arid or the most humid conditions. The Anasazi and Puebloan traditions of the Southwest are illuminated in this way by a few finds of material which include extraordinary basketry, superb cotton textiles, and painted wood ceremonial artifacts, including masks (Coe 1976:203; Vivian et al. 1978). In Florida, the sites of Key Marco and Fort Center have produced evidence of woodworking traditions with artistic qualities, particularly realism, that equal those of anything we know from the historic period (fig. 139; Gilliland 1975; Sears 1982). Most of this material, however, whether from wet or dry sites, is of ceremonial significance. In this respect, the high proportion of archaeological artifacts of great artistic quality is paralleled by that of early museum collections, which often concentrated on acquiring the beautiful and unique rather than the implements of everyday life.

A different situation exists at the Northwest Coast Makah wet site at Ozette, Washington, which was perfectly preserved by mud slides (Kirk with Daugherty 1974; and 1978:88–107). Most finds from the area date to the late precontact period, the seventeenth and eighteenth centuries. Numbers of superb, highly decorated artifacts survived, including wood bowls, wood boxes, combs, engraved ceremonial screens, staffs, and spindle whorls. However, these things are a very small proportion of the approximately fifty thousand worked objects recovered from the site. Perhaps most significantly, neither masks nor rattles were recovered, although the Makah were great carvers of these things in the historic period. This discrepancy cannot be explained by variations in archaeological conditions, although it may be possible that the place where such objects were stored did not survive, or else that they were in use elsewhere at the time of the principal mud slide. Alternatively, access to metal tools sped up the carving process and may have stimulated far greater artistry after Euro-American contact. Further, the historic record is skewed, since Euro-Americans collected only those things which appeared to be of artistic interest, ignoring the bulk of material artifacts. We thus have a very poor understanding of traditional art because we tend to view it not only outside the ideal

Pipes for smoking tobacco and herbs were used in the ancient ceremonies of many North American Indian people. Among the Hopi and their prehistoric ancestors, pipes were used as "cloud blowers," to imitate the sacred breath in prayer offerings to the supernaturals. Among the Plains people, sacred pipes known as *calumets* were essential in acts of worship or propitiation of the gods and in ritual exchanges between individuals or tribes enjoining peace or declaring war. The beautifully sculpted effigy pipes of Spiro Mounds and the ancient high civilizations of the Mississippi River were likely to have functioned in this way.

51. Pipe bowl. Ojibwa (Chippewa). 1800–1840, slate, 3½ inches. Philbrook Art Center, Tulsa, Ellis Soper Collection, 42–1390.

50. Lucifer pipe. Mississippian (Spiro Mounds). Ca. *1250–1350, carved bauxite, 9 inches in height. Stovall Museum of Science and History, University of Oklahoma, Norman, LF CRi B99–3.*

This delicately carved black slate pipe bowl probably depicts an Indian artist's interpretation of a white man, although the carving technique and materials are indigenous.

whole of a precontact culture, but also outside the general context in which the art objects were used. In other words, without a full picture of native objects, artistic and functional, we cannot comprehend the full traditionalism of native artistic endeavors, any more than we can appreciate the traditional in art without reference to the nontraditional.

When an artifact is viewed, the beholder selects a personal frame of reference for it. Sometimes information necessary for understanding an object's symbolic content may still be available from present-day followers of ancient traditions. This is particularly true for Puebloans in the American Southwest, and for cultures in the Northwest Coast and Arctic. But among other traditions, especially those of eastern North America, no ethnographic data exist to illuminate the ancient past. Appreciation of Puebloan architecture and recognition of the central importance of the kiva—a circular ceremonial room still used today—is a relatively straightforward matter. An understanding of the ancient Serpent Mound, or comprehension of the significance of the mounds in Mound City, both in Ohio, is very different. While both the Ohio sites derive from archaeological traditions related to historic cultures, the use of ethnographic parallels is insufficient as a basis for explanation. Instead, an archaeological and ethnographic explanation may need to be imported from general sources to help us interpret the great wealth of art objects recovered from Adena and Hopewellian burial sites. On the other hand, in the southeastern United States, Mesoamerican influences are fundamental to an explanation of the late prehistoric architecture of the Mississippian traditions of sites such as Etowah and Cahokia. The basis for appreciation of prehistoric North American artifacts is, however, often aesthetic, historical, and archaeological, rather than cultural.

The most commonly collected and most overwhelmingly prevalent artifact is the flaked stone point, or arrowhead. These things are of course excavated by archaeologists who meticulously record their cultural context, but they are also collected in vast quantities by amateurs whose interest in them is primarily aesthetic and historical. Collectors of stone artifacts in the United States amass thousands and tens of thousands of points, without archaeological motive, and arrange them in satisfying patterns to frame as pictures. Similarly, while many collectors of pottery and more com-

52. Pipe bowl. Southern Great Lakes/Ohio River. Ca. 1850, catlinite, 3⅞ × 6½ × 1¾ inches. Thomas Gilcrease Institute of American History and Art, Tulsa, 6126.6798.

Sharply aquiline features, an elongated neck, and a small caplike hat are elements of Indian iconography characterizing this figure as a white man interpreted by a native sculptor.

53. Pipe bowl. Micmac. Late 1800s, carved slate, 3 × 2

inches. Philbrook Art Center, Tulsa, Elizabeth Cole Butler Collection, L82.1.378.

Pipe bowls of wood and stone elaborately decorated with realistic and mythic creatures are known to have been produced among the Micmac during the nineteenth century. Many incorporate geometric compositions featuring hexagons, concentric circles, and other motifs that recall the decorative wood-carving styles of the early Dutch, German, and Swedish immigrants.

plex stone artifacts may scrupulously record provenance of the finds, many more do not, and so the acquisition and accumulation of the artifacts mitigates against the furthering of knowledge and resulting cultural explanation of their beauty. Even when artifacts such as Hopewellian stone pipes (fig. 105) or Mississippian flaked chert maces (fig. 7) are excavated by professionals, their explanation is limited by the almost complete absence of most of the kinds of cultural data usually employed to elucidate ethnographic artifacts (Evans 1977:111–112). We don't know, for instance, how long it took to make a Hopewellian pipe or whether the Hopewellian carving tradition was confined to small portable stone and occasional wood artifacts. We don't know whether the carving tradition was a funerary art, or whether the pipes and ornaments were carved for use in life. We don't know whether, if the pipes were used by the living, they were carved for everyday use or for specific ceremonial occasions. We don't know whether only chiefs were permitted to use the pipes, or whether they might be smoked by a group of people participating in a ceremony, or by members of a social or political organization such as a clan, lineage, or family. More importantly for the artistic tradition, we cannot explain the symbolism of the birds or animals depicted in the pipes. We might suggest that it derives from a personal spirit obtained by the user in spirit quest at an early age, since this is an explanation of symbolic content common in historic ethnography. Such explanations are, however, speculative. The significance of many prehistoric Indian traditions must, therefore, remain unknown. Particular types, such as monitor pipes, can be defined by reference to the archaeological description of the physical remains of prehistoric cultures. But in the end, our reconstruction and appreciation of them as art must depend on an aesthetic judgment based on non-Indian values. To suggest otherwise is to blind oneself to the reality that Indian art and many other aspects of Indian culture have largely been taken over and incorporated into Western society.

There are many categories of Indian art for which ethnographic explanations are incomplete or nonexistent. The significance of porcupine-quill decoration on early historic Woodlands artifacts, of the engraved designs on Beothuk antler pendants, of the painted designs on the skin coats of the Central and Eastern Subarctic are not known. This does not mean that we cannot define them as an art tradition, but merely that we can only say that they derive from Indian traditions which we comprehend on the basis of technology and fragmentary ethnographic data.

Reliance on the techniques which define categories of objects as a means of grouping and defining art traditions is a further reason for emphasizing the limitations of the concept of traditional art. Examples of this are provided by the atlatl, or throwing stick, and the toggle harpoon, a harpoon point which detaches from the foreshaft; both are common from prehistoric times. The atlatl was employed over much of North America. In historic times it was used principally in the Arctic and Northwest Coast, and in most areas it was hardly decorated at all. Among the East Greenland Eskimo, however, throwing sticks were and still are decorated with small, applied three-dimensional ivory carvings of mammals. In Alaska, the Aleut and Pacific Eskimo decorated throwing sticks with beads and inlaid ivory figures; the Pacific Eskimo also carved their throwing sticks with figures of sea otters, often highly abstract. There can be no general explanation for the varying embellishment of these things, and the cultural symbolism must remain relative to the traditions from which they spring. On the Northwest Coast, the few Tlingit throwing sticks that survive are carved with the crests of the people of high status who owned them, rather than with the animals that were hunted. Similarly, the toggle harpoon was decorated by only a few groups, such as the Makah and the Nuu-chah-nulth (Nootka) on the Northwest Coast. Their whaling harpoons, owned by the chiefs of high status (the only people permitted to hunt whales), were sometimes decorated on the barbs with crests. As these two technologies spread throughout the Arctic and Northwest Coast, we must assume that their symbolic significance varied and evolved within cultures and from one culture or group of people to the next. In the Arctic they were associated with subsistence activities; on the Northwest Coast, with the crests of chiefs. There is no reason to assume that an Indian art tradition will survive transference from one culture to the next with its symbolic, rather than physical form intact. It may be that as technologies or techniques such as those used in quill embroidery on skin and birchbark (fig. 57), or in false embroidery on twined baskets, were transferred from one location to another, their aesthetic content was adapted in meaning and, thus embellished, they began a new life in a new culture.

TRADITION, TRADE, AND EXCHANGE

Another break in tradition occurs when artifacts created within one tribe or culture are transferred by exchange, trade, or war to another. This can occur at many levels. At the most basic level, alteration of meaning takes place when a raw material travels from its place of origin. We can assume that this occurred for the wide variety of materials, such as copper, sharks' teeth, and marine shells, that were traded extensively in precontact times. Examples of altered symbolism of raw

54. Jar. Zia. Ca. 1930, polychrome pottery, 9½ × 10½ inches. Philbrook Art Center, Tulsa, Clark Field Collection, PO 300.

This water jar fits comfortably into the Zia's turn-of-the-century ceramic style, with the exception of the incongruous Asian tiger. The animal suggests non-Indian influence, but its integration into the painted composition of the pot is totally native.

materials are rather rare in ethnographic literature, and most are confined to variants on the same kinds of material. Catlinite, the red claystone mined by the Santee at Pipestone, Minnesota, occurs in various colors. The Santee preferred the pure red stone for their own pipe bowls and traded the speckled or apparently less pure stone to other tribes. At a different level, we may assume that artifacts traded on the Northwest Coast, such as bentwood boxes and canoes made by the Haida and traded on the mainland for *oolachen* grease, altered in symbolic significance upon transfer to their new owners, the various Nishga- and Gitksan-speaking peoples.

Another kind of adaptation of Indian art traditions, and consequently of our concept of what is traditional in the symbolism of Indian art, occurs when ceremonies are transferred from one tribe to another. The acquisition of the *Hamatsa* ritual by the Southern Kwakiutl from the Northern Wakashan (Kwakiutl) in the late nineteenth century, for example, provided a ceremonial base for the development of the great art of the Southern Kwakiutl in the late nineteenth and early twentieth centuries. In this case, the authentic tradition apparently altered more than did the symbolism of the artifacts.

Indian art traditions cannot, even when viewed as a whole, within a totally Indian context, be seen as discrete entities that develop independently. At every stage of transfer, raw materials and finished artifacts that were traded or captured in war, and even whole ceremonies, could be transformed symbolically or physically by their integration into indigenous art traditions. Another agent of change was the creative force of individuals who originated symbolic meanings through personal or social experience, and adapted and created art forms. Part of the unstated basis for using the binary opposition of "traditional" and "nontraditional" in analyzing Indian cultures is the assumption that individuality was not significant. While it is difficult to appreciate the importance of an individual's work in changing art traditions in precontact times, it becomes increasingly clear, in fields such as basketry and Northwest Coast carving, that individuality must have played a highly significant role in the adaptation of art traditions in the late nineteenth and early twentieth centuries, the period of maximum collection of Indian artifacts. For example, there was a relatively small number of carvers of argillite among the Haida in the early nineteenth century; nevertheless, within a few decades, especially after the devastating smallpox epidemics of the middle of the century, a thriving souvenir industry developed, involving sizable numbers of carvers. In another case, the Micmac of Nova Scotia are known for the carving of pipe bowls, yet it seems likely that a single carver was responsible for all the finely finished bowls embellished with figures of mammals, perhaps of totemic significance, and geometric designs including the double-curve motif. Because of their great beauty, the pipes of this one artisan have come to epitomize Micmac carving traditions (fig. 53). Through the creation of this ideal type, our perception of Micmac art has been distorted; we could even say it has been falsified, since artifacts appearing superficially to be traditional were in fact transitional, having mostly been sold or given to Euro-Americans rather than used indigenously.

TRADITION AS AFFECTED BY EARLY CONTACT WITH EURO-AMERICAN CULTURE

The question of what is traditional and what is not becomes even more complex when the overwhelming influence of the European and Euro-American colonization of North America is taken into account. The central problem here is that many artifacts commonly regarded as nontraditional are in fact nontraditional only in use. As we have seen, raw materials, finished artifacts, and ceremonial complexes were commonly transferred among indigenous groups in precontact times. The question is then whether or not the contact between European and Indian society was of a different nature, and so rendered European influences on Indian art different in some way from other influences.

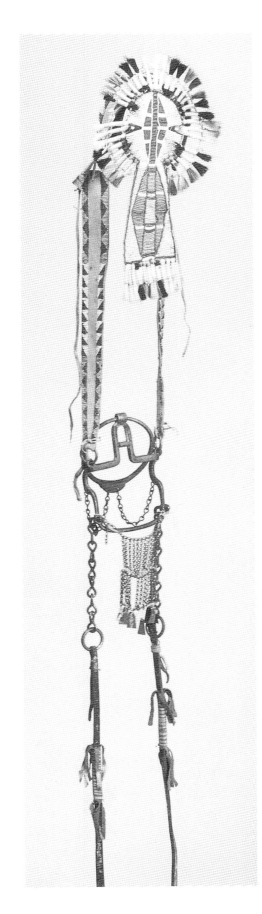

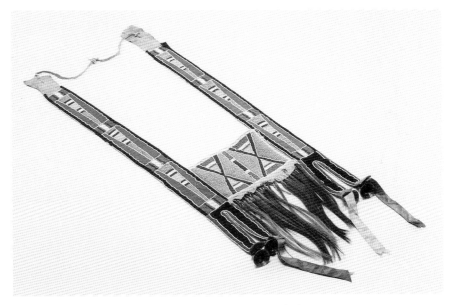

55. Headstall. Crow. Ca. 1890, metal, beadwork on hide, cord-wrapped horsehair tassels, 33½ × 8 inches; keyhole forehead ornament: 13 × 8 inches. Woolaroc Museum, Bartlesville, Philip R. Phillips Collection, IND 1311.

Since the horse was introduced into native North America by Europeans, the various types of saddles, cruppers, martingales, bits, and bridles are also derived from European prototypes. Most such Indian-made objects are purely decorative. This ornate Crow bridle incorporates a functional bit of Hispanic derivation.

56. Horse breast ornament. Crow. Late 1800s, hide, beadwork, stroud cloth, bells, ribbons, 34 × 13½ inches. Philbrook Art Center, Tulsa, Elizabeth Cole Butler Collection, 82.1.13.

The importance of the horse to Plains people is emphasized by the attention given to elaborate riding gear. The Crow people have always been noted both for their handsome dress and accoutrements and for their fine horses. Decorated collars, probably derived from functional martingales, were worn by women's horses, along with elaborate saddle cruppers and headstalls. This collar is typically Crow in design.

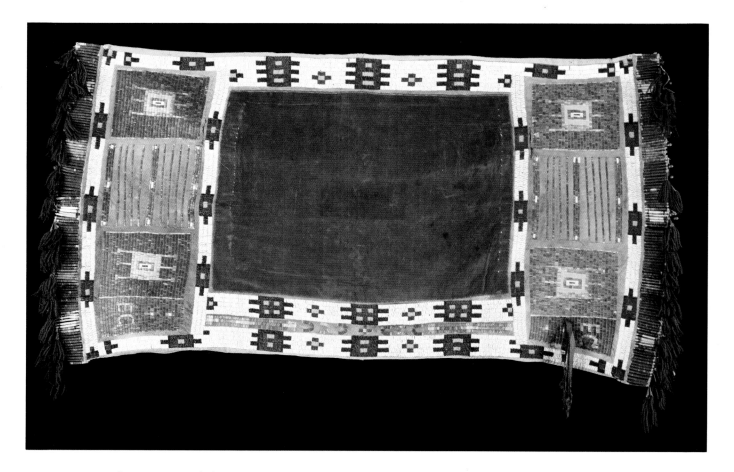

The concept of the "nontraditional" is a value-laden judgment. It reflects stereotyped ideas about Indians and expectations of the art appropriate to noble savages untainted by Western society, which in turn altered (if it did not devastate) their ideal products. The extent to which Indian material culture complexes, and therefore art traditions, internalize Western technology and ideas provides a standard against which it is possible to judge the extent of foreign influence. But this judgment is, in the end, of no use since it is based on unworkable ideal types of what Indians should be in order to be traditional, and these ideal types, like that of the Noble Savage, depend on the imposition of Western standards on Indian art. As with the description of the precontact era, that of the postcontact can be divided into a series of situations in which different kinds of non-Indian influences are brought to bear. Sometimes these influences relate to simple technologies, such as the tools that were acquired in trade from the earliest years of European contact and which wrought immediate, radical changes upon material culture and art. Sometimes these influences brought with them whole techno-logical complexes which had a more profound effect than mere tools; an example of this is the arrival of the horse, which radically altered the subsistence base of Plains society, and ultimately revolutionized Plains art (figs. 55–57; Ewers 1955). Sometimes Western trade introduced new materi-als whose acquisition influenced art without necessarily altering the form of artifacts or their sym-bolic content; the most significant of these trade items were beads, paints, and dyes, wool cloth and silk ribbon, and metals such as silver and copper, which were used for decoration and ceremonial artifacts. At a more fundamental level, Western intrusion into Indian society produced social and political responses which, although resulting from the colonization of North America, did not neces-

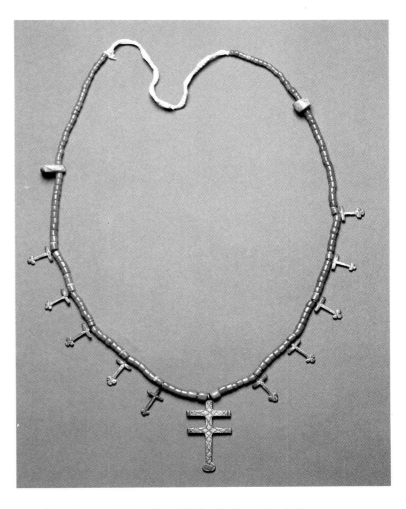

57. *Saddle blanket. Sioux. Ca. 1880, beadwork and quillwork on hide; velvet, yarn fringe, bells, tin jingles, 53 × 28½ inches. Philbrook Art Center, Tulsa, Elizabeth Cole Butler Collection, 82.1.51.*

Artworks like this quilled and beaded saddle blanket were meant solely for display. In the native style of riding, such cumbersome objects would have greatly hindered movement. Their real value was as art, and to signify the wealth and prestige of their owners.

58. *Necklace. Rio Grande, probably Santo Domingo. 1880–1890, coral, turquoise, silver, 19½ inches. Thomas Gilcrease Institute of American History and Art, Tulsa, 8437.1408.*

The double-barred cross dominating this Pueblo necklace is a native modification of the Spanish form commonly known as the caravaca cross. Its prototype was given to the Puebloans by the Franciscan fathers of New Spain. The fathers were surprised at the eagerness of Puebloans to take up the symbol of the cross, thinking this signified conversion of the ancient farmers of the Southwest. Later anthropological studies revealed that the Puebloans associated the cross not so much with Christianity as with the ancient fertility symbol of the dragonfly that adorns kiva murals and sacred medicine bowls.

sarily incorporate Euro-American ideas. Movements such as the traditionalist Midewiwin cult of the Western Great Lakes, and the Ghost Dance and Native American Church of the Plains produced ceremonial art that was new and in a sense nontraditional, but which in fact had its roots in ancient Indian society (figs. 19, 20).

Finally, there are two more superficial levels at which Euro-American society affected Indian art. The first is the adoption or adaptation of European design and its incorporation into Indian art. The second is the development of art forms, in basketry, embroidery, and carving, designed for Euro-American purchase but using Indian techniques and symbolism. The adoption by Indians of apparently European media should also be included, since this again obscures any clear division between traditional and nontraditional art (figs. 58–61).

In the Northeast, the acquisition of large quantities of metal in the seventeenth century produced rapid changes in Indian material culture. Most of these can only be guessed at because of the paucity of Indian collections from this period. The simple acquisition of metal tools such as scissors, needles, and awls, however, permitted immediate changes in skin clothing, which were and still are one of the primary media of Indian art. Skins could be cut and tailored more exactly and sewn with greater ease after metal tools became available. Clothing, we may assume, used fewer complete animal skins. Western styles were adopted, including frocked coats in the eastern Subarctic from the eighteenth century onward. On the Northwest Coast, art also changed significantly because of the acquisition of metal tools. There, iron had been available for centuries before the arrival of Europeans—either through trade with China and Euro-American societies to

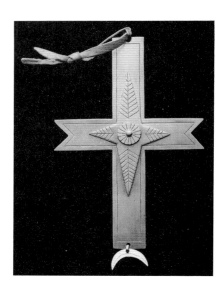

59. Cross. Robert Cruickshank (active 1790–1805), Canadian. Ca. 1800, sterling silver, beads, 11½ × 8⅛ inches. Denver Art Museum, 1959.150.

The exchange of gifts and presentation objects dates to the earliest Indian-European contact. European-made medallions, "peace medals," and decorative crosses like this one were lavished on Indian notables by white men to mark the making of peace treaties, the exchange of land, or other significant events. From the eighteenth century on, crosses made specifically for the purpose were often distributed by Europeans among other peoples. This Christian symbol became the prototype for designs used in Native American decorations and objects of personal adornment.

60. Cross with crescent. Southern Plains, possibly Kiowa. Ca. 1880, silver, hide thong, 9¾ × 6 inches. Thomas Gilcrease Institute of American History and Art, Tulsa, 6026.3a & b.

Large pendant crosses became common among the tribes of the Southern Plains in the latter part of the nineteenth century. As metalworking spread throughout the area, native artisans adapted European-made crosses, adding native iconography such as the sun and crescent moon, as well as originating their own metal jewelry. The adoption of the Christian symbol of the cross does not necessarily mean that the borrower was Christian, but rather illustrates the Native American propensity for incorporating the power objects of other cultures into their own repertoire of protective spiritual devices.

61. Cross. Kiowa. Ca. 1880–1900, German silver, hide thong, 7 × 5 inches. Fort Sill Museum, Fort Sill, 068.1.81.

This beautifully crafted Kiowa cross, made of German silver, is soldered with the overlay of a rosette and a radiating central star. The technique came relatively late to Plains metalworking, thus indicating this object's approximate date. The iconography of the piece also supports its date: stars, crosses, and crescent moons are associated with the Ghost Dance and with the later Native American Church.

the south and east, or through the collection of metal from wrecked Japanese junks that had drifted across the Pacific on the Japan Current. However, the new ease with which metal tools could be acquired apparently acted as stimulus to Northwest Coast art; the result was the creation of more and larger totem poles, house posts, and other major artifacts decorated with the crests and legends of the chiefs and families who saw to their creation. In short, simple European technology—metal tools—altered and expanded material culture and its embellishment.

The European and Euro-American colonization of North America also provided new materials through trade, which affected art and so in a sense made it less traditional. The fur trade, for instance, made wool cloth widely available to replace the skins and furs that were acquired for disposal in the east, and in Europe and Asia. Whereas skins had often been painted and decorated with moosehair and porcupine-quill embroidery, cloth was more often decorated with glass beads

62. Bandolier and bag. Delaware. Ca. 1850–1860, fabric, beads, wool tassels; bandolier: 47 inches total length; bag: 15½ × 14⅞ inches. Philbrook Art Center, Tulsa, Roberta Campbell Lawson Collection, MI 2016.

The Christian Delaware leader Journeycake owned this bag. Typical of its period is the use of heavy European-produced trade beads (pony beads), wiry-napped commercial wool known as bayeta or strouding, and bold asymmetrical floral motifs.

63. Coat. Oto. Late 1800s, floral beadwork on a wool coat, 39½ inches. Philbrook Art Center, Tulsa, George M. Tredway Collection, TR 30.

Although it was collected among the Osage and identified as a bride's coat, the distinctive motifs beaded on this European-cut frock coat suggest an Oto origin. The bisymmetrically divided fleurs-de-lis and the three-petalled flowers suggest French influence, which was much more pronounced among the Great Lakes tribes than among those of the Southern Plains.

from Italy and Bohemia (figs. 62, 63), also provided by the fur trade. Many other substitutions occurred over time; for instance, the replacement of bone, antler, and shell ornaments by silver ones. These apparently simple changes produced artifacts which were still primarily used by Indians within Indian society, and yet by their very nature seem to be nontraditional. A slightly different effect occurred with the appearance of specifically European versions of Indian tools. The best example of this is the pipe-tomahawk, a weapon and ceremonial artifact which combined the qualities of the hatchet (which had to some extent replaced the ball-headed club [fig. 142] as a weapon) with those of the smoking pipe, an object of great importance in all major and minor events. While pipe-tomahawks were almost always non-Indian in origin, they no doubt acquired symbolic value in Indian hands, something which is shown by the conservative retention of earlier forms during the nineteenth century. Pipe-tomahawks also acquired Indian embellishment, for example, the addition of feathers or burnt decoration to their stems, most of which we may assume were made by Indians rather than non-Indians. In this way, a non-Indian artifact came to be incorporated into Indian art and provided with Indian attributes. In no meaningful sense can the pipe-tomahawk be regarded as a nontraditional artifact, even though it is non-Indian. The extent to which the pipe-tomahawk came to acquire an Indian identity is apparent in the fact that during the late nineteenth century it was one of the types of artifact carved in catlinite, the Minnesota pipestone, for sale as souvenirs to non-Indians.

A separate series of incorporations occurs when non-Indian designs are taken for Indian use. The preeminent example of this is the use of European floral motifs and designs in Woodlands and Subarctic beadwork and moosehair embroidery (fig. 64). In the eighteenth century, Quebec religious orders such as the Ursuline nuns taught Indian girls to embroider in European techniques. This seems to have been in part the origin of the floral styles which appeared in the nineteenth century. Other styles perhaps came from the patterns commonly used by nineteenth-century Euro-American women in embroidery. Still, a certain proportion, mostly the more abstract designs, were certainly indigenous to native groups. The influence of French religious orders is, however, more complex and more interesting than the mere transferal of techniques and designs to Indians suggests. Because of shortages of European materials such as silk in Canada in the eighteenth century, French-Canadian nuns used Indian materials such as porcupine quills and moosehair. These materials were then incorporated into a syncretic art form, which was then taught back to the indigenous people from whom it had in part been learnt. The center of this work was the community of Lorette, which had been founded for Christian Huron dispersed from their original homeland in Ontario during the seventeenth-century wars with the Iroquois over access to fur sources (Brasser 1976:42–43; Morissonneau 1978). By the beginning of the nineteenth century, the Lorette Huron were producing large quantities of skin moccasins ornamented with floral embroidery in moosehair, as well as birchbark souvenir artifacts, such as boxes (fig. 43), trays, fans, and napkin rings decorated with figurative scenes of Indian life designed to appeal to visitors and tourists. It is reasonable to say that by the middle of the nineteenth century these were characteristic of the Huron, and so in a sense were traditional Huron artifacts, even though their beginnings were extremely complex, and by no means entirely Indian in origin or design.

TRADITION AND COMMERCIALIZATION

So far we have discussed the Indian acquisition of tools, techniques, materials, and design elements. More interesting, perhaps, are the occasions when Indians learned new technologies that used new materials and new aesthetics. Two examples of this phenomenon are the adoption in the North-east of splint basketry technique, which is possibly Scandinavian in origin, and the development of ribbon patchwork and appliqué for decorating cloth and creating clothing, which may be related to Euro-American traditions of patchwork and patchwork quilting (Abbass 1979; Brasser 1975). Another example of Indian adoption of outside influences is provided by the development of Navajo textiles in the Southwest. The Navajo had come south within the last millennium, separating from the main body of Athapaskan-speaking peoples in the Central and Western Subarctic. In the seventeenth century they were not weavers. However, after the expulsion of the Spanish during the Pueblo Revolt and the subsequent Spanish reconquest of the Southwest in the late seventeenth century, they obtained weaving technology, probably from the Hopi, and began to weave wool and to herd sheep.

Few Navajo textiles survive from before the middle of the nineteenth century. Most of those that exist are simple in design and consist largely of bold compositions of stripes in natural brown,

64. Saddle. Cree. Ca. 1900, beadwork on hide, yarn tassels with beads, 16¾ × 17 inches. Philbrook Art Center, Tulsa, Elizabeth Cole Butler Collection, L 82.1.393.

The Cree pad saddle was a direct adaptation of European military riding gear. As with other examples of métis-influenced floral beadwork traditions, this saddle beautifully illustrates a fusion of Native American and European aesthetic ideals.

white, and deep indigo (fig. 90). In the middle of the nineteenth century, and especially after the effective military defeat of the Navajo in the 1860s by the United States, the aesthetics of Navajo textiles began to undergo a series of far-reaching changes. In particular, geometric stepped designs, probably of Mexican origin, came to be used on blankets woven for Indian use. Increasing American influence brought other significant changes, especially after the arrival of railways in the 1880s. Rugs for use in American homes came to be the primary textile form, and designs began to incorporate foreign motifs, particularly from Mexican Saltillo serapes, with their vivid stepped and wedge-edged geometric designs (figs. 91, 94). These designs, known as Eye Dazzlers, are visually mobile and highly detailed, contrasting with the strong, simple designs of the earliest known blankets. At the same time, new dyes were introduced, and aniline dyes came to be more important than the old and more traditional colors, including the imported indigo. Newly introduced yarns began to replace ancient natural yarns; some were raveled from imported cloth, others purchased from eastern North America, for instance from Germantown, Pennsylvania, whose name is now synonymous with non-Navajo yarns of the late nineteenth century (fig. 94). These influences on Navajo textiles were absorbed without non-Navajo intervention. After a period of decline in textile quality at the end of the nineteenth century, a succession of Euro-American traders became involved in the development of technical quality and the introduction of new patterns and designs outside the Navajo repertoire. Traders such as J. B. Moore acquired trading posts and set about improving the quality of wool and dyeing. From 1897, when he purchased the trading post which he renamed Crystal, Moore tried to promote Navajo textiles through refinements not only in quality but also in design and motifs. Some of these, such as the swastika or "whirling logs" design, which derived from Navajo sand paintings, were traditional (Rodee 1981:19–24); others were new. Moore was also instrumental in introducing the Oriental design principles of Caucasian rugs, particularly that of a border design with a central pattern, to Navajo weavers. This was in line with his avowed intent of making Navajo textiles more commercial, in this case by making them competitive in design with imported Asian rugs. Perhaps the most significant design alteration to Navajo weaving was, however, the introduction of religious designs, particularly from sand paintings or dry paintings, in the form of Yeis, the supernatural figures portrayed in the paintings. While this idea had begun in the nineteenth century, it only developed into a substantial tradition with the work of Hosteen Klah, an important medicine man from near Newcomb, New Mexico, during the 1920s and 1930s. This introduction of religious material into an art form made entirely for commercial purposes is perhaps a direct parallel to the Haida introduction of shamans and shamanistic rituals into the subject matter of argillite carving. The Navajo still feel uneasy about the sacrilegious aspect of this tradition (Rodee 1981:103–104).

The tenacity of Indian art traditions is combined with a cohesive sense of culture in many areas. One such area is that of the Puebloan pottery traditions. Acoma was an important center for the production of superb glazed pottery during the early historic period, particularly before the 1680 revolt against Spanish rule. After the reconquest, glazed ware declined, and it ceased to be made in the eighteenth century. During the first millennium A.D. the use of paints that vitrify in the firing had been accidentally discovered, although pots were never wholly and intentionally glazed except from the fourteenth to the seventeenth centuries. By the eighteenth century, the technique and materials for glazing were abandoned, even though other mineral pigments were still used to decorate ceramics. Surprisingly, then, the use of glazes was not an introduction from Europe but an indigenous tradition which declined and disappeared, for reasons, we must assume, connected to the colonization of New Mexico. From the early eighteenth century, when mineral pigments came to replace mineral glazes, styles became more figurative, and began to include birds and flowers, perhaps under the influence of other pueblos. By the middle of the nineteenth century, a single superb decorative tradition had become established, known as McCartys polychrome. The water jars of this tradition have a smooth, swelling form, without marked differentiation of neck and base sections (fig. 65). They are decorated in bold geometric designs which incorporate deer and parrots and sometimes include figurative scenes. At Acoma, then, the tradition of glazed wares on a green or brown ground disappeared at the time of uncertainty occasioned by the Pueblo Revolt, and was replaced by another tradition which evolved into McCartys polychrome.

Finally, in the same way that modern Hopi pottery was influenced by the ancient Sikyatki tradition in the late nineteenth century, so was Acoma influenced by Mimbres pottery in the twentieth (figs. 66, 67). The use of Mimbres designs was encouraged at Acoma by members of the staff of the Museum of New Mexico. Despite this white involvement, which parallels similar interactions in so many other Indian arts of this century, Acoma pottery can be viewed as a single, coherent whole, in which coiling technique and the use of ground potsherds as temper are two aspects of a conservative, yet extremely flexible art tradition (Frank and Harlow 1974:121–133; Harlow 1977:75–80).

Aesthetic and ceremonial traditions may respond to acculturation differently, even within the same community or tribe. Material culture traditions concerned with subsistence activities are often the first to disappear, particularly when these depend on very time-consuming manufacture, such as

65. McCartys polychrome jar. Acoma. Ca. 1900, poly-chrome pottery, 11½ × 14½ inches in diameter. Stovall Museum of Science and History, University of Oklahoma, Norman, NAM 15–1–1.

From prehistoric to historic times, Pueblo pottery styles were extremely stable within given traditions. In the twentieth century, however, the rate of stylistic change has been greatly accelerated, primarily through the influence of the tourist trade. From the 1870s until the turn of the century, Acoma water jars showed considerable Spanish influence in their rosette and checkerboard designs. During the 1930s, white patrons such as Kenneth Chapman reintroduced prehistoric shapes and black-on-white pottery designs to Acoma potters. Currently, twelfth-century Mimbres designs and historic nineteenth-century designs dominate Acoma ceramics.

66. Seed jar. Lucy Lewis (1898–   ), Acoma. Ca. 1959, black-on-white painted pottery, 6½ × 10 inches. Philbrook Art Center, Tulsa, Clark Field Collection, PO 531.

Lucy Lewis ranks in many minds as the Acoma equivalent to San Ildefonso's brilliant potter Maria Martinez. She is unquestionably a twentieth-century master. Lewis integrated a variety of prehistoric designs into her ceramics, among them the ancient walnut black-on-white, as in this jar, and other western New Mexican and central Arizonan prehistoric pottery motifs. Recently she has concentrated on ancient Mimbres and Zuñi designs.

67. Jar. B. J. Cerno, Acoma. 1981, polychrome pottery, 5½ × 8 inches. Private collection.

This superb seed jar celebrates the fusion of ancient Mimbres figurative elements with geometric designs. No Mimbres vessel ever incorporated such a complex series of positive and negative motifs, yet the inspiration derives directly from the genius of these ancient Pueblo people. The jar is not a copyist work exhuming a dead tradition, but rather a revitalization of Mimbres achievements and a legitimate successor in the natural evolution of this brilliant twelfth-century tradition. The only European influence upon it is that it was made for sale.

68. *Basket. Sarah Hunter, Panamint. Ca. 1930–1940, willow, martynia, tree yucca root, 8½ × 23½ inches. Philbrook Art Center, Tulsa, Clark Field Collection, BA 616.*

This Panamint fancy basket, made for sale, is traditional in medium and technique, but adapted to a changing lifestyle and a changed relationship to the Euro-American world. Sarah Hunter, the weaver, demonstrates her characteristic use of many diverse pictorial images in a single piece of work.

69. *Basket with lid. Nootka. Ca. 1930–1950, cedar bark, grasses, 2 inches high × 3⁵⁄₁₆ inches in diameter. Thomas Gilcrease Institute of American History and Art, Tulsa, 7137.579a & b.*

Trinket baskets like this one were probably adapted from forms of imported ceramic jars. These commercial baskets were meant for coins, jewelry, or any items white curio collectors might wish to store. To fully Anglicize their appeal, the baskets were woven with American designs such as the eagle clutching arrows.

the basketry artifacts used, for instance, in the gathering of nuts or acorns. An example of this is provided by the twined basketry traditions of the Panamint Shoshone, a Central-Numic-speaking people of southeastern California. The Panamint live in an exceptionally arid area around Death and Panamint valleys, so that much food traditionally came from the mountains above the valleys. The most important food resource was the pine nut, although acorns and mesquite beans were also very significant. Twined willow baskets were made in forms for use as water ollas, winnowing and parching trays, and conical carrying and seed baskets. Basketry hats and cradles were also made. Coiled basketry, on the other hand, although comparatively finer, continued to be made in larger quantities as a tourist art after twined basketry had ceased to be necessary for purely subsistence purposes (fig. 68).

Panamint coiled baskets usually have a three-rod foundation, often of willow, but also including sumac and grass. The withes are cut in winter and prepared with a knife. The coiling element, also of willow, incorporates decorative sections of baltic rush, a light brown alkali bulrush, dark brown devil's claw, and the inner root of the joshua tree or tree yucca, which is red-brown. In the nineteenth century it is likely that all baskets were made with geometric designs for ceremonial usage. In this century, with tourist and other non-Indian activity in Panamint lands, figurative designs were included that appear to be of Euro-American derivation. These designs consist of lizards, birds, butterflies, and conventionalized animal and floral patterns. The favored and more traditional geometric designs included vertical rows of triangles and diamonds touching each other. Perhaps the most significant change, however, was technological. Whereas, aboriginally, stone knives had been used to shape basketry elements, punctured tin lids, through which the withes were drawn, came to be used for fancy baskets. This permitted quicker production of raw materials and consequently also of what had traditionally been the basketwork of highest status (Kirk 1952; Steward 1941:333–339).

On the Northwest Coast, among the Nuu-chah-nulth people of West Vancouver Island and the Makah of Washington, slightly different adaptations were made in the production of twined fancy baskets sold as souvenirs. Metal tools were introduced; parts of razor blades were used in specialized knives to produce uniform widths of grass. Figurative designs had always been a feature of basketry, particularly on the whaling hats worn by chiefs. In the nineteenth century, traditional and nontraditional motifs came to be used in large numbers on baskets made for sale (fig. 69). More unusual is the alteration in the pattern of use of particular species of grass, which occurred in this century. Most of the fine white grass used on basket exteriors was obtained in Washington and traded to Vancouver Island. With less aboriginal trade and the decline of labor opportunities in Washington, the Nuu-chah-nulth began to use more easily prepared but less fine local grasses. In this way, not only were they able to continue their souvenir art when the supply of grass declined, but they were also able to increase productivity because of the use of more easily worked materials. In no sense, however, can this substitution, or that of metal blades for knives, be regarded as altering the traditionalism of the twined souvenir baskets still produced in large numbers today. Indian artifacts, even when created for sale, contain clues about change, information about diachronic processes of which they are part, and evidence that the easy division of art into traditional and nontraditional categories is misleading.

A good example of this confusion is provided by the souvenir art of the Haida, argillite carving. In the nineteenth century, the Haida of British Columbia created a new smoking pipe, a dish form, and other objects of carved shale (fig. 120). These were all made for sale to Europeans and other non-Indians. It is commonly assumed, although scholars know otherwise, that argillite carving played no part in indigenous Haida art. A recent exhibition of argillite carving was entitled "Pipes that Won't Smoke, Coal that Won't Burn," even though the first argillite pipes probably were carved for smoking, and other artifacts such as shaman's charms were also carved for native use (Sheehan 1981). The confusion stems in part from the mistaken notion that the Haida suddenly started to carve shale souvenirs that had no reference to their indigenous culture. Compounding the error is the isolation of argillite carving from other forms of souvenir creation, particularly the carving of wood artifacts, whether pipes, bowls, or figures; and the too exclusive association of argillite carving with the Haida, even though numbers of pipes were also carved by the Kwakiutl and others on Vancouver Island, of shale taken from local coal mines. Haida argillite carving should be seen in the context of a wide range of artistic phenomena on the Northwest Coast which occurred as reactions to the European colonization of Indian peoples. If native art is seen in the context of its political and cultural situation, then the need to distinguish "traditional" from "nontraditional" art disappears and is replaced by a more subtle understanding of the way in which art traditions emerge, flourish, and decay within the context of Indian society, whether or not they are influenced by white cultures during the process.

In a common usage, the word "traditional" is applied to artifacts that were meant wholly for native use, as opposed to those that were not. By this definition, an artifact may be entirely traditional in technique and symbolic content, and nontraditional only in that it was sold rather than used. This simplistic definition avoids consideration of the political and economic context in which art objects are produced, and without which we cannot say art exists. Haida argillite is an apparently nontraditional art form because it was made for sale, and very often included Euro-American motifs which were non-Haida. But because it fully represents in a more general manner Haida society at a time of devastating change, it is very much part of the complex whole of Haida society of which art was and is an aspect. The "nontraditional" label in this, as in most other cases, derives

from the most common Euro-American affectation, that of pretending that Indians and other native peoples somehow cease to exist, or at least lose their souls, if they employ white man's materials or symbols, or create art to sell to the white man. White society does not accept Indian society as it exists at any one time: it is a part of this denial of Indian existence to denigrate postcontact adaptations in art and material culture as nontraditional.

THE EFFECT OF WHITE INSTITUTIONS ON NATIVE AMERICAN TRADITIONS IN THE MODERN PERIOD

More extreme forms of Euro-American influence occurred in the middle of this century, with the institutional fostering of Indian art, either with or without the financial and other support of the federal government. Perhaps the earliest and most direct example of this concerns the projects that arose as part of the New Deal, during the Depression of the 1930s. One of these encouraged the preservation and recarving of totem poles in Alaska. While this had a direct relationship to tourism, another project, the Seneca Arts Project in New York, was more purely centered on the cultivation and re-creation of Iroquois arts. Between 1934 and 1941, the Seneca project led to the creation of five thousand works of art at Cattaraugus and Tonawanda reservations, under the direction of Arthur Parker, the part-Seneca director of the Rochester Municipal Museum, now the Rochester Museum and Science Center. The intention of the project was to redevelop Iroquois artistic genius, long threatened and nearly overwhelmed by Euro-American political and cultural domination. Funding came from a number of different sources, particularly TERA (Temporary Emergency Relief Administration) and later the WPA (Works Projects Administration). Approximately one hundred artists worked in a variety of different media, some purely traditional and some apparently nontraditional. The former included the carving of false-face masks, bowls, spoons, and cradleboards, the weaving of baskets and burden straps, beadwork, moosehair and porcupine quillwork, and the making of silver jewelry. The apparently nontraditional aspect centered on painting and drawing in a variety of media (Hauptman 1979). However, Iroquois employment of European painting techniques was at this time at least a century old (see Sturtevant, chapter 1, this volume), and so was as traditional as, for instance, the use of European beads to decorate American fabric for ceremonial clothing. While this project was created by Parker, a man with idealistic views on the worth of Indian art, many others were set up at the time to provide work for artists of all cultural groups and in all media. From the taxpayer's point of view, the significance of the Seneca Arts Project was that it kept artists off the streets; however, TERA and the WPA helped lead to the emergence of the New York School of Abstract Expressionism and to the creation of superb watercolor drawings of Indian artifacts on the catalogue cards of the Denver Art Museum.

Perhaps the most successful and best-known examples of the institutional fostering of native arts occurred among the Inuit or Eskimo in Canada during the 1940s and early 1950s. The initial interest in Eskimo sculpture was stimulated by a Canadian artist, James Houston, who purchased carvings in the Port Harrison–Povungnetuk regions while on a painting trip to the Arctic in 1948. Houston's collection attracted the interest and material help of the Canadian Handicrafts Guild, the

Hudson's Bay Company, the Anglican Arctic Diocese, and eventually the Canadian government. These institutions, for diverse reasons both artistic and economic, helped stimulate the emergence of a full-fledged Inuit school in the 1950s (Swinton 1972:123–126). In all of this, James Houston's charismatic presence acted as a catalyst. In some sense, then, the white impact upon this art form may be considered nontraditional, particularly in terms of the kinds of artifacts produced, which were non-utilitarian sculptures created for sale outside the community (fig. 254). Additionally, while most Inuit men were carvers, stone carving, the principal medium for this work, was a minor tradition more or less confined to the production of stone lamps and cooking pots. However, the easy label of "nontraditionalism," as applied to Inuit sculpture and graphic productions, distorts their context and, because of Euro-American prejudices, even taints the art as somehow non-Inuit. The reasons for this label are similar to those identified in the rejection of other apparently nontraditional art

70. *Pipe, front and back views. Inuit (Eskimo). Ca. 1890–1900, engraved walrus tusk, seal oil soot, 9 inches. Philbrook Art Center, Tulsa, Ellis Soper Collection, S-263.*

Siberian-style pipes made of wood with lead inlay were introduced across the Bering Strait to Eskimos in the eighteenth and early nineteenth centuries with Russian expansion into Alaskan territory. In the elaborate ivory pipes that the Inuit carved later, traditional engravings of native daily life were combined with European naturalistic animal forms. Pipes such as these were usually intended for the developing nineteenth-century tourist trade.

71. *Knife. Inuit (Eskimo). Late 1800s, engraved ivory, 12⁷/₁₆ × 1³/₈ inches. Thomas Gilcrease Institute of American History and Art, Tulsa, Frank Engles Collection, 8336.1119.*

Though of late-nineteenth-century manufacture, this engraved snow knife adheres both aesthetically and functionally to native styles and traditions. Its elegant simplicity and sculptural form contrast markedly with the exuberantly decorative embellishment of the curio objects produced for commercial trade.

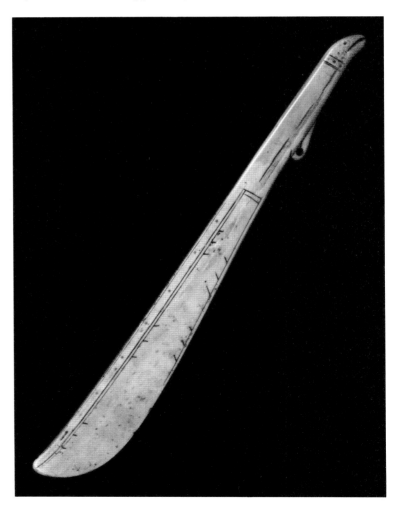

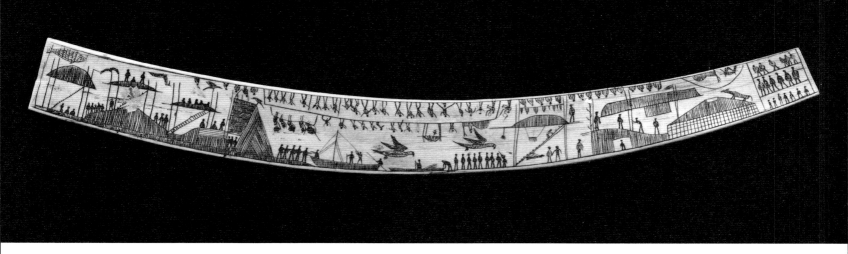

72. *Tusk, front and back views. Inuit (Eskimo). Late 1800s, engraved tusk, seal oil soot, 12 inches. Philbrook Art Center, Tulsa, Ellis Soper Collection, S–288.*

Bow drills, cribbage boards, and other elaborate objects such as this tusk and the pipe in figure 70 were made for the nineteenth-century tourist trade. They reflect a consummately synthetic art in which Eurasian, Russian, Siberian tribal, and British and American tourist influences all have an impact on Alaskan Eskimo aesthetics.

forms as non-native. And, as in other cases, it again implies a refusal to accept that the Inuit, like other native North Americans, have kept many aspects of their culture at a time of extreme economic and political change. The retention of many aspects of subsistence traditions, family networks, and linguistic and oral traditions are three basic attributes of the artistic context without which specific sculptures representing these traditions cannot be viewed. The use of the words "traditional" and "nontraditional" suggests a black-and-white situation, when reality is much subtler. The maintenance of native traditions provides an unbroken continuity which is often hard for the Euro-American to perceive.

CHANGE IN NATIVE AMERICAN TRADITIONS RESULTING FROM COLONIZATION

A different situation occurred when Indian art was the product of a cultural development arising as a response to the devastation wrought by the colonization of North America. One such development was the revitalization movement, seeking to reaffirm cultural values in a period of extreme change. Examples include the founding of the Handsome Lake religion among the Iroquois at the beginning of the nineteenth century. This religion was based on traditional Iroquois religion but was adapted to the changed circumstances of Iroquois life, after the tribe's defeat at the time of the American Revolution. A century earlier, among the Algonquian-speaking people of the Western Great Lakes, a similar development had taken the form of the Midewiwin cult, which combined traditional shamanism with the teaching of ancient beliefs (Wallace 1978).

While there is relatively little documentation of new art forms for these religions, for the Native American Church there is a substantial body of information relating to symbolism and new artifact types which were and are produced for use by members. Also unlike the Midewiwin, there is concrete evidence of the incorporation into the Native American Church of Euro-American ideas and symbols, particularly from Christianity. At the center of the Native American Church is the ritual consumption of peyote, a hallucinogenic cactus. Peyote has been used since precontact times, but only in the nineteenth century did it come to be associated with aspects of Christianity (fig. 60). The cactus is eaten on the occasion of services held by the Church to pray for an individual's recovery from illness, or in honor of a birthday, holiday, or other important occasion. Meetings take place in a tipi. Other equipment also derives from Plains prototypes but is usually decorated in idiosyncratic fashion. The rattles used are made of small gourds but the fans are of exotic bird feathers with brightly beaded handles (figs. 19, 20). Most of the unusual symbolism is, however, concentrated in the pins and other silver, German silver, and brass jewelry. These ornaments or badges are an early-twentieth-century phenomenon, and so relatively late, although they became

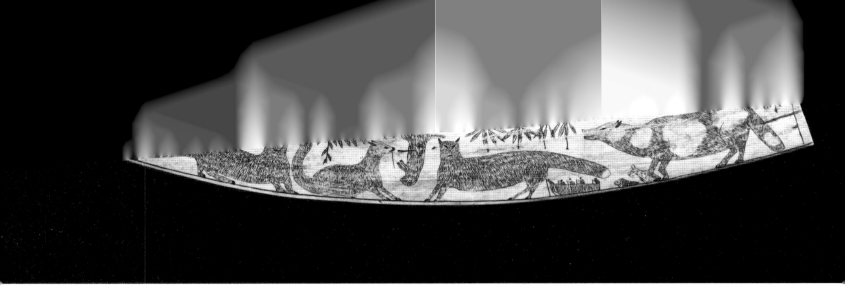

established before the Native American Church was formally incorporated during the 1920s. While the jewelry is directly related to the Plains tradition of jewelry manufacture, much of the symbolism is new. Designs derived from both the peyote cactus and Christian symbolism decorate buttons, tie pins and clips, rings, handkerchief slides, and earrings as well as fans, tipis, and drums, which are used in the ceremony (Douglas and Mariott 1942). In this instance, an art has developed from a syncretic religion to proclaim a highly moral and even conservative way of life, through the incorporation of apparently nontraditional elements into an Indian ceremony.

73. *Painted hide. Kill Eagle (1820–?), Cheyenne/Sioux. 1870–1875, buffalo hide, native and commercial pigments, 87 × 97 inches. Philbrook Art Center/University of Tulsa, 84.8.*

Early painted buffalo, elk, and deer hides of the Plains emphasized either heavily incised and painted geometric compositions, particularly favored for children's and women's robes, or autobiographical scenes of battle, horse-stealing, and visionary events for warrior's robes. The figurative decorations often narrated an individual's professional career with serially clustered scenes. The decoration of such hides was totally different from the scenes of idealized tribal life painted on curio hides from the 1890s to the present.

Related to the question of art that has been instigated or influenced by white institutions is the issue of the so-called traditional schools of Indian painting which emerged between the two world wars. The two main schools, the Santa Fe and the Oklahoma, are descended from entirely aboriginal painting techniques whose traditional qualities cannot be doubted. The Southwest traditions of the Santa Fe school were stimulated by a mixture of teachers, anthropologists, and artists who encouraged the realistic depiction of Indians, or in the case of J. Walter Fewkes, of Hopi Katcinas (Fewkes 1903). More generally, the paintings represent scenes from traditional life in a mixture of Western and indigenous art traditions (Brody 1971). These productions, and their Oklahoma equivalents, in a sense form the traditional school of Indian painting, having derived from realistic Plains or Southwest traditions and representing the first cohesive emergence of so-called fine art suitable for general patronage. In this as in other traditions, the relativism of traditional Indian art becomes apparent. Ledger drawings from the early reservation period of the Plains (figs. 162–167) are less traditional than earlier depictions of calendric winter counts and war exploits painted on skin (fig. 73). In turn, the paintings of the Kiowa Five, of the 1920s, are less traditional than ledger drawings, and contemporary, postmodern Indian artists are less apparently traditional than the Kiowa Five. Yet here again the use of the word "traditional" is in most senses meaningless because all the artists from these distinct periods or schools were Indians working within an Indian context. To describe one school or period as less traditional than another is to take one particular aspect of the paintings, whether materials, media, or motifs, and divorce it from the intention of the artist (see also Young, Warner, and Highwater, chapters II, V, and VI, this volume).

TRADITIONALISM IN INDIAN ART AS A COMPLEX AND SUBTLE PHENOMENON

Traditionalism, then, is not an attribute that can be easily identified in Indian art. Specific traits, whether technical or aesthetic, whether derived from new materials or a new social and political context, may develop in an ancient society without rendering its art nontraditional. Indian art must be made by Indians, but in all other attributes it can only be defined as Indian and traditional by the maker or beholder. To compartmentalize Indian art artificially as "traditional" or "nontraditional" is to deny the continuity of Indian society by specifying a particular point at which it breaks from the past. To do this is to idealize precontact societies and to imply that in adopting Euro-American ideas, materials, and markets, Indian societies are absorbed. The crucial term in Indian art is "Indian"; without it, Indian art has no existence, whatever the apparent traditionalism of the artifacts to the European or American beholder.

Note

1. "All the evidence leads to the conclusion that any autonomous cultural system is in a continuous process of change. The change that is induced by contact therefore does not represent a shift from a static to an active state but rather a shift from one sort of change to another. Contact often stimulates change more adventitiously, more generally, and more rapidly than do internal forces. The particular effects of a conjunction of two cultures will depend upon antecedent modes of internal change together with the nature of the intercultural contact profile and the influences that are communicated through its network" (Barnett et al. 1954).

European Influences on Plains Indian Art

NORMAN FEDER

Plains Indians, like most Indians from other areas, were extremely conservative and in general tended to resist change. They were ethnocentric as well and therefore eager to retain their tribal identity, firmly believing that their own ways of doing things were best. But change, however slow, is inevitable, and comes about through influences from outside the tribe as well as from within.

Change caused by influences from within the tribe is a continual process but usually a subtle one, as is indicated by slight changes in decorative patterns or the choice of newfound decorative materials. While changes from within the tribe could at times be profound, as in the case of vision-inspired religious art or decorative ideas, the most profound changes were generally the result of outside influences—ideas borrowed from other tribes and, later, from Europeans. Even in the precontact period, Plains Indians participated in a vast intertribal trading network which brought new materials and new ideas thousands of miles from their sources: seashells came from the Pacific and from the Gulf of Mexico (fig. 21); catlinite was traded from Minnesota all the way to the Plateau; and some religious ideas and manufactured goods came from the Valley of Mexico.

Perhaps the first influence of the Europeans on the Plains was the introduction of new materials —cloth, metals, bright paint pigments, dyed wool yarns, mirrors, hawk bells, brass tacks, and glass beads (figs. 74–76). At first these materials were distributed as gifts, valuable for their novelty and rarity; but later they were supplied in exchange for furs. For the most part, these new materials were simply adapted to old art forms, resulting in items that were more colorful but basically unchanged in form. Some of these new trade goods, however, gradually replaced the native materials in craft production: black cloth replaced black-dyed buckskin; glass trade beads and silk ribbons replaced porcupine quills. One of the indications of Indian conservatism is that the items most often requested in trade were either scarce precontact trade goods (like dentalium, abalone, and conch shells) or European-made copies of Indian items that were hard to manufacture (such as wampum beads or shell hair pipes). The Indians soon realized that some trade goods were superior to their native products; as metal cooking pots gained favor, for example, the art of pottery-making gradually died out on the Plains.

Up through the period of the American Revolution, the French, British, and Americans bestowed lavish gifts on Indian tribes in an effort to gain their allegiance. Indians became the recipients of prestige items, including a wide variety of silver ornaments, such as brooches, crosses (fig. 59), bracelets, medals, and even silver smoking pipes and tomahawks. Elaborately decorated officers' coats became common gifts, as did bolts of cloth and blankets of the best quality available. After the early American wars, the Indians continued to demand quality goods in exchange for their furs, and competition between the various fur traders was fierce. Gradually, the Hudson's Bay Company assumed control of trade in the North, as did John Jacob Astor in the South. Astor continued to dominate the trade in the United States until 1832, when he retired and the field was opened to a host of independent traders. During the period of Astor's control, however, the lack of competition led to a deterioration in the quality of trade goods, and Indians learned to manufacture some items, such as

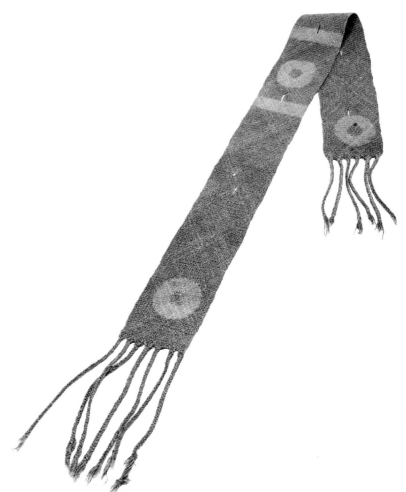

74. *Sash. Osage. Mid-1800s, dyed wool yarn, 55 × 3¼ inches. Philbrook Art Center, Tulsa, Roberta Campbell Lawson Collection, MI 2216 A.*

Various elements of European costume—coats, pantaloons, bandolier bags, caps, and sashes—influenced the native dress of North American Indians. Among some groups, such as the Seminole, Choctaw, and Cherokee, a luxurious adaptation of eighteenth-century colonial dress displaced native clothing. Others, notably Plains tribes, adopted only a few articles of European dress, which were often compatible with simpler native forms.

75. *Sash. Osage. Ca. 1925, wool yarn, beads, 86 × 7½ inches. Philbrook Art Center, Tulsa, 76.9.4.*

This richly beaded commercial yarn Eye Dazzler sash contrasts strongly with the simple woven and resist-dyed one shown in figure 74. The simpler sash reflects Osage tastes as they existed only seventy-five years before this sash was produced.

76. *Sash. Southeastern Woodlands. Ca. 1870–1890, commercial wool yarn, beads, 130 inches. Philbrook Art Center, Tulsa, Alice M. Robertson Collection, 31–430.*

Although documented as having been worn by a Seminole in an 1890 photograph, this sash is much like others common throughout the Southeastern Woodlands of native America. Although its heavy beadwork and geometric patterns suggest stylistic preferences of the mid-nineteenth century, such a sash also reveals the great range of individuality in Native American art. No two sashes, even in the same tribe or community, were ever exactly the same.

silver ornaments, for themselves. After 1832, with increased competition, more and better-quality materials were again available, but furs for trade were more scarce.

The first three hundred years of European advancement into the New World created a slow but continuous upheaval in the status quo. With the increase of the European population in the East, tribes were forced westward, displacing the other Indians in their paths. This westward migration was accelerated because Indians living in close proximity to the Europeans had greater access to guns and horses, and thus had a tremendous advantage in warfare with their western neighbors. The warfare caused by migration, coupled with the devastating effects of disease and alcohol introduced by European contact, caused extinction of some tribes and the amalgamation of others into new alliances. Due to the many long migrations, some large tribes formed into several smaller and scattered splinter groups. The Delaware, for example, who originally lived in the area from southeastern New York to eastern Pennsylvania and through New Jersey and Delaware, were forced by migrations into Ohio, Indiana, Kansas, Texas, and Missouri. Today, in addition to individuals who live scattered among the Chippewa in Minnesota and elsewhere, the Delaware live primarily on two reservations in Oklahoma, among the Stockbridge in Wisconsin and in three groups in Ontario, Canada.

77. Cradle. Kiowa. Ca. 1880, beadwork on hide, wooden frame, brass tacks, 43 × 10½ × 10 inches. Philbrook Art Center, Tulsa, Elizabeth Cole Butler Collection, L82.1.319.

Starting in the eighteenth century, the Delaware were forced to migrate from their Atlantic seaboard homeland in what is now New Jersey. Eventually they settled in scattered reservations throughout Oklahoma, Wisconsin, and Ontario. As they wandered, they disseminated their aesthetic and religious views among many tribes, with results such as this Kiowa cradle, which shows distinct Delaware influence. The Kiowa-Delaware contact probably occurred in the 1820s, when the two tribes shared territory in Texas. By the 1870s, Delaware floral motifs and asymmetric compositions had displaced much of the earlier Kiowa design.

Quite apart from the obvious hardships endured by the Delaware people during these forced migrations, it is important for our purposes that the Delaware disseminated their ideas of art, decoration, and religion wherever they traveled. For example, the Delaware lived with or in close proximity to the Kiowa as early as 1820, when they were in Texas; by 1874, 30 Delaware were living on the Kiowa and Comanche Reservations in Indian Territory; and by 1890 there were 102 Delaware living with the Kiowa (Wright 1951:147). That these Delaware influenced Kiowa art is obvious from various traits, such as the use of abstract floral designs in Kiowa beadwork and the use of bilateral asymmetry on Kiowa cradleboards and moccasin cuffs. It should be understood, however, that even though the Kiowa borrowed certain Delaware design elements, the designs were adapted to typical Kiowa forms. For example, the Kiowa did not adopt Delaware-style soft-sole moccasins; they maintained their Plains-type hard-sole moccasins and simply added Delaware-style cuffs with bilaterally asymmetrical designs. The same is true for their cradleboards: the Kiowa did not adopt the Delaware-style solid wood board with hoop and footrest; they maintained their traditional form of a leather sack on a slat-board frame, but decorated the leather sack in Delaware-style floral beadwork, using a different background color for each side (fig. 77). In short, ethnocentrism allowed the Kiowa to adopt Delaware decorative ideas, but basic Kiowa forms were maintained.

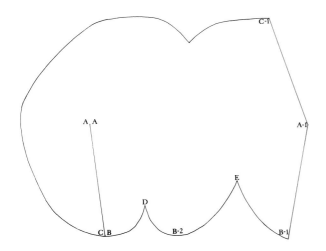

78. *Moccasin pattern. This pattern (actual size approximately 10 × 15 inches), used for Omaha/Ponca-style moccasins, produces a one-piece soft-sole moccasin with a cuff that can be worn turned either up or down. 1. Cut the line from* AA *to* CB *2. Sew edge* AB *to edge* A–1/B–1. *3. Sew edge* AC *to edge* A–1/C–1. *4. Sew edge* BD *to edge* D/B–2. *5. Sew edge* B–1/E *to edge* E/B–2.

79. *Moccasins. Ponca(?). Ca. 1890, hide, beadwork, wool yarn tassels, 10 inches. Philbrook Art Center, Tulsa, Bright Roddy Collection, 31–48.*

This pair of Ponca-style moccasins was originally catalogued as Sioux and later changed to Osage and then to Omaha, but they are just as likely Ponca. They are two-piece, hard-sole types in the general Osage pattern, but the decoration is in the Ponca/Omaha style. They were collected by Bright Roddy in Oklahoma.—N. F.

Because the factor of ethnocentrism is so important as an element of resistance to change, one more example will be presented here. In general, moccasin types are among the last tribally distinct clothing forms to change. In fact, it is often possible to identify the tribal origin of an Indian in an undocumented photograph solely on the basis of moccasin style. At one time, most of the Prairie tribes wore one-piece, soft-sole, black-dyed moccasins, although they are not common in museum collections today. These are known from the Iowa, Osage, Pawnee, Omaha, and Ponca.[1] Because this was such a distinctive item of dress, pictographic drawings of Southern Plains origin always indicate Pawnee, Osage, and Kaw enemies as wearing black moccasins with upturned flaring cuffs (Petersen 1971:290–291). The Omaha and Ponca were at one time a single tribe, splitting into two groups probably in the early 1700s (Howard 1965:15–16). Both tribes wore identical moccasin types, although the Omaha continued using the style longer than did the Ponca (fig. 78). Perhaps for this reason, there is a tendency among ethnologists to label any undocumented pair of Omaha/Ponca-style moccasins as Omaha (fig. 79). In fact, even in the case of a pair of well-documented Ponca moccasins at the Oklahoma Historical Society, the attribution was somehow changed from Ponca to Omaha and then back to Ponca (fig. 81). Figures 80–82 show a series of Ponca moccasins, from an early black-dyed pair collected in about 1830 by Maximilian, Prince of Wied Neuwied to a pair placed in the cornerstone of the Ponca–Nez Percé Industrial School in White Eagle, Oklahoma, in 1880 by Child Chief. Another documented pair of Ponca moccasins was collected by M. R. Harrington in Oklahoma as late as about 1913.[2] This older tribal style is not worn today by either the Omaha or Ponca, but the type persisted long after most other elements of costume were changed to conform to the styles of the neighboring Sioux.

80. Moccasins. Ponca. Collected by Maximilian, Prince of Wied Neuwied, ca. 1830, black-dyed buckskin, 10 inches. Linden Museum, Stuttgart, Wied Collection, 36–077.

81. Moccasins. Ponca. Mid-1800s, hide, 10 inches. State Museum, Oklahoma Historical Society, Oklahoma City, OHS 4051.

These well-documented moccasins were placed in the cornerstone of the Ponca–Nez Percé Industrial School at White Eagle, Oklahoma, in 1880 by Child Chief, a Ponca chief. They were recovered when the building was demolished in 1934.—N. F.

82. Moccasins. Ponca. Ca. 1870, hide, beads, fabric, 10 inches. Woolaroc Museum, Bartlesville, IND 787.

These Ponca-style moccasins are part of the Finney Collection, made mostly in the Bartlesville area, and so most likely are of Ponca origin.—N. F.

83. *Pipe stem. Western Great Lakes. Ca. 1850, cane, ivory-billed woodpecker throats and bills, eagle feathers, cotton string, horsehair(?), bird wing-bone mouthpiece, 31½ × ⅝ inches. Philbrook Art Center, Tulsa, Bright Roddy Collection, 31–395 B.*

One indirect impact of European contact on Native American art was the extinction of certain species of wild birds and land animals whose images had been used symbolically and physically in the making of sacred implements and clothing. After the extinction of the ivory-billed woodpecker and the Plains grizzly bear, artists often attempted to bleach or paint the body parts of related species in imitation of the animals favored by their forefathers.

84. *Necklace. Central Plains/Ohio Valley. Ca. 1850, bear claws, otter fur, bone beads, crystal beads, hide, fabric, 34½ × 14 inches; tail: 19 inches. Thomas Gilcrease Institute of American History and Art, Tulsa, 8437.2159.*

The introduction of new garments was one of the direct influences of the Europeans. Partly as a result of European notions of modesty, Indian women began to wear cloth blouses patterned after European prototypes. Open-front jackets, sometimes patterned after the earlier presentation officers' coats, became fairly common from the Southern Plains to Alaska. Other garments such as vests, gauntlet gloves, chaps, and even pants (replacing leggings) were adopted by some tribes.

European influence was felt less directly as well, in the elimination of some raw materials previously basic to native production. With European encroachment, some animals such as the Carolina parakeet, the ivory-billed woodpecker, and the Plains grizzly bear became extinct, so that items like grizzly-claw necklaces could no longer be made (figs. 83, 84). Other animals, such as the bison, were greatly reduced in number; and bison robes were replaced by wool blankets or robes made from the skins of domesticated cattle. Sometimes, too, Indians forced to relocate could no longer obtain the raw materials they had once considered basic and so were forced to substitute new materials for the old. A classic example of this can be found in the case of the Kickapoo: originally from Wisconsin, the Kickapoo migrated to Coahuila, Mexico, and there learned to use split sotol leaves to replace basswood bark as a craft material.

Two of the most basic elements of Plains Indian culture—dependence on the bison as a major food source and warfare as a way of life—were disrupted by European contact as well. Every Plains boy was brought up with the concept that being an honorable man entailed going against the enemy as often as possible and achieving as many war honors as he could in the process. He was also responsible for hunting the bison and thus for supplying the tribe's major source of food. The European introduction of the horse and the gun had a radical effect on these aspects of Plains Indian life. With horses and guns, warfare suddenly became a more deadly pastime, particularly in the early years, when some groups had access to these resources and others did not. In fact, in many cases, the inequality in the availability of horses and guns was responsible for the forced relocation of some tribal groups. Horses and guns also made hunting both easier and more effective, eventually leading to the virtual extinction of the bison. With horses, too, the nomadic life-style became easier, allowing for the transportation of more material goods. There were other effects as well. When the Plains Indians adopted horses and guns, they also adopted copies of European horse gear, including saddles, bridles (fig. 55), cruppers, and martingales (fig. 56), and items such as gun scabbards. While these were mainly patterned after early Spanish prototypes, the Indians soon altered them into something uniquely their own, so that a Crow saddle blanket, for example, can be differentiated from a Sioux saddle blanket.

For the Indians of the Plains—who were a nomadic, buffalo-hunting, war-oriented people —the most dramatic changes came about in the 1860s, when they were forced to live sedentary lives on restricted reservations. Reservation life marked the end of war and hunting. There was no longer a need for war-related military societies, and the emblems and paraphernalia of these societies ceased to be manufactured. The end of war and hunting also deprived the Plains Indian of his principal means of gaining prestige and thus self-respect. It was a period of difficult readjustment: the government trying to encourage assimilation by turning hunters into farmers; and the missionaries, who had been present from an early date, renewing their efforts to convert all Indians to Christianity. Some Indians were able to make this difficult transition and become horse breeders, cattle ranchers, or trading post operators. Some seemed to assimilate almost completely and went on to obtain university degrees and to compete in the non-Indian world, but others resisted the changes and clung to their old values.

The introduction of Christianity and later of the various messianic cults, such as the Ghost Dance[3] and the Native American Church, or the Peyote Cult, influenced the Indians to give up

85. *Shield. Comanche. Ca. 1870s, painted hide, cotton fabric, wool, eagle feathers, down, 17 × 17 inches. State Museum, Oklahoma Historical Society, Oklahoma City, 166.*

True hide war shields were painted with vision-induced sacred images which told of the bearer's encounter with a supernatural protector. This shield's eagle feathers, crescent moon, buffalo bull, and wolves refer symbolically to beings met by the warrior in his vision quest. Their power and strength were thought to work against the enemy's weapons.

86. *Roach and spreader. Osage. Ca. 1880s, dyed hair,*

carved antler; roach: 13¼ × 9 × 2½ inches; spreader: 5⅞ × 2 × 1¾ inches. Thomas Gilcrease Institute of History and Art, Tulsa, 8427.797a & b.

The elusive concept of tradition is dependent on the interpreter's point of view. When this spreader was made of antler in the 1880s, it harked back to a traditional form of the 1840s. By the 1900s, similar objects were made (see fig. 87), employing not antler but a white man's shoehorn made of bone, a material thought by some to be offensively modern. But from our perspective in the 1980s, this object and the one made with the shoehorn are both traditional in that they played legitimate roles in the life of their originating culture.

their old religion-related crafts and to produce instead new crafts for use in the new religions. Peyote jewelry in nickel silver, decorated gourd rattles, and feather fans (figs. 19, 20), for example, were a few of the special items made for use in the service of the Native American Church. At the same time, medicine bundles (fig. 11) with special powers in war and hunting, war shields (fig. 85), and items that had been used in important religious ceremonies like the Sun Dance were no longer manufactured or used by many tribes.

Gradually, artistic production on the Plains shifted from traditional crafts to fancy-dress

87. Roach and spreader. Plains. Ca. 1900; roach: dyed deer hair, trimmed feathers, stick, 11⅞ × 12 × 3 inches; spreader: bone shoehorn with decal, 15 × 1¾ inches. Thomas Gilcrease Institute of American History and Art, Tulsa, 8427.792 and 8327.1023.

88. Painted hide. Washakie or Katsikodi (active mid-1900s), Shoshone. Ca. 1890, elk hide and pigments, 71½ × 52 inches. Philbrook Art Center, Tulsa, Elizabeth Cole Butler Collection, 82.1.78.

The Shoshone artists Washakie and his son Katsikodi were among the earliest Native American painters to adapt traditional arts to the decorative tastes of white patrons. During the two generations of their painting careers, hundreds of painted buffalo and elk hides depicting the Sun Dance, Ghost Dance, buffalo hunts, public and sacred ceremonies, and battle scenes passed into the hands of white buyers. In style, these painted hides are balanced between the earlier ledger-book works and the later watercolor and tempera paintings.

items made for use in Wild West shows and intertribal powwows (figs. 86, 87), and the manufacture of decorative items for sale to tourists became a major craft activity. The production of souvenir tourist art probably began with the arrival of the first non-Indians, or at least with the Indians' early realization that non-Indians were eager to obtain artifacts to take home as a record of their travels. At first, pieces made for sale were simply copies of the items that Indians were making for their own use. Later, however, special craft items such as a variety of smoking pipes and other novelties in catlinite were developed strictly for sale. Earlier pictographic paintings on bison robes were replaced by paintings on muslin, paper, or even deerskin, produced for sale to non-Indians (figs. 73, 88). During the reservation period, these craft items included dolls, small pouches, model tipis, and beaded brooches and finger rings.

Production for tourists was never a full-time occupation, but rather a home industry used by Indians to supplement their income. Trading-post owners tried to develop markets for these tourist crafts and in a way determined what the Indians produced by requesting some objects and refusing to buy others that they did not like or could not sell. Craft production and marketing were also controlled by missionary organizations such as the Mohonk Lodge at Colony, Oklahoma, under the direction of Reese Kincaid. Kincaid ensured the production of a quality product by insisting that the Arapaho and Cheyenne continue to make traditional-style moccasins, using Indian tanned skins sewn with sinew thread. Still later, the Indian Arts and Crafts Board, a branch of the Department of the Interior, established Indian cooperatives and museums to encourage the sale of quality crafts.

In the modern period of about the last thirty years, the process of assimilation and acculturation has been even more rapid. The government tried to encourage the termination of the reservation system, but without success. Another major government program, the relocation of Indians from reservations to urban areas, was developed in an effort to alleviate overcrowding on the reservations and to place Indians in areas where employment was more readily available. Many of the relocated Indians have made a concerted effort to become fully acculturated into the mainstream of American society, but others, such as those who develop Indian community centers in the midst of urban areas, still cling to whatever they can in the way of "Indianness."

There have been changes, too, on the reservations, where the phenomenon of pan-Indianism has developed (see Howard 1955). This is true particularly in Oklahoma; with so many tribes living in close proximity, the Indians have begun to assume a common Indian style, rather than maintaining individual tribal identities. The change is obvious at any typical intertribal powwow in Oklahoma today, since it is usually impossible to identify the tribe of a dancer by the costume he wears. Some individuals and tribal groups, seriously concerned with the acceleration of assimilation and the resultant loss of identity, have countered by reintroducing older dances, tribally distinct costumes and other indications of general pride in their cultural backgrounds.

All of these modern movements are reflected in modern art. Some modern Plains art is the result of a conscious effort to retain as much as possible of the past; but more and more of the current artistic production shows the effects of acculturation. Indian artists are now trying to compete simply as artists, rather than as Indian artists, and the result is art by Indians that is essentially indistinguishable from non-Indian art.

Notes

1. Examples of black-dyed buckskin moccasins in museum collections are as follows: Ponca—Linden Museum, Stuttgart, catalogue number 36–077, collected by Maximilian, Prince of Wied Neuwied circa 1830; Omaha—Museum of the American Indian, Heye Foundation, New York, catalogue number 15/5610, collected by Melvin R. Gilmore, and catalogue number 20/1408, collected by De Cost Smith; Iowa—Museum of the American Indian, Heye Foundation, New York, catalogue number 12/3917; Pawnee— several pairs at the Field Museum, Chicago; Kaw/Osage —one pair (presently attached to a Pawnee medicine bundle) at the Colter Bay Visitor Center Museum, Grand Teton National Park, Wyoming.

2. Museum of the American Indian, Heye Foundation, New York, catalogue number 3/6739.

3. For a wide discussion of a variety of messianic cults, see Mooney 1896.

III

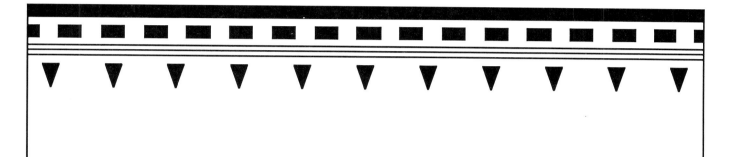

AESTHETICS

Aesthetics in Native American Art

WOLFGANG HABERLAND

THE QUESTION OF UNIVERSALITY
IN AESTHETIC SYSTEMS

Because the concept of aesthetics is European in origin,[1] our first question must be, Can this concept be applied worldwide? Is there a set of rules by which one can judge a work of art, regardless of its cultural connections? Has aesthetics been the same among Greeks, Chinese, Aztec, Haida, and Dogon; during Olmec times as well as during the European Renaissance? In short, can somebody confronted for the first time with an art object appreciate it regardless of its origin?

No system of aesthetics applies to all art, in spite of the fact that discovering such a universal system remains a goal of philosophical endeavor. Historically, the presence of a "universal aesthetics" was posited by anthropologists concerned with the art of nonliterate peoples. Douglas and d'Harnoncourt (1941:11) wrote, "In theory, it should be possible to arrive at a satisfactory aesthetic evaluation of the art of any group without being much concerned with its cultural background. A satisfactory organization of lines, spaces, forms, shades and colors should be self-evident wherever we find it." Robert Redfield (1959:16) also expressed the ideal of the universality of aesthetics, quoting from the writing of Eliseo Vivas: "For him who experiences an object only as art its meanings are immanent in the object." However, Redfield—and with him many others—was at the same time unsure of the existence of a universal aesthetics.

> With primitive as with other art one may begin to state to one's self and to propose to others elements that compose the standard of excellence which the artist has at first only suggested to you, the viewer, as implicit in his work. I am by no means sure that such elements are discoverable that apply to all styles and kinds of art. I do not imagine that our understanding appraisal may ever be reduced to a check list whereon we mark off, *seriatim*, failures and successes. The considered understanding of aesthetic worth is more probably an interminable dialogue (Redfield 1959:30–31).

Certainly there is and always has been a universal aesthetic taste, an innate human ability to develop aesthetic feeling. This basic characteristic of human nature, however, is so general that for purposes other than philosophical speculation it is without consequence.

Although appreciation of the beautiful is a worldwide phenomenon, the definition of beauty differs from one culture to another in space as well as in time. Every group, at a given time, has had a model, an ideal of beauty that was its very own and was rarely shared with other groups, at least before the advent of film and television. Since the aesthetics, or taste, of one group may differ radically from that of another, it may be difficult for an outsider to appreciate the beauty in an

89. *Child's blanket. Navajo. Ca. 1860s, homespun wool, natural and indigo dyes, 54½ × 37 inches. Woolaroc Museum, Bartlesville, IND 410.*

Men's ponchos and children's blankets stood at the pinna-cle of Navajo weaving, both technically and aesthetically, with the most competent of these surpassing all other Native American woven goods in both complexity of design and fineness of tapestry-quality weave.

object regarded as highly aesthetic by those to whose culture it belongs. As Melville Herskovits (1959:54) wrote, "In art, familiarity breeds appreciation, which is to say that it takes time and experience to perceive, internalize and respond to the aesthetic values in the art of peoples whose culture differs from one's own." The same ideas were earlier expressed by Leonhard Adam (1949:30), to whom it seemed that "a complete enjoyment of beauty is possible only when we are confronted with a work of art which either belongs to our own kind of culture, or is at least superficially related to our own ideals of artistic beauty. The combinations of form and color evolved by foreign civilizations may have many attractions, but they remain shrouded in an uncanny, mysterious atmosphere which is entirely alien to us."

This shroud of mystery suggests the major reason why Native American, African, and Oceanic art, so-called primitive art, is rarely included in art histories—at least, in those not written by or with anthropologists. For an art historian or critic raised and educated in the West, the aesthetic context of primitive art is so foreign that he is rarely able to comprehend the beauty of its forms. As Herskovits (1959:55) pertinently remarked, "Our [Western] fixation on pseudo-realism contained a hidden, culture-bound judgment wherein the values of our own society, based on our particular perceptual modes, were extended into universals and applied to art in general. . . . The 'natural' world is natural because we define it as such; because most of us, immersed in our own culture, have never experienced any other definition of reality."

Ultimately, while there is an aesthetic sensibility in every human being, the particular aesthetics of a given culture can only be accurately appreciated by its members. What one group may judge as beautiful, aesthetically pleasing, another may regard as horrible, aesthetically repugnant. Further, "aesthetic experience is direct and personal. The thing speaks; one hears and is moved" (Redfield 1959:29). The beauty of an object of art may, therefore, be appreciated by only a few members of a group. Redfield (1959:29) probably had this in mind when he defined art as, "in its public product, controlled experience with personal qualities for both artist and appreciator." These ideas are also present in modern art history, expressed, if not invented, by Aby Warburg, Erwin Panofsky, and E. H. Gombrich.

> The evolved forces of a living portrait art cannot be searched for exclusively in the artist; one has to keep in mind that an intimate contact occurs between [the] paintings and those portrayed in any epoch of higher taste, [and] brings about a sphere of impeding or encouraging interrelations. . . . It is one of the basic facts of the culture of the Florentine Early Renaissance that art objects owe their creation to the social and sympathetic cooperation of customer and artist [and] therefore, from the first, have to be regarded as a product compounded of [the wishes or ideas of] patron and executing master" (Warburg 1902, as cited by Ettlinger 1971:16; my translation).

What Warburg, a great art historian, and one of the few to consider Native American art in his studies, wrote about the Early Renaissance in Florence could have been written with equal justification about several American Indian groups. The designer of a Chilkat blanket or other paraphernalia of the Northwest Coast took into account the wishes of his customer, but composed the final object according to tradition and his own aesthetic ideas. This was one reason why different people saw different emblems in the designs, as Boas (1927:212–216) has shown. The same was obviously true for the traditional protective designs—as opposed to later scenic designs—on shields and tipi covers among the Plains Indians. Here, the complete symbolism was known only to the painter or, if he painted his images for another person, the owner. The arrangement of design elements, and the resultant aesthetic control, fell completely under the jurisdiction of the artist.

There may be several kinds of aesthetics, not hierarchically ordered, but coexistent. "Universal aesthetics" embraces the general human ability to create and appreciate objects of beauty. "Group aesthetics" embodies a given culture's ideas about beauty. It is shared by all or most members of the group and is frequently called a "style," especially in archaeology. It is often said that the styles of nonliterate peoples are long-lasting and all-pervasive; this conservatism results partly from the fact that, in nonliterate cultures, the group aesthetics and individual aesthetics are in accord with one another. "Individual aesthetics" refers to the individual ability to appreciate, or, in the case of an artist, to create beauty. This ability is innate in every person and can therefore be partially equated with universal aesthetics. It is, however, conditioned by individual inclinations and, probably much more important, by education, experience, and surroundings.

Anthropologists, art historians, and art critics interested in non-Western art are always trying to explain foreign group aesthetics through European-formed views of individual aesthetics which, especially in the twentieth century, have little in common with one another. Further, it is questionable whether in contemporary Europe and North America there still exists a group aesthetics. Granted, it is possible for some individuals of Western origin to admire the group aesthetics of North American Indian groups, as the Surrealists, for example, newly immigrated to New York, admired Eskimo masks and Northwest Coast carvings (see Holm and Reid 1976:9). But they are the exception, not the norm. Even today, the criteria by which Western-educated art collectors select their purchases often differ widely from those considered important by Eskimo and Indian artists.

CONSERVATISM IN NORTH AMERICAN INDIAN ART

Perhaps now we can understand why North American Indian art has rarely been appreciated as art outside anthropological circles, and why it has engendered so many misunderstandings, misinterpretations, and misconceptions. Paramount among these is the notion that the art of nonliterate peoples is conservative (Adam 1949:29–30; Redfield 1959:21; Haselberger 1961:345). The reasons are twofold. First, to outsiders, especially those who casually flip through illustrations in primitive-art books or wander through museum exhibitions without intensive study of a specific style, all art objects of a group look alike. All Katcina figures are interchangeable, for example, as are all Plains beaded objects or Chilkat blankets. But if the same casual viewer were to rush through an exhibition of Gothic sculpture, it too would appear homogenous. For this uninformed viewer, only the labels pointing out different artists would allow, perhaps, some understanding. Anonymity seems to create an illusion of uniformity.

Equally damaging is the misconception arising from the lack of historical perspective. Since most art fashioned in ancient North America was created from organic material that deteriorates easily, and since serious collecting began rather late (essentially in the nineteenth century), few art styles can be traced back more than two hundred years. Among the exceptions are a disproportionate number of sculpture and ceramic traditions, which have lasted due to the physical durability of their materials (fig. 125). The assumption that art traditions are fleeting, maturing in a century or less, is false; art styles do not change that rapidly; at least, they did not in former times. Old World styles like the Romanesque and Gothic endured through several centuries. The same can be seen in Greek and Egyptian art and in Chinese styles in periods such as the Han or Ming. Why, then, should we assume that North American Indian art changed more rapidly?

Still, change it did. A good example is Plains figurative painting. While general subject matter and composition remained more or less constant throughout the eighteenth and nineteenth centuries, the drawing of the figures themselves gradually and subtly changed, becoming increasingly realistic, while retaining its general character. Without knowing all the intermediate stages the style passed

90. First Phase blanket. Navajo. Mid-1800s, homespun wool, natural and indigo dye, 70 × 51 inches. Woolaroc Museum, Bartlesville, IND 2.

Though generally thought to be pristinely distinctive of the Navajo, the Chief's blanket was nevertheless produced as a trade item. Long after Navajo taste moved away from the simple Ute-style First Phase blankets and toward the more flamboyant Mexican styles, Plains tribes were still eagerly seeking the earlier blankets as prestige items. The evolution of the Chief's blanket within Navajo society was an economic phenomenon in which the Navajo adapted their tastes and designs to the tastes of their native customers.

through, one can still recognize that the late-eighteenth- or early-nineteenth-century painted hide robe collected by Lewis and Clark, and the ledger drawings of the early-twentieth-century Sioux artist Amos Bad Heart Bull come from the same tradition, and probably even from the same group. Whether these changes occurred through outside influences or through internal development by gifted artists, or both, is not central to this argument. The point is that Plains Indian painting, like all other North American Indian art, shows development, sometimes subtle, slow, and hard for the uninitiated to detect; sometimes rapid, substantial, and vividly evident.

Illustrative of such radical change is the Navajo blanket, whose style changed so thoroughly that only a specialist would relate a modern Two Gray Hills rug to the blanket fragments from early-nineteenth-century Massacre Cave. It is even difficult to establish the link between a wedgeweave blanket of 1880–1890 (fig. 91) and an early Chief's blanket of 1850 (fig. 90), without knowing the intermediate steps. The change in the aesthetic concept is considerable. All early blanket styles included, as a basic motif, parallel stripes distributed symmetrically around an imaginary center line (fig. 90). When the blanket was worn, this center line ran parallel to the spine of the wearer. In Chief's blankets, there was a wide ornamental strip on either side of the center line, which was ordinarily repeated at the right and left borders. These border strips formed another center line when held together in front—which was, however, rarely done—creating a bisymmetrical effect. Symmetry was an important aesthetic principle of the Navajo and can also be seen in their sand paintings. A similar design formula was used when elements other than stripes were incorporated. Though skewed, it is still present in a saddle blanket from about 1880 (fig. 94). This blanket has stepped triangles at the left and right borders but, contrary to what one would expect, there is no

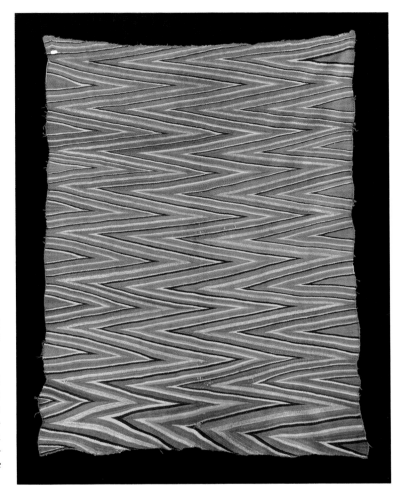

91. *Wedgeweave blanket. Navajo. Ca. 1880–1890, unplied natural wool yarn, native and commercial dyes, 69 × 49 inches. Woolaroc Museum, Bartlesville, IND 16.*

The wedgeweave was an aberration of Navajo transitional blanket design, whose exaggerated serration and zigzags stem from New Mexican and Mexican weaving, which used contrasting colors, optical illusions, and an undulating pulled-warp technique to create an effect of motion and rhythmic symmetry. By the 1880s, this exuberant abstraction would evolve into the blanket style called an Eye Dazzler.

stepped diamond in the middle, perhaps because it would have been covered by the saddle or the rider. However, the two lines to the right and left of the center still run parallel to an imaginary center line. If this were a wearing blanket, the lines would run parallel to the spine, and the stepped triangles at the borders would form a diamond when held together in front. Still, the design is symmetrical; when on the horse, both sides showed exactly the same pattern, and the animal's spine formed the center line. This basic aesthetic idea has been lost in the pattern of the wedgeweave blanket. Here, the motif covers the whole blanket. One may construct a center line, but it is without significance and does not show when worn. While there is still symmetry, a fundamental change in ornamental composition has occurred, which can be explained by a change in aesthetic values.

But was it a true change? We always assume that the striped blanket arose from Navajo aesthetics. This assumption ignores the fact that the Navajo learned weaving from the Puebloans during colonial times, perhaps within the final decades of the seventeenth century: roughly during, or just after, the Pueblo Revolt of 1680. They probably copied not only the weaving techniques of the Puebloans but also their textile patterns. Prehistoric Puebloan textiles were much more elaborate than historic ones, as can be seen in the few remnants recovered archaeologically and in costumed figures in precontact kiva murals (Kent 1957; Hibben 1975). Because of this, the relationship of earlier to later textiles is difficult to trace. A further obstacle is the fact that no colonial-period textiles from the pueblos have survived, leaving a gap in our knowledge about the evolution of textiles in that region. However, while there are no Puebloan striped cotton textiles from the historic period, such designs nevertheless show up in historic-period woolen blankets. Apparently the Navajo had already adopted aesthetic values from another ethnic entity early in their history. Whether the borrowed patterns

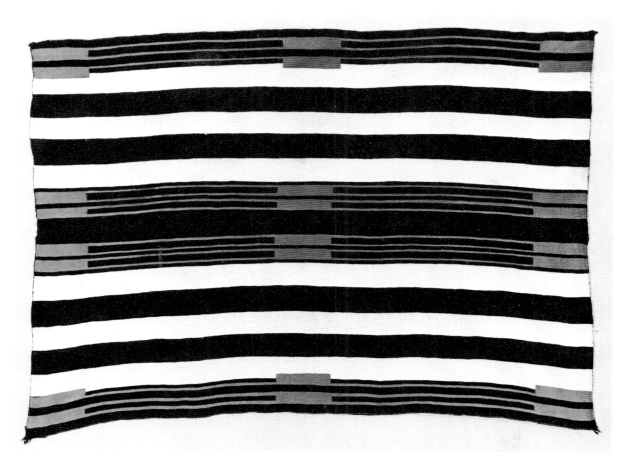

92. Second Phase blanket. Navajo. 1860–1870, homespun wool, bayeta commercial yarn, indigo dye, 53⅛ × 73⅝ inches. Thomas Gilcrease Institute of American History and Art, Tulsa, 9736.26.

Navajo blankets changed radically between 1850 and 1900. First, Second, and Third Phase Chief's blankets formed three distinctive design traditions, evolving in response to the tastes of non-Navajo Indian patrons. The serape-blanket style favored by the Navajo owed much to the Moorish-inspired Hispanic weaving of New Spain. With late-nineteenth-century Anglo colonization of New Mexico, a host of other forms and decorative motifs appeared in Navajo weaving. The most pronounced changes were the transition from wearing blankets to tapestries and floor rugs, and the shifting of the design axis from horizontal to vertical.

93. Moki blanket. Hopi. Ca. 1880, native wool yarn, aniline dyed American flannel, 73½ × 54 inches. Woolaroc Museum, Bartlesville, IND 393.

Although the Navajo learned the art of weaving from their Pueblo neighbors, the Hopi, Zuñi, and Rio Grande farmers never achieved the excellence in weaving exhibited by the nomadic Navajo. Moki blankets are a heavier-gauge nineteenth-century Hopi adaptation of the classic Navajo step-serrated, banded wearing blanket. This style of weaving disappeared by the end of the nineteenth century, although the simple banded blankets of the Hopi persist to the present.

conformed to early Navajo designs will never be known. The balancing of the design on the back and, perhaps, front views seems to have appealed generally to North American Indians and could therefore easily have been transmitted from one group to another. This predilection is indicated not only by the spread of Navajo-manufactured blankets over large regions during the nineteenth century (Bennett 1981), but also by the symmetry of designs on the blankets and garments of several other groups.

A good example is the Chilkat blanket seen in figure 95. Here, too, the main design is in the middle and centers on the back of the wearer (Emmons 1907; Boas 1927:212–216). It is important that, here again, the main design is on the back, on that part of the garment which shows the least movement and where the motif can be distinguished even when the wearer moves. This principle has been kept alive on the Northwest Coast even to the present, though many other elements have

94. Saddle blanket. Navajo. Ca. 1880, Germantown and bayeta commercial yarn, cotton, 30 × 24½ inches. Woolaroc Museum, Bartlesville, IND 406.

Heavy, functional woven saddle blankets appeared soon after the Navajo adoption of the horse, but decorative blan- kets like this one were rare until the 1890s. Though the design field of this blanket maintains the horizontal axis of the classic wearing blanket, the design, with its serrated bands interspersed with floating motifs, points to the breakdown of classic blanket design and the rise of more freely interpretive styles in the commercial-yarn period.

95. Chilkat blanket. Tlingit. Ca. 1900, yellow cedar bark, mountain goat wool, dye, 73 × 36 inches; fringe: 19 inches. Woolaroc Museum, Bartlesville, IND 707.

The central panel of this fine example of Northwest Coast weaving shows a diving whale. The two large, eyelike patterns at top center are the joints of the tail flukes, and the large eyes near the lower border are the eyes of the whale. The deep fringe is designed to undulate when the robe is worn by a ceremonial dancer.

changed: for the last hundred years, blankets have been made from imported cloth, mostly in the form of European-made woolen trade blankets, which are ornamented with mother-of-pearl buttons (fig. 96). The designs have changed, too, not so much in content as in style. Today, they are more naturalistic, easier to "read" than the old Chilkat blankets. Nevertheless, the composition is still centered in the middle of the blanket and, when worn, on the back of the owner.

The frontality of Northwest Coast garments (figs. 97, 98, 101) was also preserved over a long period, even on costuming of differing shapes. Motifs on the ankle-length Chilkat shirts are always placed in such a way that at least the main figures, and often the complete compositions, are seen on the front or back, or both. They never appear on the sides.

Whether the paintings and other ornamentation on the poncholike war shirts and the hide robes of the Plains Indians can also be included here is an open question. Certain decorations, like the sunburst or feathered-circle pattern on bison-skin robes, were painted so as to be centered on the back of the wearer, but the well-known battle scenes usually cover the entire surface of a robe and had therefore, at least in part, to be viewed from the side (fig. 73). The war shirts were painted on front and back, but this might have been from pure necessity, since the sides were more or less open,

96. Button blanket. Kaigani Haida. Ca. 1890, wool, flannel, mother-of-pearl buttons, 67 × 52¾ inches. Philbrook Art Center, Tulsa, Elizabeth Cole Butler Collection, 82.1.81

During the last half of the nineteenth century, the button blanket became the standard ceremonial robe throughout the Northwest Coast. Woolen trade blankets, usually dark blue, were the foundation for dramatic compositions appliquéd in red flannel and mother-of-pearl buttons. Button blankets always had a red border on the upper and lateral edges and often a crest animal displayed in the central field. Here a beaver is shown, semihuman, but with ears, incisors, and tail to establish his identity. Typically, button blankets were worn over the shoulders with the crest design falling on the back, but they were worn in other ways as well, depending on the activity of the wearer. They were never displayed as hangings, except at the funeral or on the grave of a chief.

and did not lend themselves to ornamentation. The long strips of quillwork, which were obviously an important part of the adornment, originally covered the seams and ran not only in front and back, but also in such a manner that they pointed to the sides. With the adoption of the European sleeve, this became still more pronounced. On the other hand, the rosettes, made originally from quills, and later sometimes from glass beads, were always situated in front and back. In sum, frontality is not a fixed element in the textile designs of the Plains groups.

The late-nineteenth-century alteration in the Navajo aesthetic principle of frontality, visible in the 1880s appearance of the allover-pattern wedgeweave blanket, coincided with two other important events: the introduction of aniline dyes or aniline-dyed yarns, and the opening of the Santa Fe railroad. The dyes suddenly made a whole new field of colors available and, as happens with new materials or techniques in any culture, the Navajo eagerly began to experiment with them. The railroad brought a large new clientele into the region, whose tastes differed from the tastes of those who had bought the "old-style" blankets. Wedgeweave blankets were manufactured almost exclusively for trade and were rarely worn by the Navajo themselves. Along with the commercial wedgeweave, the Eye Dazzlers (fig. 100), and pictorial rugs (fig. 99), conventional striped blankets (figs. 90, 91) continued to be produced, not only for Navajo use but also for trade with other North American Indian groups. Bennett (1981: figs. 1, 2, 5, and 6), for example, shows Chief's blankets from the 1880s, as well as photographs of Plains Indians from the 1890s, wearing rather new-looking First Phase-style Chief's blankets. The Navajo clearly continued to produce them because they were in demand; they were simultaneously weaving in two different styles for two sets of customers. The group's aesthetic values probably did not change, or at least changed very little, but were subdued by commercial incentives. Even after the rather sudden switch, after about 1895, from blanket to rug weaving, from traditional and experimental ornamentation to the heavily Orientalized designs promoted by traders, the sense of symmetry continued, reflecting, perhaps, the group's basic, inherent aesthetics.

It has been proposed that allover-pattern designs are the result of the issuing of Rio Grande Spanish blankets to the Navajo during their 1860 imprisonment at Bosque Redondo (Wheat 1977:13), but it is unlikely that the wedge motif and the serrated diamond have their origin in that particular event. The Navajo were certainly familiar, before that date, with Saltillo serape-style blankets of colonial production, and had already incorporated some of those designs into their weaving, if our present dating of the different blankets and their styles is correct. One can detect the gradual change

97. Dance apron. Kwakiutl. Ca. 1890, wool cloth, beads, puffin beaks, brass thimbles, 32½ × 22½ inches. Philbrook Art Center, Tulsa, Elizabeth Cole Butler Collection, L82.1.301.

Aprons decorated with pendant rattles were worn ceremonially throughout the Northwest Coast and are still made and used today. The Kwakiutl form was rectangular, with rows of pendants (often beaks of the tufted puffin) interspersed with beadwork. The designs were generally floral or curvilinear and were primarily decorative, though crests were often included. The trade cloth and beads were obtained from trading companies, as were the brass thimbles, popular as adjuncts to, or substitutes for, puffin beaks.

98. *Leggings. Tlingit. Ca. 1880, wool cloth, beads, buckskin, porcupine quills, 12½ × 15 inches each. Philbrook Art Center, Tulsa, Elizabeth Cole Butler Collection, 82.1.62c.*

Beadwork was never as important on the Northwest Coast as elsewhere on the continent, but spectacular beaded ceremonial regalia were made there, beginning early in the nineteenth century. Many beaded pieces reproduced the form and decoration of earlier painted or quilled skin pieces. The most splendid were made in the latter part of the century, when traditional art systems were breaking down. The designs do not follow the classic conventions either in form or color use, but comprise a completely new tradition. These frogs illustrate the flamboyant quality of the style; an elegant feature taken straight from early skinwork custom is the fine porcupine-quill wrapping on the fringes.

until about 1880, that is, until well after Bosque Redondo. It was later that the rapid, but not exclusive, appearance of the new styles occurred: an explosion of colors and ideas certainly furthered, if not initiated, by new materials and trade opportunities.

It is quite possible that each of the new types was first made by only one weaver, whose work was imitated by others after successful sales to whites. Whether the production then spread over a whole reservation or was restricted to those parts near the railroad and non-Indian settlements cannot yet be ascertained. Here, as in other cases, lack of knowledge about particular artists is a considerable handicap. While in Europe and Asia and the regions of their influence artists have signed their work since medieval times, North American Indian artists have remained nameless until the modern era. This anonymity greatly impedes the unraveling of the development of aboriginal North American art. It would be much easier to recognize specific contributions to the art of Navajo weaving, and to the development of the art in general, if we knew the foremost weavers' names.

Since nearly every Navajo woman was and is a weaver, thousands of blankets and rugs are still extant, preserved in museums and private collections, in spite of the fact that most of those woven before the turn of the century have disappeared through wear and other circumstances. Nevertheless, it is possible that a dedicated specialist will be able to ascribe a number of blankets or rugs to a specific, if unnamed, weaver of outstanding talent, as has been done by Cohodas (1976; 1979a; 1981; also chapter v, this volume) in his work on Washoe basket weavers.

Another impediment to our study is inherent in the kind of collections in which Navajo blankets are normally found. These collections are almost exclusively ethnological, not art oriented, and there is a critical difference between the two. When ethnologists and anthropologists collect representative examples of a given object, their concern is with the "normal" product, not with artistic masterworks. The telling object is one that is considered to be, whether rightly or wrongly, average, not outstanding or perfect. Contrariwise, art museums collect—or at least exhibit—only objects of the best quality, the products of established or promising artists. Until recently, anthropologists, rather than art connoisseurs, have dictated importance within non-European art. The result is that even poorly made Navajo rugs and blankets from the turn of the century are not only exhibited but are sold dearly at auction to museums and collectors alike. The same is true of all North American Indian works of art, with the exception of the most modern ones. Poorly executed or conceived European paintings of the same period, on the other hand, scarcely sell, since no museum and few collectors will buy them. Apparently, ethnologists are not yet discriminating enough with regard to quality and artistic value. The occasional exceptions are those temporary or permanent exhibitions that concentrate exclusively on the artistic aspect of ethnological specimens. As for the collectors, they have only their own tastes as a guide, and the education of taste is a long and slow process. Collectors of European and East Asian art have the artist's signature as a talisman of quality, reassuring even to a beginner.

AMERICAN INDIAN OBJECTS AND THE FINE ARTS

Related to the issue of aesthetics in Native American art is the basic question, Are Navajo blankets and other utilitarian objects art? Western art history has conceived of the fine arts as having three or four main branches, as in the *Webster's New Collegiate Dictionary* definition: "Painting, drawing, architecture, and sculpture; and sometimes, poetry, music, dancing, and dramatic arts" (Webster 1959). More or less the same idea appears in one of the dictionary's many definitions of art: "Application of skill and taste to production according to aesthetic principles; specifically, such application to the production of beauty by imitation or design, in painting and sculpture." While our example, the Navajo blanket, falls within the first part of this definition of art, it does not correspond to the second part and certainly not to the definition of fine arts. Utile objects, such as blankets, are sometimes included in a category called "applied art," or are considered to be a craft or handicraft, something much less noble than art. From our standpoint, this division between fine arts and applied arts is unfortunate, for it is not based on aesthetic values, and sometimes not even on function, but on medium. For instance, the painted bison-skin robes of the Plains may be thought of as painting or drawing, that is, as fine art, while the equally advanced Chilkat blankets, because they are woven, belong to the category of applied art. This distinction has been controversial even in European art history, as demonstrated by the fact that tapestries are sometimes included in the fine arts, and sometimes not. The decisive factor is often the identity of the artist: a wall hanging designed by Oskar Kokoschka would be included in an art exhibition, as would a ceramic by Picasso, while wall hangings or ceramics by John Craftsman, European or native, would not, regardless of their aesthetic value. It is, therefore, often the name that causes art historians and critics to say a work is artistic enough to be called art. Again, most North American Indian artists of both former and modern times are at a disadvantage because their names are unknown.

Closely connected to this issue of art versus craft is another misconception about the art of nonliterate peoples. Allegedly, no art for art's sake exists among them. This misconception is even

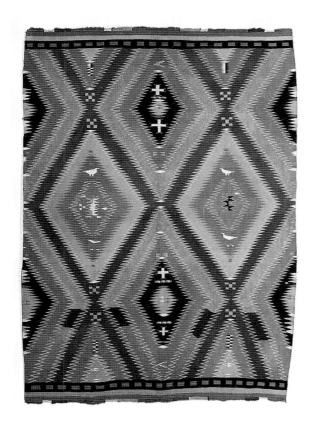

99. Pictorial blanket. Navajo. 1885–1900, Germantown commercial wool yarn, 74 × 57½ inches. Woolaroc Museum, Bartlesville, IND 365.

This eloquent Germantown pictorial is a consummate expression of the Eye Dazzler tradition. Pictorial representations were commonly associated with tourist-market products and infrequently found among works the Navajo made for themselves. In its composition, the secondary asymmetrical design elements, and the overall color field, this blanket bears a striking resemblance to Middle Eastern kilims. Such a similarity is not surprising, since trading-post operators in the 1890s encouraged native weavers to incorporate Oriental textile designs into their works.

100. Blanket. Navajo. Ca. 1890, Germantown commercial wool yarns. 86½ × 56½ inches. Woolaroc Museum, Bartlesville, IND 403.

In addition to exuberant color and scintillating compositions, the Germantown period also saw the addition of optical illusion to the Navajo design repertoire. Masterful skill was required to counterbalance contrasting color blocks with multidirectional design elements, to create a composition that changed with the viewer's changing point of visual reference.

perpetuated by anthropologists with a special interest in art, but that does not make it any truer. Douglas and d'Harnoncourt (1941:13), for instance, said of North American Indian art:

> Fine art in the sense of art for art's sake is a concept that is almost unknown in Indian cultures. There are very few aboriginal art forms that have no established function in tribal life. Some of the miniature ivory carvings of the Eskimo may be an exception to the rule since there is no evidence that they serve any specific purpose, but by and large every product made by an Indian artist has a function and is created by him primarily to serve a given end. Artistic merit is simply considered a necessary by-product of good workmanship.

On primitive art in general, William Fagg (1961:365) remarked:

101. Chilkat tunic. Tlingit. Ca. 1900, yellow cedar bark, mountain goat wool, commercial wool, 50 × 24 inches. Philbrook Art Center, Tulsa, Elizabeth Cole Butler Collection, L82.1.309.

Much less common than Chilkat blankets are heraldic tunics woven in the same technique and materials. Chilkat weaving using formline animal motifs was perfected around the beginning of the nineteenth century; previously, designs had been geometric. Late in the century, configurative animal designs like the ravens on this tunic began to find favor. In many cases, as here, some of the long-established rules of composition and design structure began to weaken, resulting in a loss of the classic logic of the northern formline system.

I think that ... "Art for art's sake" exemplifies ... a long-standing fallacy about tribal art—that it can be divided into works of purely ritual or other utilitarian purpose and those—a small and anomalous group—of purely aesthetic purpose. In fact all tribal art (like all true art anywhere) has an artistic purpose in that the artist intends to make it beautiful, but at the same time it is always an expression of belief, art and belief being for any true artist inseparable and coterminous; only when their unity is undermined by intellectualization or aestheticism does the concept of "art for art's sake" begin to have any meaning, and this never happens in tribal art—indeed, it may mark the end of it.

If such statements are made by anthropologists, one should not be astonished that art historians adopt them and promote the idea that nonliterate peoples have no true art. As an example, consider the opening statement of an introduction to primitive art in the catalogue for the exhibition *Weltkulturen und moderne Kunst* (World Cultures and Modern Art), presented during the 1972 Olympics in Munich. The author is a well-known art historian with an interest in the art of nonliterate peoples, a history of publication on the subject, and a reputation among his peers as an authority in the field. He writes:

The character of primitive art can only be understood through its function within the life of primitive peoples. While there can be no doubt about its classification as "art" and [about the fact that] our aesthetic consciousness has absorbed it as art, and while, furthermore, aesthetics without doubt played a role during its creation, its nature is essentially functional. Beyond its use, the work of primitive art is without function, *without meaning*. It is never kept because of its beauty, nor even because of certain representational qualities. Indeed, often enough, a carving is destroyed after use; its function has been carried out (Schmalenbach 1972:428; my translation and italics).

102. Horse breast decoration. Crow. Ca. 1910, beadwork, bells, red cloth on canvas, 41 × 21 inches. Philbrook Art Center, Tulsa, Elizabeth Cole Butler Collection, 82.1.118.

The late-nineteenth-century Crow style of beadwork persisted well into our century, and this horse collar is a fine example of the style in its late bloom. Some characteristics suggest that the collar may have been made on the Columbia Plateau, where beadworkers developed a style closely related to that of the Crow. Non-Crow elements are the sewing of beads directly to the red cloth, the color scheme of the central panel, and the width of the straps. These features, however, may be due to the late date of the collar.

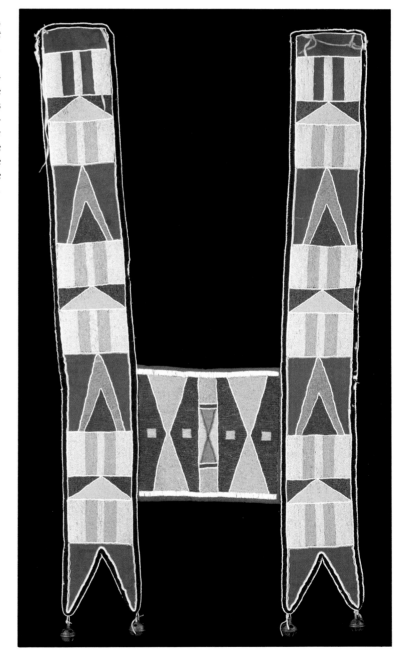

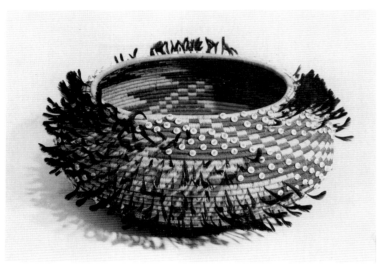

103. *Basket. Evelyn Lake Potter, Pomo. Ca. 1900, willow, sedge, bulrush root, 4½ × 12½ × 10¾ inches. Philbrook Art Center, Tulsa, Clark Field Collection, BA 686.*

Basketry among the Pomo of California was a refined art, whose many formal designs and weaving techniques were clearly named and classified. Partially and fully feathered baskets were cherished as heirlooms and treasure objects. Tightly woven willow coiled baskets like this one and the one in figure 104 were the canvas upon which Pomo artists wove intricate compositions. The abstract pictorial elements they chose, and the way they combined them, had definite and discernible meanings for members of the tribe.

104. *Basket. Pomo. 1900–1920, willow, sedge, bulrush root, shell beads, redheaded woodpecker feathers, quail topknots, 5¼ × 12½ inches in diameter. Philbrook Art Center, Tulsa, Clark Field Collection, BA 164.*

Thus art, in conventional wisdom, has no purpose other than to delight audiences and to release the energies or frustrations of the artist—often, in today's individualistic society, the legitimation of artistic expression and meaning. Anything with a purpose, a function, is suspect. But is this true? The notion of art for art's sake was an emancipatory idea popular in the last century, and may not be universally applicable. Certainly much medieval art was functional: What is the difference in artistic value between sculptures of Gothic saints, Zuñi war-god figures, and tiki figures from the Marquesas Islands; between a Renaissance sarcophagus and a Haida carved grave box; between the Bayeux Tapestry and the painted muslin by Silverhorn (fig. 33)? All are functional, but the European examples are considered fine art, while the others are not. American Indian fine arts can be viewed in much the same manner as the arts of medieval Europe. Like the frescoes of a Gothic church, the wall paintings in a Pueblo kiva have both an artistic and a ceremonial function—though, in fact, that function has not been identified. Too often, however, Europeans and Euro-Americans are unable to understand the art of other groups, to see beyond their own cultural heritage, which suggests a sort of arrogance. Works of aboriginal art from North America and other continents are measured against European conventions, European ideas of art and beauty, and are found lacking. It is rarely understood that there are other conventions besides those developed in Europe; that, for example, it is not necessary to create a "photographic" image of an object or an event, that one-point perspective is not a necessary sign of skill. Perhaps a Western art historian or critic would grant that certain kinds of North American Indian art, in spite of being functional, can be included among the fine arts, but he would probably maintain that the bulk of it—Navajo blankets included—is still

105. Beaver monitor pipe. *Hopewellian. Ca. 300 B.C.–A.D. 700, carved stone, pearls, 5 inches. Thomas Gilcrease Institute of American History and Art, Tulsa, 6124.1140.*

Hopewellian sculptural arts refute the often-held misconception that naturalistic art did not exist in native North America. This sensitively rendered beaver is anatomically realistic. Its rich embellishment, through both subtle modeling and the incorporation of pearl for the eyes, recalls the depiction of animals during the European Middle Ages.

106. Raccoon Priests gorget. *Mississippian (Spiro Mounds). Ca. 1250–1350, carved shell, 7¼ inches maximum diameter. Stovall Museum of Science and History, University of Oklahoma, Norman, LF CRi I 108–4.*

The significance and meaning of the delicately fashioned Spiro shell gorgets remain unknown, though the excellence of their manufacture clearly attests to the skill of

professional artisans. The works illustrate lavishly attired mythic beings and ceremonial performers, as well as symbolic glyphs of anthropomorphic and zoomorphic beings. It is probable that they form part of the visual vocabulary of a prehistoric cult.

"applied art." But what, we may respond, is functional in the blanket *designs*, or other ornamentation? A blanket can function without ornament; in fact, the decoration does not even perform the abstract function of carrying religious, social, or other connections. It is therefore purely supplemental, added for its aesthetic value (Blackwood 1961:360; Goldwater 1973:6–7). What, other than aesthetics, can induce one to adorn and elaborate riding gear as most Plains groups did? The large, beaded horse collars of the Crow (fig. 102) and others are, in fact, actually antifunctional, since they encumber the horse and hamper its movements. We have here a twilight zone between finery or adornment and art, in which a historian of European art would also encounter difficulties. Ornament and jewelry are at times—especially before A.D. 1000, and during the second half of the nineteenth century—considered art, though more frequently they are not. It is particularly interesting that even as the slogan "art for art's sake" was becoming familiar, jewelry and other Art Nouveau objects were commonly considered art, as were those objects later designed by members of the Bauhaus. Here, in theory, the anthropologists and the art historians think alike. In practice this is often not true, probably because European products are thought to be of a much higher standard than are those of non-European, and certainly of nonliterate, cultures. A comparison of the use of "noble" materials like precious metals and precious stones with that of lowly ones such as glass beads and porcupine quills may also play a role.

It is sometimes said that art for art's sake could not exist in North American Indian art, since there were no professional Native American artists. The implication is that only professionals can fashion real art, a premise which one can and should contest. However, even if we accept this dubious assumption, we can challenge the idea that there were no professional artists in precontact

North America. A number of pre-Columbian objects are of such a perfection that it is difficult to believe they were fashioned by mere farmers. I should like to single out, from among many possibilities, the Hopewellian monitor pipes, with their often perfect renderings of animals (fig. 105), and the elaborate paraphernalia used in connection with the Mississippian Southern Cult. The engraved and cutout shell objects from the Spiro Mounds are another instance of such professional expertise (fig. 106), as are the copper objects (fig. 2) and the monolithic axes (fig. 4) from the same area. Archaeologists have been curiously reluctant to call these objects art. At the utmost, they claim that they might have been made by "specialists."

Certainly the question remains whether these and earlier artists worked full time, but is this a necessary condition of art? Who, for example, will claim that Frank Lloyd Wright or Walter Gropius were not professional artists because they taught architecture for money? It is curious that visual artists are conceived of as doing nothing other than create art, while poets and writers have often maintained a second profession. I do not suppose that there were professional artists in aboriginal North America in the sense indicated above, but there were certainly masters.

An anecdote concerning a living Native American artist will illustrate this. Not long ago, a Northwest Coast carver was working at the Museum für Völkerkunde in Hamburg. The weather was beautiful and the work rather tiring, and he suddenly remarked, "At home, I wouldn't be carving today, in this weather. I would be out fishing." Now, fishing for food is a common profession on the Northwest Coast, and nearly all Northwest Coast artists spend considerable time pursuing it. Does this make them part-time artists, or nonartists? It is often extremely difficult to draw an exact line between a professional artist, working full time, and one who creates art but does something else too. By any serious measure, a Pueblo potter, a Navajo weaver, and a Northwest Coast carver are as professional as are the painters and sculptors of modern Euro-American society.

Professionalism was much more present in the original North American societies than we now imagine. Among the Plains groups, for example, there were individuals who practiced art for payment—a rather clear mark of professionalism. This is demonstrated by the statement of an Oglala in 1909: "Formerly I made shields magical in many ways. They gave me a horse for it as payment. Really, I painted them in such a way that they became protective [talismanic] and so they were" (Haberland 1973:86). There were probably many more instances of professionalism in the Plains and elsewhere in aboriginal North America than we can document.

Besides practicing art as a full-time occupation, two other criteria are often named for professional artists: formal training, and a critical attitude toward one's own and other artists' creations. Both traits are again said to be missing among the aboriginal North American groups, but once more these claims are misrepresentations.

Let us begin with the issue of training. Artistic training among Native American tribes was usually rather informal; it occurred within the family, clan, or other small social entity. Among the Navajo weavers and Pueblo potters, for example, the mother, or some other female relative who was well versed in the art, instructed the younger woman in its technical aspects. Members of other families and even complete strangers might also receive instruction, if they asked for it. This was, however, the rare exception, since most persons desiring instruction could obtain it within their family or clan. The content of the training was still less rigid than its form. As Bunzel showed in her landmark investigation of Pueblo pottery, teachers did not—and probably still do not—ask apprentices to copy designs. One potter said:

In painting I should tell her to use her own brain and to paint any kind of design she likes,

107. Jar. Tonita (1892–?) and Juan Cruz Roybal (1887–?), San Ildefonso. Ca. 1940, polished redware, 11 × 12½ inches in diameter. Philbrook Art Center, Tulsa, Clark Field Collection, PO 150.

The husband-and-wife team of Tonita and Juan Roybal were the last San Ildefonso ceramicists to specialize in the old black-on-red style of pottery decoration, which had been produced for over a millennium in the Southwest. Because twentieth-century Anglo taste favored the flamboyance of polychrome or the classicism of black-on-black ware, the Roybals "modernized" their work by incorporating the pan-Puebloan designs first introduced by the Martinezes, and converting to their commercially successful burnished surface treatment. Their greatest achievements were elegantly shaped vases whose angular Art Deco–style motifs counterbalance the fluidity of serpents and rain clouds.

whatever she can think of. I should not tell her what to put on, but I should say to her: "Use your own brain and paint anything you like, only put it on straight and even." She would learn the different designs by watching the other women paint and by using her own brain and making the kind she wants (Bunzel 1929:61).

In spite of this, it is astonishing to see the consistency—at least to the eye of an outsider—of Pueblo pottery designs. In the past, and to a certain degree even today, each pueblo had its own group of unmistakable designs, patterns of design distribution, color combinations, and shapes. Families, too, had characteristic designs, often handed down from mother to daughter informally, through observation. Again and again, potters told Bunzel in interviews that certain design patterns came from their mothers, but were re-created by themselves. "This is a new design. I learned the different parts of it from my mother, but they are put together in a new way" (Bunzel 1929:52). The designs obviously belong to the family. "I never use other women's designs, and they never use mine," they often said (Bunzel 1929:52). This may go far to explain the conservatism discussed earlier. Family tradition, however, does not exclude the invention of new styles, as exemplified in modern times by Nampeyo and her daughter Fannie Nampeyo of Hano (figs. 150–156), or Maria and Julian Martinez of San Ildefonso Pueblo (figs. 157, 159). Furthermore, these new styles, if they are thought to be pleasing, may be copied by others, at least in technique. In general, however, a consistent style suggests that a certain family is involved; an example is the jar from San Ildefonso decorated in a red-on-red technique (fig. 107), similar to the black-on-black Martinez style. It was made in about 1940 by Tonita and Juan Roybal, who were related to the Martinez family through their niece Santana, and therefore had a certain right to use the Martinez technique and design. The jar itself is an excellent example of the continuity of shapes in Pueblo pottery, which are often traceable to prehistoric times. This can be seen if we examine a Zia jar from the early twentieth century (fig. 108) side by side with a precontact Gila polychrome jar dated 1300–1400 (fig. 109). It may be added that the design of the Gila jar appears again today on comparable pottery vessels made by the Nampeyo family.

Is such training professional? Surely it is. That the training often took place within the family does not speak against it; in fact, many European artists also received instruction from family

108. Jar. Zia. Ca. 1930, polychrome pottery, 16½ × 20½ inches in diameter. Woolaroc Museum, Bartlesville, IND 22.

Nineteenth-century Zia potters were overshadowed in popularity by their Acoma and Zuñi neighbors. Yet during the first three decades of this century their ceramics gained national fame. While pueblos like San Ildefonso adopted modernistic, non-Indian motifs, the Zia consciously returned to and refined their earlier traditions, experimenting with gold, white, and tan slips, and vessel forms ranging from delicate long-necked vases to huge bulbous storage jars. Design systems included intricate geometric compositions and flowing rainbow bands, punctuated with floral and animal designs.

members. Whether this pattern was present in other North American regions has scarcely been investigated. It is likely to have taken place among the basket weavers of California and other regions. Information is lacking on formal apprenticeships or training in painting, beadwork, quillwork, and other art activities on the Plains, but there can be little doubt that such training was present.

We have more complete knowledge of art instruction on the Northwest Coast, which has probably the most formal system in aboriginal North America. As in the Southwest, the teacher is traditionally a relative and, in conformity with the lineage system, often a mother's brother. However, a father may also teach his son, at least in current practice. Apprenticeship is a long and arduous process. The boy first learns to fashion the instruments he will use, then how to carve with them, and only then to create designs, i.e., to depict a certain animal or other motif. Having learned all this, the apprentice finally begins to perform the activity we would call "creating."

From the European standpoint, it is only too easy to ask, In what way is he creative, when all the essentials of his art are prescribed? When carving a killer whale, he must include an upright fin with a hole in it, a symmetrically split tail, and a big head with a broad mouth and blow hole, as well as a number of smaller standardized elements, such as the form of an eye, the outline of a feather, various round and oblong shapes, and prescribed crooked and straight lines (fig. 110). We are forgetting that in traditional European painting there were also "essentials," signals without which one could not recognize the intended image; that a human head had to have a nose, eyes, mouth, and ears, that these had certain shapes, and that a European apprentice had first to learn to draw a tree, a flower, a house in a manner considered "natural." These essentials have been questioned only in the last century, and are still often used, even in paintings that are thought to break from tradition. Ultimately, in the art of both Europe and the Northwest Coast, it is not the detail that is most important, but the manner in which the elements are combined, integrated in a harmonic whole that is pleasing, aesthetic, unique. This is the basis for the desire of the artist to achieve a personal style. Again and again, on the Northwest Coast, I was told that only those who have developed their own unique style are considered masters, that only after one's work is distinguishable from that of other carvers is he ending his apprenticeship, and able to teach others. This is not so different from the remarks of the Pueblo potters mentioned above: only the basic matters are taught, and from this base the gifted student can develop and become an artist in his own right.

The further question remains, When is a carver on the Northwest Coast considered to have

109. Jar. Gila. Ca. 1300–1400, polychrome pottery. 7¼ × 10¼ inches. Museum of the Red River, Idabel, 2262.

A comparison between this prehistoric polychrome vessel and the Zia jar in figure 108 shows that even though stylistic evolution and fads have altered the general appearance of Puebloan ceramics, an essentially conservative taste in form and design has still maintained remarkable continuity over the centuries.

developed his own style? I have been told that his peers, the established masters, decide this; and herein lies a clear example of art criticism among Native Americans. It is rare for an outsider to hear these judgments, since it is often considered impolite to talk negatively about an absent person, especially in the presence of a foreigner. Anybody, however, who accompanies a Northwest Coast artist through a museum exhibition will be exposed to a running commentary on the merits of the objects on display. Bill Holm and native artist Bill Reid (1976) offer an example of such art criticism in print. Another glimpse can be caught in Bunzel's (1929:58–60) work with Pueblo potters, but she, too, noted that people were reluctant to comment on the ceramics they were shown. Among themselves, their remarks were no doubt much more lively. The same kind of criticism—or apparent lack of it—has recently been described among the Saramaka, an Afro-American group in Surinam (Price and Price 1980:38–40). Open art criticism in the absence of the artist may be a European trait, perhaps even a rather new one, related to the advent of mass media. It is certainly not a criterion for determining the presence or absence of art criticism, or true art, or artists among North American Indians.

Up to this point, Native American art has been discussed in terms of isolated objects categorized as paintings, sculpture, and so forth. However, the classic definition of the fine arts may also include—and certainly art often incorporates—poetry, music, dance, and drama. These, too, are elements of aboriginal North American art, and often are intimately interrelated. Masks, for instance, are part of a whole complex in which music and dance, and sometimes also drama and poetry, play a role (figs. 110–112). We usually see masks in well-lit showcases, isolated from one another. There they may appear to us flat and lifeless. How different it is to see them used in dances, even under modern conditions with glaring electric lights on! Suddenly they come to life, as part of a greater aesthetic concept. They are animated not only through the movements of the dancers, but also, as in the case of the Northwest Coast masks, through their own mobility. Northwest Coast art is kinetic. Beaks and mouths of masks open and shut, eyes roll, whole figures are suddenly changed with this opening up of features, transformed from one being into another. Even the buttons of the blankets and leggings (fig. 96), and through them the animals they depict, seem to move, glittering, catching the light and the shadows. This kinetic quality lends the figures a sense of vitality appropriate to the life force said to be present within them. Still more life was given to them in former times, when the flickering firelight played upon masks and dancers, on costumes and other paraphernalia (see the

110. Whale mask. Kwakiutl. Ca. 1900, carved and painted wood, 14 × 56½ × 15½ inches. Philbrook Art Center, Tulsa, Elizabeth Cole Butler Collection, L82.1.881.

Kwakiutl carvers were masters of kinetic sculpture. In their transformation masks, one being was transformed into another through the hidden mechanics of the mask. In articulated animal masks such as this one, the physical motion characteristic of the portrayed animal was actually a part of the mask, heightening the effect of mimicry dances.

description of such a performance, virtually unchanged since earlier times, by Bill Holm in the following essay). The dynamism and vitality of the mask are of course lost in a museum exhibition, even one that uses photographs or live film. Not only drama is lost, but also the mask's aesthetic reality. In fact, in terms of its kinetic quality, North American Indian art is much more advanced than that of Europe, which has only discovered kinetic art in modern times. Certainly Europeans could learn much, and perhaps recover knowledge lost over time, by looking carefully at the art of non-Europeans.

The intimate relationship between fine arts and performing arts is not peculiar to the Northwest Coast, but can be found in many other parts of aboriginal North America, although perhaps in a less elaborate form. One has only to remember the Katcina dancers of the Pueblos, or the masked performances of the Iroquois (fig. 144), Cherokee (figs. 113, 114), and many other groups, to see this unity. Kinesis in art is by no means restricted to dance and religious performances. It can also be seen in the quillwork and beadwork on blankets of the Plains, in which the movements of the wearers, man and horse, create a constantly changing interplay of color and design, becoming a living, mobile, three-dimensional picture. Even the well-known headdresses of the Plains Indians, with their feathers, streamers, and dangles moved by wind and the wearer's motion, are kinetic (figs. 86, 87).

Finally, there remains the question, Why is non-European art so little appreciated outside its own regions? The limits of appreciation are perhaps more pronounced in Europe than in the United States, and certainly we cannot generalize with regard to East Asian art. However, the art of nonliterate peoples is, as a whole, greatly undervalued.

There are several answers to this question. An important one has to do with European art history and art museums. Here, Eurocentrism is still prevalent. This attitude neglects not only the art of nonliterate peoples, but also often the work of literate non-European artists as well. An example is the paucity of European art museums that own or exhibit works of the great Mexican muralists. Even special exhibitions on such a theme are rare, and usually financed and promoted by the country of origin. The situation in art history books is somewhat better, but even here non-European

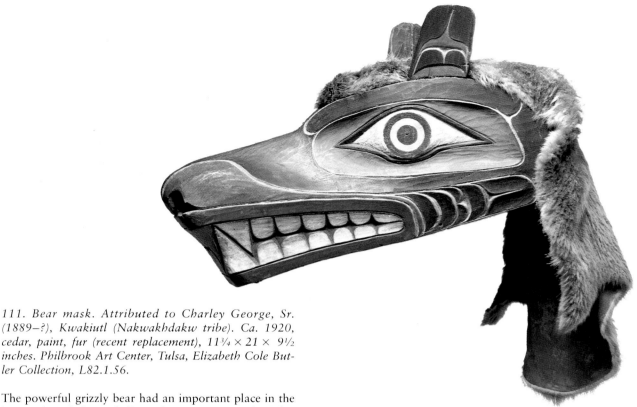

111. Bear mask. Attributed to Charley George, Sr. (1889–?), Kwakiutl (Nakwakhdakw tribe). Ca. 1920, cedar, paint, fur (recent replacement), 11¾ × 21 × 9½ inches. Philbrook Art Center, Tulsa, Elizabeth Cole Butler Collection, L82.1.56.

The powerful grizzly bear had an important place in the lives and mythology of all Northwest Coast peoples. This mask, worn in the *Tlásulá* ceremony of the Kwakiutl, dramatizes the original acquisition of a crest animal by an ancestor. The bear dancer represents the *Tlásulá* initiate, who takes the form of his crest animal.

112. Raven mask. Kwakiutl. Ca. 1930, cedar, red cedar bark, paint, leather, 11 × 47 × 11 inches. Philbrook Art Center, Tulsa, Elizabeth Cole Butler Collection, 82.1.82.

In the Winter Ceremonial of the Kwakiutl, the principal dancer represents a man-eating supernatural being from whom his ancestor has acquired the right to songs, dances, and masks. The masks of the man-eater's associates have the form of great, voracious birds. This raven mask is part of such a set. The beaks of the masks are articulated, so that they can snap shut resoundingly during the dance, performed during the ritual taming of the new privilege-owner (called *Hamatsa*), just returned from a sojourn with his supernatural motivator, the cannibal spirit.

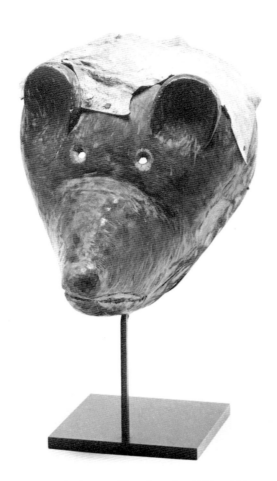

113. Bear mask. Eastern Cherokee. Ca. 1850–1880, carved wood, hide, 10½ × 9¼ × 6½ inches. Philbrook Art Center, Tulsa, Elizabeth Cole Butler Collection, L82.1.359.

Although tribal traditions hold that the Cherokee once used carved wooden dance masks like those of their Iroquois relatives to the north, there is little historical evidence of wooden masks before the late 1800s. It was then that Will

West Long began to carve masks like this one and the one in figure 114 and to incorporate them into the dances of the North Carolina Cherokee religious system. Known as booger masks, they are more often human than animal, depicting Europeans and other foreigners. By the early twentieth century, booger dances by bear-, buffalo-, wasp-, and human-faced dancers were an integral part of Eastern Cherokee ceremonialism.

114. Buffalo mask. Eastern Cherokee. 1850–1880, carved wood, fur, 12½ × 8¼ × 7¾ inches. Philbrook Art Center, Tulsa, Elizabeth Cole Butler Collection, L82.1.360.

artists are relegated to a lesser place and often scarcely considered. Even the expression "mainstream art," used in modern books on North American art (as in Wade and Strickland 1981), fails to take into account the larger part of the world population, and generally refers to art that is dominant in Europe and North America, with small numbers of adherents on the other continents.

Certainly, conditions for the art we are discussing here are much worse. No European art museum seriously collects primitive art and few exhibit it, except under very special circumstances, as when showing the influence of African art on certain European artists. Even in comprehensive art history book series, primitive art is often relegated to a minor place, where it is likely to get approximately as much space as the art of the baroque period in Europe, despite its enormous scope.

The effect on the public of this lack of formal attention to the art of nonliterate peoples is to invalidate it as art. For the proverbial Man in the Street, primitive art is, therefore, not art at all but a curiosity to be examined together with shrunken heads and poisoned darts. This attitude begins in school, with art education based on the principles of European art, especially those of past centuries. Naturalism and one-point perspective are basic axioms learned in drawing lessons; similarly, introductory courses in art history are often devoted exclusively to European art.

Is there a chance to alter this attitude? After many years of involvement in the field, I am rather skeptical about the possibility of change. We ourselves tend to preserve this attitude by too often insisting that this art can only be understood by a trained observer who knows all of its real or imagined meanings (see, for instance, Redfield 1959). Is it necessary to be so well versed? Does each viewer enjoying a Brueghel painting know the Flanders of Brueghel's time?

Another fault is our failure to apply classic art historical methodology, commonly used with European art, to the primitive arts. As mentioned before, we have been unable or unwilling to investigate North American Indian art in such a way as to attribute works to specific artists or to schools. We know, for instance, of at least three paintings by the early-nineteenth-century Mandan chief Mato-tope. Although these are often published, his name, if mentioned at all, appears only in the text, rarely in the caption. Instead of "Mato-tope, *Battle Count*," the caption is likely to read "Painted robe, Mandan," which is a significantly different form. And who has ever tried to analyze Mato-tope's style, his influence on fellow painters, or other such matters? Similarly, we have made only a feeble start in much basic necessary research, such as the ordering of all paintings on hide by style. That such work is not undertaken may result from the misconceptions that "all natives were artists," or that "no Indians were true artists." We have shown, of course, that this is not true (see also Young, chapter I, this volume).

Our main obligation is, on the one hand, to convince art historians that the art of aboriginal North American peoples is "Art with a capital A." On the other hand, we should show that European, or mainstream, thought systems, categories, and values cannot be applied to North American Indian art, or to the art of any other non-European people, and that they are culturally biased and not universal truths, contrary to the opinion of many art historians and art critics. Only after we have accomplished this can we hope that the general public will begin to give North American Indian art the place it deserves. When this happens, the use of the term "aesthetics" in the study of American Indian art will no longer be subject to question.

The importance of Native American art is expressed in a statement by a Laguna potter to Bunzel (1929:51), and may stand as a fitting conclusion: "Some people do not think that pottery is anything, but it means a great deal to me. It is something sacred. I try to paint all my thoughts on my pottery." What more could a European artist say about his work?

Note

1. Aesthetics as a branch of philosophy is European in essence and Greek in origin. *Webster's New Collegiate Dictionary* defines it as "dealing with the beautiful, chiefly with respect to the theories of its essential character, tests by which it may be judged, and its relation to the human mind." Plato and Aristotle were the first to investigate this notion systematically, and major philosophers throughout the ages have pursued it. Their ideas about aesthetics have been as varied as their thought-systems, often mirroring their time and its ambience. They were, however, concerned with art of the literate cultures and were, therefore, heavily influenced by the arts and tastes of their contemporaries. To review the fruits of their investigations here would have no bearing on our theme. More central to our concern is the issue of whether or not there is a universal aesthetic.

The Dancing Headdress Frontlet: Aesthetic Context on the Northwest Coast

BILL HOLM

A blue-green flash catches the eye of a museum visitor. Looking closer, he sees it is light reflected from abalone shell set in the rim of an intricate wooden carving. Abalone plaques border the carving and accent the features of a sculpted bird, fancy and fanciful, or perhaps a monster, with jutting beak, round, metal-rimmed eyes, and feet thrusting forward to flank a small man's head. Another head crowns the rim (fig. 115).

The visitor knows nothing about this sparkling object, or perhaps what he thinks he knows is not true. Even so, he responds to the dramatic force of this small chunk of an unfamiliar world—to its workmanship, richness, and imaginative content. The headdress frontlet will stand as a piece of art and be judged according to a foreign aesthetic.

On the museum wall it is torn out of context and exhibited, along with its kin, as simply the trappings of an unfamiliar culture. Even the complex headdress from which it is properly inseparable is often missing. The headdress is hard to display, or perhaps moths or carpet beetles have long ago reduced the swanskin, flicker feathers, scores of ermine skins, and sea-lion-whisker crown to an unsightly shambles. A conscientious and knowing curator may have reconstructed part of the frontlet's context through the use of captions, illustrations, or film. But its true context, its larger setting, is more than just a richly fashioned headdress of exotic feathers and fur—it is an intricate composite of costume, dance, rattle, and song. It is movement, accent, style, and the sounds of drum, tone, voice. It is the dance house, with its own atmosphere of carved crests and shadows, smoke, flame, swirling sparks, and eagle down. And it is history—long, convoluted family narratives delineating the track of the dance and its striking headdress down the generations, through inheritance, marriage, and war, back to a time when the ancestors of humans and the creatures of myth interacted to establish these emblems carved in the frontlet and emblazoned on dancing blankets.[1]

Appreciation of the frontlet as an art object is not wrong. The Northwest Coast native connoisseur recognized—and still recognizes—the skill and beauty in it. But his notions of proper style were not developed universally. They are peculiar to his region. Masks, totem poles, all sorts of sculpture, and even surface painting and engraving conform to regional concepts of form (figs. 116–120; Holm 1972a:77–83). Perhaps, long ago, an innovator at Talio, or some other Bella Coola town, carved a face more to his liking than what had been done before. Maybe it reflected the features of a noble Bella Coola, stylized with bold planes and curves. Other carvers admired it and incorporated its forms into their own sculpture. "Bella Coola style" evolved and it was different from the taut features of the masks of the Gitksan, with their open, smooth orbs, aquiline noses, and narrow lips.

115. Frontlet. Bella Coola. Ca. 1880, alder, abalone shell, iron, paint, ermine, sea-lion whiskers, canvas, rabbit fur, wool flannel, crown 13 × 11 inches; trailer 57 inches in length. Philbrook Art Center, Tulsa, Elizabeth Cole Butler Collection, L82.1.284.

Carved plaques representing crest animals or mythical beings were part of many Northwest Coast headdresses. The headdresses are remarkably similar over their whole range, invariably consisting of the carved plaque, usually inlaid with abalone shell, an upstanding crown of sea-lion whiskers, and a trailer of ermine skins. Bella Coola examples are bold and deeply carved, commonly representing birds; this frontlet illustrates the type well.

116. Mask. Bella Coola. Ca. 1880, carved and painted alder, 9½ × 7 × 4¼ inches. Philbrook Art Center, Tulsa, Elizabeth Cole Butler Collection, 82.1.61.

Bella Coola mythology is peopled with an enormous number of fabulous beings, mostly humanoid, and all are represented by masked performers in ceremonial dance dramas. The differences between them are subtle, so that most cannot be specifically identified today. The masks are carved boldly and directly, with great skill. Adz and knife marks often show clearly. The style is distinctive and, combined with the blue, vermilion, and black painting, is easily recognizable as Bella Coola.

It had more in common with the carvings of the tribe's seaward neighbors, the Bella Bella, or even the Bella Bella's more southerly Kwakiutl relatives.

It is impossible to establish just when that way of carving became the accepted Bella Coola style. The earliest white men who managed, like Vancouver's survey parties, to penetrate the labyrinthine channels to the Bella Coola country or to pierce its mountain barriers, as Sir Alexander MacKenzie did, left us no record of the art. The first systematic collections were made in the closing decades of the last century, and by then a powerful local sculptural tradition had been set.[2]

Why is Bella Coola style so distinctive? How is it that Kwakiutl sculpture, which is neighboring and related, is yet so distinct from it? Something, a principle of proportion, or perhaps some underlying concept of form, has tied the sculptural creations of Indian artists the length of the Northwest Coast into a cognate body, yet each part has diverged in its descent from the common, ancestral art (Holm 1983:32–45). Bella Coola artists evolved a thrusting form. A face slopes back from its center, the nose, snout, or beak protruding forward (fig. 116). Eyebrows, often exaggerated in Northwest Coast sculpture, are expanded and sweeping. On a man's face, pursed lips push forward. A beast's or bird's lips are vermilion bands lining the mouth, with bulging, crescent nostrils arching above. The whole face slants back: forehead, cheeks, chin. Eye orbs are strong, and look outward and downward, never straight ahead. The cheek may thrust upward against the lower corner of the orb, in a typically Bella Coola rendering of the zygomatic arch (fig. 116). This cheek bulge, though very much a mark of the style, is not always present; at times the socket conforms to the prevailing

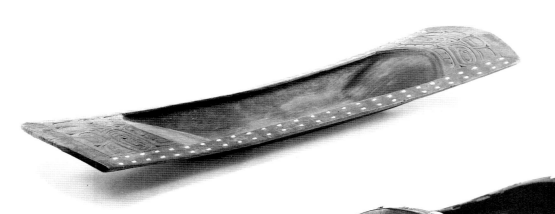

117. *Feast dish. Tlingit. Ca. 1875, alder, operculum shells, 5½ × 52 × 13 inches. Philbrook Art Center, Tulsa, Elizabeth Cole Butler Collection, L82.1.302.*

Alder-wood bowls and trays of many forms were used at feasts on the Northwest Coast. Long trays like this one were carved in shallow relief at the ends and were often inlaid with opercula, the shell-like plates covering the opening of the marine snail's shell. This material was also prized for use in inlaid box lids and the teeth of masks.

118. *Oil bowl. Haida. Ca. 1850, carved wood, operculum shells, 3¾ × 9 × 7 inches. Philbrook Art Center, Tulsa, Elizabeth Cole Butler Collection, L82.1.287.*

A technical achievement of the Northwest Coast wood-carvers was the construction of containers—boxes, chests, and bowls—using a single plank for all four sides, grooved and bent at the corners. A second plank was fitted and joined for the bottom. This small bowl is unusual in that it is carved of solid wood in imitation of an actual bent-corner bowl. Even the bottom plank, which appears to have been fitted, is a part of the solid carving. Sea-snail opercula decorate the rim. The shallowly carved design must represent an abstract animal form known to the carver and the owner. The bowl's black surface results from impregnation with the oil it once held.

northern coastal ovoid form (fig. 115). The ovoid eyesocket is firmly embedded in the repertoire of Northwest Coast artists. Even Bella Coola sculptors, who tended to avoid its carved form, honored it in painting. A band of paint, usually the ultramarine blue favored by these artists, crosses the face at eye level, ignoring the sculpted ridges delineating nose and cheekbones (fig. 116). Its outer painted edges, however, conform to the ovoid curve. Blue paint may spread beyond the socket, even over the whole mask, but the ovoid socket corner is defined by a gap in the blue; this T-shaped delineation, in natural wood color or vermilion paint, ties the painter's conception to the sophisticated system of two-dimensional design followed by artists of the northern coast for over a thousand years.[3]

Bella Coola artists relished the blue-vermilion contrast. Background was usually left unpainted, in the natural wood color, sometimes with relieving dashes in vermilion. The Bella Coola seldom used white paint as a background or accent, though the Kwakiutl artists to the south often have, at least for the last century (fig. 111).[4] But borrowing of all sorts did take place through the diffusion channels of marriage, trade, and war. Bella Coola dances were strongly influenced by the ceremonial dramas of the Wakashan speakers (Bella Bella, Nootka, and Kwakiutl; Jacobsen 1895:2), and many a Bella Bella noble name was acquired through marriage and borne proudly by a Bella Coola chief. In its turn, the bold sculpture of the Bella Coola made its mark on Kwakiutl and Bella Bella art. Many masks and headdress frontlets of undoubted Bella Coola origin were put to use in dance dramas on northern Vancouver Island, to the south. More often than not, these exotic objects were eventually given a new look, in keeping with the flamboyant tastes of their new owners: white accents and background, perhaps a coat of the more acceptable green paint for the eyesockets, a general brightening up.[5] The strong Bella Coola sculpture was and is accepted, even admired, by the Kwakiutl, but the typically restrained color scheme, with its often predominantly blue surface, is not

119. Amulet. Tsimshian. Pre-1850, carved antler, 2¾ × 1⅛ inches. Philbrook Art Center, Tulsa, Elizabeth Cole Butler Collection, L82.1.295.

Amulets of ivory, bone, and antler were used by Northwest Coast shamans to cure illness. They were thought to concentrate the power of the spirits they represented, and to direct it toward the patient. The figures on shamans' charms are hard to identify, since they represent arcane beings known to them, and not the more public figures of the crest system. This elegant object, whose color and wear suggest considerable age, combines sculptural form and two-dimensional formline detail.

their choice. To suit their tastes, a mask or headdress frontlet should stand out in the firelight of the house.

It is in that firelight that the frontlet comes into its proper setting. For the Kwakiutl, the headdress is a principal insignia of a ceremonial complex called *Tlásulá*.[6] It was acquired by the Southern Kwakiutl over a century and a half ago by marriage with the Awikenokhw and Bella Bella, who call it *Dluwúlakha* (Boas 1897:630; 1921:866–875, 1352), and it corresponds closely to *Sisaokh*, a Bella Coola ritual complex. All these have a common origin, most likely with the Bella Bella, to judge by the detailed family narratives, which describe the transfer of the dance among families and tribes, from generation to generation, and its spectacular regalia and associated names (Boas 1897:621–632). The headdress frontlets of the different tribes of the coast are distinguishable from one another not only by the stylistic features of sculpture and painting, but also by the choice and arrangement of subject matter. There are variations aplenty, but Tlingit frontlets, for example, are usually rectangular, with one large, main figure and one supplemental figure, while Haida frontlets, also typically rectangular in outline, usually feature a single large figure (Holm and Reid 1976:172, 174–175). The face of the Haida creature is frequently left unpainted, except for black eyebrows and red lips and nostrils. Tsimshian headdresses are similar in composition to Haida examples, but often display the rim elaborately detailed with a row of small faces or figures (Hawthorn 1967:fig. 227; Macnair et al. 1980:fig. 31). Frontlets from the tribes to the south, Bella Bella, Bella Coola, and Kwakiutl, are often round or pentagonal in outline and a common arrangement consists of a large head of an animal or bird as the central figure, with smaller faces above and below. These supplementary faces are not haphazardly chosen, but relate to the central figure and the mythical background of the carving (see Hawthorn 1967:pl. xi, figs. 216, 218, 219; Holm 1972b:28–29; Holm and Reid 1976:181).

The structure of the headdress itself, although basically similar all along the coast, shows discernible differences. While northern headdresses are almost always constructed on a framework of thin baleen splints, many southern examples are based on a cylindrical cap, sewn of cedar-bark matting. Kwakiutl headdresses sometimes substitute thin shafts carved of amber-colored baleen for the traditional sea-lion-whisker crown. The southern groups often cover the foundation of the head-

120. Platter. Charles Edenshaw (ca. 1839–1924), Haida. Late 1800s, carved argillite, 2 × 8¼ × 6⅜ inches. Thomas Gilcrease Institute of American History and Art, Tulsa, 6137–6942.

Although the black slate called argillite was known to the Haida of the Queen Charlotte Islands before the arrival of the Europeans in the late 1700s, its use as a carving material appears to have been a nineteenth-century development in response to the growing trade in European-oriented curios. Initially, the Haida adapted the traditional imagery and compositions of their wooden pipes to argillite, but by the 1840s their subject matter had expanded to include whimsical caricatures of European ship captains and their possessions and activities, intermixed with ancient Haida designs.

dress with swanskin, with its thick pile of down, and the trailer of ermine hanging below it is longer and wider than in the northern form. Northern headdress makers often use the brilliant orange and black tail feathers of the red-shafted flicker interspersed with the whiskers, or framing the frontlet, while a Tlingit practice is to set the frontlet against a rectangle of heavy red trade cloth and to cover the edge of the headdress below it with the iridescent green feathered skin of the mallard's neck and head. All of these variations illustrate choices that have become integrated into tribal aesthetic codes.[7]

Just as the carved and inlaid frontlet cannot be separated conceptually from the headdress, with its ermine trailer and crown of sea-lion bristles, neither can the regalia and the dance be isolated from the stories that explain their origin and ownership. These stories are as much a part of the headdress as are the whiskers and furs. Without them, there would be no headdresses, nor would there be songs. The songs of the Kwakiutl *Tlásulá* are much different from the songs of their Winter Ceremonial. They are sung in a natural voice, not in the deep, resonating tone that marks the songs of the Cedar Bark dances—the Man-Eater Songs, the Songs of Reckless Dancer who destroys fire, and the others, with their pulsing rhythms. The *Tlásulá* songs are driving and unaccented, with a steady beat that is sometimes chopped by incomprehensible breaks and changes in rhythm.[8]

In the *Tlásulá* ceremony, the readiness of the headdress dancers is signaled to the line of singers at their time-beating plank by an attendant's rattle, and the song leader begins striking the cadence. As he sings the first chorus alone, the dancers file out from behind a painted curtain. The extravagantly furred trailers of their headdresses half cover dancing blankets of red appliqué on blue or green. Iridescent buttons rim the designs and the broad red borders of the blankets (fig. 96). Dancers of the northern coast, Tlingit, Haida, or Tsimshian, traditionally wear the Chilkat dancing blanket with the headdress (fig. 95). This most elegant of chiefly robes is worn by Kwakiutl dancers as well, but here it is considered a prerogative of those who can claim descent from the northern tribes. Although recognized as foreign, the Chilkat blanket is admired for its striking design and color, as well as for the dramatic effect of the swirling, sumptuous fringe. Each dancer wears an apron embroidered with crest designs or fanciful floral patterns and hung with copper pendants, brass thimbles, small bells, or the beaks of the tufted puffin (fig. 97). Striking together with each movement,

121. *Bella Coola dancers performing in Berlin, January,*
1886.

the ornaments produce a rustling underlayer of sound, which floats beneath the staccato of the singers' batons, the deeper peal of the drum, and the voice of the song leader.

At first the row of dancers faces the singers and the back wall. Ermine trailers reflect the fire. The sea-lion-whisker crown, enclosing a loose handful of white eagle down, rustles and glistens as the figures bob in time to the first chorus. Then the singers all join their leader, and with this rush of sound, the dancers turn and match in vigor the new force of the song. Now the abalone-shell coronas of the frontlets flash firelight. Each crowns a proud face framed in swirling ermine. The dance itself is deceptively simple. The dancers, legs slightly spread and knees flexed, make short, barely perceptible jumps, both heels striking the ground at each beat of the singers' batons. This elemental jumping step is only the foundation on which the style of the dance is built. The most admired performances convey a sense of deep tension and control. Head and headdress move with the stress of the song. A short bow, followed by a quick upward swing, throws the headdress back, releasing a flurry of eagle down through the crown of sea-lion whiskers. The loosely hung rows of ermine bounce in response to the dancer's rhythmic motions. His elbows, or even his arms, are spread, stretching the blanket wide to display whatever part of the design is not concealed by the ermine mantle. He turns slowly in place, always maintaining the rhythm, gaze fixed on a point. Again, a bow and swing of the head, or a quick tilt to the side, releases another snowstorm of down. It flies around him, whipped and stirred by the rattling whiskers, drifting across the floor in windrows. If he uses a rattle, it is the raven rattle, held upside down and to the side, vibrating throughout the whole dance. Its complex iconography and formline detail, in constant, rapid motion, are hardly visible in the firelight (Holm 1972b:30–31).

A great dancer is appreciated and remembered. All parts of his performance fit together: his response to the rhythmic batons and drum, and to the stress of the song; the steady vibration of his rattle; the controlled tension of his body, and especially the movements of his head and headdress—a

122. Bag. Apache. Ca. 1865–1895, hide, red flannel, beads, 51 × 14 × ½ inches; fringe: 23 inches. Fort Sill Museum, Fort Sill, 067.89.1.

Though the Apache share linguistic and tribal origins with the Navajo, the development of their aesthetic has followed its own cultural course; this double saddlebag is uniquely Apache. Various appliquéd layers of commercial red flannel and pinked and pierced hide create a vibrant geometric frieze. It has been suggested, though not confirmed, that such techniques derived from Spanish influence. Regardless of their origin, the resultant artworks create dramatic optical collages, with a timeless but modern feeling.

sudden tilt and turn, trailing slowly off, then another, reversing; and his proud expression. All are part of the setting of the headdress frontlet (fig. 121).

For all its richness, this headdress dance is only a preliminary to the main performance, the display of a mask representing an ancestral being. One of the line of dancers is heir to the privilege embodied in the mask. The power of the unseen being hovers near him, and when he is teased by an attendant, his control dissolves and he bolts from the dance house, disappearing into the darkness. The attendants who hurry after him return empty-handed, except for his regalia, which they volunteer to don to complete his dance. In their comic, burlesque performance, the noble headdress is profaned, worn backward or upside down. The clowning attendants are as expert as the most serious dancer and their antics are enthusiastically appreciated by the audience who, moments before, sat spellbound by the power and skill of the headdress dancer.

After this, there is an interval of quiet, broken by the distant wail of a reed horn. This is the voice of that supernatural being, the abductor of the dancer, or perhaps of the dancer himself, transformed. The sound approaches the house and the reluctant attendants investigate. One announces the identity of the creature to the singers, and a masked figure is escorted through the front door and onto the firelit floor. A new song begins, the Song of the Mask. The creature moves according to his character: the underwater undulation of a sea animal; the heavy, fluid power of the grizzly bear (fig. 111); the hunched rustling of the great Thunderbird; or the furtive crouch of the ghost chief, Man of the Ground.

This is the true setting of the headdress frontlet that we see isolated on a museum wall or in the pages of a book. The context of the headdress is as important as the headdress itself to natives of the Northwest Coast, who never displayed it, as we might, for its artistic merit alone. Only in an array of goods to be transferred at marriage, or among the lineage emblems and treasures flanking the body of a deceased chief lying in state, was the headdress seen separated from a dancer. Instead, it leapt into life as part of a complex ritual, the nexus of an intricate interweaving of sensation, myth, and meaning, inseparable from the dancer and the dance, and integral to the expression of the life of a people.

Notes

1. There are many published accounts of the origin and function of the ceremonial complex of which the headdress dance is a part. The earliest of these which recognizably describe the dance are Dunn (1844:242–254) and Tolmie (n.d.:295–296). Dunn's account was published in 1844 and Tolmie's was written in November of 1834, 150 years ago. Others that are of importance are Boas (1897:621–632, 646–652; 1921:866–875, 1352–1354), Curtis (1915:271–279, 243–244), Drucker (1940:205–222), Holm (1972b: 28–51), Jacobsen (1895:2–23), and Olson (1954:246–249; 1955:330–333).

2. The most significant collections of Bella Coola sculpture were made by the Jacobsen brothers, Adrian and Fillip, in 1885 and by Franz Boas and George Hunt in 1897. Most of the Jacobsen collection is in the Berlin *Museum für Völkerkunde* and the Field Museum in Chicago. The Boas-Hunt collection is in the American Museum of Natural History in New York.

3. Recent recovery of well-preserved carved wooden and bone objects from sites on the northern coast of British Columbia, especially in the Prince Rupert Harbor area, have established the very early existence of a design system based on principles closely related to those governing nineteenth-century northern Northwest Coast art. A bone comb with a wolf depicted on the handle has been dated to A.D. 800, nearly 1200 years ago (MacDonald 1983:107–108).

4. This observation is based on my comparison of hundreds of documented carvings, and on conversations with native artists and traditionalists.

5. There are many such repainted masks in collections and still in native use. While some of the pieces have been repainted merely for the sake of renewal, many were acquired from neighboring tribes and repainted to conform to the local aesthetic.

6. *Tlásulá* is the name commonly used by the Kwakiutl today. They also use the Bella Bella name *Dluwulakha*, which is the term used in much of the literature. Various orthographies render it *ḺEwElaxa, Laō'laxa, dlūwulaxa, glualaxa,* and *Tlŭ'wŭláhŭ*.

7. These observations are based on my comparison of several hundred dance headdresses from various Northwest Coast tribes.

8. This description of the character of *Tlásulá* songs, like the following description of the dance, is based on personal observation of, and participation in, many Kwakiutl *Tlásulá* dances since 1959. I would like to acknowledge the cooperation and assistance over the years of the many Kwakiutl friends who have given me, by word and example, what understanding I have of the *Tlásulá* dance. Chief among them are the late Mungo Martin, Herbert Martin, Peter S. Smith, Charley George, Jr., Tom Hunt, Bill Scow, Joe Seaweed, and Sarah Smith Martin; and Katherine Adams, Agnes Cranmer, Adam Dick, Henry George, Helen Knox, James Sewid, and Tom Willie.

IV

QUALITY

Determining Quality in Native American Art

EVAN M. MAURER

Relative judgments of quality are intrinsic to the creation of an object and to its critical reception. In Native American cultures, judgments of quality were based on sets of rules or conventions passed on by example and teaching from one generation to the next. Daughters joined their mothers in daily tasks, which usually included making what we now consider works of art, such as weavings, baskets, or ceramics. As a girl grew older, she was expected to help in the process of producing these objects, and so learned the criteria of quality through observation, instruction, and criticism. There were rules governing the production of every type of object in all media, rules that directed the selection and preparation of materials; the methods and techniques by which they should be manipulated; and the shapes, surfaces, and methods of decoration.

The proper application of these rules and techniques required repeated experience in all phases of the process, and through this participatory learning, an individual acquired skill, which was expressed in technical excellence. In "The Pueblo Potter: A Study of Creative Imagination in Primitive Art," Ruth L. Bunzel reports that among the people with whom she worked, the concern for technical skill in the creation of an object ranked even higher than the aesthetic evaluation of its decoration. When she asked one of her Hopi informants to choose ceramics from the pueblo for her to purchase, the primacy of this criterion became apparent:

> I soon discovered that the selection was made entirely on the basis of technical excellence of the ware. A handsome bowl by one of Nampeyo's daughters was discarded because one side had a slightly mottled appearance, showing that not all the water had been expelled in the firing. "It will break when you use it." She admitted that the painting was good, but this seemed too unimportant to be commented upon until directly questioned. The prophecy was, alas, correct. I purchased the bowl for the sake of its design, and although I did get it to New York unbroken, it crumbled the first time it was used (Bunzel 1929:60).

Bunzel's crumbling bowl is a perfect example of the importance of technical excellence in determining the quality of an object from Native American cultures, in which most things that we consider art had a functional purpose, or were based on utilitarian prototypes. In the eyes of the Hopi, the beauty of the bowl's shape and painted design were negated by the poor quality of its technique. How could it be considered beautiful when the essential fabric of the vessel was itself wrong?

The primary definition of the word "art" in the English language refers to skill, which is the result of knowledge and practice. The term was at first generally applied to a great variety of

123. Dress. Sioux. Ca. 1880, hide, beadwork, tin jingles, 58 × 40 inches. Philbrook Art Center, Tulsa, Roberta Campbell Lawson Collection, MI 2062.

The delicacy of Plains costume design belies its massive construction. This dress, which weighs approximately thirty-five pounds, was worn only on festive social occasions. Its broad tee-shaped configuration is accented by a heavily beaded yoke that extends from the neckline down the arms. The massive color block so delineated, and the simple floating geometric motifs, suggest the design influence of the Sioux's northern neighbors, the Piegan and Blackfoot.

124. Ramos polychrome effigy jar. Casas Grandes. Ca. 1200–1340, polychrome pottery, 7½ × 8¼ inches. Museum of the Red River, Idabel, 058.

Ceramics of the Casas Grandes, like those of their northern neighbors the Mimbres, are enigmatic. These two traditions are similar to each other but have little in common with any other culture of the greater Southwest. Both traditions are filled with fanciful, imaginative, and transformational figures, but where the Mimbres favored painting, the Casas Grandes potters favored sculpted and painted effigies. Casas Grandes figurines like this Janus-faced effigy jar characteristically depict faces with crescent-shaped ears, tattoo marks, minimal protruding tattooed chins, concentrically ringed eye knobs, truncated pendant noses, and coffee-bean-shaped mouths with paint overlaid. Such faces float amid a collage of asymmetrically balanced geometric motifs.

activities, embracing the sciences and technological crafts, as well as the creation of things of beauty. Not until the latter part of the nineteenth century did the words "art" and "artist" begin to change in emphasis and meaning. In modern Western cultures, artists are no longer seen as ordinary people, highly skilled and gifted in the accomplishment of their work, but as unusual individuals isolated from general society, who seek new, personal modes of expressing their sense of the beautiful, and of representing the life around them.

Few Native American languages have words that correspond to our terms "art" and "artist." However, when the word "artist" does occur, it usually has a primary reference to talents involving skill and craftsmanship. In the Choctaw language, the term for an artist is *to" kṣali imponna*, the first word meaning work and the second connoting skill, workmanship, talent, and understanding (Byington 1915:355). Our modern willingness to consider aesthetics and beauty apart from qualities of technical skill is one symptom of the separation of art from life that exists in our culture, a separation that has promoted a general misunderstanding of the purpose and meaning of art, and led to the estrangement of the artist from his own society. However, in traditional Native American cultures, art was totally integrated into the social fabric, and many individuals of both sexes produced some sort of object that reflected a concern for the harmonious union of beauty and function. To live and work properly, according to tribal ideals and rituals, was an affirmation of one's spiritual world view.

In Native American cultures, a properly and skillfully made object that adhered to conventions of ritual, material, and style reflected the sacred nature of the people's lives and the harmony of the world's forces. The aesthetic and technical quality of the object was a visual metaphor for a spiritual attitude, a mental state of being; consequently, even functional objects, such as spoons, bowls, robes, or moccasins, could be regarded as symbols of spiritual power or personal feeling. A well-documented illustration of this relationship among quality, function, and meaning can be seen in the quillworker society that was found among first the Northern and then the Southern Cheyenne, before their culture was drastically affected by ever-increasing white incursions into the Plains during the second half of the nineteenth century.

The women's quillworker society, known as *moneneheo*, "the selected ones" (Petter 1915:97–98), produced porcupine-quill-decorated robes, moccasins, containers, lodges, lodge liners, ornaments, and other objects that were sometimes associated with special individuals or groups, such as priests or tribal societies, or with the fulfillment of certain personal vows. The technical production of these quill-decorated objects was regulated by a carefully followed set of rituals, and the objects themselves were in many ways thought to be sacred. Initiation into the quillworker society included learning the proper rituals and techniques to create the objects, as well as the meanings and usage of the traditional abstract designs, representational images, and colors. The objects created by the "selected ones" were considered to be among the highest in quality because of the consummate skill that their makers had gained through long experience and through strict adherence to the traditions governing style and decoration. The high cultural value of the art produced by this society was recognized by all in the tribe, and a woman's feats in creating such aesthetic utilitarian artifacts were parallel to a warrior's acts of bravery and the counting of coup in battle (Grinnell 1923:161–162).

The most complete description of the traditional quillworker society is found in George Bird Grinnell's classic study of the Cheyenne. His investigations demonstrated that mistakes were not tolerated in the creation of the quilled decorations made by members of the society. When a mistake was detected, it had to be removed according to a carefully prescribed ritual in which a proven warrior cut away the defective work with a knife. The warrior recited his personal battle honors as he severed the stitches, ending the process of removing the faulty quills from the hide with the phrase, "And when I scalped him, I did it in this way" (Grinnell 1923:166). The older Cheyenne women who had been members of the society were, by their own account, as concerned with the overall visual quality of their work as they were with proper ritual technique. The clean, even surface of the robe was an important element in their concept of quality and aesthetics, and they took great pains to ensure the pristine aspect of their creations. They reported that when a finely tanned buffalo robe was being decorated with quillwork, the society member took the precaution of covering her hands with white clay or gypsum, and that she kept the robe in a protective sack, only taking out the portion on which she was working (Grinnell 1923:164).

The quillworkers were one traditional group that adapted to new conditions brought about by the advance of white culture into the Cheyenne's traditional homelands. Alice Marriott continued Grinnell's work by demonstrating how this important women's society changed, though it also continued to maintain its central purpose. Natural materials such as buffalo hides and porcupine quills were no longer available to the people, so they substituted canvas and glass beads obtained through purchase or barter. However, one factor that remained constant was the strong emphasis placed on personal accomplishment, ritual, technique, and design (Marriott 1956:20). The people no longer possessed the freedom they had previously enjoyed, but they still clung to traditional values of quality in their lives and work.

The integration of creative activity with daily life was even characteristic of those Native American cultures that developed a specialized class of artists, whose principal work was to create art objects, usually on commission. The best example of this phenomenon was found among the tribes of the Northwest Coast, where unique social, economic, and religious systems fostered a magnificent creative tradition, employing the skills and genius of professional artists.

There also seem to have been individuals singled out on the basis of technical skill and aesthetic prowess in nonspecialized Indian cultures, where most adults were expected to engage in the production of objects. Archaeological evidence has established that in many areas of the ancient Southwest ceramic vessels were produced by specialized individuals for trade to other, often distant, villages.

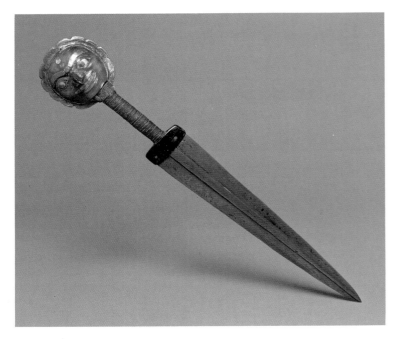

125. *Dagger. Tlingit. Ca. 1870–1890, copper, mountain-sheep horn, abalone shell, wood, hide, whale baleen, 21 × 3¾ inches. Thomas Gilcrease Institute of American History and Art, Tulsa, 6337.229.*

On the northern Northwest Coast, daggers were often much more than functional weapons, though they did have a place in intertribal warfare. Sometimes masterpieces of design and craftsmanship, they achieved the status of prestigious clan emblems. In the late 1800s, most functional daggers were of trade iron, but later in the period copper, the dagger material used in ancient times, was again a favorite for elaborate, mainly decorative, weapons. The face on this piece probably represents the sun, which is frequently portrayed in the art as a hook-beaked human face surrounded by radiating beams.

That this tradeware was generally of good quality is indicative of the shared aesthetic standards and mutual appreciation of fine workmanship that existed between producers and buyers. In the contemporary Southwest, this phenomenon is perhaps best represented by the San Ildefonso artist Maria Martinez (fig. 157), who worked from about 1900 to the 1970s. The ceramics of great technical quality and beauty that she created during her long and active life were enthusiastically appreciated by both Indians and whites, who provided her with a ready commercial market for over fifty years.

A survey of any large museum collection of Native American art will demonstrate that by no means all Indian objects are of high quality. As in any culture, there is great variation in technical capability and aesthetic genius among Native American artists. To be sure, a large percentage of those who made objects produced work of good quality. But it seems to be universally true that only a small number of artists in any culture produce works that go beyond average skill and sensitivity into the realm of artistic genius.

Native American societies, like Oriental cultures, maintained an essentially academic art, governed by systems of conventions. But while artists in such traditional civilizations must respect these conventions, they are still free to express their creative individuality within the confines of the general rules. These personal inventions and subtle nuances in the manipulation of forms separate the ordinary object of good quality from the spiritually evocative work of a gifted artist. (For the best presentation of this issue, see Holm and Reid 1976.)

Observations on the relative quality of Native American arts were often made by European travelers who visited North America. In 1787, an English captain praised the sculpture he encountered among tribes of the Northwest Coast as "well proportioned, and executed with a considerable degree of ingenuity, which appears rather extraordinary amongst a people so remote from civilized refinement" (Dixon 1968:243).

During his famous expedition to the Northern Plains in 1833–1834, Prince Maximilian of Wied Neuwied gave an enthusiastic description of the aesthetic quality of the shirts, dresses, and

126. Slave killer or dagger. Nootka. Pre-1778, pecked and ground basalt, native pigment, hide strap, 11¹³/₁₆ × 3³/₄ inches. Museum für Völkerkunde, Vienna, Captain Cook Collection, 210.

This dagger is a type of hand-held mallet with a stone blade. Slaves were known to have been killed ceremonially at important events with weapons such as these; hence the Anglo-derived name "slave killer."

127. Mask. Nootka. Pre-1778, wood, native pigments, shell inlay, 4³/₈ × 9 inches. Museum für Völkerkunde, Vienna, Captain Cook Collection, 222.

These works were acquired by Captain Cook on his exploratory voyage in 1778 to Nootka Sound, in what was to become British Columbia. These important objects provide a rare insight into the design and style traditions of

late prehistoric, precontact art of the southern Northwest Coast. The mask shows remarkable stylistic continuity with objects produced during the late nineteenth and early twentieth centuries by the Nootka and Southern Kwakiutl. Both the mask and the sculpted stone slave killer (fig. 126), which is structurally compatible with ancient petroglyphs found along the coast, indicate the enormous time span of this tradition.

robes made by women of the Crow tribe. However, the prince had developed a connoisseur's appreciation of Plains Indian art and preferred the "graceful" and "highly original" costumes of the Minetaree, calling them "the most elegant Indians on the whole course of the Missouri," and judging that their work even surpassed that of the Crow (Thomas and Ronnefeldt 1976:36–37). Individual women in Plains culture were also singled out for the skill and quality of their creative decorative arts, as was observed by Samuel Weygold among the Lakota beadworkers at the turn of the century, when the traditional life-style of the tribe was replaced by that of the reservation (Haberland 1981:29–56). We should also note that these arts continue today among the Crow, who carry on the creative traditions admired by Prince Maximilian one hundred fifty years ago.

The relative percentage of objects of extreme technical skill and artistic quality varies widely in North America, according to region, tribal group, and time period. In the Southwest, for example, the ceramics made at Acoma are, for many reasons, of a consistently higher quality than those from Picuris to the north. However, even famous ceramic centers such as the Hopi and Zuñi pueblos have experienced serious fluctuations in the quality of their wares. At Zuñi, the art of making pottery, which had been a vital tradition for hundreds of years, fell victim to the pressures of social change and had virtually died out by the time Bunzel published her work on Pueblo potters in 1929 (Bunzel 1929:62).

A non-Indian observer unfamiliar with Indian art might not recognize those details expressive of technical skill which were hallmarks of quality immediately apparent to a Native American artist's peers. However, it would be fair to say that both the Indian and the non-Indian would have a high regard for generally observable skills in the technical production of an object. While there has not been extensive research on the subject, studies have shown that universal, cross-cultural standards of aesthetic quality do seem to exist (Child and Siroto 1971). Non-Indians will never fully comprehend the complex cultural, religious, and metaphysical associations of a traditional Indian art object, but they can derive pleasure from its technical and aesthetic excellence and, if they are receptive, experience some limited appreciation of its spiritual force. Many Western philosophers, especially since the eighteenth century, have written at length about the nature of judgments of artistic taste and quality, and it is generally agreed that the response to a work of art depends more on the mental state and experience the viewer brings to the act of perception than on any definable physical characteristics of the work itself. Nevertheless, most philosophies of aesthetics also agree that the great work of art is that which, through some ineffable configuration and combination of forms, colors, and materials, is most powerfully evocative, expressive, and suggestive. In the final analysis, what determines the quality of a work of art is its capacity to act on man as nature does: setting the mind and spirit in motion. In the following pages, we will look at examples in some traditional Native American media of objects which attain that power through excellence.

To be able to make informal comparative judgments about the quality of art objects, one must be familiar with a wide selection of works in the same media, and understand the technical and aesthetic conventions that governed their creation. While a complete description of the range of media used by Native American artists is beyond the scope of this essay, the following observations on objects of high quality will demonstrate the close relationship of technique to aesthetics in the art of Native America.

The critical ranking of media in order of relative importance has been integral to European art for hundreds of years. In the official art academies, the "noble" arts of painting, sculpture, and architecture were regarded as possessing far more innate value than the graphic arts or the so-called "decorative" arts of textiles, ceramics, metalwork, glass, and furniture. Objects in these latter media were closely related to more purely utilitarian productions in the same materials; therefore, the quality of workmanship and design and the use of precious materials were, and often still are, the principal factors used to differentiate between the ordinary object and the work of art.

In effect, this traditional bias against certain media has led to a misunderstanding of the artistic value of certain types of objects produced by non-Western cultures. As in the more recent case of photography, many Western observers still argue the question whether a basket or pot is a craft object or a work of art. However, this question would not arise from members of Native American cultures, for whom the value of an object rests more on its artistic success and utility than on its creator's choice of medium. In this context, "craft" must be defined as the technique of making the art object, rather than as the end product of that process. A comparison can again be made between the arts of North America and those of Oriental cultures, where people also understand and appreciate the great aesthetic potential of media other than painting and sculpture. In the following pages, examples of woven textiles, basketry, and ceramics will be discussed to illustrate some of the basic determinants of technical and aesthetic quality in Native American art.

128. Bowl. Haida. Ca. 1830, carved wood, 7¼ × 12 × 10¼ inches. Philbrook Art Center, Tulsa, Elizabeth Cole Butler Collection, 82.1.75.

One of the most significant aspects of Northwest Coast culture was the development of the seagoing canoe. So important were canoes to native life that they were even imitated in elaborate oil bowls used for feasts. This fine example illustrates the principal features of the northern canoe—flaring sides and upswept ends with finlike projections. The stern, now cracked, sweeps upward at an angle from the keel, while the bow line is interrupted by a notch, which defines the projecting wave cutter. The shallow groove inside the gunwales is a feature both of canoes and of many forms of bowls.

TEXTILES

In the Southwestern region of North America, the art of weaving cotton textiles on a loom can be dated to approximately A.D. 700. During the ensuing centuries, the art spread through the region, reaching its apogee with the work of the Navajo weavers of the mid-nineteenth century. These women worked with fine wools prepared from the fleece of sheep first introduced by the Spanish, as well as with commercial yarns obtained from traders. The well-deserved reputation of the tradition rests on the elegant garment known as the "Chief's blanket" (figs. 90, 92); however, the Navajo also made serapes, which were woven in the longer-than-wide format adopted from the Spanish. By the end of the eighteenth century, the Spaniards themselves were duly impressed by the quality of these great weavings and reported that the Navajo "made the best and finest serapes that are known" (Wheat 1979:26).

The art of weaving requires a substantial degree of technical skill in the preparation of raw materials. The wool must be gathered, cleaned, carded, and then spun into yarn. The skeins of yarn

129. Serape. Navajo. Ca. 1860, natural-dyed native wool yarn, cochineal-dyed bayeta, indigo, 73¼ × 47¼ inches. Thomas Gilcrease Institute of American History and Art, Tulsa, 9736.115.

Classic Navajo serapes at their finest equal the delicacy and sophistication of any premechanical loom-woven textile in the world. Quality is indicated by the weaver's mastery of a number of attributes. Fineness of weave (as indicated by weft and warp count) allowed greater complexity and graphic cleanness of design. Symmetrical balance, with borderless, floating overlays of banded designs accentuated by primary colors, created vibrating fields of composition. And, in the most sophisticated blankets, weavers experimented with vegetable and commercial dyes, as is evident in this textile, where the spent indigo used to color the deep cobalt bands has been reused to yield a vivid pastel turquoise.

are then dyed, using either vegetable dyes prepared by the weaver, or, in more recent times, commercial dyes. Using a large upright loom, the artist works carefully to produce a fine, even, tight weave that will make a practical as well as beautiful garment, strong yet soft and supple. Illustrated here are two superb examples of the Navajo serape (figs. 129, 130). Both demonstrate the so-called classic design elements that are the basis of their reputation as the most expressive vehicle of Navajo textile art. The main elements of the classic design are the horizontal stripe and the terraced, or stepped triangle. In the weaving, the arrangement of these elements in varying shades of red, blue, and sometimes pink, yellow, and green is contrasted to similar motifs in a natural white yarn. The success of the serape design depends upon the creative interrelationship between the active stepped triangle and zigzag, and the more stable horizontal line. By the careful yet inventive balancing of design and color, the artist creates a unique solution for each woven object and, despite the visual complexity of the pattern, the artistic integrity of the object is maintained by the harmonious proportions of individual units to the whole.

BASKETRY

The creation of a basket as a work of art also requires considerable skill in the proper selection and preparation of the natural materials with which the artist works. The fibers used as the weft form the visible surface of the basket and must be very carefully peeled and split so that all strands are as uniform as possible. These weft fibers must then be precisely coiled around the larger bundles, or

130. Child's blanket. Navajo. 1860s, bayeta, homespun wool, natural and indigo dyes, 46½ × 30½ inches. Woola-roc Museum, Bartlesville, IND 379.

Children's blankets, primarily those intended for young boys, were miniaturized versions of men's serapes. They rank among the finest examples of Navajo weaving, often rivaling the sophistication of prehistoric, Basketmaker Phase (A.D. 200–400) hair and cotton textiles.

rods of the warp, so that each horizontal line of the basket is of a regular thickness, and each vertical stitch is a perfect repetition of the one it follows. Thus, the skillful replication of small parts unifies the surface of the object as it builds toward a three-dimensional whole.

The essence of the subtle art of basketry lies in the harmonious relationship of the form of the object and its two-dimensional decorative motifs. A superb example of this creative process can be seen in the large and imposing basket woven by the famous Washoe artist Louisa Keyser, also called Dat So La Lee (fig. 131). This full, round shape, known as a *degikup*, gradually rises from a narrow base until it reaches a maximum breadth at about three-quarters of its height. From that widest point, the form curves smoothly inward, ending in an open neck, slightly larger in diameter than the base.

Integral to the conception of the three-dimensional form is the abstract design that the artist has woven into the structure of the basket, using black and red natural fibers that contrast with the predominant light tan of the background. This design is known as the scatter pattern, and consists of a series of stepped triangles arranged vertically on a narrow black band. The sloping sides of these triangles support smaller, acute triangular forms that begin at the point of each step segment and extend upward on three rows of coils. The stepped triangles grow in size as the form of the basket widens, and diminish as the form curves inward at both top and bottom. These motifs are arranged in four groups of three, evenly spaced around the form of the basket. The central element of each group is aligned on a vertical axis, but the two flanking elements gently bow outward, to compen-

131. *Basket. Louisa Keyser (Dat So La Lee, 1850–1925), Washoe. Ca. 1917–1918, willow, redbud, bracken fern, 12 × 16¼ inches. Philbrook Art Center, Tulsa, Clark Field Collection, BA 666.*

Considered by many the consummate expression of Native American basketry, this masterwork of Louisa Keyser perfectly fuses classic sculptural form with surface decoration. The unique woven columns expand and contract in relation to the swelling of the vessel's form in the manner known as *entasis* in Greek architecture.

132. *Basket. Maggie James (ca. 1870–1952), Washoe. Ca. 1915–1920, willow, redbud, dyed and undyed bracken fern, 3⅝ × 8½ inches in diameter. Philbrook Art Center, Tulsa, Clark Field Collection, BA 78.*

This woven vessel by Maggie James illustrates several stylistic traits typical of the weaver's work in the middle of her active career. The dramatically bulging shoulder, flattened wide top, and narrow base are characteristic of the shape she developed by exaggerating Louisa Keyser's *degikup* basket form (fig. 131). Fine stitching and lightweight, dynamic designs, arranged diagonally, also mark Maggie James's style. Though technically brilliant, this basket does not exhibit the extraordinary fusion of decoration and three-dimensional form seen in Louisa Keyser's work.

sate visually for the perspective changes that result from the curving surface. This subtle and sensitive adjustment is comparable to the ancient Greek architects' use of a similar swelling of the column, called *entasis*, which serves the same visual purpose when the viewer looks down the exterior column line of a temple. In this way, the decoration is not only totally integrated into the very fabric of the basket, but also serves to emphasize the harmony of its surface with that of its form.

Another Washoe basket of high quality (fig. 132), though less expansive and organic than the example by Louisa Keyser, also shows a high degree of technical skill and control. Upon close examination, it can be seen that the weft fibers of this basket are even thinner and finer than those used by Keyser, resulting in a weave count of approximately ten more stitches to the inch. However, a tour-de-force technical achievement does not necessarily make this basket a finer work of art than the *degikup* made by Keyser. The design elements on this basket have very little relationship to one another and almost no integral relationship to the form of the basket itself. Skillful technique, or craft, can produce a beautifully detailed form, but only an overall harmony of form and design can result in a truly superb work of art.

CERAMICS

The production of ceramics is the oldest continuing artistic tradition in North America. This is especially evident in the Southwest, which has long been regarded as a center for quality ceramics. Archaeologists have identified over one thousand different Southwestern pottery types, from the earliest examples of circa 100 B.C. to the establishment of a strong Spanish presence in the area during the seventeenth century. Even today, the people of the Pueblo farming communities have retained ceramics as part of their strong cultural heritage, in the face of increasing pressure to adopt a Western life-style. While the number of active ceramic artists has significantly decreased during the last hundred years, objects of high quality are still being created by the ancient methods passed down from generation to generation for two thousand years.

Proper and skillful technique is crucial to the successful creation of ceramic wares, as the smallest mistake in the long and careful process can result in total loss of the object. Each artist has her favorite source of special clay, which must be laboriously gathered and prepared with a tempering agent of fine sand or carefully ground fired pottery shards before it can be mixed with water and used to create the work of art. All Native American pottery is made by hand, without the use of the potter's wheel; the wheel was never used in North America prior to the coming of the Europeans. Knowing this, we must marvel all the more at the consummate artistic control of these ceramicists, who are able to produce large, thin-walled, round vessels of graceful yet powerful form.

A very fine example of the high-quality ceramic tradition of the ancient Southwest is the large Tularosa-style olla that was made in northern Arizona or New Mexico in about 1100–1250 (fig. 133). The artist who made this piece built up the beautifully controlled shape from the bottom, adding coils of clay which were then smoothed to form the growing wall of the vessel. Because of the consistent thinness of the wall and its relatively large dimensions, there was an ever-present danger of collapse while the piece was being made. After the shape of the vessel was carefully completed and sun-dried, the artist applied a thin clay slip to the surface and burnished it until it was regular and smooth. At this stage, the artist applied her design directly to the surface of the vessel, without first making drawings. Different tonal values were achieved through the creative use of wide black

133. Olla. Tularosa. Ca. 1180, black-on-white pottery, 13 × 17 inches. Museum of the Red River, Idabel, 745.1.

This jar is a superlative example of the ceramic brilliance of the ancient Puebloan potters of New Mexico. In its complex composition, banded and negatively outlined, interlocked step-frets delicately meld into the serrated concentric spirals of the upper shoulder. As with Louisa Keyser's basket (fig. 131), the expansive designs perfectly complement the vessel's sculptural form.

134. Jar. Nampeyo (1860?–1942), Hopi. 1910–1915, poly-chrome pottery, 8¼ × 14½ inches. Thomas Gilcrease In-stitute of American History and Art, Tulsa, 5437.4396.

The Hopi potter Nampeyo ranks with Maria Martinez as one of the greatest known Indian ceramicists of the twenti-eth century. Nampeyo adapted prehistoric motifs to then-contemporary Hopi designs, creating an entirely new visual vocabulary. She also experimented with ancient and mod-ern design techniques such as stippling and the use of mul-tiple lines of various widths, drawn on a white surface, to approximate values of gray. All these considerations are present in this unique five-color water jar.

lines, groups of thin parallel lines that read as areas of medium gray, and white slip as a background and a positive design element. The painting was rendered with fine yucca brushes, using mineral or vegetable pigments prepared by the artist, and then the vessel was ready to be fired in the open, using wood and dried dung for fuel. Tularosa artists excelled in the creation of overall abstract patterns that were made up of the straight, zigzag, and spiral lines that formed their decorative vocabulary. Each pot bears a unique combination of those basic motifs, which have been manipulated according to the vision of the individual.

The finely rendered geometric designs used on this vessel are repeated in a varying orientation over most of its surface, so that they emphasize the unified and organic form of the vessel itself. These two-dimensional patterns are freely and creatively expressed, yet they remain subordinate to the general visual effect, achieving a delicate balance that is indicative of the vessel's quality.

Around the turn of the century, there was a renascence of the potters' art among the ceramicists who lived on and around the Hopi First Mesa, in northern Arizona. This resurgence involved the revival of vessel shapes and decorative patterns from the fifteenth-to-seventeenth-century Hopi site of Sikyatki. The most famous artist of this period was a woman named Nampeyo, whose grand-daughters are among the finest contemporary pottery artists working today at Hopi.

The vessel by Nampeyo featured here (fig. 134) was created in about 1915 and is a prime example of Hopi pottery at its finest. Its walls are of an even thickness and describe a shape with a wide shoulder that slopes directly from the high waist to a perfectly formed circular neck. As in the Tularosa olla (fig. 133), the comparatively high midline gives an animating sense of muscularity and lift to the form. This emphasis on the upper part of the vessel is reiterated in Nampeyo's painted design, which is anchored by a thick black line running around the vessel several inches below its widest point. The large painted elements arranged above this line consist of two pairs of designs, one based on a spiraling curve and the other on a large, broken-topped triangle. Both forms are them-selves subdivided into smaller components, parts of which seem to be totally abstract, while others, like the bottom sections of the triangles and the ends of the spirals, are generally interpreted as symbols of feathers. Nampeyo's palette usually consisted of various shades of red and black. However, this pot is distinguished by the artist's use of an unusual five-color scheme of dark red-orange, light orange, dense black, stippled black (medium gray) and thinly painted black (charcoal gray). As in the Tularosa olla, these painted designs are proportionately suited to the size and shape of the vessel on which they are painted. While each design can command an independent visual presence, to-gether they are part of a larger aesthetic unity.

CONTEMPORARY WORK

The contemporary Native American artists who express themselves in essentially nontraditional formats are also affected by the values and experiences of their Indian heritage. They may have been trained in contemporary Western methods and means, but their art is very much related to their individual sense of cultural background. The long and successful career of the Chippewa artist George Morrison provides a meaningful example of this, and is exemplary of contemporary Native American art at its best.

Morrison was raised in a small town in the dense woodlands of northern Minnesota. His father and grandfather were trappers and woodsmen and the family still practiced many traditional activities, making certain objects, hunting, and gathering wild rice. As a young man, Morrison decided to pursue a career in art. He graduated from the Minneapolis School of Art and went on to win several major fellowships and teaching positions while establishing a well-deserved reputation in the competitive world of contemporary painting and sculpture.

For over ten years, George Morrison has been exploring the medium of collaged wooden sculpture. In 1977, he created the first in a series of *Red Totem*s (fig. 135). The large scale of *Red Totem* makes an immediate impact on the viewer, who is forced to relate the sculpture to the surrounding spatial environment that he shares with it. In its general form, the tall, vertical shaft is reminiscent of Native American sculptural traditions such as the totem poles of the Northwest Coast and the decorated sacred center pole of the Plains Sun Dance ceremony. As their name implies, the works in Morrison's *Red Totem* series are all stained a rich, mellow tone that recalls the ceremonial earth paint used for centuries by Native Americans.

The skillfully rendered patterns of wood that cover the surface of *Red Totem* have two basic stylistic precedents. They can be traced to Morrison's earlier personal style, beginning with his paintings of the 1940s (Kostich 1976:47, 51), as well as to traditional Chippewa and Great Lakes decorative motifs historically found in quillwork, beadwork, and ribbon appliqué (Maurer 1977: figs. 105–106, 113, 127, 134, 145). These associations emphasize the thematic role of the interlocking curves of the design, which reflect the ubiquitous harmony of a traditional nature-oriented world view. These barklike patterns enclose, yet seem to emanate naturally from, the core of the sculpture that stands like a tall tree in the gallery space. By achieving this evocative and suggestive image, the artist presents us with a self-sustaining work of art—an imaginative and nonconceptual natural metaphor that is rooted in his personal genius and in the traditions of his Native American cultural experience.

135. Red Totem. *George Morrison (1919–   ), Chippewa. 1980, wood, paint, 16 feet × 20 × 20 inches. Collection of the artist, Minneapolis.*

Morrison is a pioneer of contemporary abstraction in Native American sculpture. His interest in the interaction of forms in a compacted space is evident in *Red Totem*, where asymmetrical components climb tier upon tier to create a smoothly columnar obelisk. This preference is also visible in his layered acrylic landscapes, whose environmental features are delineated through graduated hues.

Sculptural Arts of Native America

CHRISTIAN FEEST

The North American Indians appear to have been as ignorant of the sculptor's art as was any race which had learned its first rudiments.... Of all the examples known of aboriginal American stone-cutting, it is doubtful whether there is a single one which could be designated even as low relief (McGuire 1894:361).

If by sculpture we mean something "above" the utilitarian level, then it may truthfully be said that few Indian tribes from Mexico to the Arctic were successful sculptors (Judd 1931:3).

In spite of such discouraging statements, Native American art has often been esteemed for its sculptural qualities,[1] particularly that of the historic Pacific Northwest Coast and the prehistoric Eastern Woodlands. The primary reason that sculpture from these two areas was appreciated by non-Indian viewers seems to have been its technical excellence, since that is the one parameter most easily measured cross-culturally. Both on the Northwest Coast and in the prehistoric East, this excellence was probably the result of the professional specialization, beyond the simple division of labor by sex, that occurs within highly ranked or stratified societies. The straightforward naturalism of some prehistoric eastern and historic Northwest Coast carving was equally important in helping foreign viewers to recognize the quality of the works. "No other objects in this exhibition," exclaimed the organizers of the 1931 Exposition of Indian Tribal Arts in New York, "are as familiar in conception, from a European point of view, as the delicate [Hopewellian] figurines.... [A Hopewellian figurine] has its own style, but the idiom is one which we can understand without effort" (Sloan and La Farge 1931:41).

In contrast to Native American sculpture, which was measurable by Euro-American standards, North American Indian painting only came to be recognized as art after it adopted the media of Western painting and graphic arts. This is evidenced by twentieth-century Pueblo Indian watercolors and late-nineteenth-century Plains ledger drawings and their contemporary descendants. Only in retrospect were most examples of native painting using traditional media regarded as art, with the exception of prehistoric Southwestern murals, which were rediscovered in the twentieth century and have influenced modern native painting styles. Thus, the major change in the perception of Native American arts has not been in the application of native standards of excellence, but in the recognition of a greater range of arts as art, plus, at least in some areas, an improved understanding of native aesthetics.

The equation of contemporary American Indian art with painting was promoted by schools, in particular, the Institute of American Indian Art in Santa Fe and the art departments of the University of Oklahoma in Norman and Bacone College in Muskogee, which devoted themselves to the

136. Smithport plain jar. Caddoan. Ca. 500–1200, smoothed brownware, 18 × 13½ inches. Museum of the Red River, Idabel, 1197.

This huge Caddoan plainware jar illustrates the artistic attention lavished on the sculptural aspect of ceramics. The sensitive modeling of the vessel's form is complemented by the variegated brown hues of its surface, attesting to the Native artist's admiration of simplicity.

137. *Dog effigy vessel. Mississippian. Ca. 1200, polychrome pottery, 8 × 10 × 4½ inches. Thomas Gilcrease Institute of American History and Art, Tulsa, 5425.2634.*

The brilliance of Southwestern ceramics, which early captured the attention of white collectors and scholars, has unfortunately eclipsed the ceramic accomplishments of the ancient Mississippian peoples. This marvelous jar shows surprising continuity with the Caddoan storage jar in figure 136 and the stone ocelot pipe in figure 140. In form, the jar is essentially an expanded version of the ocelot pipe, but where a bowl (opening) exists in the back of the cat, in this work there is a flaring jar neck. The surface painting of red and white interlocking spirals is typical of designs seen on similarly necked spherical jars.

teaching of painting. Consequently, prestigious Indian art shows, such as the one at Philbrook Art Center in Tulsa, from 1946 to 1979, refused to accept works of sculpture well into the 1950s. By this time, however, several Native American painters, Allan Houser and Willard Stone among them, had begun to experiment with nontraditional sculpture, transferring themes and some stylistic principles of what had become the generally accepted mode of Indian painting into three-dimensional work. Since 1962, when Allan Houser became the first teacher of sculpture at the Institute of American Indian Art in Santa Fe, a number of other contemporary artists have turned to three-dimensional art. Nonetheless, the two-dimensional arts continue to dominate the art market and the amount of contemporary sculpture produced is still negligible when compared with the continued output of traditional forms of native sculpture.[2] The strength of a sculptural tradition like that of the Northwest Coast has even attracted members of other tribes (as well as non-Indians), who have adopted it as their own. Lelooska is the best known of these (Blair 1976). Though his origin is Cherokee, he lives and works in the Seattle area, and is thought of as a Northwest Coast artist (fig. 258).

This tradition has also strongly influenced one branch of contemporary Native American sculpture, represented by a range of artists, including the self-taught John Hoover (fig. 269) and Bill Prokopiof, both Aleut, who studied with Houser at the Institute of American Indian Art, and Ted Garner, a Sioux who grew up on the Northwest Coast and was influenced by Bill Reid, the famous traditional Haida artist. A second branch of contemporary sculpture features that Santa Fe–derived pan-Indian carving style, largely in alabaster but also in other materials, represented by Allan Houser and his students, including Douglas Hyde, Don Chunestudy, and Bruce Wynne. Other artists, like Richard West of the older generation, and Michael Naranjo of the middle one, have independently developed broadly comparable carving styles. Not unexpectedly, the counter-tradition represented by Fritz Scholder, heavily influenced by mainstream Western iconography, has found adherents in three-dimensional art as well; this group includes ceramic sculptors such as Glen La Fontaine, Estella Loretto, and Bill Glass, as well as Allan Houser's son Bob Haozous (figs. 211, 226, 263, 264). Finally, there are artists like George Morrison (fig. 135), whose sculptures reflect their native heritage in a highly abstracted manner, and who consequently do not fit the narrow definitions of the Indian art market (Monthan and Monthan 1978; Wade and Strickland 1981; Amerson and Gordon 1981:12, 13, 24).

The obvious resurgence of interest in contemporary Native American sculpture by both artists and the market is welcome in view of the richness and variety of traditional sculptural arts. However, before an attempt is made to survey these in terms of quality or excellence, the question of how excellence is measured should be addressed. From an anthropological point of view, it is doubtful that a single measure of excellence can apply across cultures or even across media and techniques within a culture, although it is equally likely that some features of the various measures will overlap and coincide. But if art is viewed as a communicative process between maker and user or viewer, one can apply a competence/performance model to this process: competence being measured by the set of rules governing acceptability of acts of communication, and performance referring to the acts themselves. In this context, quality would be defined as the approximation of performance to competence; that is, of actual product to ideally defined shape. The set of rules includes, besides the religious, social, and caste-based, those dealing with aesthetics: meaning, function, originality, and technique. All of these rules are continually subject to change and are, of course, culturally specific. Technique must be considered here because of the varying levels of technology possible. The carvings of someone who uses only stone tools cannot be fairly compared to those made with the help of electric power and metal tools; nor can hand-built pottery be properly evaluated against the product of the potter's wheel.

As a communicative process, the understanding of art is usually based on shared competence (active and passive, respectively) by the maker and the user of the art. In the case of Native American prehistoric, and many of the historic arts, the modern viewer does not share the maker's competence, and while the rules governing the creation of an object may be partially reconstructed by an outsider or modern viewer, they cannot be fully and experientially grasped. This is the inherent antinomy between the universality and cultural specificity of art.

Quality thus defined is rarely revolutionary in form or content. Only those innovative works which had helped to bring about change, and whose deviation was later canonized by changes of the old rules, would in retrospect be classed as excellent. The European tradition of art criticism, by contrast, stresses uniqueness and individuality as part of excellence. White influence on the arts of Native Americans thus extended from sixteenth-century collecting of "artificial curiosities," stressing rarity as the primary measure of worth, to the emergence of signed artworks by known individuals during the past century of Indian art.

That subcultural differences can lead to conflicting evaluations is nicely illustrated by a scene from a seventeenth-century German novel, in which the picaresque hero, at best an occasional viewer of art, visits the chamber of curiosities of a nobleman who is a connoisseur of art. When asked to select his favorite piece in the collection, the hero finally chooses a rather mediocre painting of *Ecce Homo*. When the surprised nobleman suggests that a Chinese map with pictures of idols should receive preference, the hero replies that he considers the image of God's son to be far superior to a pagan object of worship. The nobleman finally shouts at the hero, "Fool! I esteem rarity!" and thus reveals his own standard of excellence, whereas the simple-minded hero had based his judgment on meaning. The moral is that judgments of quality can be made on various grounds, and that it helps to specify one's basis for making them (Grimmelshausen 1977:73–74).

It follows from these premises that changing measures of excellence in Native American art cannot be separated from the history of Indian-white relations in North America, for these have had lasting effects on the maker-user relationship in native art, as well as on both performance and competence. The impact of the increasing interest taken by a non-native audience in native arts, entailing an application of different standards and an imposition of different expectations, has quite obviously changed both the face and nature of native arts and the communication process involved. This is true of contemporary art, in which the adaptive struggle is mutual, but also of historic traditional arts, where changing attitudes of the public redefine past rules.

138. Polikmana Katcina. Hopi. Ca. 1890, cottonwood root, native pigments, 10½ × 12 inches. Museum für Völkerkunde, Munich, 38–8–1.

Unlike the increasingly realistic contemporary Hopi Katcina carvings, nineteenth-century *tihus* were columnar in form, with minimal articulation of limbs. *Polikmanas* often sported elaborately carved piercework *tablitas*, surmounted by feathers and occasionally by shell or stone.

White influence on native performance and competence in art operates on a different level. If, according to our definition, quality is the successful attempt to come as close as possible to a model created by the mind, quality is partly a matter of skills. As has been noted, occupational specialization certainly helps to improve skills, those both of the average and of the unusually gifted individual. Inasmuch as the market for native arts has drastically changed over the last two hundred years, specialization has occurred where it was unknown before. Performance has likewise been improved by new technologies (especially iron tools) introduced by Euro-American civilization, and by new raw materials. All of this is as true of the sculptural arts as it is of other arts, and should be taken into account in the following brief overview.[3]

THE SOUTHWEST

The Southwest is not generally regarded as an area of high development of the sculptural arts. This is even more true if the term "Southwest" is used in its wider sense, to include California and the Intermontane Basin, two areas almost devoid of sculpture.

The absence of stone sculpture as a major art is a little surprising in an area connected in several respects with the Mesoamerican civilizations of Mexico. Neither the sculptural efforts of the prehistoric Hohokam culture, nor the highly stylized stone fetishes of the Zuñi and other historic tribes offer much in terms of excellence on a continental scale. Southern Californian stone carving, usually attributed to the prehistoric Chumash, depicts aquatic fauna in soft stones, and easily ranks first in the area, when rated for elegance and finish by Euro-American, rather than native, standards. Together with Hopewellian pipes, Chumash stone carvings are among the Native American works of art most widely faked (Burnett 1944).

Both effigy and clay sculpture have been minor arts in the southwestern heartlands since prehistoric times, but have never approached pottery painting in importance. As the tourist-art market of the late nineteenth century began to develop, some prehistoric shapes came into more frequent use, but their quality was diminished. Tesuque "rain gods" (a purely touristic invention) serve as a good example that professional specialization does not necessarily lead to higher quality: here, specialization for a low-cost, volume-oriented, mass-production market encouraged a machine-made look, as opposed to the earlier spontaneous individuality of the original figurines. Cochiti clay figurines (fig.

139. Mask. Key Marco. Ca. 1500, wood and pigment, 13¼ × 7⅝ inches. The University Museum, University of Pennsylvania, Philadelphia.

The remarkable turn-of-the-century discovery of wooden masks and sculpture in a submerged site located in the inhospitable wetlands of Florida indicates that during prehistoric times elaborate masking and wood-carving traditions may have flourished throughout the North and the Southeast. Their absence in archaeological sites is most likely a consequence of adverse preservational conditions, and not indicative, as many have maintained, of the paucity of sculpture in this region.

195) developed differently from a similar base, but here specialization resulted not in bulk but in higher quality. Individual makers modeled and painted their figurines more carefully, and made each one look unique enough to avoid suspicions of assembly-line production. Droll, but slightly sterile, they exchanged some of their spontaneity for neatness.

Greater naturalism, neatness, and technical quality also resulted from the most dramatic development of the sculptural arts in the Southwest, that of Hopi Katcina dollmaking. Wooden sculpture did not develop easily in an arid and often treeless environment, and the only traditional woodcarvings known from the area are the fairly big, but stylized figures of the Twin War Gods made by the Zuñi for short-term ceremonial use, and afterward allowed to rot. The formal variation within the type is narrow, and quality judgments of individual pieces seem to be based mostly on their state of preservation—or even patinated decay—rather than on sculptural distinction. As a type, however, Zuñi war gods have always ranked fairly high on the quality scale of non-Indian connoisseurs, thanks both to their striking abstraction and their uniqueness in the area. Always regarded as sacred and therefore unmarketable by the Zuñi, pressure for their removal from public display in institutions has risen continually over the years.

While the ultimate origin of Hopi Katcina carving (fig. 138) has not been established beyond doubt, it is known that by the middle of the nineteenth century, both flat and cylindrical pieces of cottonwood root were painted to represent Katcinas, supernatural beings embodied by masked dancers of the pueblos. Two factors have contributed to the evolution of Hopi Katcina carvings from these humble beginnings: the availability of better carving tools, and the development of new markets. Before the end of the nineteenth century, when the majority of Katcina dolls were still made for use by the Hopi themselves, better tools led to an increased variability of the type and greater formal complexity within it, such as articulation of the limbs. Once sale to tourists became economically important, other formal changes occurred in those carvings made for secular and commercial purposes: indications of genitals were removed and figurines conformed to a static stereotype, even though dolls showing action had been made before. These changes should not be misconstrued as simply the result of market demand, for in fact they originated from an interaction with the market. The final reemergence of action-oriented Katcina dolls after World War II was likewise not so much a function of improved skills (witness the much earlier appearance and disappearance of the type), but of changing expectations. While improved naturalism has obviously not harmed sales, it is doubtful whether quality has risen (Erickson 1977).

THE EAST

The quality of the sculptural arts of the prehistoric eastern North American Mound Builders, as it appeared to nineteenth-century European eyes, must have contributed to the early suspicion that these people were of a different stock than modern Native American populations. Of course, we have known for some time that there is nothing un-Indian about the populations that constructed mortuary (Adena and Hopewellian) mounds and temple (Middle Mississippian) mounds. The reason that Hopewellian clay figurines and both Hopewellian and Middle Mississippian stone sculpture achieved a naturalism and technical precision unsurpassed in the area during the historic period is twofold. First, local cultures of the East—not unlike those of Mesoamerica—moved from a classic to a postclassic period, a development involving a shift away from stylistic standards more easily compatible with those of Western art; second, the impact of European colonization hit the East early and hard, cutting off flourishing traditions of wooden sculpture, of which little has been preserved. As if to remind us of what has been lost, the late prehistoric wooden remains recovered from Key Marco in Florida document the technical excellence and stylistic sophistication of at least one such vanished tradition (fig. 139; Gilliland 1975).

140. Ocelot effigy pipe bowl. Mississippian. Ca. 1200, carved stone, 4 × 5¹/₄ × 2¹/₂ inches. Thomas Gilcrease Institute of American History and Art, Tulsa, 6125.1204.

This unusual depiction of an ocelot shows the concern of Mississippian sculptors with the realistic portrayal of both the exotic and the commonplace creatures of their world. The uses of such a pipe remain unknown, but we are tempted to posit a ceremonial significance not only because of the unusual iconography, but also because of the locations of excavation. A pipe nearly identical to this one was found in Alabama and is now in New York, at the Museum of the American Indian, Heye Foundation.

141. Human effigy pipe. Ohio, Adena Mound. Ca. 800–100 B.C., carved stone, 8 × 2½ inches in diameter. Ohio Historical Society, Columbus.

Anthropomorphic figurines, especially those approaching portraiture, are rare in prehistoric North America, but those we know provide valuable glimpses into the customs, personal adornment, and culturally mandated perceptions of self of the extinct peoples. This exquisite pipe bowl not only tells us of the costuming of the ancient Adena people, including earspools and stylized hairdos, but also illustrates the sculptural sophistication of ancient North Americans, equal to the brilliance of ancient Mesoamerica.

Most stone sculptures from the prehistoric and historic East are effigy figures carved on the bowls of tobacco pipes (fig. 140), usually out of fairly soft stone, such as steatite or a variety of clay stones. While a unique tubular pipe of the earlier Adena culture is anthropomorphic (fig. 141), only animals are portrayed in Hopewellian pipes. Birds, amphibians, and mammals were acutely observed and naturalistically portrayed (fig. 105). Both their ultimate meaning and the native standards of quality according to which the several hundred surviving pieces might be graded remain inaccessible to modern viewers. But their naturalism gives us the illusion of understanding them. Animal effigy pipes recur in Mississippian times, but human effigy pipes (fig. 50), often showing scenic compositions, are less conventionalized and on the whole technically superior to both animal effigy pipes and contemporaneous stone masks. The larger stone sculpture that appears during this period betrays the strongest Mexican influence discernible in native North America.

What remains in the historic period is a continued tradition of scenic effigy-pipe carving throughout the Eastern Woodlands. Examples from, or attributed to, the Cherokee, Ojibwa, Wyandot, and Eastern Dakota tend to illustrate subject matter that is less traditional and more oriented toward the early tourist market (figs. 51–53). Folk pornography and drinking scenes depicted on pipes were often the work of already specialized craftsmen no longer producing primarily for their own use. Another factor contributing to the rise in technical quality was, here as elsewhere, the availability of superior iron tools (King 1977; Ewers 1978).

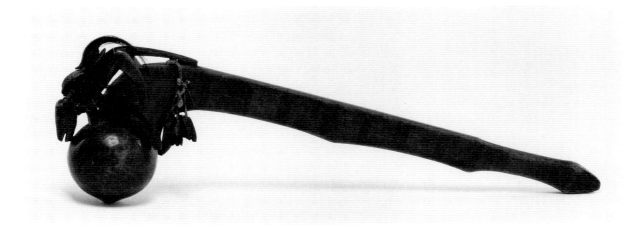

The modest scale and utilitarian nature of most surviving wooden sculpture of the Eastern Woodlands make it easy to compare to the stone pipes of the same area. Handles of crooked carving knives, ball-headed war clubs, staffs, bowls, and ladles (figs. 142, 143) were among the items embellished with three-dimensional carving. The function of most of these anthropomorphic and zoomorphic carvings, as distinct from the function of the objects on which they appear, is unknown, and thus native standards of excellence and even of effectiveness remain hidden. Well-dated seventeenth- to late-nineteenth-century clubs with the most intricate carving were the least effective as weapons. In losing their utilitarian function, these objects certainly move toward the realm of art in a Western sense.

While virtually none of these types of carvings continued to be made into the twentieth century, others connected with native ritual were—at least in some areas, like the Great Lakes region. Small wooden figurines, mostly of human but sometimes of animal shape, were made for magico-religious uses by specialists in several tribes, including some of those which had moved out into the Plains area in historic times (figs. 9, 10). Most are stylized and, since they never entered the tourist market, remain immune to the changes affecting other types of carving (Ritzenthaler 1976).

Iroquois false-face masks (fig. 144) have become almost synonymous with eastern North American mask-making. Used in curing ceremonies by medicine-society members, including both doctors and patients, these masks realistically represent a variety of supernatural spirits whose (by human standards) often grossly distorted facial features exhibit a great deal of individuality. Even though the tradition is very much alive, morphological classifications intended to bring order and comparability into this universe seem to be based largely on non-native criteria. Hence, their value for establishing excellence by native standards must remain in doubt (Ritzenthaler 1969; McElwain 1980).

Cherokee masks (figs. 113, 114) represent the only surviving Southeastern masking tradition, evidence for which is otherwise limited to literary sources and the Key Marco finds. Cherokee booger masks caricature potentially harmful aliens, and were used in burlesque dances. Their native aesthetic background is even less well understood than that of the Iroquois masks, to which they do not compare well in average technical quality (Fogelson and Walker 1980).

Masklike faces appear on the only surviving type of monumental wooden sculptures of the East: the interior house posts carved by the Delaware in their Oklahoma exile. Since we have nothing but early literary descriptions and a few old illustrations to compare them to, the high esteem in which they are rightly held is largely a function of their accidental uniqueness.

142. Club. Oto. 1780–1850, carved wood, horsehair, dewclaws, 23½ inches long, 3½ inches diameter of head. Philbrook Art Center, Tulsa, MI 2681.

Ball-headed clubs, characteristic of contact-period Eastern Woodlands tribes, became notorious during the French and Indian Wars (1754–1763), when the aboriginal form was adapted to more lethal, European-produced metal knife blades and spikes. Despite this object's elegance, with its elliptical ball, elongated and scalloped handle, and delicately carved crouching beast, it was an offensive weapon. The minimalist handling of the animal effigy, emphasizing massive head and limbs, is typical of early Algonquian sculpture and fits comfortably with pieces collected in the late 1700s among the Kaskaskia and other Illinois tribes.

143. Ladle. Mohawk. Ca. 1754, carved wood, 8¾ × 5¼ inches maximum diameter. Philbrook Art Center, Tulsa, anonymous loan.

This ladle was brought to Oklahoma from New York State during the early 1840s and, according to records of the original owner, had been acquired in the mid-1700s. Its style is compatible with these dates. Even though Mohawk, the form of the object recalls the Oto club of figure 142. The graceful, curvilinear sweep of the bowl and elongated handle is accentuated by the minimalist, but naturalistic,

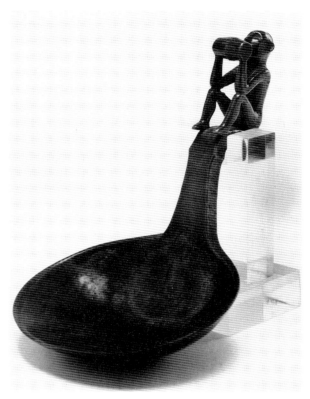

Indian man drinking from a European keg. Though now cherished as an artwork, the ladle was clearly used, as attested by many years' patination and buffing of the carved features, and by the permeation of oils into the wood, creating the illusion that the object is carved from horn.

THE NORTH

Walrus ivory is the carving material most universally and plentifully available in the American Arctic. The hardness that makes it difficult to manipulate has also helped to preserve prehistoric examples necessary to a history of Eskimo carving. Even the earliest ivory carvings in both the eastern and western Arctic exhibited a pronounced sculptural quality. An initial realism, especially in the human figurines produced by the Okvik culture of Alaska, later gave way to a more abstracted and two-dimensional treatment of carved ivory surfaces. It reappeared in late prehistoric and early historic Eskimo sculpture, and was further promoted by the tourist market that developed even in the Arctic during the nineteenth century.

While ivory carving has been given up in most parts of the Eskimo area during this century, it has become the specialty of East Greenland carvers, whose figures of *tupilaks* (spirits) have become their major product for a non-native collectors' market since the 1930s (Smith 1980).

It has been reported that, at least for some Eskimo carvers, carving means the detection and release of images preexisting in the ivory. Quality, then, would involve the closest possible congruence between the preexisting model and the released figure. Unfortunately, viewers lacking the original, archetypal vision will have a hard time applying this native criterion of excellence (Carpenter 1973).

Much less is known about the development of wooden sculpture in the North. The only areas in the Arctic in which wood carving was not seriously limited by the scarcity of trees were the Bering Sea, the Pacific coast, and Aleut regions. Here, carved boxes, bowls, floats, and a variety of other intricately sculpted wooden items were made, and an extremely versatile masking complex originated, in which the separate reality of the spirit world was portrayed in anthropomorphic and zoomorphic masks, based upon the visions of shamans. Masks ranged in basic approach from abstract through naturalistic to surrealistic. Indications point to a fairly recent origin of this complex in the mid-1800s, which is all the more remarkable since the masks encountered at the other end of the Arctic, those of East Greenland, are very similar in their basic inclination toward distortion and asymmetry (Ray and Blaker 1975; Gessain 1978).

The comparatively late appearance of wooden masks in Alaska is paralleled by the even later flourishing of monumental mortuary sculpture in roughly the same area. In both cases, the change was obviously not caused by the tourist-art market, but by technological, economic, and social changes initiated by white contact (Ray 1982).

Stone sculpture has an even less traceable history in the Arctic than wooden sculpture. Oil lamps were the major product carved from stone until small soapstone carvings of humans and animals made their appearance in the tourist-art repertoire of both Alaska and Greenland. This late-nineteenth-century tradition, soon dropped in Alaska, lingered on in Greenland, though it did not become a major art form. Soapstone carving, introduced as a new art form among the Hudson Bay Eskimo by white artist James Houston in 1948, met with unprecedented success in the white collectors' market. The case of Eskimo soapstone carving is quite revealing of the question of quality, since its whole development was largely guided by external market expectations, which varied in several respects from native standards of excellence (fig. 254). The primary criteria for Eskimo soapstone carvings include hardness of the material carved, boldness of the carver in making holes right through the stone, and contrast in surface treatment between polished and dulled areas. Many pieces that would be considered first-rate by Eskimo carvers and critics have a hard time in Western markets. Eskimo art in soapstone as accepted by non-Eskimo viewers is plainly a phenomenon different from Eskimo art as conceived of by its makers (Graburn 1976:39–55, especially 49–54).

THE NORTHWEST

Stone sculpture is of some antiquity on the Northwest Coast, though problems of dating still limit our knowledge of its role in the history of Northwest Coast sculpture. Due to the plentiful availability of wood for carving, stone sculpture never attained great importance, especially in the northern and central parts of the area. During the early years of the nineteenth century, however, a theretofore little-used soft stone, argillite, began to be carved by the Haida into souvenirs for white sailors. The earliest such carvings were certainly not regarded as quality products by either producers or buyers. The sailors lacked the ability to discriminate between correct and incorrect, or between good and indifferent, in a style that was exotic to them. Argillite carvers were not constrained by any necessity to produce meaningful art in a traditional context, but derived the structure, style, and iconography of the new type of carving from traditionally carved spoon handles. By the 1840s, European motifs began to dominate the imagery of argillite art, apparently following the general trend of tourist arts toward better recognition of images by buyers, as well as reflecting the increased inclination of Haida carvers to poke fun at the strange ways of the white man. Only after the late 1860s, when disease and heavy acculturative stress were threatening their social structure, did Haida carvers return to traditional motifs. Without totally abandoning the exotic subject matter, they began again to produce carvings that made sense to themselves, even though the market remained a non-native one (fig. 120). While the return to native topics may be seen as an attempt to preserve a threatened heritage, in the long run reproductions of totem poles—the one stereotype of Northwest

144. False-face mask. Seneca. Ca. 1900, carved and painted wood, horsehair, tin eyes, 10½ × 6¾ inches. Philbrook Art Center, Tulsa, MI 3332.

The diversity and individuality of Iroquois false-face masks rival the complexity of the more celebrated masking traditions of the Northwest Coast and the Southwest. Particular features proclaimed supernatural personages; here, the double-spoon-shaped mouth and protruding tongue connote the Doorkeepers, mythic figures in the curing ceremonies of the Seneca, thought to possess potent power to exorcise disease. The associations did not always hold, however, as masks were traded and sold among members of the Doorkeepers' medicine society, and a new owner could give a mask the identity of the being he was currently to represent.

Coast art recognized by even the least knowledgeable white buyer—sold best and became the mainstay of argillite carvers. Only with the general revival of native arts in the area in the 1880s and 1890s did argillite carving become a living and lively art once again (Kaufmann 1976; Wright 1980; Sheehan 1981).

The history of argillite carving, though interesting, is minute in importance compared with that of wood carving on the Northwest Coast. The most striking fact about wooden sculpture of the area is its tremendous diversity, despite the presence of both early and late stylistic similarities across tribal boundaries; these make it one of the most easily recognized arts of native North America. This has partly to do with the indebtedness of sculpture to the classic two-dimensional Northwest Coast painting style.

Labels derived from Western art history and attached to tribal carving styles (such as "classic" for Tsimshian, or "rococo" for Tlingit) do not really provide a better understanding of the differences among them, but give some indication of stylistic range (Wingert 1950:93). Since many of these differences occur gradually, and carvers from neighboring tribes have certainly influenced one another, the reconstruction of the history of Northwest Coast carving styles in historic times poses greater problems than the study of argillite carving, which was always monopolized by the Haida.

Nevertheless, enough is now known about wooden sculpture of the Northwest Coast to allow us to identify individual nineteenth-century artists, even though they did not sign their works in a Western sense, and to trace some of the changes in tribal styles during the historic period.

Northwest Coast sculpture ranges in size from the miniature (horn spoon handles or shamans' amulets, fig. 119) through the portable (rattles, staffs, and masks) to the monumental (house posts and totem poles). In particular, the efflorescence of totem-pole carving among the Haida and others was caused by external influences, such as the supply of better metal tools, but it also responded to the influx of new wealth through the trade in sea-otter fur, enabling the local nobility to patronize the arts and so aggrandize their kinship groups.

The period between 1840 and 1870 is often referred to as the golden age of Northwest Coast sculpture, because the advantages of improved tools and the increased native and external demand for carvings combined to create an ideal situation for the flourishing of the arts. While among some groups, like the Haida, this climax was followed by oblivion, the southern Kwakiutl not only continued to carve in order to fill their own need for ceremonial paraphernalia, but even developed a flamboyance that surpassed earlier carvings (Holm 1972b).

The current revival of carving among tribes whose art had been more or less lost in the recent past has produced an extraordinarily large number of excellent carvers, who have reestablished wooden sculpture as a living tradition. These sculptors have continued to work in the traditional mode, gradually adding innovations as well. While their market will necessarily always be different from that of either pan-Indian or mainstream modern art, it will be there—and from all indications, it will be bigger than even that of the golden age of Northwest Coast art.

Notes

1. Donald Collier's selection for the 1959 Chicago exhibition, *Indian Art of the Americas*, for example, featured twenty-two items that could be classified as sculpture (three-dimensional art). Of the twelve items illustrated in the catalogue, eleven were sculptures (Collier 1959). Twentieth-century European artists attracted by Indian art seem to have shared this preference for sculpture in their collecting habits.

2. *Native American Art at Philbrook*, published in 1980, includes twenty-four contemporary paintings, but only one sculpture. The same institution's 1981 Native American art exhibition, *Magic Images*, showed eighteen sculptures out of a total of seventy-eight works, but these eighteen included six pieces of jewelry and three sculptures in the Northwest tradition (see Wade and Strickland 1981).

3. A slightly different overview, arranged by materials and techniques, may be found in Feest 1980:158–197.

V

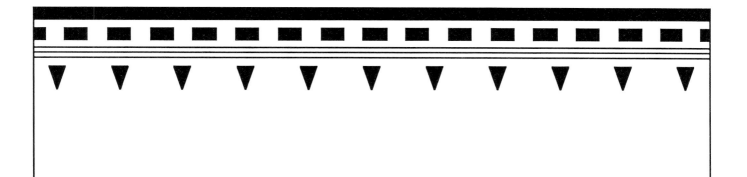

INDIVIDUALITY

145. *Ceremonial shawl. Hopi. 1920, cotton, commercial yarns, aniline dyes, 24¾ × 33¾ inches. Museum of the Red River, Idabel, 1888.*

In a small-scale society, where everyone in the community was known or related, applying the owner's or maker's name to an object was unnecessary. Still, certain objects required some mark of ownership, either for functional reasons (as with arrow points and shafts) or because of ceremonial constraints (as with Pueblo Katcina sashes and robes). A Hopi ceremonial textile was identified through the convention of the weaver's mark, a personalized design pattern. It occurred between the white undecorated field and the decorated part of the sash, or was suspended below the upper geometric decorated band of a shawl or robe. In this piece it is in the geometric line between the colored and blank fields.

The Individual in Native American Art:
A Sociological View

JOHN ANSON WARNER

Human beings are by nature social. They learn, via the socialization process, the attitudes and behavior of a distinctive social milieu. Because of this, what it means to be an individual is always a question of what society one grew up in. Further, it is a question of where one's society is placed in history, and what relationships it sustains with other cultures. In speaking of the relationship between the individual and society, the late C. Wright Mills (1959:3) argued for the importance of what he called "the sociological imagination," by which we may "grasp the interplay of man and society, of biography and history, of self and world." Mills's sociological imagination is particularly important to an understanding of the role of Native American individuals in the creation of art objects.

Because the individual is the result of social circumstances, art, too, is a social product. Art can be defined as what results when a member of a society personally interprets his society's values through matter, movement, or sound (CRM 1971:571). Nevertheless, many cultures have looked upon art differently. Among most Indian and Inuit peoples, for example, there was no special word or concept for art. Among the Inuit, all man-made objects were grouped together and called *sanasimajanga* ("that which has been made"), without reference to aesthetics or beauty. In societies where no special artistic or artisan class existed—the typical situation in aboriginal Indian cultures—no concept of art existed. This is not to say that in such cultures there were no concepts of aesthetics or beauty, but rather that most objects produced were valued primarily for their utility. In most Indian societies, art functioned within the religious system, teaching people about traditions, morals, ideals, and the natural world. The creativity of native individuals in aboriginal societies must be understood from this point of view.

Further, it is crucial to recognize that Indian individuals did not work in a vacuum. Ruth L. Bunzel illuminates the relationship of an artist to his or her society in her classic volume *The Pueblo Potter: A Study of Creative Imagination in Primitive Art*, in which she remarks on individual creativity among Pueblo pottery-makers. Despite the manifest examples of individuality apparent in the work of Puebloan potters, Bunzel recognized that its expression took place within the narrow confines of what Puebloan society allowed. She argued:

> Like all other forms of human behavior, art forms are not the direct response of the individual to the esthetic impulse. It might be assumed that a man painting a box to contain his personal belongings, and wishing to adorn it in some fashion pleasing to himself, would use this opportunity for individual expression. To some extent he does this; yet even the individual of marked originality operates within narrow limits, limits much narrower than those set by the exigencies of the technique. These limits are socially determined, just as are the methods of designating kindred. Language in order to fulfill its function as symbols of communication must be cast into accepted forms. The need for formalizing expression in art is more difficult to understand; even among primitive peoples art is recognized as primarily an individual function. Yet the tendency of artistic activity to become set in definite modes of expression characteristic of different social groups is so marked that when ethnologists

were seeking a convenient term by which to designate the socially determined limits of acceptable behavior, they borrowed the word "pattern" from the terminology of decorative art (Bunzel 1929:1).

This view of individuality and art is widely accepted in sociological circles. According to Janet Wolff (1981:1), it "argues against the romantic and mystical notion of art as the creation of 'genius,' transcending existence, society and time, and argues that it is rather the complex construction of a number of real, historical factors." What are these "real" and "historical" factors necessary to a comprehension of art as social production? They are many in number and can be approached through three central questions.

First, what is the role in society of individuals who are artistically active? Second, what is the function of art in the society? And finally, for whom is the art intended? Or, in other words, who are the consumers of art and what are their needs? The matter of the individual in American Indian art can be examined through the use of some of these concepts, based on the notion that individuals and the art they produce can best be understood within the context of the society (inclusive of its social structures and culture) in which they live. The argument on behalf of this thesis holds that Indian artists have been subject to varying social conditions over the last four hundred years or so, and hence their art has changed accordingly. In tracing these changes, it can be seen that there are, historically, at least three major sorts of individualism with respect to native arts: the aboriginal, that of the reservation, and the modernist.

Aboriginal individualism developed during the time when Indian cultures were autonomous from white culture or only minimally influenced by it. This condition existed at different times for different culture regions and even for different tribes. Aboriginal individualism varied from one culture to another, as some Indian societies were more individualistic and others more collectivistic in their cultural orientations. Whatever the case, however, individuals in this category were responsive primarily to the needs of the social group.

For the past three or four hundred years, artistically active Indians have been exposed more and more to non-Indian concepts of the nature of art and the role of the artist in society. Indian art history, consequently, is the study of how, and to what degree, individuals in the field of Indian art have gradually been assimilated into the non-Indian world. Even in the reservation period, many Indian artists straddled two cultures: their own and that of the white man. In modernistic individualist art, the process has gone farther. In the most extreme case, the Indian artist occupies a role in the art world not unlike that of other artists.

ABORIGINAL INDIVIDUALISM

Aboriginal individualism was not the same everywhere among Indian cultures in North America. Further, within a culture or tribe, the particular sort of aboriginal individualism that prevailed was not always static over time. Since Indian peoples traded and warred with each other, they also exchanged ideas and influences. In talking about any culture, sociologists are interested in whether it promotes an individualistic way of life, called a self orientation, or a collectivistic one, called a collectivity orientation (Parsons 1966).

A self orientation is one commonly found in the culture of modern, industrial Western civilization. In this kind of social system, it is expected that people will pursue private interests independently of the welfare of the group. A collectivity orientation, on the other hand, teaches people to subordinate their own interests to the benefit of the group. Instead of fostering individualism, this value orientation urges people to think of "we" and "us," not "I" and "me."

While Indian cultures, in their empirical reality, are not perfect examples of either orientation, it can be said that some of them are closer to the first type, while others approach the second. As a specific example, the Pueblo Indians of the Southwest were closer to the collectivity-orientation pole, while the Plains Indians of the grasslands were closer to the self-orientation pole. The effect of these differing patterns of culture on the arts of these peoples was quite significant.

Among the collectivistic Puebloans, for example, consider the ancient tradition of handcrafted pottery, originally the domain solely of women. It is notable that Puebloan pottery was anonymously produced, never signed by its maker. While everyone in the village might recognize who had made a certain pot, by virtue of its shape, size, or design, no actual mark publicized the artisan's name. This fact is consistent with the culture pattern of Pueblo society. Further, every pueblo produced pottery with distinctive shapes, sizes, design motifs, colors, and decorative layouts for the placement of designs, and every woman in a pueblo was expected to adhere to her village's pottery type. While individual touches and slight modifications were countenanced if they did not threaten the integrity of the style, conformity to the general style itself was expected.

Pueblo culture witnessed a high degree of conformity and social control, which was tangibly expressed in the uniformity of pottery styles. At no time would an individual potter wish to stand out from her peers as different, for that would violate the ethic of uniformity which was cultivated so strongly. Since new ideas and innovations in pottery-making issue from an audacity of imagination, change among the conservative Puebloans was very slow. As Francis H. Harlow (1977:7) has said about Pueblo pottery, "within the time and region for a particular type, there is a remarkable uniformity in its features, attributable to a rigidly conservative outlook that has characterized the Southwestern Indians until the most recent decades."

Perhaps the last word on the role of the individual woman in Pueblo pottery-making should be reserved for Ruth Benedict. In her classic work, *Patterns of Culture*, she noted that the Puebloans were a people who, in their style and approach to life, avoided taking chances, preferring safety from error or mishap. In thus characterizing the Puebloans as Apollonians, she said:

> The known map, the middle of the road, to any Apollonian is embodied in the common tradition of his people. To stay always within it is to commit himself to precedent, to tradition. Therefore those influences that are powerful against tradition are uncongenial and minimized in their institutions, and the greatest of these is individualism. It is disruptive, according to Apollonian philosophy in the Southwest, even when it refines upon and enlarges the tradition itself. That is not to say that the Pueblos prevent this. No culture can protect itself from additions and changes. But the process by which these come is suspect and cloaked, and institutions that would give individuals a free hand are outlawed (Benedict 1934:80).

Hence, the individual imagination of the Pueblo potter is circumscribed at best—in point of fact, it must be subservient to collective needs and wishes.

The Plains Indians embraced a culture that in relative terms was much more self oriented than that of the Puebloans. Plains Indian society was actually very short-lived, prospering only from 1750 to 1875 or so. Thus, in essence, the golden age of the Plains Indians lasted less than 150 years. However, while it lasted, it provided enough romance for Euro-Americans to absorb the legend of the dashing, mounted warriors and buffalo-hunting horsemen of the Plains. Plains culture incorporated the buffalo as the staff of life, as well as the horse, the hide tipi, the cult of the warrior, military societies, vision quests and sacred bundles, and the Sun Dance ceremony. As Peter Farb (1968) and others have pointed out, the Plains culture was actually made possible by the presence of the white man on the continent, through his introduction of the horse, firearms, and trade goods. It was not until after 1850 that the non-Indian presence became overtly disruptive.

Most people know that the quintessential tribes of the American Plains were the Sioux, Cheyenne, Arapaho, Kiowa, Comanche, and Blackfoot. Although this does not exhaust the list of Plains tribes, it highlights those destined to become prominent in American history through their resistance to white intrusion in the late nineteenth century. It is an anomaly that while these tribes are considered to be the "ideal" Plains Indian peoples, they originated elsewhere on the continent and did not come to dwell in this area until the eighteenth century. In any case, the concept that best illuminates their culture is the cult of the warrior.

Like the Puebloans, Plains Indians divided labor by sex, but the Plains male dominated tribal social life. The entire culture of the classic Plains Indians was devoted to the individual celebrity, notoriety, heroism, and glory of the male hunter and warrior. Young men sought fame as warrior-hunters to gain a degree of prestige unequaled elsewhere in society. Successful warriors were the boyhood heroes of every young male. In discussing the life of a Crow warrior named Two Leggings, John C. Ewers observed:

> He was above all else a Crow warrior. And his story tells us quite as much of tribal values that motivated and guided his actions as it does of his personal escapades. The successful warriors of his tribe were his boyhood heroes. And in his doggedly persistent efforts to win a name for himself by risking his life on repeated war parties over a period of more than two decades, he reflected the strong cultural compulsion upon the males of his tribe to seek to emulate or surpass the brave deeds of older Crow heroes (Ewers 1967:ix).

In such a society it was important for a warrior to record his great deeds, so that all might know of his greatness. These were often depicted on painted hides, which could be worn or displayed outside a man's tipi, accurately, one hoped, since any exaggeration or inaccuracy in the retelling was sure to be noticed by his peers and called to his attention. It was commonly accepted that the individual would paint the narrations of his own achievements. However, if he felt inadequate to the task, he might ask a man known for artistry to perform it for him. An arrangement would be made and the talented artist would execute the appropriate scene on the hide for the man who had actually earned the honor. This practice also applied when a man wanted to paint a tipi with sacred, or power-invoking, designs.

The distinctive form of hide narrative is well known to most devotees of Plains Indian art (see Young, chapter 1, this volume). In his important study of possible white influence on Plains painting, Ewers (1939:25–26) has said that the art of painting on hides antedates the period of white contact with the Plains tribes, although, "to date neither painted hides nor the peculiar bone brushes used by the Indians to paint upon them have been found in prehistoric sites.... For the earliest detailed information on the appearance of a painted hide we are indebted to the intrepid American explorers, Lewis and Clark [1805]." It is likely that the naturalistic or quasi-realistic stick figures on painted hides were inspired by examples of late-eighteenth- and early-nineteenth-century European art. It is speculated that in the period 1832 to 1834, Karl Bodmer and George Catlin may have played a role in stimulating the imagination of Plains Indian men, prompting them to depict their achievements realistically on hides.

With respect to naturalistic painting, Wolfgang Haberland, in *The Art of North America*, has characterized individualistic hide paintings by males in this fashion:

> Turning first to the naturalistic style, the finest work appears on the so-called bison robes.

These are skins that are worn with the smooth side against the body in summer and the reverse in winter. The smooth side of these robes was frequently painted, above all with human figures, animals and objects, supplemented by a series of symbols. The process of making them was as follows: the outlines of the figures intended were first pressed or embossed into the leather with a blunt tool. Then the artist applied earth or vegetable colours, filling the areas defined by the lines with the aid of a brush made of a frayed piece of wood. The imagery of the paintings, which at first appears confused, becomes comprehensible as soon as one learns something of the meaning, which is closely connected with the art of war as practiced by the Plains Indians. The paintings on the robes recount the deeds of the owner-wearer—his special feats, his battles and, if of importance, the gifts he has distributed. Thus they amounted to public documents subject to constant inspection so that it was impossible to get by with fictional exploits. At the same time the paintings had a narrative value, serving as an aid to memory. In this sense they recall pictographs, a term that is sometimes applied to them, though not entirely correctly. . . . Basic to their aesthetic is the fact that perspective is entirely absent, as are such details of landscape setting as mountains or trees. The individual scenes that make up the paintings—a single scene covering the whole hide is unusual—are often arranged in strips one above the other. Oddly enough the native animals, particularly the bison, are better drawn than the men and horses. The latter are often quite stiff and the human figures, which recall those of children's paintings, can often be described as "primitive." But it may be that the effects of a certain tendency towards abstraction are evident here. Real profile views are rare and if present probably reflect European influence. The pictorial problem of the horse and rider was rarely solved, for the legs of the rider are often omitted, or else both legs were shown on the flank visible to the observer. It is, however, quite possible that the concept of the X-ray view may have been operative here. Its effect may be noted in other scenes where the body of a man is shown beneath his clothing and shield. Protective spirits and visions are also depicted in naturalistic fashion on robes (Haberland 1964:154–157).

Therefore, while the designs on Pueblo pottery featured abstract figures of various sorts and were anonymously executed, the designs on Plains Indian hides featured quasi-realistic images of real individuals. There is a sort of individuality in both types of art. Nevertheless, while Pueblo pottery was intended for the private use of family (or possibly for friends through gifts, or neighboring peoples through trade), the Indian art of the Plains was designed for display. Why such a difference? As has already been suggested, differing cultures brought forth differing forms of individuality in aboriginal times.

RESERVATION INDIVIDUALISM

Aboriginal individualism among American Indians was not destined to last forever. In some cases by the eighteenth century, and in all cases by the end of the nineteenth century, Indian peoples were placed on reservations by government authorities and forced to undergo culture change. In most cases, reservation society differed to a marked extent from aboriginal society. While some tribes were able to retain certain continuities with their pasts, most were profoundly altered by the change from aboriginal to reservation conditions. In the case of the Puebloans, the change was not as great as it was for the Plains Indians. Still, by the end of the nineteenth century most Indians were living in a world that differed significantly from that which they had once known.

146. Basket. Minnie Lacy, Yavapai Apache. Ca. 1950, willow and martynia, ⁷/₈ × 14¼ inches. Philbrook Art Center, Tulsa, BA 890.

This basketry plaque was intended as an object of art even though its shape is reminiscent of nineteenth-century functional winnowing trays. The intricacy of the design, with its dominant male and female figures, reflects the commercial influence of the early trading-post operators at the Fred Harvey Company. To enhance appeal for white buyers, they encouraged more flamboyance in the Apache design system, which had traditionally been austerely geometrical.

147. Basket. Pima. Ca. 1920–1930, cattail coil, willow, martynia, 2 × 11⁷/₈ inches. Philbrook Art Center, Tulsa, Alice M. Robertson Collection, 31–452.1.

Even within so standardized or traditional a design scheme as the Pima squash blossom, there is room for individuality and artistic expression, particularly in the subtler aspects of balance and proportion. The artists who made important strides in these areas were imitated, allowing the style to evolve slowly. In such a traditional society, although each woman would weave the same design, every member of the village could easily identify the maker of a basket according to stylistic particulars.

148. Basket. Paiute. Ca. 1920–1930, willow, redbud, bracken fern, 9 × 14 inches in diameter. Philbrook Art Center, Tulsa, Elizabeth Cole Butler Collection, L82.1.546.

As did other native basket weavers of California, Arizona, and Nevada, the Paiute rapidly adapted their ancient functional weaving traditions to embrace innovative pan-Indian "fancy" designs, in the hope of attracting the attention of white basket collectors. Though no provenance exists for this basket, certain of its attributes suggest the work of Leanna Tom, aunt of the famous weaver Lucy Telles. A variety of design influences can be read in the work, including Maidu influence in the offset plumed terrace, Washoe influence in the eight-pointed star, and Pomo derivation in the feather-banded head ornaments atop the human figure.

149. Baskets. Mrs. Cruz I. Billy, Pomo. Ca. 1930, willow, feathers, shell beads, 4 × 13½ × 7¾ inches; 3 × 8¼ inches; 3 × 8¼ inches. Philbrook Art Center, Tulsa, Clark Field Collection, BA 997; BA 969; L82.1.538.

Pomo feathered *e-pi-ka*, or treasure baskets, won renown among nineteenth-century collectors as the artistic apex of Native American basketry. Producing such baskets took masterful skill and very costly aboriginal resources, such as rare mallard duck, quail, woodpecker, flicker, and other luminescent feathers. A substantial amount of time was invested in hand-grinding and polishing abalone pendants and shell disks (*kaia*). Originally such treasure baskets were intended as honorific gifts and mortuary offerings, but by the late nineteenth century their appeal to the collectors' market, and the fabulous sums willingly paid to acquire them, prompted certain weavers to begin imitating these semisacred baskets as objects for the market trade.

Most aboriginal economic and political structures were torn asunder by the reservation system. The changes brought about by reservation life are clearest when seen in terms of contrasting social values. It was the intention of American authorities, after the advent of the reservations, to resocialize their Indian charges into rural agrarian or urban working-class equivalents of the white population. In order to do this, they sought to introduce dominant white values of the time. First, the Indian should learn to accept the same achievement values and the "Protestant work ethic" that were so predominant in the society at large. This sort of individualism, of course, was very different from any sort of aboriginal individualism prevailing before; it emphasized such matters as personal possession of property, accumulation and investment of money, a personal "get-ahead" ethic, competition, materialism, the intrinsic value of hard work, postponement of gratification, and so on. While some tribes possessed aboriginal values that could accommodate these concepts, others found such ideas totally foreign. Second, missionaries from every denomination descended upon the reservations in order to convert Indian peoples to Christianity.

These resocialization efforts met with mixed results. True, much of the aboriginal economic and political lifeway was destroyed or significantly altered. But in social and cultural realms the Indians, with varying degrees of success, usually managed to retain at least some vestiges of their traditions. The effects of white resocialization varied, depending on the tribe involved and the general circumstances obtaining. Among the Puebloans, the effects of white dominance were somewhat less devastating than they were, for instance, among the Sioux.

In any case, virtually all Indians in the reservation period had to make a living in a new way. Nomadic Plains warrior-hunters were expected to settle into a sedentary life of farming and herding. This kind of disjuncture between old and new could not have been easy, no matter how well handled by white authorities—and the transition often had tragic results. Hence, most Indian tribes came to live in impoverished backwaters of the American continent. Opportunities to make a viable living were few and far between, and as a result a great many came to depend upon government welfare, missionary philanthropy, and charity. By any standard, this was an unsatisfactory state of affairs.

For a few Indians, the production of arts and crafts offered the possibility of some additional income. Two major sorts of artistic production thus arose during the reservation period: individually produced art that was associated with an aboriginal tradition, and individually produced art that was white-influenced in its nature.

On the reservations, many Indians, both male and female, produced artworks directly associated with or descended from aboriginal traditions (figs. 88, 162). During this period, which for our purposes lasted from the turn of the century through World War II, many individuals produced what Christian F. Feest (1980:12) has termed "ethnic art." Ethnic art was and is produced by members of a tribal society primarily for the use of members of another group; in the case of North American art, mainly for white Americans. It is generally not thought of as art by its makers, who still live in a social context that does not recognize art as separate from the commonplace. The technology of manufacture is largely traditional, though new kinds of tools and raw materials received from the buyers' group may be used; in some cases, this substantially changes the form the art takes. The maker of ethnic art often does not know why his products are bought, or what possible use the buyer may make of them. For him they are first of all a source of income; in the long run they may become an important symbol of the maker's ethnic identity. Forms and decorations tend to be a mixture of native traditions and foreign expectations, so that the art is "sufficiently native to be recognized as exotic, and sufficiently foreign to be acceptable to the buyer. There are only a few transitional cases where tribal art has continued to be made, without changes, for an outside market" (Feest 1980:14–15).

As Feest has observed, much of the art of this period was produced to be sold to white people for the purposes of income. Given the impoverished conditions on most reservations (especially during the first half of the twentieth century), the economic motivations for artistic production are undeniable. It is also noteworthy that the goods produced for sale were tradition-oriented.

Such a contention is seen to good advantage in the production of beadwork items by Plains Indian women. Indeed, perhaps the real golden age of traditional Indian beadwork arrived in the period between 1880 and approximately 1930. With the passing of many arduous and difficult prereservation tasks, women had more time to engage in the elaborate embroidery of wearing apparel. Not only were they freed from the grinding necessities of tipi life, but now their beadwork was also freed from the constraints of severe practicality. Beauty became a great concern. Sioux women began to produce dresses with heavily beaded yokes (fig. 123), some of which weighed over fifty pounds, and fully beaded baby cradles. In the old days of migratory life, such items would have been impractical and nonfunctional. But under the circumstances of reservation life, the situation changed. Women during this period not only perfected beadworking techniques and attempted projects theretofore impracticable, but they also refined and definitively worked out distinctive tribal styles of beadwork designs.

Beadwork produced during this period shows strong evidence of white influence in the choice of materials and design ideas. While glass seed beads were made available to Plains Indians by fur traders after 1850, their use for decorative purposes was accelerated during the reservation days. Seed beads were much more flexible and easier to use than the porcupine quills that had commonly been employed during aboriginal times. In addition, contact with whites introduced the Sioux to new design ideas, such as the floral motif and the realistic portrayal of mounted horsemen and flags. It seems clear that the floral motif in the decorative arts emerged out of contact with French culture in eastern Canada and spread westward among the Plains tribes, via such culture bearers as the Cree and métis fur traders. Sioux women were much taken with the colorful flags of the Americans and Europeans and sometimes employed these flag designs as decorative motifs in their beadwork. The realism and representationalism of Euro-American art was also introduced to Sioux artisans in the nineteenth century, and women sometimes portrayed hide-painting-like representations in their beadwork. It can also be argued that during the reservation period Sioux women were introduced to rugs from the Middle East as a result of visits to white homes, and that they copied some of these carpets' filigree and scroll-like designs in their beadwork. All in all, then, non-Indian influence was a considerable factor in the art of beadworking, both during and after the aboriginal period (Lyford 1940).

Of equal importance is the fact that much of the beadwork produced was destined for the marketplace. Sometimes Sioux women made elaborately beaded pieces for the sole purpose of sale to local non-Indians, and sometimes, during a period of economic need, they sold pieces originally produced for their families. Whatever the case, there is no question that the reservation period witnessed a vast outpouring of material that eventually found its way into white ownership. Without doubt, some of the objects identified in museum cases as "aboriginal Indian art" are actually ethnic-art pieces produced during the reservation period. This is as true for objects from other culture areas as it is for Sioux beadwork (fig. 98).

The consumers of this ethnic art were whites who harbored a romantic and nostalgic image of the North American Indian. Native Americans have often had to face the fact that they are perceived by whites as either the Noble Savage or the Bloodthirsty Savage. Europeans in particular have maintained special affection for the dashing heroism of the Plains Indian. The image of the mounted hunter chasing down buffalo, or the warrior attacking an enemy village, has had an appeal for many that transcends mere facts. Even during the reservation period there were many whites who appreciated Indian artifacts out of romanticism, nostalgia, a proclivity for exotic cultures, or a combination of these. Indian objects were sometimes collected as curios or as souvenirs of a sojourn to the American West. They were purchased as colorful and appealing reminders of a past culture. It is significant that these consumer motivations are still prevalent in today's market.

During the reservation era, non-Indian patrons were the primary agents for ethnic art. White people living near a reservation, often storekeepers, would specialize in the purchase of ethnic art which they, in turn, sold or made available to consumers who lived some distance away. This was a very individualized sort of patronage and oftentimes a quite personal relationship grew up between

150. Jar. Nampeyo (1860?–1942), Hopi. Ca. 1910, polychrome pottery. 7¼ × 13¾ inches. Thomas Gilcrease Institute of American History and Art, Tulsa, 5437.4409.

151. Jar. Nampeyo, Hopi. Ca. 1910, polychrome pottery, 3 × 8 inches. Thomas Gilcrease Institute of American History and Art, Tulsa, 5437.4407.

Nampeyo was celebrated as one of the earliest and most versatile of Puebloan ceramicists. The Fred Harvey Hotel and Tourist Service Company early recognized her unique skill and willingness to adapt her art to white taste. Among Nampeyo's favorite compositional motifs were the abstracted feathers and body parts of birds. The designs of these two vessels experiment with the bird form, which floats freely, without the typical interconnected radial shoulder design. Such compositions, which were radical departures from the more common geometric formulae of Hopi pottery decoration, illustrate Nampeyo's unceasing personal innovation and quest for artistic expression.

the Indian producer and the non-Indian patron who was the principal purchaser of his or her work. While Indian producers often sold work door to door in nearby white communities, those who excelled in artistic production more commonly traded regularly with one or more established dealers in their work. While some of these purchasers were collectors themselves, others merchandised the art as a livelihood.

With the advent of non-Indian patrons for Indian art came a new emphasis on individual attribution. Consumers in the tradition of Euro-American culture wanted to know who had made a particular piece. In the Euro-American art world, of course, individual attribution of artworks was a great measure of the value and prestige of any acquisition. The indifference of Indian artisans to such concerns did not matter, since it was the white middlemen, or patrons, who took the responsibility for communicating such information to consumers.

The development of Southwestern Pueblo pottery is a good example. With the establishment of railroad travel and the popularity of tourism in the Southwest in the late nineteenth century, there

152. Jar. Nampeyo, Hopi. 1912, polychrome pottery, 10½ × 13½ inches. Thomas Gilcrease Institute of American History and Art, Tulsa, 5437.7774.

Nampeyo, and in the beginning her daughter Fannie, cream-slipped their vessels with the finest kaolin clays. This trait was a holdover from the earlier tradition of Hopi pottery known as Polacca polychrome. Daughters typically assisted their mothers and maternal aunts in the potter's trade, learning the art as they worked. The celebrated commercial illustrator William Leigh, original collector of this jar, maintained that it was made by Fannie, but this is suspect. Such meticulously designed jars, featuring prehistoric systems, were favored by Nampeyo, and irrespective of the degree of work Fannie may have done on this piece, the conception is stylistically her mother's.

was a growing demand for this pottery among tourists who wanted souvenirs of their exotic trips into Indian Country. The Fred Harvey Company, associated with the Sante Fe–Atchison–Topeka Railroad in what would later become New Mexico and Arizona, was especially prominent in the effort to obtain inexpensive bric-a-brac from the Puebloans. The Harvey Company, having established several hotels and eating establishments in the Southwest along this railroad line, sought to expand the opportunities for tourists to part with dollars, by opening curio shops where Navajo rugs and pottery could be purchased. As a result, local traders to the Puebloans asked for and obtained pottery pieces that were oriented to the tastes of an untutored buying public. Indian women were encouraged to make small pottery pieces in the shape of ashtrays, pitchers, jugs, cups, and so on. Though traditional designs were often utilized in the decoration of such wares, the function of the pieces was wholly disassociated from Puebloan tradition.

In some cases, completely new types of pottery arose. Among the women of Tesuque and Jemez pueblos, for instance, there was an impetus to develop a new kind of ware, whose decorations were

153. Seed jar. Nampeyo, Hopi. Ca. 1910, polychrome pottery, 3¾ × 11 inches in diameter. Philbrook Art Center, Tulsa, anonymous loan.

Nampeyo was fascinated by the technical challenge of sculpting a flattened seed jar. No functional value is associated with physical forms such as this, but they posed a consummate technical problem for even the most masterful of potters. Sheer weight and density of clay were precariously balanced against gravity, which threatened to collapse these vessels under their own weight. Though such flat-topped vessels offered interesting new design possibilities, it was the ingenious technical feat involved that drew the admiration of other potters.

154. Jar. Nampeyo, Hopi. 1910–1915, polychrome pottery, 8 × 14¼ inches. Museum of the Red River, Idabel, 2160.

The design of this jar shows a red rectangular block encasing a narrow upthrust lip, from which four pendant feather motifs, extending down over the jar's shoulder, are interspersed with four curving feather designs. It was a favorite of Nampeyo, and many contend that it was her innovation. The motifs were adapted from fifteenth- and sixteenth-century Sikyatki polychrome vessels, which continue to be a hallmark of the work of Nampeyo's descendants. This composition found such great favor among white patrons that soon other Hopi potters began to adapt it freely, and similar vessels of less technical virtuosity were commonly produced by Nampeyo's daughter Anna.

no longer applied before firing. Instead, very bright poster-paint colors were applied to the pot after firing. Naturally, such colors would run if they were exposed to water or any other diluting agent. Along with this new technique came the advent of small figurines which became known as "rain gods." These small figures, usually molded in a sitting position and holding a small jar in their hands, became extremely popular throughout the Southwest.

Not all forms of patronage were frivolous, however. In the Santa Fe region, for example, there were a number of scholarly institutions established for the serious study of Indian culture. Even before the turn of the century, the Southwest was alive with anthropologists and archaeologists researching the past and present of American Indians. Any student of Southwestern Indian culture is familiar with the names of Alfred Vincent Kidder, Earl Morris, J. Walter Fewkes, Harold S. Colton, Kenneth Chapman, Edgar L. Hewitt, and Adolf Bandolier, among others. Several of these scholars played important roles in encouraging the maintenance of quality in Pueblo pottery.

The case of Nampeyo is particularly instructive. Nampeyo was a woman of the Hopi First Mesa pueblo of Hano (actually a Tewa pueblo founded after the 1680 Pueblo Revolt by refugees from the Rio Grande). Nampeyo had learned pottery-making at an early age, but was unfamiliar with the distinguished designs on ancient Sikyatki pottery (1375–1625) until the 1890s or so. Although reports are contradictory here, it would appear that Nampeyo became familar with these

155. Jar. Nampeyo, Hopi. 1910–1915, polychrome pottery, 2½ × 5½ inches. Thomas Gilcrease Institute of American History and Art, Tulsa, 5437.4413.

156. Jar. Nampeyo, Hopi. Ca. 1920, polychrome pottery, 6½ × 14 inches in diameter. Philbrook Art Center, Tulsa, Clark Field Collection, PO 378.

The final stage of Nampeyo's stylistic experimentation,

during which her daughter Fannie took an increasingly commanding role, emphasized an angular, Art Decoesque refinement that reduced the vitality and spontaneity of the designs to a handsome, but less forceful, decoration.

designs when J. Walter Fewkes excavated the ruin of Sikyatki in 1895. Through the efforts of her husband, Lesou, the potter was able to obtain sketches and sherds of this pottery. Impressed by the artistry of prehistoric potters, she began to incorporate designs inspired by Sikyatki pottery into her own work. Thus, Nampeyo is credited with the revival of Hopi pottery-making in the early twentieth century, and Fewkes too is given much credit for his role as facilitator in this process (figs. 150–156).

Patrons other than Fewkes also appear to have helped the career of Nampeyo. In 1898, Nampeyo and Lesou demonstrated pottery-making at the Santa Fe Railroad Exposition at the Coliseum in Chicago under the auspices of that company. In 1904, Nampeyo was employed by the Fred Harvey Company to demonstrate her art at the Grand Canyon Hopi House, a curio center owned by the firm. It is probable that the agent for Nampeyo in this project was Lorenzo Hubbell, Jr. Nampeyo also worked for the Harvey Company at the Canyon in 1907 and finally, in 1910, she and her family went to Chicago once again to demonstrate pottery-making.

In the case of Nampeyo, we are witness to several important developments. First of all, it is apparent that she was individualistic and audacious enough to want to experiment and innovate in her pottery-making. This in itself reflects a difference between her and her aboriginal predecessors, who would probably have been more inhibited about such a project. However, it is clear that much of Nampeyo's interest in producing an appealing product for consumers arose from real economic needs in her family. One of her daughters, Nellie Douma Nampeyo, is quoted as saying:

> Nampeyo told me to teach my daughters how to make pottery and to keep the pottery making alive. Marie and Augusta have kept it up. I hope it never goes away. All the ladies do it. I use my pottery for a living and my son Douglas makes dolls [Katcinas] (Maxwell 1974:30).

157. Jar. Maria (1886–1980) and Julian Martinez (1897–1943), San Ildefonso. Ca. 1940, black-on-black pottery, 16¾ × 23½ inches in diameter. Philbrook Art Center, Tulsa, Clark Field Collection, PO 313.

During their long, innovative careers, the Martinez family of San Ildefonso have experimented more widely with ceramic styles and techniques than any other known group

of potters. Around the turn of the century, Maria first perfected the then-traditional polychrome-on-cream-slipped style she had learned from her maternal aunt Nicolosa. Her husband Julian's inadvertent burning of a firing of pottery resulted in the now-famous black-on-black ware. Though this style has changed considerably since its inception in the 1920s, through the addition of stone inlay, carving, duotone oxidation and reduction firing, and color reversal designs, still, the basic style remains the mainstay of both San Ildefonso and Santa Clara pottery-making. Unfortunately, popularity of the ware among white patrons, and their lack of sensitivity to the Puebloan aesthetic of the functional full-size water and storage jar, has resulted in the contemporary miniaturization of this tradition.

158. Plate. Maria and Santana (1909–) Martinez, San Ildefonso. 1946, black-on-black pottery, 2 × 15 inches in diameter. Philbrook Art Center, Tulsa, Clark Field Collection, PO 335.

Following Julian's death in 1943, Maria continued to produce pottery typically undecorated and bearing the signature "Marie." Her daughter-in-law Santana, wife of Adam, began to assist her, contributing a new vitality to the system developed by Julian. During this time, meticulously crafted, classically harmonious plates were perfected. The earlier, exuberant Art Deco design gave way to a concern for pristine symmetry, balance, and forms often associated with Greek Attic ware. It was also during this time that Adam and Santana began to attract their own patronage and recognition as celebrated potters.

To this evidence, John E. Collins has added the following observation:

> One of Nampeyo's great-granddaughters told me, "The Old Lady [Nampeyo] told us that we should learn to make pottery because it would be something to provide us a living. She knew this was true for her children and grandchildren and also for all Hopi potters. She had the vision to know this, and it has proven to be true. She was concerned with all the Hopi, not just with her own family" (Collins 1974:32).

Nampeyo stands out in Hopi history as an innovator who changed the course of pottery-making among her people. Her work was particularly sought by connoisseurs and collectors of art, and it still is. But a real part of the individualism of Nampeyo is attributable to the excellence and artistry of her work. Bunzel expresses this judgment clearly:

> The work of Nampeyo and her daughters, for instance, is quite unmistakable. She makes no modern white forms, no worthless trifles. She makes only dignified pieces in the best traditional style. Technically, her work is superior to that of any other Hopi potter. Her vessels are more symmetrically and gracefully molded with great subtlety of line in the flare of the lips. Her designs are executed with greater delicacy and precision, and her line work is superior to that of her fellow workers. Furthermore, her designs are of a different character. There is less design per square inch of pot. At times her patterns are almost impressionistic in their economy (Bunzel 1929:68). . . . Undoubtedly the original stimulus came from

outside, but it was Nampeyo's unerring discrimination and lively perception that vitalized what would otherwise have been so much dead wood. She did not copy Sikyatki patterns, her imagination recreated the Sikyatki sense of form (Bunzel 1929:88).

The world-famed Maria Martinez of San Ildefonso Pueblo, who, with her husband, Julian, developed the famous polished matte black-on-black ware around 1919 (figs. 157, 158), was also encouraged in her pottery-making by anthropologists and archaeologists in the Santa Fe area. The most prominent of these were Kenneth Chapman and Edgar L. Hewitt. In actuality, the polished black ware of Maria was a revival of a style of pottery originally produced by ancient peoples of the adjacent Pajarito Plateau. The School of American Research in Santa Fe was instrumental in encouraging local potters like Maria to recover this style (Marriott 1948).

In the 1920s, there was a movement to get the most notable potters (Maria primary among them) to sign their work. White consumers were anxious to validate the fact that they possessed a genuine Maria Martinez pot, and were convinced that works signed by her would fetch a better price. Therefore, they sought to persuade her to sign her works on the bottom. Maria, however, anxious to help the other women at San Ildefonso to make a living from their pottery, obligingly

159. Jar. Maria Martinez, San Ildefonso. Ca. 1930, black-on-red pottery, 6½ × 10 inches maximum diameter. State Museum, Oklahoma Historical Society, Oklahoma City, 3157/8.

Maria and Julian produced very little work in the black-on-red style that was, from the 1920s to the 1940s, the consummate domain of fellow San Ildefonso potters Juan and Tonita Roybal. Julian's sensitivity to design is apparent in the eloquent simplicity of this jar's decoration, which he painted. By the 1920s, he had visited both public museums and other pueblos, and his sketchbooks were storehouses of motifs and layout configurations common to prehistoric, historic, and then-contemporary Zuñi, Zia, and Acoma pottery traditions. The central element of this vessel is a streamlined interpretation of the feather motif common to Zuñi food bowls. Julian purposely offset and bent the design, creating a vibrant circular motion. In both shape and elegance of design, this work is the Native American extension of European Art Deco, which attests to the popularity of that style among white buyers during the 1930s.

160. Plate. Maria Martinez and Popovi Da (active 1956–1971), San Ildefonso. 1956, polychrome-on-cream pottery, 1½ × 13½ inches. Philbrook Art Center, Tulsa, Clark Field Collection, PO 521.

Julian and Maria continued to produce polychrome vessels sporadically throughout their long careers, but neither they nor any other potters working in the tradition ever matched the perfection of vessels by Maria's son Popovi Da. During his brief career, Popovi was rightfully celebrated as the outstanding ceramicist of his time. This eloquent, educated man, recipient of two Guggenheim Fellowships, approached his art not only as an aesthetician, but also as a scientist intimately concerned with the properties of clay, pigments, and firing techniques. This plate, made by Popovi with his mother, is one of the earliest examples of his work.

161. Jar. Maria Martinez and Popovi Da, San Ildefonso. 1956–1960, polychrome pottery, 7 × 9¾ inches. Thomas Gilcrease Institute of American History and Art, Tulsa, 5437.7900.

Popovi's experimentation led him to develop varieties of firing atmospheres that created sienna and duotone surface finishes. Polychrome ceramics, however, remained his favorite, since their neutral backgrounds provided a canvas for his increasingly complex multicolored compositions.

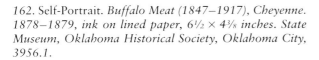

162. Self-Portrait. Buffalo Meat (1847–1917), Cheyenne. 1878–1879, ink on lined paper, 6½ × 4⅜ inches. State Museum, Oklahoma Historical Society, Oklahoma City, 3956.1.

Ledger drawings arose from two very different traditions. The first was the ancient Plains pictorial style common to painted hides, bone and wood etchings, and rock carvings. In its purest form, cultural, personal, and zoomorphic information was provided through the stereotypic exaggeration of a dominant attribute. Buffalo, for example, were identified by their massive humps; tribal affiliations by costume and hairstyle; and individual identity by shields, horse trappings, and dress. The second major influence was European. In the 1830s, frontier artists like George Catlin and Karl Bodmer encouraged warriors to use paper and colored pencils to depict their accomplishments. By the late 1860s, these influences resulted in a florescence of autobiographical picture narratives. The richly detailed, impressionistic portrayals of native life by native artists such as Buffalo Meat are refreshing glimpses of the pride and historical perceptions of the vanishing Native American experience.

signed not only her own pots but sometimes theirs too. Understandably, she received strong advice against doing this from local traders and collectors. Maria's generosity notwithstanding, there was a growing momentum toward greater individualism throughout the reservation period (figs. 157–161).

Another example of reservation-period art that is ethnic or traditional in nature is found in the ledger drawings of the Plains Indians. In 1875, a number of captured or surrendered Cheyenne, Kiowa, Arapaho, and Comanche warriors were interned at Fort Marion, Florida. Considered hostile, and held as hostages for the good behavior of their people, these warriors were placed in a strange environment, where they had a great deal of time on their hands. In order to provide them with an activity, and to help them earn extra money, an officer at the fort gave the warriors paper and drawing materials. They were encouraged to draw scenes of village life and other typical activities. A number of the ledger-drawing artists achieved some renown for their work; these include Howling Wolf and Buffalo Meat of the Cheyenne (fig. 162), and Etahdleuh Doanmoe and Zotom, both Kiowa.

Ledger drawings stand as a transitional form of art between the traditional hide paintings of aboriginal times and the easel paintings of the 1920s and 1930s. They were first encountered in the 1860s, when some Indians obtained account-ledger paper from traders or storekeepers for the purpose of drawing pictures. While it is possible that many ledger drawings produced near the turn of the century were intended for private or family use, most seem to have found their way into the hands of non-Indian purchasers. Certainly it is true that the ledger drawings produced by the Fort Marion prisoners were made for a non-Indian audience. In any case, the subject matter tends to focus upon domestic, hunting, and warfare scenes that glorify the old days. It is noteworthy that most of the artists put some kind of a signature on these works, even if only a symbol or sign for their names (see Petersen 1971).

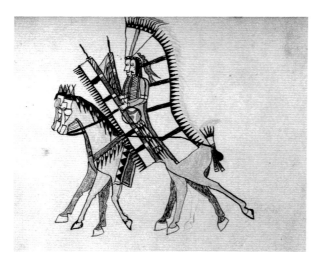

163. Two Young Cheyenne Warriors. *Making Medicine (1844 or 1851–1931), Cheyenne. Ca. 1875–1878, colored inks, colored pencil, lead pencil on paper, 6½ × 8¼ inches. Philbrook Art Center, Tulsa, anonymous loan.*

164. Buffalo Hunt. *Making Medicine, Cheyenne. Ca. 1875–1878, colored inks, colored pencil, lead pencil on paper, 6½ × 8¼ inches. Philbrook Art Center, Tulsa, anonymous loan.*

The Cheyenne artist Making Medicine was a fellow inmate of Buffalo Meat at the military prison of Fort Marion at St. Augustine, Florida. Following the unauthorized abandonment of the reservations by a hostile minority of Cheyenne, Arapaho, and Kiowa warriors in 1874, there arose a brief period of hostilities between the tribes and the U.S. government, known as the Red River war. By 1875, it had been quelled by U.S. cavalry forces. Under the pretense of purging native troublemakers from the tribes, seventy-two Indian men and one woman were accused of war crimes and incarcerated in the prison at Fort Marion for three years. In prison, a number of warriors came to produce picture books depicting their former lives, deportation to the East, and eventual pacification, as souvenirs for the Anglo visitors of the day. Though many of these drawings were little more than crude sketches, some of them were significant artworks. In figures 163 through 167, Making Medicine personally takes us from his former life in Indian Territory (Oklahoma), through the appearance of the U.S. military and the transportation overland, by train, of the warriors sentenced to prison, to their reeducation by whites in European skills and modes of behavior.

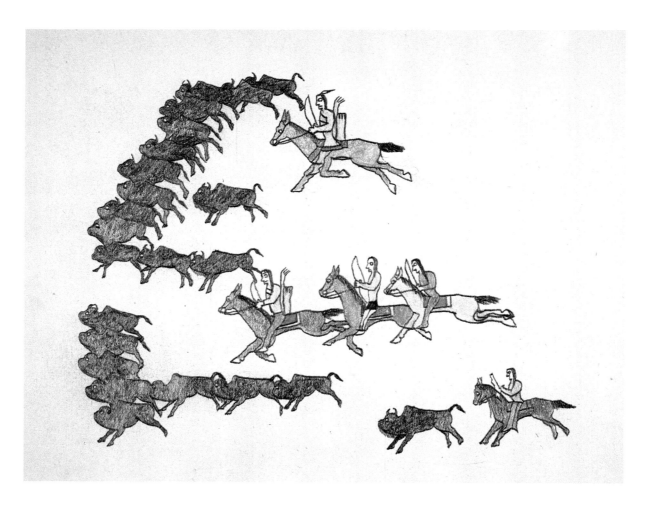

165. U.S. Cavalry. *Making Medicine, Cheyenne. Ca. 1875–1878, colored inks, colored pencil, lead pencil on paper, 6½ × 8¼ inches. Philbrook Art Center, Tulsa, anonymous loan.*

166. Train to Fort Marion. *Making Medicine, Cheyenne. Ca. 1875–1878, colored inks, colored pencil, lead pencil on paper, 6½ × 8¼ inches. Philbrook Art Center, Tulsa, anonymous loan.*

167. Indians Shingling Their Barracks. *Making Medicine, Cheyenne. Ca. 1875–1878, colored inks, colored pencil, lead pencil on paper, 6½ × 8¼ inches. Philbrook Art Center, Tulsa, anonymous loan.*

168. Kiowa Scalp Dance. *Stephen Mopope (1898–1974), Kiowa. 1946, watercolor on paper, 10⅞ × 15 inches. Philbrook Art Center, Tulsa, 46.45.6.*

The bisymmetry of this painting and its depth of perspective reflect the muralist tradition of which Mopope was a part.

169. Eagle Dance *(mural). Tonita Pena (Quah Ah, 1895–1949), San Ildefonso. 1934, oil on canvas, 70 × 120 inches. Private collection.*

170. Basket Dance *(mural). Romando Vigil (Tse-Ye-Mu, 1902–1978), San Ildefonso. Ca. 1934, oil on canvas, 56 × 111 inches. Private collection.*

In the 1930s, with the founding of WPA and CCC projects, a new social consciousness arose in America, led by a federal government that encouraged architectural and artistic movement toward celebration of the virtues of the common man. This was the major muralist period for both white and Indian artists. Commercial works adorned libraries, post offices, police stations, and public buildings. Plains artists such as Woodrow Crumbo, Archie Blackowl, and Stephen Mopope looked toward Euro-American models for their compositions, but the southwestern muralists, such as Tonita Pena and Romando Vigil, found their inspiration in ancient precedents from their own cultures, including the ceremonial kiva mural, which depicted processions of regal figures, dancers, and priests along with lush fertility symbols of the Southwest.—E. L. W. with Arthur Silberman.

Nonetheless, traditional or ethnic art of the reservation period was not the Indians' only sort of output. In addition to these objects, they developed white-influenced arts such as easel and mural paintings, which were individually produced and signed. What distinguishes these from ethnic art is that they were definitely generated by outside interest. As with the traditional or ethnic art, however, they were made to augment the incomes of reservation Indians, and again the buyer's main motivation was romantic and nostalgic.

Easel painting crystallized in the 1920s with Indian artists in the state of Oklahoma. Out of this movement came what are known as the original Kiowa Five—Spencer Asah, James Auchiah, Jack Hokeah, Stephen Mopope (fig. 168), and Monroe Tsatoke. In the period from 1917 to 1926, an Indian Service field matron, Susan Peters, had organized an arts club for young Kiowa students near Anadarko, Oklahoma. It seemed like the logical thing to do, since they were indifferent to their studies but liked to draw and sketch whenever they could. On the basis of the early evidence, it would appear that the young Kiowa artists were already conscious of art from their home environments.

In any case, around 1926 or 1928 these Kiowa were enrolled in special courses at the University of Oklahoma and came under the tutelage of Edith Mahier and Oscar B. Jacobson. The amount and kind of influence exerted on them by Mahier and Jacobson is the subject of much controversy, but it is clear that they were introduced to the elements of the American Art Deco style so popular in illustrative arts from 1920 to 1940 (see Brody 1971:120–126).

It would appear that the Kiowa Five developed a hybrid style, one that had some strong ties to the traditional forms of hide and ledger drawing, yet took a modern approach to expression. What emerged was a style of painting emphasizing flat colors, clear outlines, and sinuous curves, with a stress laid on line, which was used to separate discrete color areas. The subject matter of the painting, in the main, was nostalgic and traditional-minded in that it depicted scenes of dancing, warfare, buffalo hunting, horses, and so on. As J. J. Brody (1971:124–125) has noted, the painting of this

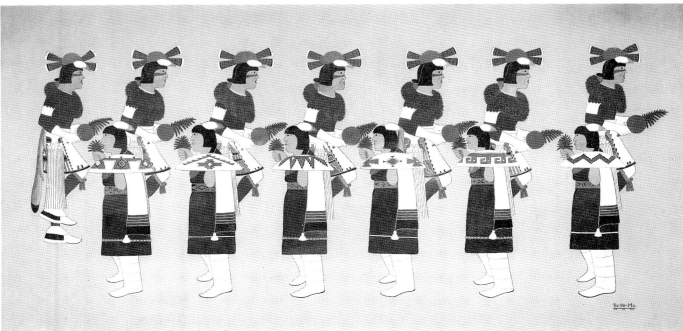

period is preeminently decorative, in the sense that it is design-conscious and often more emblematic than narrative. The Oklahoma style of painting influenced later developments in the Southwest, affecting the so-called Santa Fe Studio style that emerged in the 1930s.

In the post-World War I period in Santa Fe, several young Pueblo artists, most of them from San Ildefonso Pueblo, were encouraged to take up watercolor painting. The local intelligentsia—including John Sloan, Mary Austin, and Alice Corbin Henderson—offered encouragement to self-taught art-

171. Pollination of the Corn. *Waldo Mootzka (1903–1941), Hopi. Ca. 1940, watercolor and pen, 15 × 10 inches. Philbrook Art Center, Tulsa, anonymous loan.*

Mootzka provides an elegant refutation of the naïve notion that North American Indian artists were not aware of mainstream art styles and that American and European artists did not look to the compositions of talented Indian artists for inspiration. The complexity of impressionistic forms and the architectural concern for curvilinear leaves, flowers, and cloud pyramids in this painting speak of Art Deco. However, as Arthur Silberman has observed, the ultimate roots of these design forms extend back to the Puebloan traditions of kiva mural painting and sacred art.

172. Koshares of Taos. *Pablita Velarde (1918–   ), Santa Clara. 1947, watercolor on paper, 14⅛ × 22½ inches. Philbrook Art Center, Tulsa, 47.37.*

Pablita Velarde's distinctive, original style is compatible with the tradition of American folk painting. Her densely clustered figures, animals, fields, and architectural features are frozen in an instant between the pulsebeats of time. Their visual texture suggests the artist's quest to detail the life and attitudes of her people and community, filling her canvas with minute documentary data.

173. Night Chant Ceremonial Hunt. *Harrison Begay (1919–), Navajo. 1947, watercolor on paper, 20 × 30 inches. Philbrook Art Center, Tulsa, 47.40.*

This hunt scene is one of the most effective two-dimensional presentations of constrained dynamics in Native American painting. It is a masterful work of contrasts. The uniformity of the bounding gray deer is balanced by the marked individuality of the gaily colored horses and their riders. The fleeing prey, who hang surrealistically in an indeterminate space, are in stark opposition to the aggressive wedge of pursuing horsemen, who are placed firmly in a real ground.

174. Navajo Woman on Horseback. *Gerald Nailor (1917– 1952), Navajo. 1942, watercolor on paper, 14 × 12 inches. Philbrook Art Center, Tulsa, 42.9.30.*

Along with Oscar Howe and Fred Kabotie, Gerald Nailor is considered one of the masters of traditional Native American painting. He walked a dangerous line between too-thin prettiness and honest reverence for beauty, particularly as expressed in his representations of the female principle.

176. Navajo Woman Weaver. *Andrew Tsinahjinnie (1918–), Navajo. 1952, watercolor on paper, 39½ × 30 inches. Philbrook Art Center, Tulsa, 52.7.*

175. In the Days of Plenty. *Quincy Tahoma (1921–1956), Navajo. 1946, watercolor on paper, 36⅜ × 26⅝ inches. Philbrook Art Center, Tulsa, 46.19.*

This seminal work by Tahoma epitomized the white vision of the virile barbarian. Though original to Tahoma, the composition would influence generations of later artists, who would finally reduce it to a stereotype. The picture was intended as an encapsulation of idealized masculine Navajo life and as a vision of the proud and fierce hunter before his subjugation by the white man.

Tsinahjinnie's weaver ranks with Howe's *Victory Dance* (fig. 179) and Tahoma's *In the Days of Plenty* (fig. 175) as a pivotal work in the twentieth-century American Indian art movement. Tsinahjinnie's painting expresses a delicate female sensuality unknown in the work of other native artists. At his best, he captures a surrealistic fluidity of perception. His paintings are not of the real world, nor are they ethnographic documents, but rather distillations of emotion and movement.

ists such as Crescencio Martinez, Julian Martinez, Alfonso Roybal (also called Awa Tsireh), Abel Sanchez, Romando Vigil, Fred Kabotie, Otis Polelonema, and Velino (Shije) Herrera (also called Ma Pe Wi) (figs. 200, 201, 216, 217). At first their work was illusionistic, representational, and realistic in character. However, under the tutelage of their patrons, the artists were encouraged to turn to Pueblo designs for more abstract modes of decorative expression.

Between 1932 and 1937 Dorothy Dunn came to the Santa Fe Indian School and developed a systematic artistic approach with her young pupils. Like the local intelligentsia before her, Dunn was hopeful that her students would develop a style of painting that was unique and somehow Indian in character. Out of her five years of work came what is known as the Santa Fe Studio style of painting. It is very much like the Oklahoma style, utilizing flatly laid colors and an especially firm line in drawing. Notable Puebloan painters out of the Studio include José Rey Toledo, Joe H. Herrera, Ben Quintana, José Vicente Aguilar, Pablita Velarde (fig. 172), Vicente Mirabel, and Juan B. Medina. Navajo artists trained there include Harrison Begay (fig. 173), Stanley Mitchell, Gerald Nailor (fig. 174), Quincy Tahoma (fig. 175), and Andrew Tsinahjinnie (fig. 176). In sum, paintings in the

177. Cheyenne Sun Dance, First Painting of the Third Day. *Richard West (1912–), Cheyenne. 1949, watercolor on paper, 24½ × 35 inches. Philbrook Art Center, Tulsa, 49.20.*

West is considered one of the major exponents of the Oklahoma Plains tradition of painting. More than any other artist, he has been committed to exploring the ethnographically correct depiction in painting of history, costume, ceremony, material culture, and individual lifeways of Cheyenne society as it existed during the nineteenth century.

Oklahoma style and the Santa Fe Studio style have now become known as traditional Indian painting (Warner 1975:84–88).

It is fruitful to reiterate our initial point that the white-influenced art of the reservation period differs from traditional and ethnic art in that the white patrons played an active or directive role—as opposed to a merely facilitative one—in the development of this art. In this connection, it is also useful to point out that this patronage tended to be institutionalized rather than individualized in nature. As we have already seen, the Oklahoma style was fostered in large part, at least initially, by the University of Oklahoma, and the Santa Fe Studio style received its impetus within the confines of the Santa Fe Indian School. After these preliminary institutional forces had served their purpose, other institutions played a role in fostering and supporting easel art of a traditional Indian nature.

One of the institutions supportive of Oklahoma-style painting was Bacone College in Muskogee, Oklahoma. Indeed, Oscar Jacobson, who was the mentor of the Kiowa Five painters, taught Bacone's first art-department director, Acee Blue Eagle. The succession of teachers who have nurtured the talents of young artists following Blue Eagle include Woodrow Crumbo (fig. 202), Richard West (fig. 177), Chief Terry Saul, Gary Colbert, and Ruthe Jones.

Philbrook Art Center, in Tulsa, has also been a very important source of institutional patronage of traditional Indian painting. For many years, from just after World War II until 1979, the Philbrook Indian Art Annual was an exhibition of major significance. It became, in the words of Rennard

Strickland, "a major force in the dramatic evolution of the world of contemporary Indian painting" (Strickland 1980:9). Philbrook made it a policy to purchase some of the best paintings from the competition each year for its own collection, and the result is one of the finest and most representative aggregations of Indian painting in the world. At the beginning of its program, Philbrook was committed to the encouragement of what is termed "traditional" Indian art, but under pressure from such adventurous painters as Oscar Howe (fig. 179), the museum opened up its annual exhibitions to broader and more encompassing and experimental categories of art.

In conclusion, it is necessary to state that while the reservation period witnessed the production of a great quantity of Indian art (often of very high quality), this was achieved amid great anguish. Indians of the reservation period were a disfranchised people. They existed in a no-man's-land between the two worlds of aboriginal and Euro-American culture. They were a part of both, but wholly within neither. This marginality, coupled with the very real poverty of most Indian peoples, bred a sense of despair among many Native Americans. It is not surprising that this state of affairs was the setting for much social pathology both on and off the reservations. Going further, it is possible to say that Indian artists often felt this state of marginality with special acuteness. Wanting to be counted among their people, many artists were nonetheless singled out for special recognition by non-Indian art patrons, a situation which could cause great stress. It is known, for example, that Nampeyo was often criticized by her Hano neighbors for the income she received from her pottery and the tributes accorded her for the excellence of her wares (see Wade, chapter VI, this volume). While she sought to encourage other women of the pueblo to emulate her example and produce

178. Prairie Fire. Blackbear Bosin (1921–1980), Kiowa/ Comanche. 1953, watercolor on paper, 23 × 33³/₁₆ inches. Philbrook Art Center, Tulsa, 53.7.

Prairie Fire is probably the best-known American Indian watercolor in existence, and has been lauded as a succinct statement of the Santa Fe Studio style, combined with innovative personal expression. The immediate appeal of the work rests in the interaction of static, frozen, and dynamic elements. The antelope form an arched bridge of stylized movement, while the hunters flee before the approaching fire in a posture that is a reversal of the typical Indian hunt scene. Below them, the disdainful wolves provide a stable ground for the frenzy of the picture, suggesting the continuation of the world even in the face of imminent disaster.

179. Victory Dance. Oscar Howe (1915–1984), Yanktonai Sioux. 1954, watercolor on paper, 19½ × 12 inches. Philbrook Art Center, Tulsa, 54.6.

The importance of this work cannot be overstated. It opened an entirely new expressive avenue for visualizing emotion and energy, beyond the meticulously detailed, yet frozen anatomical realism of traditional Indian painting. In his cubistic approach, Howe masterfully captures the depth and personal significance of the visionary experience; here are expressed the confusion and glory of living between the seen and the unseen, as the dancer is transformed from the ordinary to the sublime.

pottery of their own, the difficulty of an artist's position in this period was keen. Within such a context, it is not hard to understand why some talented artists had difficulty with alcoholism and other personal troubles (fig. 197).

MODERN INDIVIDUALISTS

In the post-World War II era of modernist individualism, a condition of pluralism exists in American Indian arts. No one particular sort of individualism predominates exclusively. Instead, there are at least three different types prevalent in the modern Indian art world: modernist individualism that is a continuation of and elaboration upon reservation art traditions; modernist individualism that employs new forms of expression but retains Indian symbolism; and modernist individualism that is assimilated into mainstream Euro-American art.

Some Indian artists prefer to retain the community-oriented art traditions that were so pronounced in the reservation period. Traditionalist Indian painting, for instance, which still persists today, has large numbers of both practitioners and consumers. At the same time, many Indian individualists are emerging who retain reservation-art traditions, but are expanding and elaborating upon them. Nowhere is this seen to better advantage than in the field of contemporary Pueblo pottery. Stylistic innovation and ceaseless artistic change are the hallmarks of this continuing tradition. Some potters—Joseph Lonewolf, Tony Da (fig. 180), Grace Medicine Flower, and others— have begun to change their pottery shapes, designs, and decorations on a regular and even frequent basis. The search for innovation and change by such potters as Joseph Lonewolf has reached extraordinary proportions. One new technique is elaboration of the pot's surface with inlays of turquoise, *heshi*, and silver. Another is sgraffito—scratching through the slip on a pot to expose the color of the clay beneath. Occasionally a pot is fired by San Ildefonso and Santa Clara potters in ways intended to produce interesting color effects. These and many other decorative ideas are tumbling in, one upon the other, enabling potters to produce new artistic effects.

Strong evidence for the foregoing was provided by a 1974 exhibition at the Maxwell Museum of Anthropology at the University of New Mexico in Albuquerque, called *Seven Families in Pueblo Pottery*, for which an illustrated catalogue of the same title was published. The matriarchs (and their husbands) celebrated as the leading individualists of Puebloan pottery in the Southwest included Marie Z. Chino and Lucy Martin Lewis, Acoma; Nampeyo, Hopi/Hano; Lela and Van Gutierrez and Serafina and Geronimo Tafoya, Santa Clara; and Rose Gonzales and Maria and Julian Martinez, San Ildefonso. Each of these seven families is in reality a dynasty, following more or less in the tradition of its predecessors. It is a notable feature of these dynasties that traditional sex-role barriers are breaking down, so that men can now not only decorate pottery, but shape it as well (Maxwell 1974).

Patronage for contemporary Pueblo pottery has grown considerably since the 1960s. Those who command high prices for their work have incomes in the corporate executive range. This, of course, is a far cry from earlier reservation days, when potters depended upon a local trading post or a few storekeepers in nearby cities. Today, some major artists sell primarily from their homes directly to their customers, without a middleman. Others retail their work through Indian specialty art shops of good reputation or through galleries. The Santa Fe Indian Market, held the third weekend of August each year, is an important market for Pueblo pottery; artists operate their own stalls. Indeed, the days when Pueblo pottery was a tourist art fostered by the Fred Harvey Company or the Santa Fe–Atchison–Topeka Railroad are long gone.

Other Indian artists, however, are committed to modernist art in all its myriad forms. In particular, many younger Indian artists are going beyond reservation-art traditions in order to pursue careers that are organically connected to the modern art world. These younger artists see themselves as very much involved with art forms that transcend what they regard as the constraints of traditional Indian art. They are searching for new forms of expression, although their work continues to be Indian by virtue of its symbolism. The imagery they employ may or may not come from the tribe of their origin.

In commenting on a 1982 exhibition of contemporary North American Indian art—including the works of Phyllis Fife, Harry Fonseca, George C. Longfish, Jaune Quick-to-See Smith, Randy Lee White (figs. 228–230, 233, 234, 244, 249, 265), and others—Saulteaux artist Robert Houle said:

> While putting to use contemporary styles, techniques and modes, the artists in this exhibition are still very much involved in leaving visual documents of their personal heritage. Nowhere is this more evident than in the diversity of creative expression found in the show. One is treated with an expression full of secular, sensuous counterpoints and mystical, existential visions. Each artist is invariably and intimately involved in recording personal experiences determined by tribal culture. This leaves the artist to create works of art traditionally inspired, but expressed through modern concepts and techniques. To deny the legitimacy of this inspirational source would be like refusing the Renaissance its Greco-Roman heritage; and to treat the validity of this creative process with deliberate reserve is sanctimonious (Houle 1982:2).

One of the most important traits of modernist art is that it is ideologically explicit. An ideology is a doctrine used to justify a group's course of action in pursuing its own interests, and here we

180. Symbols of the Southwest. Tony Da (1940–   ), San Ildefonso. 1970, casein on paper, 19½ × 15 inches. Philbrook Art Center, Tulsa, anonymous loan.

The artistic prowess of the Martinez family of San Ildefonso continues to express itself in the most contemporary of Native American art circles. Tony Da, son of Popovi Da and grandson of Maria Martinez, has in his time been celebrated internationally as a ceramicist, designer, and painter. In this composition, Da explores ancient ceremonial beliefs and anthropomorphized forces of nature as depicted in Hopi, Navajo, and ancient Mimbres cultures, fusing them in a collage that speaks of the recycling of fertility and life. Those seen here are stylized Yei figures, a counterpart to the Pueblo Katcina.—E. L. W. with Arthur Silberman.

are dealing most commonly with an ideology that proclaims a sort of Indian nationalism. Quite obviously, there is a certain amount of palpable mythmaking here about the Indian past, and this time it is the Indians themselves who are creating it. This artistic mythology holds that the Indians of aboriginal times were intensely spiritual people who were attuned to nature and its rhythms, and were committed to peaceful and harmonious living with their neighbors. Such mythology is surely ideological in nature.

The converse side of this ideology declares that the Euro-Americans exemplify the opposite of these aboriginal Indian traits. Moreover, the ideology also holds that Euro-Americans have pursued evil policies with respect to Native Americans and that these practices demand a moral atonement.

Hence, the subject matter of modernist art often affirms Indian life in very positive ways and denounces middle-class American values in very negative ways. Specifically, contemporary Indian art of a modernist nature will sometimes express a sense of alienation on the part of the artist from the so-called American way of life, thus functioning as social criticism. These individuals also see themselves as proclaiming traditional Indian values. This point was expressed by Lloyd Kiva New, former director of the Institute of American Indian Arts (IAIA) in Santa Fe:

In recent years, through education, political cognizance, and the prestige of their art, Native Americans have acquired considerable strength as a people. Out of this has billowed a wave of neo-traditional revivalism and cultural nationalism that has permeated Indian society and has motivated many Indian groups to make vigorous efforts to retrieve what has been lost of their unique culture. In this context Indian art has become increasingly important as a tool by means of which to reaffirm cultural identity and to reinforce national pride (New 1980:5).

In a larger sense, Indians who are involved with modernist art have adapted themselves to the Euro-American conception of what an artist is. In the nineteenth century, European artists found themselves largely without the patronage of the nobility, the court, and the wealthy bourgeoisie. Instead, they were a part of an art marketplace where buyers and sellers interacted. No longer required to flatter the rich or the highborn, artists, in conjunction with other intellectuals, developed a special idea of their role in society. Intellectually, they saw themselves as solitary, isolated, alienated individuals who, in their existential splendor, were destined to denounce the world that exists and to point the way to worlds not yet created. In particular, this put them in a position to be critics of the middle class and to adopt the role of disfranchised commentators. Their official role was that of rebels and outsiders. Tom Wolfe describes this state of affairs in *The Painted Word*:

> What held the *cénacles* [artistic fraternities of the nineteenth century] together was that merry battle spirit we have all come to know and love: *épatez la bourgeoisie*, shock the middle class. With Gautier's *cénacle* especially . . . with Gautier's own red vests, black scarves, crazy hats, outrageous pronouncements, huge thirsts, and ravenous groin . . . the modern picture of The Artist began to form: the poor but free spirit, plebeian but aspiring only to be classless, to cut himself forever free from the bonds of the greedy and hypocritical bourgeoisie, to be whatever the fat burghers feared most, to cross the line wherever they drew it, to look at the world in a way they couldn't *see*, to be high, live low, stay young forever—in short, to be the bohemian (Wolfe 1976:14–15).

Translated into the language of the modern Indian artist, this means that he is alienated from American society and expresses his isolation by reaffirming a native identity. Indeed, it is even possible that the Indian might be used as a symbol of white alienation from all that is organic and natural. In the 1970s, for example, Fritz Scholder's paintings, and those of his followers, depicted Indian history and modern Indian life with bitter humor and sardonic images. Utilizing such modernist approaches as Abstract Expressionism and Pop Art, Scholder and a host of other painters delivered moral homilies about Indians to bourgeois white consumers (fig. 212). The Indian artist of modernist, individualist convictions considers himself not so much existentially alone as part of an old and oppressed ethnic community. In New's words:

> Perhaps the most profound effect on Indian art lay in its change from being essentially a tribally oriented expression serving tribal needs to being essentially an individually oriented expression serving individual needs. Included among the many consequences bred of this change was the rise of the star system within which the work of name artists was keenly sought after by collectors, a phenomenon most uncommon to Indian tradition within which art was integrated into the overall social order and unfolded at a gradual pace within tribal containment. Thus the Indian artist came to perceive of himself and his world in new dimensions which gave leeway for novel and experimental expressions. The Indian artist's concept of art was further altered by the introduction into his world of the technology and materials of the white man. The various directions which the Indian artist pursued were defined to a significant degree around the turn of this century by a belated public acceptance of Indian artwork—as art, rather than merely as anthropological artifacts or tourist curios.

181. His Hair Flows like a River. *T. C. Cannon (1946–1978), Caddo. 1970s, color woodblock print, 20½ × 15¾ inches. Philbrook Art Center, Tulsa, 81.7.*

Cannon has been lauded, along with Fritz Scholder, as a profoundly influential force affecting contemporary American Indian painting. Rising above the polemical concerns of 1960s "Indian message art," Cannon wedded a wry, satiric vision to the Op and Pop of mainstream art.

This served to give Indian art a *bona fide* place within the hierarchy of the universal world of art and propelled it into the stream of American commerce (New 1980:5).

There is no question that the Institute of American Indian Arts in Santa Fe was a major force in legitimizing the new modernist art for Indians. Established in 1962, the IAIA sought to dispel the notion among young would-be artists that traditionalist painting was the only legitimate Indian two-dimensional art form. Featuring teachers like Fritz Scholder, who produced students like Kevin Red Star and Earl Biss, the IAIA became the mecca for the so-called new Indian art. The establishment of the IAIA was preceded by a Rockefeller Fund–sponsored conference held in the late 1950s at the University of Arizona at Tucson, where an assessment was made of the state of Indian art. The consensus of that conference was that traditionalist art was "moribund," and "new directions" were required in the field. The IAIA has been a source of controversy throughout its existence, since there are many persons, both Indian and non-Indian, who cannot accept the ideology and the modern-art forms of the new Indian art. Nevertheless, during the heyday of its influence in the 1960s and 1970s, the IAIA stimulated much thought and artistic production. In the 1980s, it is quite possible that the singular influence the IAIA has exerted through its patronage will be diluted as other educational institutions seek to offer themselves as educators of young Indian artists.

It is significant that the current social milieu for the reception of modernist art also differs somewhat from previous conditions. Consumers of the new Indian art tend to be individuals who possess a more liberal political and artistic temperament than the devotees of the more traditional arts. They purchase these works from established art galleries in urban centers, replete with the hoopla of openings, receptions, and art notices in the newspapers. During the 1960s, the Scottsdale national annual exhibition and sale in Arizona played a prominent role in introducing these innovative artworks to the sometimes doubtful buyers of Indian art, but now many art museums assume the challenge of exhibiting the works of these artists (both in solo and in group shows) before a new art public.

An important legitimizing function for this new art is performed by art critics who comment on the respective virtues of individual artists. Increasingly, the analysis of the new Indian art is being taken out of the hands of anthropologists and aficionados, and coming to rest in the hands of various sorts of art critics, who are introducing new canons of art judgment. Indeed, the provocative interpretation of J. J. Brody (1971) in his groundbreaking study, *Indian Painters & White Patrons*, can now be understood as one of the first steps toward this new sort of art criticism. In Brody's case, it is clear that his specific agenda was to validate and promote the new Indian painting coming out of the IAIA with the argument that the older, traditional painting was insipid, artificial, tourist oriented, and the product of a demeaning paternalism. Critical value judgments like these, however couched in analytical terms, were a novel development for the normally placid field of Indian art scholarship. Since Brody's book, they have become more commonplace.

Finally, there is a third force among Native American artists today, and that is the lure of individualism itself. Individualist Indian art pursues a uniquely personal approach, with no necessarily discernible Indian symbolism. It is an assimilated art that is as much a part of the Euro-American art world as anything produced by a non-Indian artist. Using a cosmopolitan approach, this art speaks to the world at large (fig. 181).

Herein we encounter an interesting question. It is clear to most observers that there is a very special art market available to artists whose work is identifiably Indian. In other words, many art products are purchased in the Indian art market because they are Indian in origin. Indian artists, therefore, are sheltered in certain ways from the ordinary standards and criteria of the cosmopolitan Euro-American art world. Will Indian art and Indian individuals continue to need such a special art market for survival? That is a crucial issue. Does Indian art benefit or suffer from its special status in the art marketplace? That is another important question. Perhaps the examination of these issues awaits the scholar who possesses the sociological imagination necessary to grasp the interplay between the Indian and non-Indian worlds.

Washoe Innovators and Their Patrons

MARVIN COHODAS

Washoe fancy basketry is a twentieth-century "art of acculturation" (Graburn 1969:475; 1976:5), owing little to traditional techniques, forms, or designs as they appear to have existed in the nineteenth century.[1] Promoted by collectors and dealers of Indian curios, it evolved rapidly to meet the demands of the marketplace. The evolution of this new Washoe style was dependent on the widespread imitation of a small number of innovative and commercially successful artists, among them Louisa Keyser (Dat So La Lee), Sarah Mayo, Maggie James, Tootsie Dick, and Lena Dick.

The contributions of these and other Washoe artists were obscured until recently. Among them, only Louisa Keyser was well known, but even she was often credited erroneously with the work of others, and at the same time denied credit for true innovations of her own. Art-historical research has allowed the identification of several other Washoe weavers, and has led to a greater understanding of their contributions to the development of the Washoe basketry style.

Accomplishing this goal has involved the study of over one hundred public and private collections of Washoe baskets. Documentation of date and weaver was compiled and museum and library archives were searched for photographs and other forms of supporting information. Local collectors and descendants of the Washoe weavers were interviewed in order to identify the photographs gathered, to learn as much as possible about the lives and careers of the weavers, and to determine the circumstances in which fancy baskets were woven and collected during the Washoe basketry florescence (1895–1935). As in other media, the styles of the greatest basketry artists were so distinctive that many undocumented pieces could be attributed to them, thus enlarging the corpus of their particular contributions for study. Copies of representative baskets were woven by this researcher in an effort to further understand a weaver's individual approach to basketry design. The results of these investigations are presented in a catalogue of Washoe coiled basket-weaving (Cohodas 1979b), a more comprehensive survey of Washoe basketry types and history (Cohodas 1983), and a series of articles on specific Washoe weavers (Cohodas 1976; 1979a; 1981; 1982; 1984).

Here, the contributions of the five major weavers mentioned above to the development of Washoe basketry art are related to the social and economic context in which they worked. From this context, it can be seen that differences in basketry style often reflect differences in life-style and patronage.

LOUISA KEYSER (DAT SO LA LEE)

That Louisa Keyser (fig. 182) was the most innovative and influential of the Washoe weavers is due in part to her unique patronage relationship with Abe Cohn, owner of the Emporium Company, a men's clothing store in Carson City, Nevada (fig. 183). For three decades, from 1895[2] until her death in 1925, Cohn provided Louisa Keyser and her husband Charlie with food, clothing, and medical care. He even built them a tiny house next to his own residence. In return, Louisa owed Cohn all the products of her labor, and she was expected to weave in public to attract the attention of customers. In thus exchanging independence and respect for economic security and paternalistic

182. Louisa Keyser (ca. 1850–1925) weaving *degikup* L.K. 81 in 1921–1922. The weaver lived with her patron, Abe Cohn (1859–1934), owner of the Emporium Company, a clothing store in Carson City, Nevada, and spent summers at his branch curio shop, the Bicose, on Lake Tahoe. Although separated from Washoe society, she was put on display for tourists as a symbol of the Washoe tribe.—M. C.

183. Abe Cohn stands outside his Emporium Company in 1924, proudly displaying Louisa Keyser's *degikup* L.K. 96 and 43. Although Cohn's first wife, Amy, was more responsible than he was for inspiring the Washoe curio trade, patronizing Louisa Keyser, and documenting the

baskets, he took credit. No photograph of Amy Cohn has yet come to light.—M. C.

184. The Cohn Emporium and its branch store on Lake Tahoe remained the only major retail outlets for Washoe basket-weaving during the period of major artistic activity, from 1895 to 1935. In this early photograph of the Emporium basketry display, ca. 1900, Louisa Keyser's *degikup* are exhibited in the center, surrounded by baskets of other Washoe weavers and other tribes. Louisa Keyser's twine-covered whiskey flasks hang on the wall above.—M. C.

protection, Louisa participated in a feudal relationship similar to those entered into by most Washoe after Anglo settlers deprived them of their territory and traditional subsistence (Downs 1966:86–88).

Although Abe Cohn took credit for the patronage of Louisa Keyser and the marketing of Washoe basketry in general, it appears to have been his first wife, Amy,[3] who expressed the initial interest in Indian culture and began investing in Washoe basketry. Under Amy's influence, the clothing store that Abe had inherited from his father was gradually transformed into a curio shop. In the late 1890s, a corner was set aside for Indian artifacts, including basketry of the Washoe and other tribes (fig. 184). The Cohns bought used utilitarian baskets from Washoe women, who had replaced them with manufactured utensils. Once divested of these wares, many Washoe women began weaving baskets specifically for sale in the Emporium. By hiring Louisa Keyser, the Cohns were able to ensure a steady supply of high-quality baskets for sale. Amy numbered and recorded all baskets the Cohns acquired, noting the name of the weaver and the date of acquisition, and she issued a certificate of documentation to the purchaser of each. Louisa Keyser's baskets were considered special: Amy recorded them in a separate ledger with its own numbering system.

185. A Washoe woman holds a storage basket which, since it was woven for home use, displays a more traditional approach to design than contemporary baskets woven for sale as curios.—M. C.

186. While Louisa Keyser was synthesizing her fancy *degikup* style, other weavers elaborated the traditional Washoe cooking and storage basket by refining the shape and stitching technique as well as creating more elaborate motifs. This basket displays the interest in negative space within motifs that developed around 1900.—M. C.

Primarily through Amy's diligence, the Cohns greatly expanded their trade in Indian curios. A brief attempt was made to open an outlet in Pasadena, where Grace Nicholson had stimulated interest in Native American basket-weaving (Nicholson seems to have greatly resented this competition). A more successful endeavor was the Cohns' summer shop at Lake Tahoe, the Bicose, located at Tahoe City, near the great Tahoe Tavern resort. The Cohns operated out of the Bicose from June to September of each year, bringing not only their baskets but also their star attraction, Louisa Keyser. Since the location gave the Cohns access to an upper-class clientele, drawn from throughout California, the Bicose probably accounted for the majority of their basketry sales.

Amy Cohn died in the winter of 1919, shortly after returning with Abe and Louisa from the St. Louis Exposition of Industrial Arts and Crafts. Cohn's second wife, Margaret, was less interested in the basketry business, so Abe was left to take over the promotional activity. In 1922, he had a film made of Louisa gathering and preparing her materials, as well as demonstrating her weaving techniques.[4] Drawn by the fame of the Emporium, Edward Curtis visited Cohn in 1925, shortly before Louisa's death. In volume 15 of his monumental study, *The North American Indian*, Curtis (1926:facing pages 96, 152, 154, 156) published a portrait of Louisa and photographs of her work. Cohn's business was still expanding in the late 1920s, when he moved his store to a new location, renaming it the Kit Carson Curio Store and decorating it with a huge mural of Louisa Keyser. By Cohn's death in 1934, however, the curio trade was beginning to decline. Margaret operated the business half-heartedly until 1937, then disposed of the remaining inventory in 1944 and 1945.

Through their marketing of Washoe basketry, the Cohns provided the economic stimulus for the transformation of traditional Washoe basket-weaving into a fancy curio style. Whether due to the harsh nature of the Great Basin environment, which made even basic subsistence a constant struggle, or to the degradation of the culture when non-Indian settlers overran Washoe lands, Washoe basket-weaving in the late nineteenth century was simple in both technique and design[5] (fig. 185). While used specimens of such traditional basketry were valuable to anthropologically minded collectors, these crude wares could not compete in the curio market with the sophisticated artistry of Californian basket-weaving. For the Washoe, commercial success demanded a new approach.

The Cohns' patronage of Louisa Keyser catalyzed the creation of such a new curio style. Secure from economic necessity, Louisa could devote a vastly increased amount of time to perfecting her art. Living with the Cohns, and isolated from prolonged contact with other Washoe, Louisa had the freedom[6] and encouragement to break with Washoe weaving tradition. More important, she was also exposed to the baskets of Californian tribes, which were on sale at the Emporium. Between 1895 and 1898, the early years of her relationship with the Cohns, Louisa transformed Washoe weaving by imitating the shape, motifs, and design arrangements of the commercially popular Pomo gift baskets. To these foreign traits Louisa herself contributed a larger scale, fine stitching, and a color scheme based on the contrasting colors of black (mud-dyed bracken-fern root, a traditional Washoe decorative material) and red (redbud branch, a Californian material used by the Miwok and Maidu). Her result was the *degikup* (fig. 183), a fabric sculpture without utilitarian function and without precedent in traditional Washoe basket-weaving (Cohodas 1982:129–132).

Other Washoe women imitated Louisa's elaborate and expansive two-color designs, applying them not only to the traditional coiled-basket shapes—truncated cones used for storing, cooking, and serving food (fig. 186)—but also to Louisa's newly invented *degikup*. This widespread adoption of Louisa's innovative shape, color scheme, and designs led to an explosion of experimentation. Inspired by Louisa's example, other weavers looked to foreign ideas and to their own creativity to evolve highly individualized styles. The Cohns provided the economic incentive, buying all worthwhile baskets for resale at the Emporium and Bicose. Eventually, many weavers found other outlets. Some acquired their own patrons among the businessmen of Carson City or the ranchers of Carson Valley. Most sold baskets to tourists at the hotels and steamer landings on the shore of Lake Tahoe, especially at Tallac, their traditional camping grounds. The fancy style of Washoe basketry spawned by the partnership of Louisa Keyser and the Cohns was fully established as a high-quality and economically viable curio ware by 1910.

Although she originated the Washoe fancy-basketry style, Louisa pursued a separate course of development in her basketry art. The high aesthetic standards that developed in the initial phase of enthusiastic experimentation soon declined under influence of the marketplace. For most weavers, real artistic achievement was of little economic value. Baskets could be made more quickly with simpler techniques and designs, and yet sell as well as a true work of basketry art. (Even today, the size and condition of a basket affect its price more than does its artistic value.) Although Louisa also wove many simple curio pieces for the Cohns, patronage helped insulate her from the degrading effects of commercialism. The Cohns' complete economic support and appreciation of her talent gave her the time and encouragement to pursue more aesthetic goals. While other Washoe weavers adopted ever bolder and more flamboyant designs to compete for the attention of tourists, Louisa retained a reserved approach of elegant simplicity, with which she created effects of profound visual poetry. While many weavers came to ignore the integration of design with basket shape, Louisa continued to grapple with this difficult artistic problem. Perhaps her greatest achievement was the creation of an illusionistic perspective in which the exaggerated curve of the design mirrors the basket profile (Cohodas 1979b:28), locking the basket and its design into an indivisible organic unity (fig. 131).

Although a source of great delight to the Cohns, the remarkable aesthetic quality of Louisa Keyser's major works made them practically unmarketable. Her application of profound artistic sophistication to a medium traditionally relegated to the category of craft created a paradox. While the Cohns refused to sell her masterpieces at craft prices, the public balked at paying fine-art prices for works of Indian basket-weaving. G. A. Steiner proved the exception when, in 1914, he purchased one of Louisa's finest *degikup*. The Cohns reported to the newspapers that he had paid nearly $2,000 for the single piece, although he actually paid only $1,400: the remainder had gone to the purchase of over sixty additional Washoe baskets. While this publicity did enable the Cohns to obtain more money for Louisa's baskets—up to $600 for a *degikup* sold in 1917—it did not greatly increase the rate at which they were sold. In 1915–1916, Cohn appealed to Steiner to purchase additional baskets, valuing them at around $2,000 each, but offering them at a forty percent discount. Abe wanted the money to build a museum to house his collection of Louisa Keyser's baskets, for which he had already purchased property adjoining his home. Although he even offered to name this museum the "Steiner Museum of Basketry Art," Steiner declined to make the purchases, and the project was never undertaken.[7] At Cohn's death in 1934, three-quarters of Louisa's major works remained unsold. Their marketability declined further, to the point where, a decade later, Margaret was anxious to dispose of the collection completely, even at ridiculously low prices. She did not even reach her goal of $5,000 for the huge inventory. In 1945, she sold the last twenty major *degikup* to the state of Nevada for only $1,500, or $75 each!

While Louisa's masterpieces were rarely purchased, they nevertheless formed the basis for the commercial success of the Emporium, and thereby of Washoe fancy-basketry development. In 1899, Amy supplied photographs and information on Louisa and her work for publication in the famous texts on Native American basketry by both James (1903) and Mason (1904). From then on, Amy worked tirelessly to promote Louisa and Washoe basketry, giving lectures, writing articles, and publishing advertising pamphlets.

In order to appeal to the customer's taste for "authenticity" in Indian curios, Amy had to invent most of what she wrote. Over the years, she wove an increasingly tangled web of falsification to create an artificial mystique around Louisa Keyser's basket-weaving. Although the *degikup* is based on a Californian basketry shape and has no precedent in Washoe material culture, and thus no indigenous function, Amy claimed that it was a traditional mortuary basket, and even published a fictitious description of its use in a burial ceremony. In order to explain the absence of the *degikup* before Louisa began weaving them in 1896, Amy claimed that the Paiute had prohibited Washoe women from weaving this form,[8] and that Louisa had only resumed its manufacture when she could depend on Cohn's protection from Paiute reprisals. Finally, to explain why no other Washoe women wove *degikup* until after 1900, Amy claimed that Louisa was a Washoe princess who alone had inherited the sacred right to weave a ceremonial basket.

Amy also satisfied the buyer's appetite for symbolism in Indian designs. Since the motifs introduced by Louisa and other Washoe weavers were not native, they could have no symbolic meaning to the Washoe. Amy had to invent a symbolic meaning for each motif. She developed an iconographic vocabulary according to which she created an interpretation for the design on each of Louisa's baskets, applying this vocabulary to the baskets of other Washoe weavers and even other tribes. Claiming that the baskets recorded traditional Washoe legends, history, and life-style, Amy tried to tailor her interpretations to fit the romanticized ideal of Washoe culture in precontact times (Cohodas 1982:126–127). What the customer actually purchased was thus equally the creation of the Washoe woman who wove the basket, and of Amy Cohn, who invented its context.

In her permanent attachment to the Emporium, Louisa Keyser was sufficiently separated from the reality of early-twentieth-century Washoe life to be transformed by the Cohns into a symbol of the Washoe tribe, personifying the two contrasting Anglo views of Native Americans embodied in the term "Noble Savage." On the one hand, Amy pretended that Louisa had been born in precontact times, and was thus free of contamination by white culture. Louisa was even supposed to have met John Charles Frémont, the first white explorer fully to record his passage through Washoe territory. Louisa's supposed cultural purity was elevated to a sacred status by Emporium propaganda, which called her a princess and the daughter of a Washoe chief, both of which positions were unknown in traditional Washoe society, since it lacked inherited status differentiation. On the other hand, Louisa was expected to fit the negative stereotype of the Native American as savage, mentally inferior, and lacking the rational constraints of civilization. In this respect the propaganda was less sophisticated. Abe Cohn frequently reported stories to the newspapers that portrayed Louisa as vain, willful, petulant, childish, devoid of common sense, and unable to control her emotions—a caricature of the negative traits that men often attribute to women. Imputations of mental immaturity or inferiority were and still are commonly used to justify lower status in society, whether it is directed toward nonwhites or women, and Louisa was subject to the stereotype on both counts.

On public display as a symbol of the Washoe tribe, Louisa was also vulnerable to the antipathy felt for Native Americans. Her weight, not unusual for Washoe women, provoked constant ridicule. Although her original Washoe name was Dabuda, and she preferred to use her English name, the Cohns publicized her entirely under the name Dat So La Lee, which means "big hips." When she requested that the Cohns buy her a corset, it was probably to make herself more acceptable to the Anglo society in which she now lived. But the idea of a fat Indian woman wearing a corset was both ludicrous to the Anglos and compatible with their preconception of the Indian's mental inferiority. The gregarious Abe Cohn, who loved to regale Emporium visitors with stories about Louisa, never tired of claiming that she had been angry with him because the corset did not transform her into the slender woman of the advertisement. Louisa and other Washoe women wove the baskets, and Amy created the artificially "authentic" context to market them. But Abe Cohn, the only male in this triangle, not only took credit for the success of the Emporium, but also determined the public attitude toward Louisa and her work. It was possible for Cohn to admire the intelligence and artistry of Louisa's weaving, yet ridicule her personality and appearance, both because an Indian could be noble as well as savage, and because a person could be an artist as well as a woman.

The image that the Cohns created for Louisa Keyser and her art was so attuned to white preconceptions of Native Americans that it still persists, repeated from time to time in newspaper and magazine articles, occasionally with fresh embroidery. The suggestion of poetic symbolism in her designs still fires the imagination of owners and dealers. Louisa's image has become larger than life, due primarily to the focus of Emporium promotion on a single individual as the symbol of a whole culture. Other artists have faded from memory, so that any fine Washoe basket might be attributed to Louisa, even by other Washoe weavers. Louisa left no descendants, and she was not a princess, but today the ability to trace descent from Charlie Keyser by one of his previous marriages is often used to claim special status within the tribe. Although some of these descendants rightly criticize the Cohns for exploiting Louisa, they owe their claims to status not only to the great Washoe artist, but also to the patrons who recognized and supported her talent, and carved for her a niche in history.

Notwithstanding Louisa Keyser's enormous artistic talent, it is clear that without the patronage and promotion of the Cohns, Washoe basket-weaving would have taken quite a different course.

The Cohns provided the support and encouragement necessary for Louisa to transform Washoe basketry and pursue her aesthetic goals, but they also created a false context for the baskets and forced Louisa into a negative stereotype of the Native American. While Amy carefully recorded the date of each of Louisa's baskets in her ledger, she also hid the truth of Louisa's life and distorted the nature of Louisa's contribution to the development of the Washoe art style. The only facts that remain are Louisa Keyser's baskets, incontrovertible testimony to the unique creative genius and sensitivity of this Native American artist.

SARAH JIM MAYO

In contrast to Louisa Keyser, Sarah Mayo (fig. 187) lived within the Washoe cultural context. Her yearly round followed the transhumant pattern of most Carson Valley Washoe during the period of basketry florescence, a pattern derived from earlier subsistence techniques, but modified by lessened availability of traditional resources (Cohodas 1979b:12). In late spring and early summer, the Washoe camped on the south shore of Lake Tahoe, near Tallac, to take advantage of the tourist presence, now that fishing rights had been denied. Like other Washoe women, Sarah performed domestic chores and sold her baskets to tourists. In winter, the Washoe returned to Carson Valley. Since the land had been carved into private ranches, they camped with permission of particular ranchers, from whom they received employment, protection, and assistance. Like other Washoe women, Sarah worked in the ranch houses as a domestic, and sold or bartered her baskets to the ranchers' wives.

While Sarah's life followed the standard pattern for Washoe women, her relationship with one women approaches patronage. Margaretta (Maggie) Dressler, whose husband, William, owned one of the largest Carson Valley ranches, acquired a large collection of Indian baskets. When Margaretta attempted to document the baskets several years later, she remembered obtaining most of them from Sarah Mayo, although few have proven to be her work (Cohodas 1979b:41–42). The special relationship of the two women is further revealed in the many photographs that Margaretta took of Sarah and her baskets (Cohodas 1979b:47). By contrast, Margaretta did not photograph either Maggie James or Tillie Snooks, whose baskets in fact made up the bulk of her collection.

Sarah also claimed a special status within Washoe society. In the late nineteenth century, Washoe men who emerged as spokesmen in dealing with the whites were called captains, after railroad-crew leaders (Downs 1966:90–92). Sarah's father was Captain Jim, the most influential nineteenth-century Carson Valley captain. Captain Jim's reputation as a tribal chief, however, reflected in his nickname "King James I" (Downs 1966:90), was a creation of Anglos, who preferred to deal with a single tribal representative, and was not accepted by the Washoe. Nevertheless, due to Captain Jim's still considerable prestige, the husbands of his two daughters, Sarah and Agnes, both came to be called Captain in the early twentieth century. In 1918, after the death of her husband, Captain Pete Mayo, Sarah took her father's name, preferring the higher status it conferred (Cohodas 1979b:47).

In 1914, Captain Pete Mayo led a delegation to Washington, D.C., to argue land claims before the federal government (Nevers 1976:72–73). Sarah wove a special basket for presentation to Woodrow Wilson on this occasion. Although the present location of this basket is not known (d'Azevedo and Kavanagh 1974), it may be studied through the many photographs taken of it by Margaretta Dressler. The unique design (fig. 187) features a long inscription, which Margaretta wrote out for Sarah. Perhaps the idea of weaving such an inscription on a presentation basket was also in part Margaretta's.

Sarah intended this basket to represent a historic communication between herself and the President, as representatives of their two cultures. In the inscription, she identifies herself as the daughter of

187. Sarah Jim Mayo (ca. 1860–1945) holds the basket she finished in 1913 for presentation to President Woodrow Wilson. Margaretta Dressler took this photograph of Sarah with her sister, Agnes Jim Pete. Their status as daughters of the renowned Captain Jim allowed their husbands, Pete and Pete Mayo (also shown), to claim the status of captains as well. The pictorial design on the basket includes a rare self-portrait by a Native American woman. —M. C.

Captain Jim, making no mention of her husband, who actually presented the basket. The full inscription reads:

> Nevada and California
> Sarah, I am his daughter
> Captain James, First chief of Washoe tribe
> This basket is a special curio, 1913

Instead of the subservience and loyal devotion that Native Americans were expected to demonstrate to white patrons and officials, Sarah's inscription is full of pride and independence, and represents a demand for fair treatment. Sarah's relationship with Margaretta Dressler, as well as her descent from Captain Jim, seems to have encouraged her proud demand for respect. Unlike Cohn, who both admired and ridiculed Louisa Keyser, Margaretta Dressler treated Sarah much as an equal. Sarah's claims to superior status within the egalitarian Washoe tribe, however, were met with resistance and ostracism: it is said that other women avoided her and considered her a witch.

The design on Sarah's presentation basket also includes pictorial imagery. Representations of eagles clutching crossed arrows, an approximation of the presidential seal, alternate with portraits of the two persons identified in the inscription, Sarah and Captain Jim. Although the Wilson basket is the earliest documented example, stylistic analysis has suggested that Sarah Mayo introduced pictorial designs to Washoe basketry between 1905 and 1910 (Cohodas 1981:53).

Sarah's pictorial baskets represent an approach that was not only entirely new to Washoe art, but was also the antithesis of Louisa Keyser's style. Louisa Keyser employed repetition of small, simple motifs to expand the design and control more of the basket surface. By contrast, Sarah introduced complex, large-scale motifs that reach the full height of the design field, and that usually alternate in an *a b a b* pattern (fig. 188). While Louisa Keyser preferred delicate, lightweight motifs repeated in contrasting colors, Sarah Mayo's images are bold, massive forms combining colors for greater richness, solidity, and depth. In fact, to Louisa's two-color innovation, Sarah added a third color: the brown of undyed bracken-fern root. Sarah even experimented with willow dyed pink, yellow, green, and gray. While Louisa remained conservative in her vocabulary of motifs, in order to concentrate on subtle problems of composition, Sarah continually expanded her repertoire of pictorial images, and even combined them in illusionistic settings and with narrative action. Finally, while Louisa emphasized fine stitching, but created patterns that were simple to plan and weave, Sarah ignored refinement of technique but attempted designs of staggering difficulty. These include not only the spiraling inscription on the Wilson basket,[9] but also asymmetric trees with hanging leaves that overlap branches. Louisa's art is profound, poetic, and reserved; Sarah's is powerful, dramatic, and active. The proud, ambitious, and defiant personality of Sarah Mayo seems directly reflected in her artistic innovations.

Sarah's innovations influenced the course of Washoe fancy basket-weaving as profoundly as had Louisa Keyser's. Between 1910 and 1925, virtually every major Washoe weaver imitated Sarah's pictorial imagery, powerful color combinations, and alternation of large-scale designs (Cohodas 1981). The same traits were simultaneously adopted by the Mono Lake Paiute and Yosemite Miwok weavers to the south, a proliferation of pictorialism that may have been due in part to the preferences of curio buyers. However, Sarah's dynamic and asymmetric images came to be delineated in a much more static and decorative fashion by other weavers.

As with Louisa Keyser, Sarah Mayo's most sophisticated design achievements were too personal to be imitated. While Louisa explored the sculptural form of the *degikup* as an abstract medium of aesthetic expression, Sarah used color, overlapping, and juxtaposition to give an illusion of depth. On the Wilson basket, Captain Jim stands on a flat ground line, while Sarah is shown on a hill; on other baskets, the figures might be positioned next to houses or under trees. This semblance of reality is most developed in narrative interaction between figures, as when a woman leads her horse by its reins, or reaches her arms toward a child (Cohodas 1981).

Sarah's baskets were not consistently innovative and few abstracted reality or events so deftly. Like most self-supporting weavers, Sarah produced many works that did not confront artistic problems, but whose boldness made a favorable impact on their purchasers. Nevertheless, Sarah stands out from other Washoe weavers for her experimentation with color, her introduction of a completely new mode of design to Washoe weaving, and her sophisticated exploration of illusionism in basketry design. Such bold innovation must depend at least in part on her proud claim to high status within the tribe, and her relationship with a patron who treated her with unusual interest and respect.

MAGGIE MAYO JAMES

The art and career of Maggie James (fig. 189) followed a more standard pattern for Washoe weavers during the full flowering of the fancy basketry style. Although she was the daughter of Sarah's husband, Captain Pete Mayo, she claimed no special tribal status, and she developed no close

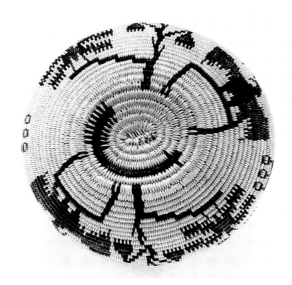

188. Basket. Sarah Mayo, Washoe. Ca. 1910, willow, red-bud, dyed and undyed bracken fern root, 3½ × 5½ inches in diameter. Philbrook Art Center, Tulsa, Elizabeth Cole Butler Collection, L82.1.543.

Sarah's innovative use of alternating, large-scale pictorial designs and integrated color schemes was imitated by most other Washoe weavers between 1915 and 1925.—M. C.

relationship with a patron. Maggie dedicated herself instead to commercial basket-weaving. Her success is seen in the large number of her baskets bought by tourists such as Mrs. George Pope and Grace Blair de Pue, during their annual visits to Lake Tahoe, and by Margaretta Dressler as well. Like Louisa and Sarah, Maggie was an innovator, imitating Pomo basketry in her experimentation with oblong shapes and feather decorations. Maggie's uniqueness lies in part in the extreme range of quality visible in her work (Cohodas 1979b:53), which runs from crude, small, and simple tourist pieces, to larger, more elaborate and refined works that, at up to forty stitches per inch, surpass those of all other Washoe weavers in technical achievement (fig. 132).

With few documented baskets, it is difficult to assess Maggie's influence on the development of Washoe style. By the 1920s, Washoe weaving had become more homogeneous, based on Sarah's innovations of alternating, massive, large-scale designs, use of additional colors, and incorporation of pictorial imagery, but made more lightweight and decorative to suit commercial taste. Since Maggie appears to have been among the first weavers to adopt and transform Sarah's innovations, and to have created the finest pieces in the derivative approach, it is likely that she bore the major responsibility for the creation and development of this decorative style. Maggie was also significant in popularizing the more quickly made one-rod *degikup* which, since it brought greater monetary return in proportion to the time expended in weaving, gradually replaced the finer three-rod technique.

In general, the style of Maggie James is distinguished by her personal taste and artistry (Cohodas 1979b:55). Maggie's designs are bold and dynamic, frequently arranged in diagonals to emphasize a dramatically tapering *degikup* shape. While Maggie may have led the way in commercializing Washoe basket-weaving, producing many simple curio baskets for quick sale, she was nevertheless one of the few weavers active during the decline of three-rod *degikup* weaving, from 1925 to 1935, still to produce major art works of high technical and aesthetic merit.

MINNIE AND TOOTSIE DICK

The patronage of the Cohns allowed Louisa Keyser to pursue an aesthetic of subtlety and refinement in her major works, whereas the lack of dependable patronage led Carson Valley weavers such as Sarah Mayo and Maggie James to create bolder and fancier designs with broader public appeal. Tootsie Dick, at one time the leading Washoe weaver in Antelope Valley, may be placed between these two extremes in both her patronage situation and her approach to basketry design.

Living to the south of Carson Valley, the Antelope Valley weavers had less access to the tourist trade at Lake Tahoe. Instead, they relied upon selling their baskets in stores. Telge and Cordelia

189. Maggie Mayo James (1870–1952) at Lake Tahoe, ca. 1913. Like several other photographs of Maggie James weaving for tourists at Lake Tahoe, this example in the C. Hart Merriam Collection shows her surrounded by baskets of other weavers.—M. C.

Hardy, owners of the general store in the main Antelope Valley town of Coleville, displayed and sold baskets of local weavers, although the better weavers took their major works to the Cohns in Carson City. The best-documented of these Antelope Valley weavers are Minnie Dick, who was selling through the Emporium by 1910; Tootsie Dick, who began around 1913; and Lena Dick, wife of Minnie's son, and Tootsie's aunt, whose earliest known Emporium basket is dated 1916.

Minnie Dick was the first of these three weavers to earn special attention from the Cohns, who photographed a display consisting at least partly of her baskets. The photograph (Cohodas 1983: fig. 4) suggests that by 1910 Minnie had already introduced traits that would later distinguish the Antelope Valley style of fancy basketry design. These traits include an emphasis on alternating motifs, which are integrated through similarity of configuration, through insertion of small intermediary or filler motifs, or through insertion into an overall zigzag pattern. When combined with a simpler, more spherical *degikup* shape, this integrated approach to design results in a more harmonious effect than was typical of Carson Valley weaving.

Some of the characteristics that distinguish the style of Antelope Valley weavers may be related to the basketry of the Mono Lake Paiute, whose weavers preferred heavier and more interconnected patterns. Families of both tribes occupied Antelope Valley, separated only by the Walker River, and Minnie Dick was actually a Paiute woman married to a Washoe (Washoe Dick). However, since there is no evidence that the Mono Lake Paiute style of fancy basketry was well established by 1910, it is possible that the more interconnected approach to design traveled southward, along with pictorial imagery.

By 1913, Tootsie Dick was becoming the most influential weaver in Antelope Valley, building on and perfecting the concepts introduced by Minnie Dick, and adding innovations of her own. Tootsie preferred complex motifs, some drawn from beadwork. After 1915, she frequently adapted Sarah Mayo's representational images (fig. 190), emphasizing decoratively abstracted bird, butterfly, and bug motifs. Tootsie also transformed Sarah's tree motif into bush- and stalklike patterns distinguished by extreme complexity and rigid symmetry.

Tootsie's most important innovation is an arrangement of design elements which, although simpler to plan and weave than either Sarah's asymmetric motifs or Minnie's zigzag pattern, is conceptually more advanced. Tootsie created alternating motifs that are formally related, yet placed at different heights on the design field, defining a zigzagging motion of visual continuity. This arrangement is more dynamic than an actual zigzag because it is more subtly suggested, relying on the viewer's eye to complete the relationship.

Little is known as yet about Tootsie's association with her patrons. Although she worked for the Hardys, Tootsie does not seem to have sold many baskets through their store. She also worked for the Chichesters, owners of a major Antelope Valley ranch, but although Ella Chichester created perhaps the largest collection of Washoe beadwork known, she did not buy Tootsie's baskets.[10] Instead, Tootsie sold virtually all her major works through the Emporium, from at least 1913 until near the time of her death in 1928.

Perhaps the most unusual aspect of Tootsie's career was a special, short-lived relationship with

190. This group of *degikup* by Tootsie Dick (ca. 1885– 1928) was photographed in 1925 at Cohn's Emporium by Edward Curtis. It was published as a comparison with Louisa Keyser's weaving, but without any mention of Tootsie Dick's name.—M. C.

Louisa Keyser that may have preceded her connection with the Emporium (Cohodas 1984). Louisa sold some of Tootsie's baskets to William Breitholle, wine steward at the Tahoe Tavern. As with the baskets by Louisa herself, which Breitholle collected, these works have no Emporium catalogue numbers, so their sale was not under the Cohns' control. Louisa may have been fulfilling some family obligation, perhaps by attempting to find a steady patron for Tootsie. We will probably never know the reasons for or nature of this relationship between Louisa and Tootsie, or the effect it had on Tootsie's career; the lack of relevant evidence is typical of the dearth of surviving information on most Washoe weavers.

Tootsie Dick's relationship to the Emporium appears to have been very similar to that of Scees Bryant, Louisa Keyser's sister-in-law. Both weavers sold virtually all their baskets through the Emporium, even though they did not live in Carson City. Both were recognized by the Cohns as outstanding artists, and were honored by having special promotional photographs taken of their work. Both were accorded laudatory comments on certificates issued with their baskets; before her death in 1919, comments on certificates for Scees's baskets call her the second-best Washoe weaver, while after Scees's death the same comment appears on Tootsie's certificates. Continuing the same approach after 1925, Tootsie's certificates carry the comment that she is the best weaver since Louisa Keyser's death. Another similarity is the clear distinction that the Cohns maintained between Louisa's exalted status and the secondary rank of Scees and Tootsie. No advertising photographs were taken of the weavers themselves, although one candid shot survives of Scees on a visit to Louisa's home. More significant, when Curtis published a photograph of Tootsie's baskets (fig. 190) as a comparison with Louisa's, he made no mention of her name.

Despite their similar economic situations, Scees and Tootsie followed completely different approaches to artistic innovation. Scees imitated Louisa Keyser so closely that some of their baskets can hardly be distinguished without documentation, and she did not contribute any important ideas to Washoe basket-weaving. By contrast, Tootsie was one of the most creative and individualistic of Washoe weavers. Tootsie Dick and, as we will see, Lena Dick illustrate the fact that steady patronage may allow artistic innovation but it cannot inspire it. This depends on the artist's own personality.

We cannot reconstruct the aspects of Tootsie's personality that led to her innovative style of basket-weaving. She was the child of a white father, but he was never incorporated into the family structure, and Tillie Snooks, who likewise had a white father, followed a reserved basketry style much closer to that of Louisa Keyser. However, the fact that Tootsie committed suicide when her six-year-old daughter died of spinal meningitis suggests a passionate and impulsive side to her nature that is reflected in the powerful impact of her art.

LENA DICK

After Tootsie's death, the major Antelope Valley weavers were Lena Dick and Lillie James. The major works of basketry art woven by these two sisters, in the face of the general decline in Washoe basket-weaving after 1925, may have resulted from their acquisition of a steady patron. First-hand information on this patronage situation is available from Fred Settelmeyer, at that time a Carson Valley rancher. On returning from his southern range around 1925, Settelmeyer stopped in the Hardys' store and admired Lena's baskets, which were on display. On a subsequent visit to Carson City, he noticed a similar basket by Lena on sale in the Emporium for five times the price. He passed this information on to Roscoe Day, an Oakland orthodontist in the process of building an Indian collection. At Day's request, Settelmeyer regularly stopped at the Hardys' and bought the best baskets.[11] He continued these purchases until 1934, when a heart attack forced Day to curtail his collecting and, since he could no longer visit Nevada, he and Settelmeyer lost touch with each other.

This patronage arrangement was unusually impersonal. Settelmeyer dealt entirely through Cordelia Hardy. He knew Lena (fig. 191), and encountered her occasionally on her visits to Carson Valley, but he did not contact her in relation to the collecting agreement. Settelmeyer only gradually became aware that some of the baskets Lena brought to the Hardys' store were woven by her shy sister, Lillie. He did not know which baskets Lillie had woven, and in fact greatly underestimated Lillie's contribution to the collection, which was about two-thirds of the baskets. Consequently, Day also did not know which weaver was the creator of each basket he received. He never inquired about Lena or Lillie, and even though he and Settelmeyer passed through Coleville on their way to camp and fish, they never stopped to meet the two artists. According to Settelmeyer, Day was pleased at obtaining fine baskets at bargain prices, and did not need to inquire further.

In this phase of declining quality in Washoe art, Lena and Lillie both responded to Settelmeyer's interest in fine baskets by retaining high artistic standards. Lena, the more gifted and individualistic of the two, vastly improved her technical and aesthetic mastery of the basketry medium under Day's patronage, distinguishing herself from all contemporary Washoe weavers. Between 1925 and 1934, Lena's approach gradually changed from somber, horizontally oriented basketry designs to a dynamic, vertically oriented style (Cohodas 1979a). Although Lena was among the first weavers to reject representational images after their great popularity, she never gave up the effect of richness created by juxtaposing red and black in the same motif, a technique that Carson Valley weavers tended to abandon around 1925. Lena did follow a general Washoe trend in delineating alternating columnar designs, but on her baskets these motifs are tightly attenuated. They also seem to grow and change as they move up the basket surface, creating an emotive semblance of organic growth. Her careful adjustment of the attenuated forms to a taut, spheroid *degikup* shape produces an effect of dynamic surface tension. In contrast to the lifeless products of many contemporary weavers, Lena created masterpieces of unequaled vitality.

The contrasts in style between Lena and Lillie are most illuminating, since the sisters shared precisely the same patronage situation. While Lena devoted herself to creating a small number of uniformly superior baskets in the decade of Day's patronage, Lillie produced a much larger number of works that show a greater range of quality. Lillie was less innovative in her designs, relying primarily on the innovations of Lena and Tootsie, but adapting them to a quieter taste. Lillie's most distinctive contribution was the imitation of crochet patterns to produce tight and repetitive banded designs.

CONCLUSION

The weavers discussed above were among the most innovative and influential artists to guide the development of Washoe fancy basketry between 1895 and 1935. Their individual approaches to basketry design derived not only from their personalities, but also from their relationships to their patrons and other consumers. While Maggie James and Sarah Mayo, who lacked wealthy patrons, increasingly compromised their aesthetic standards to appeal to the tourist taste in curios, Tootsie Dick, Lena Dick, and Louisa Keyser were able to devote much more of their energy to the increasing excellence of their art.

The importance of these patrons is further revealed by their effect on the decline of Washoe fancy basket-weaving in the 1930s. This decline was in part precipitated by the changing economic situation: young Washoe no longer learned to weave because their native heritage had become

191. Lena Frank Dick, ca. 1943. With the stable income provided by her husband Levi Dick and the steady patronage of Roscoe Day, Lena Dick increased the artistry

of her basket-weaving while other Washoe weavers allowed theirs to decline.—M. C.

192. Basket. Lena Dick, Washoe. Ca. 1930–1935, willow, redbud, and bracken fern root, 7¼ inches high. California Department of Parks and Recreation, Sacramento. B.H.W. 17–B.Z.–1.–S. L.

Lena Dick's technical and artistic achievement, exemplified by this elegant and dynamic *degikup*, which was collected by Roscoe Day, seems to have gone unnoticed by her patron.—M. C.

an obstacle to economic advancement. At the same time, Washoe weavers were losing their major patrons. The year 1934 saw both the end of Day's collecting and the death of Abe Cohn, who, as both patron and entrepreneur, had been most responsible for developing the market for Washoe basketry. With their support system extinguished, and with, in more than one case, their eyesight severely impaired, the elderly Washoe weavers abandoned the creation of basketry art for simpler work. They concentrated on the rapid manufacture of one-rod vessels, beaded baskets and bottles, and twined utilitarian wares, often in miniature, which to tourists were equally acceptable as Indian curios.

Although their encouragement was clearly a deciding factor in the creation of fine works of Washoe basketry art, the patrons of this work did not actually consider the baskets art, nor did they treat the weavers as artists. As a result, the aesthetic achievements of Washoe basketry were completely forgotten. Louisa Keyser's invention of the *degikup* and origination of the Washoe fancy-basketry style were purposely obscured in order to make her works appear more "authentic." Her artistic achievements were overshadowed by a notorious public personality fabricated to fit non-Indian preconceptions. The artistic achievements of Sarah Mayo and Maggie James were likewise forgotten. No one remembered that Sarah had introduced pictorial imagery to Washoe weaving, and Maggie James was remembered only by the Washoe, not for her artistry or her unequaled technical excellence, but for the mallard feathers with which she often decorated her crudest tourist pieces. Even Sarah's presentation basket, designed as a demand for respect and admiration, was casually treated and so lost: to government officials, it was probably just another Indian basket. Tootsie Dick had the dubious honor of having her baskets published in the great work by Curtis —without mention of her name. Last, the attitude of Roscoe Day toward Lena Dick may be the most illuminating. Although he received a steady supply of ever more breathtaking creations, Day

193. Fred Settelmeyer on horseback at Gardnerville, Nevada, in 1935.

never showed an interest in meeting the artist or inquiring about her life. With no knowledge of their origin, he cannot have considered these masterpieces anything more than fine examples of Indian curios, anonymously produced. Until quite recently, Lena's baskets were actually displayed as the work of Louisa Keyser.

Lamentably, the attitude of collectors has not changed appreciably in the last half-century. Despite the apparent cult of the Indian artist, the commercial value of a work still lies primarily in the race of its maker, not in its inherent individuality or creativity. Until we learn to judge Native American art according to the aesthetic standards with which we judge Western art, we are still just consumers of Indian curios.

POSTSCRIPT: WASHOE BASKETRY TODAY

Washoe basketry has both declined and ossified in the half-century since the abandonment of three-rod coiling. Most of the remaining weavers learned from their mothers or grandmothers before 1935, and are now quite elderly. Twined basketry has virtually disappeared, except in the manufacture of baby carriers. The one-rod *degikup* survives as the standard form of coiled basket-weaving, still practiced by four weavers in 1983. Beaded baskets and bottles, the most popular curio item through the 1950s, are today produced primarily by two women.

With only a few elderly weavers remaining active, Washoe basketry is in danger of extinction. Realizing this, some collectors are attempting to acquire all the baskets made by the best contemporary weavers. The Washoe tribe hopes to interest young people in taking up basket-weaving as a profession. This historical study should serve as a reminder that it takes hard work on the part of both weavers and collectors to revive a basketry style: neither can succeed without the full participation of the other.

Notes

1. "The Washoe are a small Indian tribe whose territory centers around Lake Tahoe . . . between the states of Nevada and California. Washoe territory forms the western border of the Great Basin, a harsh and sparse environment inhabited primarily by the Paiute tribes, neighbors of the Washoe on the north, east and south. To the west are the California tribes, such as the Miwok and Maidu, who live in a much richer and more secure environment.

"Before non-Indian settlement of their land, the Washoe were hunters and gatherers, ranging throughout their territory in a strict seasonal round. . . . Washoe women made many types of basketry containers, light objects which could easily be carried as the Washoe moved between the lakes, mountains, hills and valley floors in their yearly gathering circuit" (Cohodas 1979a).

2. The beginning date of this patronage is known only from the Cohns' often distorted records: it cannot be corroborated by other means. There is a possibility that before 1899, when Louisa's technique and approach were fully synthesized and Amy began recording her work in the ledger, the relationship was much looser. Louisa was originally hired to perform domestic chores for the Cohns, and may not have switched to full-time weaving until 1898–1899.

3. Cohn married Clarisse Amy Lewis on April 8, 1891 (Stern 1983:292). Although photographs of Cohn frequently appeared in newspaper and magazine articles publicizing Louisa and her work, photographs of Amy never appeared.

4. "Washoe basketry is woven primarily from willow, which is abundant on the valley floors of their territory. The Washoe employ two techniques to weave these basketry containers. The conical gathering baskets, flat winnowing, and parching trays, were made by the technique called twining, in which the vertical willow spokes form the structure of the basket and are held together by the horizontal willow weft. Two wefts are employed simultaneously, with one passing in front of and one behind each warp spoke. The two wefts cross each other between the spokes, so that they become intertwined. The large storage baskets, watertight cooking baskets, and *degikups* (small spherical baskets for ceremonial use) are woven in the coiling technique. In coiling, the rigid element or warp is formed of a spiraling foundation composed of one or three willow rods. The flexible weft is employed both to wrap the foundation and to stitch each rod of the foundation to the previous round. In the sewing technique, an awl is used to make the hole in the previous round, and then is removed to allow the passage of the weft thread. While the larger storage baskets may be woven with the looser one-rod foundation, the watertight cooking baskets and the *degikups* must be woven in the tighter weave made possible by the three-rod foundation" (Cohodas 1979a).

5. "Originally, the designs on these coiled baskets were quite simple, emphasizing zig-zag lines and isolated motifs executed in the mud-dyed root stock of the bracken fern. The design is made by substituting the fern root weft for the willow weft, not by an overlay technique. The basketry tradition was very similar to that of the neighboring Paiute tribes of the Great Basin, but decidedly inferior to the artistic products of the Californian tribes" (Cohodas 1979c).

6. Given the disintegration of Washoe culture in the late nineteenth century, it is not likely that tribal sanctions still significantly affected the nature of innovation in basketweaving.

7. The correspondence between Abe Cohn and G. A. Steiner was supplied to me by Steiner's grandson, William Huff.

8. Amy adapted an old story to a new purpose. While the Paiute adopted many aspects of Plains Indian culture, including the horse, their Washoe neighbors did not. To explain this difference, it was said (Fowler and Fowler 1970:124) that after defeating the Washoe in a great war, the Paiute prohibited them from owning horses. The war and the prohibition are equally fictitious (Cohodas 1982:124).

9. The difficulty of weaving this inscription would have been great for Sarah, who was illiterate.

10. Tootsie Dick may have produced several of the beaded bottles collected by Ella Chichester.

11. Although denied by the Hardys' daughter, Clarice Williams, Settelmeyer's claim that Cordelia Hardy gave him the right of first refusal on Lena's and Lillie's baskets is supported by the general absence, in other collections, of fine baskets woven by Lena during this period.

VI

CONTROVERSY

of the art style taught by Dorothy Dunn, and he has constantly interrelated his work with the art forms that came into sharp focus in New Mexico and Oklahoma during the 1930s and 1940s (see Warner, chapter v, this volume; Highwater 1976).

What is most controversial about Howe's seminal work in the modernist manner is the relationship he attempted to establish between the strongly nationalistic bent of the style known as traditional Indian painting, and the highly idiosyncratic approach of modernists. Howe is saying that both in pictorial presentation and in the expressiveness of an individual vision there is a great deal of common intent in ancient Dakota and modern non-Indian art. Unquestionably, Howe's argument possesses a good deal of merit, at least for the Plains tribes, for even the most traditional artists of this region were never particularly interested in realistic detail. They tended to use the eye in conceptual, nonimitative ways that produced a "marvelous reality." They were intent upon an artistic conceptualism that gave great emphasis to the essence of reality rather than to its appearances—in contrast with the realistic trend that dominated non-Indian naturalism in the nineteenth and early twentieth centuries. In this context, the controversy between the various groups of Indian artists, collectors, promoters, and dealers has, in part, been little more than the outdated contest that raged internationally between naïve realism and the various forms of modernism; or, to put it another way, between illusionist and nonillusionist art.

The ramifications of this situation are considerable. There are many religious, historiographical, and psychological facets to the way these controversies have affected the world of Indians, but the resulting crisis of identity is most central. What makes the whole matter of tradition and modernization such a distressing conflict in the native arts is the way numerous contradictions tend to interact to produce nagging and unresolved questions for artists, critics, and art historians about the ultimate value of Indian art.

THE CONTROVERSY OF IMAGERY

Behind the conservative insistence on a status quo in Indian art is the common belief that traditional art has the power to preserve a threatened culture. There is much reason to contest this viewpoint, since the painting and sculpture produced by many Indians during the first half of this century were framed upon a stereotypical idea of Indianness and an attitude about the "proper" media for Indian art that have absolutely no basis in history. There is, for instance, nothing indigenous about watercolors, tempera, illustration board, or paper—the standard materials used since about 1915 by traditional Indian painters. Likewise, it needs to be pointed out that there is nothing native about seed beads or silver; these are elements introduced from Europe, which were thoroughly Indianized by North American native craftspeople. Cultures are dynamic, not static; there is no reason for us to listen to reactionaries who say they want to keep Indian culture "pure" or to debate the question of what materials are appropriate to Indian artistic efforts. A far more complex and immediate question, which we must address, however, is the matter of what images and what emotional attitudes are appropriate in Native American painting and sculpture.

To deal with this problem it is necessary to depart momentarily from the specific case of the Indian artist, and to deal with the production of art in a more general way. The life of any artist balances upon several creative axes, but two of these apparently direct much of the energy of contemporary painters and sculptors, whether Indian or not. If what artists see and feel fits comfortably within the common cultural context, then they are very likely to use conventional materials and styles to manifest their art. But if artists see the world in terms of a vision or emotion that is remote from their societies, then they are inclined to invent new styles and to search for new materials that

197. White Man's Bad Medicine. Jerome Tiger (1941–1967), Creek-Seminole. 1966, tempera and pencil on poster board, 10½ × 15 inches. Philbrook Art Center, Tulsa, anonymous loan.

At his best, Tiger chronicled the twilight world of the transitional Native American caught between pride and despair. *White Man's Bad Medicine* is a pointed indictment of the double-binding effect of white society on Indian masculinity. To reinforce their masculinity, the Indians, now itinerant ranch hands, crop pickers, and odd-job men, must drink. In the process, they provide the white world with the demeaning stereotype of the drunken Indian, eroding further the pride of these ancient warriors. Jerome Tiger died at the age of twenty-six.—E. L. W. with Arthur Silberman.

make it possible for them to realize their uncommon and individual visions as works of art. This process seems to be the expressive imperative of all transitional twentieth-century societies: Anglo-American, African, Oceanic, Hispanic, and others. The American Indian also lives in a dynamic and transitional culture, and Indian artists have necessarily responded to the same expressive imperative.

The Indian artist in our day faces exactly the same aesthetic challenges as does an artist of any ethnic background. The resulting art will doubtless be distinctive because of the cultural imprint of a particular ethnic group, but the mandates that confront twentieth-century art are the same for all artists. Unfortunately, however, this internationalism is often missing from conservative discussions of Indians as artists.[1]

With this recognition of Indian art as an intrinsic part of the international art mentality, it is possible to return to the question of what images and what emotional attitudes are appropriate in Native American painting and sculpture. The answer appears to be this: the images and feeling of any kind of art are the sole province of the artist, and no ethnic or nationalist mandate should be allowed to divert painters or sculptors from whatever they determine to be the vision inherent in their work. The late Caddo-Kiowa Indian painter T. C. Cannon (fig. 181) made this point very clearly:

> First of all, let me say that an Indian painting is any painting that's done by an Indian. Today, however, I really don't think there is such a thing as "an Indian painting." There are so many modes that people are working in that it seems beside the point to call a painting *Indian* just because the artist is an Indian. People don't call a work by Picasso a Spanish painting, they call it a Picasso. After all, Picasso spent most of his life in France anyway. Does that make him a Spanish painter or a French painter? I say it makes him Picasso (Highwater 1976:177).

Hidden behind this debate about who has the right to define contemporary Indian art is the question of who has the right to define contemporary Indian society. It seems unarguable that the determination belongs solely in the hands of the diverse tribes of American Indians and those individuals who are Indian. That response may seem self-evident, but it is contradicted by historical fact, for never since the era of contact have Indians been allowed to define themselves. Even the fundamental process of recording Indian history has been given over to non-Indians. The curious result is that Indians have been segregated by the intrusion of "experts" (scholars, missionaries, scientists, bureaucrats)

198. Indian Prisoners in Costume. *Buffalo Meat (1847–1917), Cheyenne. Ca. 1878, colored inks on paper, 4½ × 6¾ inches. State Museum, Oklahoma Historical Society, Oklahoma City.*

Frank H. Taylor recorded on the front of a battle scene by Buzzard which was mounted alongside this drawing: "These drawings were given to me by Apache prisoners at Fort Marion, St. Augustine in 1879." Though first attributed to Buzzard, the drawing was reattributed to Buffalo Meat, partly on the basis of style, in 1982. According to Taylor, it was drawn "to show his squaw how the bunch [of Indians dressed in military garb] looked as artillery men."

who insist that they must speak on behalf of Indians, who are not considered capable of speaking for themselves. On the other hand, it would be less than accurate not to point out that it is exceptionally difficult in our era of Indian progressives and traditionalists, activists and conservatives, to identify either an Indian leadership or Indian spokespersons who have the approval of a truly wide constituency and are not the target of considerable internal or intertribal factionalisms.

THE CONTROVERSY OF HISTORY

The history of artistic individuation among Indians has been visible through the past two or three decades, but the rise of the idiosyncratic artist has been under way for at least a hundred years. It commenced with those uncommon prisoners of war at Fort Marion, St. Augustine, Florida, in the 1870s who used pencils, crayons, and accounting ledgers to vivify memories of their Oklahoma homelands, and to make a pictorial record of their lives while they were interned (figs. 162–167). This so-called ledger art was the means by which an ancient pictographic Plains Indian tradition found its way into our century; and Indians like Buffalo Meat, Buzzard, Bear's Heart, Zotom, Howling Wolf, and Etahdleuh Doanmoe were the first "artists" among tribes that had produced pictures for centuries (see Highwater 1976; Petersen 1971).

The Indian artist as historian—as *individual witness to history*—dates back at least to the beginning of the nineteenth century. By the 1870s, native artists had produced a vast archive of images which now serves as an alternative historical form, often providing a drastically different view of events from that we have come to know from books, and to accept as fact. The Fort Marion artists provide us with a substantial body of work in this category of alternative history. An example is the benign portrait *Indian Prisoners in Costume* (fig. 198), produced by Buffalo Meat in about 1878. Similarly, there are lavish scenes of the battle of the Little Bighorn, produced by anonymous artist-historians such as the painter of the Cheyenne muslin, ca. 1880, as well as by such illustrious painters as Kills Two, Katsikodi, Amos Bad Heart Bull, Kicking Bear, and Red Horse.

The controversy surrounding these historical pictographic works is not easily resolved, for the simple reason that most institutions and intellectuals do not even recognize the possibility, let alone the necessity, of accepting them as factual documents. That these nineteenth-century drawings are precious reservoirs of an alternative history has gone almost unrecognized in America, and this

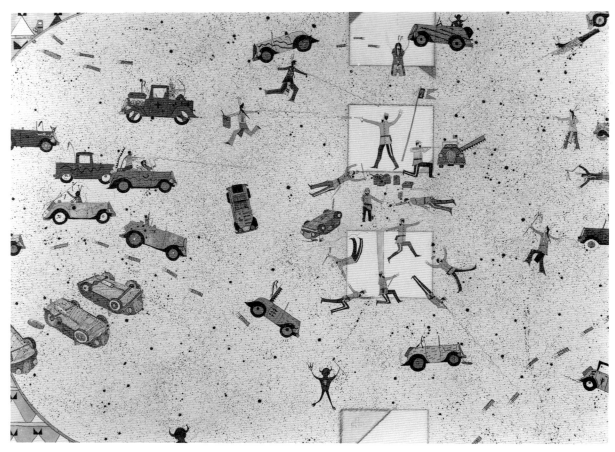

199. Custer's Last Stand Revised. Randy Lee White (1951–), Sioux. 1980, mixed media, 72 × 96 inches. Collection of the artist, New Mexico.

This painting uses the nineteenth-century Plains pictorial style to record a modern-day event—the trouble that ensued when unwary Rosebud Sioux were sold junk cars by white dealers, not knowing that the automobiles would eventually need gasoline to be kept running. Though White uses airbrush and acrylics, he is true to the symbolic integrity of early Plains art. Cars replace horses, tire tracks replace hoof marks, and a gas pump stands in place of shield tripods, but the aerial perspective and iconographic approach spring directly from ancient conventions of Plains aesthetics.

situation alone makes them highly controversial. And yet, from the Native American view, such pictures possess great strength of conviction and credibility, and have inspired some young artists of today, like Randy Lee White, to rediscover the art of recording history in graphic forms. The result, works such as White's *Custer's Last Stand Revised* (fig. 199), can be a stingingly candid means of directing our attention to a neglected genre, in which Indians kept alive the truth they saw in their own lives.

THE CONTROVERSY OF INDIVIDUALITY

In the American Southwest, the process of individuation was complex and troublesome. Artists of the pueblos were not easily allowed to become individual witnesses to history. The sedentary desert tribes of Arizona and New Mexico had an organized priesthood at the center of a persistent tribalism, which discouraged the expression of individuality. This was quite a different social context from that of the nomadic hunters of the Plains, who quested for a personal vision and who carried almost all aspects of their cultures as individual acquisitions.

This is not to suggest that Plains Indians were unresponsive to the concerns of the group. As the Southern Cheyenne artist Archie Blackowl told me in 1975:

Y'know, we have to go ask permission from the elders. That's right, we got to get their

200. Buffalo Dance. Crescencio Martinez (?–1918), San Ildefonso. Ca. 1916, watercolor on paper, 27 × 21 inches. Philbrook Art Center, Tulsa, 81.5.

Crescencio Martinez is generally considered to be the father of contemporary Native American painting. Whether or not the title is justified, his stylistic influence and the rapid acceptance by whites of his renderings of traditional Puebloan life did have a monumental impact on the Indian art of his time, and ultimately catalyzed what became the Santa Fe and Oklahoma schools of Native American painting. Martinez was self-taught and he depicted with great sincerity a lifeway which, though rapidly passing, still briefly surrounded him in his native San Ildefonso. His paintings are joyous in their naïveté, abounding in an unexpected dynamism that animates their dancing figures. When looking at these innocent images, it is hard for white viewers to fathom the theological controversy they generated in Pueblo society, but the depiction of the sacred impersonators in Martinez's works was considered by many to be a sacrilegious act.

permission. The dances are all right and the buffalo hunt, things like that are all right. But when it comes to ceremonial subjects, that's another matter, 'cause they're sacred. . . . In a roundabout way the elders used to object to some of my paintings. There were a lot of things I started but I let them go. Because they didn't like it so I let it go. I was raised in the true Indian way, and you have got to listen to the elders (Highwater 1976:170, 172).

Despite such prohibitions, the painters of the Plains were relatively free to act as individuals simply because much of their cultural world view resided in the vision of the individual. No such ego assertion was possible in the American Southwest, among the Puebloan peoples. In the 1920s, for instance, the Zia Pueblo painter Velino Herrera allegedly provided drawings of the sun symbol of his tribe to officials of New Mexico, who adapted it as the logo of the state of New Mexico,[2] thus betraying a sacred image. Even if this event were only a Southwestern legend, it would represent the Puebloan attitude toward individuality. Presumably, therefore, what made his behavior unacceptable was its outrageous individuality. Herrera's legendary error was not simply a matter of having given away secrets to non-Indians; his most fundamental mistake, from the Puebloan viewpoint, was his inclination to act out a personal conviction. There was, in short, something extremely

201. Hopi Ceremonial Dance. *Fred Kabotie (1900–   ), Hopi. 1946, watercolor on paper, 18 × 22 inches. Philbrook Art Center, Tulsa, 46.15.*

By the turn of the century, Hopi society was economically dependent on the burgeoning tourist trade. Between 1900 and 1920, as a desperately needed alternative to their fail-ing traditional economy, Puebloans allowed many once-sacred images to be secularized, in response to the demands of the curio market. These included Katcina dolls and the public depiction of supernatural beings. The Hopi and Zuñi eventually succumbed fully to this pressure, but the Rio Grande Puebloans to this day censor the artistic depiction of their sacred ceremonies and personages.

controversial about the Southwestern native artists who wished to depict Pueblo ceremonial life and the Katcina beings which are the central power-figures of their ritual life.

When J. Walter Fewkes (1903) commissioned Hopi men to provide drawings for his study of Hopi Katcinas, the artists' work was printed anonymously.[3] When, in 1936, Dr. Elsie Clews Parsons commissioned watercolors depicting daily life at Isleta Pueblo, she had to assure the artist, in response to his urgent request, that his identity would never be divulged. The artist wrote, "These paintings you will never see anywhere because no one [else] could do them, it is too hard. They are afraid to die if they do them. . . . I am not afraid of sickness or dying. I am ready to die any time as long as I have a little good time with this little money" (Parsons 1962:1–2).

It is in this context of tribal secrecy that we must understand the emergence of Pueblo Indian art. When Edgar L. Hewitt (chair of the Department of Anthropology of the University of New Mexico, ca. 1915–1917) commissioned Crescencio Martinez, a San Ildefonso Indian, to paint tribal ceremonies and dances (fig. 200), he was inevitably infringing upon a very sensitive aspect of Indian sensibility. Hewitt, however, was aesthetically inclined and admired Martinez's work for its artistic value rather than its ethnographic significance. Thus, he did not press Martinez to expose tribal secrets—evidenced by the fact that none of the paintings in the Hewitt series illustrates secret

202. Land of Enchantment. *Woodrow Crumbo (1912–), Creek-Potawatomi. 1946, watercolor on paper, 17¾ × 23½ inches. Philbrook Art Center, Tulsa, 46.45.4.*

Some contemporary Indian artists in recent years have accused their preceding generation of passivity and a lack of willingness to confront social and polemical issues through art. However, the fact is that artists like Crumbo, Kabotie, Tahoma, and others did directly address many such issues in moving and sometimes humorous commentaries about the difficulties of native peoples in transition. The absence of this art from many white histories and collections reflects the preference of the dominant culture not to deal with it.

dances. The relationship between Hewitt and Martinez was sensitive, but it did not result in tribal conflict for the artist. Crescencio Martinez was the first in a line of Pueblo artists to work for Hewitt. Another such artist was the Hopi painter Fred Kabotie (fig. 201). The relationship between artists and scholar evidences a sincere concern by Hewitt to avoid compromising his informants. As Kabotie told me, Hewitt "would let me come into the museum and work during the summer months.... In the afternoon I had a studio up on top, on the second floor, where I painted.... I have tried to be perfect in my painting.... [But] I only painted the public ceremonies" (Highwater 1976:143).

This bit of history provides the framework in which the first Indian artists emerged as individuals, and it gives us insight into the tension and the potential conflict that existed between an artist and his or her tribe. This delicate situation makes it especially ironic that non-Indians eventually became strongly involved in efforts to pressure Indian artists to conform to what the non-Indians arbitrarily considered the "proper" province of Indian art. A review of this history perhaps makes it easier for us to understand the brilliant satire that dominates Woodrow Crumbo's painting, *Land of Enchantment* (fig. 202), in which he uses pictorial irony to depict an Indian view of white tourists. And it is likewise clear that Oscar Howe was sacrificing all alliance with such tourists when he returned from World War II and embarked upon a lifelong experiment with Cubism.

203. Making Wild Rice. *Patrick Desjarlait (1921–1973), Ojibwa (Chippewa). 1947, watercolor on paper, 14¾ × 19 inches. Philbrook Art Center, Tulsa, 47.22.*

205. Pueblo Green Corn Dance. *Fred Kabotie, Hopi. 1947, oil on canvas, 29½ × 25½ inches. Thomas Gilcrease Institute of American History and Art, Tulsa, 0137.192.*

Desjarlait revealed both the great potential and the lost hope of American Indian painting. An acute architect of composition, he transcended the limits of ethnicity. His murallike compositions draw on European and particularly Latin American traditions, as expressed by Diego Rivera and others, to portray the dignity of the humble and the commonplace. His great gift was the ability to instill in the image of the common man a heroic character that sweeps across his canvases. Unfortunately, some fundamentalist thinkers of his time execrated his work, seeing it not as a poem to the human spirit but as a threatening statement of socialist philosophy.

204. Maple Sugar Time. *Patrick Desjarlait, Ojibwa (Chippewa). 1946, watercolor on paper, 15½ × 20⅜ inches. Philbrook Art Center, Tulsa. 46.31.*

There is still insufficient recognition of the artistic versatility of many native painters. Due to the selectivity of scholarship and philanthropic support for exhibitions, only one genre of art—that conforming to the traditional style of the 1930s—has been widely published as Indian art. Kabotie, Blue Eagle, Crumbo, Mootzka, West, and innumerable others freely experimented with and mastered mainstream art techniques and styles. Kabotie's painting realistically captures the solemnity of a Rio Grande ceremony in the style of the Santa Fe–Taos school, at the same time incorporating a note of social comment in the procession of the people flowing away from the pre-Christian kiva, toward the Franciscan priest and all that he represents.

206. View of Taos. *Albert Looking Elk (?–ca. 1941), Taos. Ca. 1930s, oil on Masonite, 5 × 7⅞ inches. Philbrook Art Center, Tulsa, anonymous loan.*

Looking Elk was a friend and model to Oscar Berninghaus in Taos in the 1920s. This color-saturated, impressionistic rendering of Taos Pueblo clearly reflects the influence of the German-born Berninghaus. Unfortunately, white patronage was unprepared to acknowledge Indian facility with European styles in a time that saw Indian painting as documenting the romance of a vanishing tribal world, rather than as art for its own sake. Whereas Kabotie returned to a traditional style of painting and created a legendary career, artists like Looking Elk and Desjarlait (figs. 203 and 204) kept working in untraditional styles and remained relatively obscure.—E. L. W. with Arthur Silberman.

Perhaps the Indian artist whose career was most dramatically diminished by the tensions of the 1940s transitional period was the remarkable Chippewa muralist Patrick Desjarlait (figs. 203, 204). Dissatisfied with the traditionalism of most Indian art of his day, he determined to use the elements of his training in commercial art to the advantage of his Indian subject matter, retaining the soul and spirit of his Minnesota background, but exploring a wider palette and a grander formal scope than any of the traditionalists. The result was his virtual eclipse. His modest modernism was considered heretical among some conservative humanist organizations and local museums and crafts shows, which restricted judging categories for art competitions and thus cast some of the most accomplished painters into a lifelong limbo. Tragically, Desjarlait was one of these artistic pioneers whose impact was never truly felt by his own artistic colleagues in the Indian world.

THE CONTROVERSY OF MODERNISM

The dominance of the non-Indian art market over Indian art began to decline by the end of World War II. Traditional Indian painting had become increasingly homogenized, and most of the regional and tribal elements had begun to disappear from it. Whatever appeal there had once been in the naïve and simplistic translation of Indian pictographic elements into European media, the mid-century art of most Indians had become trite, cute, self-effacing, and non-Indian in style, emotion, and content. Indian artists were no longer close enough to their tribal roots to withstand the influence of non-Indian aesthetic mediocrity—nor were they close enough to sophisticated non-Indian art to benefit by its example. What surfaced in this declining era of traditional Indian art were the sentimentality and decorative excesses of calendar art, Walt Disney-style cartooning, and the kind of sanitized imagery that abounded in greeting cards, magazine ads, and billboards.

As is often the case among tribal peoples whose art cannot be supported by their own economy, a tourist mentality began to intrude upon the sensibility and taste of many Indian artists. Despite the faltering of traditional style, many artists retained the high standards of the idiom and a few still paint in the traditional manner today (fig. 210). But an alternative approach to Indian art was also in the wind. By 1960, when the Indian Art Project Conference at the University of Arizona examined the future of American Indian art, the way was already prepared for a drastic new current in Indian aesthetics. The result, in 1962, was the founding of the Institute of American Indian Art (IAIA), in the same buildings in Santa Fe where Dorothy Dunn's famous studio had ushered in a grand era of traditional Indian painting in the 1930s.

The IAIA was something new and highly controversial. In theory, art students at the IAIA were given both traditional and modernist instruction, but the fact is that the temperament of the students was strongly inclined toward the new wave of individualistic Indian art (figs. 211, 212). From the outset, this focus was repudiated and scorned by those whose experience in art was extremely limited, both Indians and non-Indians. There had always been an unofficial boycott of Indian modernism among the so-called conservative humanists (a contradiction in terms but, like so many

207. Woman and Animals. Wa Wa Chaw (1888–1972), Mission. Date unknown, India ink on paper, 16½ × 13½ inches. Philbrook Art Center, Tulsa, anonymous loan.

The expressionistic works of Princess Wa Wa Chaw (figs. 207–209) reveal the scope and complexity of the twentieth-century American Indian art experience, yet to be fully acknowledged or deciphered. Her work is virtually unknown and exists in few places, principally the Heye Foundation, Philbrook Art Center, and a private American collection. Wa Wa Chaw, born in 1888, was a psychic reader, a feminist and a proponent of Native American political rights even before the 1920s, a streetcorner marketer of her own work from the 1940s to Beat culture Greenwich Village in the 1950s. Toward the end of her life, she returned to mystic pursuits, delving into automatic writing, out-of-body travel, and personal visions.

She died penniless in 1972. Her art reveals a hauntingly dark vision of beings who merge into one another, an existential abyss, and an intensely all-embracing, even absorptive, mother figure. Such deeply primal and emotionally forceful images are relatively rare in any art tradition. Among European work, we have seen them in Käthe Kollwitz, Edvard Munch, Emil Nolde, and in the work of some Jewish concentration-camp artists.—E. L. W. with Arthur Silberman.

208. Woman. Wa Wa Chaw, Mission. Date unknown, oil on cardboard, 11¾ × 5⅝ inches. Philbrook Art Center, Tulsa, anonymous loan.

209. Woman and Children. Wa Wa Chaw, Mission. Date unknown, India ink on cardboard, 24 × 28⅜ inches. Philbrook Art Center, Tulsa, anonymous loan.

contradictions, a perfect summation of what was actually in the minds of the multitude of regional art collectors and merchandisers during the 1950s and 1960s). The most powerful institutions disavowed nonillusionist and nontraditional art almost as if it did not exist, or as if its existence among Indian artists were some kind of blight on all the realistic and wholesome aspects of Native American culture. Important art competitions framed rules that expressly excluded modernist efforts. This institutional sanction of a reactionary attitude was easily adapted as a cause célèbre by collectors and dealers seeking approval of their disdain for modern art in general. The advent, however, of the Institute of American Indian Art made it clear that a countermovement was underway, and that the heretics were no longer a few random modernists. Although the IAIA staff was largely committed to the method of training established by Dorothy Dunn (most faculty members were alumni of her studio), the organizational intent of the Institute and the aesthetic disposition of its students were clearly progressive. In this way, the IAIA represented a vote of confidence for Indian modernism by a government-subsidized institution with clout and a good deal of respectability. The conservative

210. Polar Bears and Seal. *Kivetoruk Moses (1903–1982), Inuit (Eskimo). 1964, pen, ink, and colored inks on illustration board, 10 × 15⅜ inches. Philbrook Art Center, Tulsa, anonymous loan.*

White influence on Native American art has been quixotic, fickle, and paradoxical. By the late nineteenth century, scrimshaw (the carved, etched, and inked sculpture done in bone or ivory by European whaling crewmen) had so influenced Eskimo art that its floral, animal, and folk-genre motifs had replaced precontact native designs. Eskimo scrimshaw artists like Happy Jack showed remarkable ability, far surpassing most of their European models. Eskimo artists who painted on paper, like Kivetoruk Moses, built on the scrimshaw tradition, but used colored inks, shadowing, and perspective to model their figures, creating the illusion of three-dimensionality. Such paintings are almost unknown. Eskimo graphic art submerged from white view, to resurface only in the late 1940s, when the influence of the Hudson's Bay Company brought about an entirely new, surrealistic lithographic style.

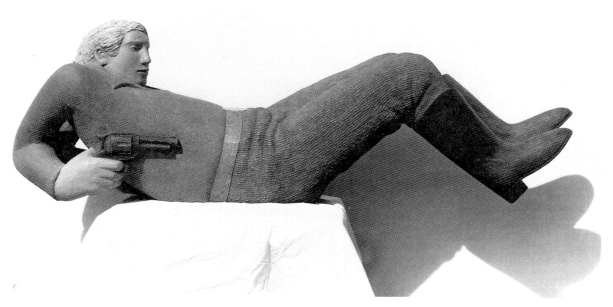

211. Neophyte Cowboy. *Bob Haozous (1943–   ), Chiricahua Apache/Navajo. 1981, painted limestone, 16 × 60 × 12 inches. Collection of Samuel C. Stone, Tulsa.*

Haozous is the leading exponent of contemporary figurative sculpture in the Native American art movement. His uniqueness of style and conscious abdication of traditional iconography generated some overdue controversy as to what—if anything—could constitute the iconographic integrity of Native American art. Haozous has long maintained that legitimate art is generated from the individual Native American experience, not from slavish adherence to ethnically prescribed styles or subjects.

status quo in Indian art was meeting organized opposition for the first time. The education of Indians with a modernist inclination was no longer a matter of a few non-Indian teachers and exceptional Indian students like Joe H. Herrera in the 1940s. (Herrera was the first Indian to have a one-person show at the Museum of Modern Art in New York City, but even he did not succeed in the reactionary Indian art market.) When the IAIA began to champion artistic experimentation, it was an organized academy of Indian and non-Indian students boasting considerable artistic experience and sophistication. Institutional acceptance of modernist trends in Indian art did not blossom suddenly at the IAIA, however; it had had a quiet but long-standing underground existence in the art community. For instance, in an interview with Jeanne Snodgrass, Indian arts curator from 1956 to 1969 at Philbrook Art Center, I was told:

> In 1959, three years prior to the opening of the Institute, Philbrook Art Center presented paintings generally considered to be taking a *new direction.* Thus Philbrook provided the first major endorsement of the evolution in Indian art and acknowledged the ever-increasing desire of artists to experiment—not to break from their culture, but to explore it and improvise upon it—to effect an integration with the demands of the present. Even the purist, if he is honest and knowledgeable, must admit that from the very beginnings of Indian art, there have been many styles, many techniques, and many approaches. The *new direction* treatment, first accepted by the Philbrook, later by more recent annual exhibitions, and certainly encouraged by the IAIA, is but one more phase in the continuous development of Indian art (Highwater 1976:116).

The controversial nature of Indian modernism was not simply an invention of the Institute of American Indian Art, but a wide-ranging institutional response to an experimental mood among many young Indian artists. The most imperative question faced by the IAIA and its teachers and students was the same kind of query that always haunts explorers: where are we going, and why are we going there? This dilemma was especially acute among Indian artists, because of their strong sense of ethnic heritage, which many voices around them proclaimed to be in direct contradiction to their experimentalism.

Lloyd Kiva New, a Cherokee and the director of the IAIA during its most influential years (1967–1980), faced this dilemma when he wrote in 1974 about the aims of the Institute:

> I believe that young Indians should be trained to the point where they will be able to make up their minds as adults of the future how they will want to present their culture to the outside world. I don't think these decisions about what Indians should do in capturing the beauties of their rich past in contemporary dramatic forms should be made by [older] people. But I do believe that I can, with the assistance of others, help Indians have the experiences that will lead them toward making sound decisions about the evolution of those institutions that will be needed to support Indian culture into the future. I am frustrated that Indians cannot gain access to at least one major educational institution where they can have an opportunity to get themselves together with the help of sympathetic mentors and attack the problem of how to go about furthering those cultural values that should not be lost, particularly as they apply to performing arts experiences. . . . I feel that the first steps that need to be taken are those that will help [Indians] become involved educationally in the problems so that they can eventually decide what they would like to do. Until this is done, I fear we risk a kind of paternalism that is rapidly going out of style (Highwater 1976:115).

As the Iroquois painter George C. Longfish has noted:

> The major change in emphasis [at the IAIA] was one which encouraged individual expression of the artists for the purpose of "the development of ego strength with which to face the world." With this change in attitude and a concomitant broadening of exposure to art through the curriculum, the Institute proceeded with its training of young Indian students of the sixties (Longfish and Randall 1982:25).

By the late 1960s and early 1970s, the students were not only using a broader range of techniques, but were also painting images that grew out of their own experienced contradictions in the Indian world. Many of the instructors, however, resisted these developments, partly because they could not grasp the intent of their students, and partly because of their loyalty to traditional forms, imprinted by their own experiences as the first-generation product of Dorothy Dunn's studio. Then, in 1964, an artist and teacher who understood the modernist impulse of his students arrived at the IAIA. His name was Fritz Scholder (figs. 212, 262). He had studied under Oscar Howe in South Dakota, and he had trained in several non-Indian institutions which put no restrictions upon imagery, style, or media, and were not concerned with ethnicity. His work quickly became a storm center in the long battle between the conservatives and the progressives. His example became a veritable beacon for countless young Indian painters, many of whom never set foot in New Mexico. By 1969, Scholder had left the Institute, but already the idea of a contemporary Indian art movement had been born. Scholder's work found its way into the mainstream art market at the very moment when misguided Indian traditionalists were demonstrating in front of Southwestern galleries against Scholder's "grotesque and shameful" depiction of Indians—a reaction, it should be pointed out, almost identi-

212. Laughing Indian. *Fritz Scholder (1937–), Mission (Luiseno). 1973, acrylic on canvas, 70 × 50 inches. Oklahoma Art Center, Oklahoma City.*

In the late 1960s and early 1970s, Scholder became the most widely known contemporary American Indian painter. According to Scholder himself, he is a non-Indian Indian artist. The idea that Indian art is art by any Indian and can take the form of any Euro-American-derived style was at one time highly controversial. But as the world becomes a global village, and art becomes an international language, issues concerning ethnicity and nationality are coming to be seen in a new light. The image of a laughing Indian counters the stereotypic idea of primitive stoicism. Scholder enjoyed introducing contradictory visual elements such as ice cream cones, beer bottles, and other artifacts of white culture into traditional Indian imagery.

cal to that of the European demonstrators at the turn of the century who had cried out against the debasement of academic art by Kandinsky, Picasso, and Matisse. This artistic confrontation became a political one: non-Indian conservatives saw the reaction of these unsophisticated Indian traditionalists as a vindication of their own insistence that paintings like Scholder's were not truly Indian. It became very popular in the American heartland to dismiss Scholder for the shoddiest reason of all: because he is "only one-quarter Indian," or, allegedly, because he is "not *really* an Indian." The racist implication of this sort of argument is too transparent to be discussed, but we may note that blood quantum became an issue in the assault against Indian modernism.

THE CONTROVERSY OF SUCCESS AND RECOGNITION

The aims of the Institute of American Indian Art had been thoroughly realized by the mid-1970s, despite provincial opposition. But it is an error to believe that all Indian painting and sculpture of the recent past have been devoted to the contemporary idiom, and that all Indian painters of value were necessarily trained by the IAIA in Santa Fe, for Indian art is highly diverse and has evolved in a great many different regions of North America. But there is no question that the Institute produced most of the important young Indian artists of the 1960s; and even among painters who did not study there, the influence of the IAIA's avant-garde ideas had a strong impact, through the brilliant success of people like Fritz Scholder and the late T. C. Cannon (figs. 181, 232).

The importance of Indian art centers such as those at Santa Fe, Scottsdale, and Tulsa cannot be overestimated, but over time the exhibitions and art circles of such centers have gradually become elitist and self-absorbed. For many reasons, new trends from other regions have been unduly neglected.

This is not only because the regionalist, conservative Southwest has failed to recognize them, but also because artists from Canada, the Southeastern United States, the Northwest Coast, and the Iroquois region of the Northeast Coast often have not been trained, as IAIA alumni were, in art marketing and career management. As a result, some of them have been unmotivated professionally and disinclined personally to try to make an impact on the Indian art scenes of the Southwest. But there are also other reasons why the dominance of the Southwest (and eventually of the Institute itself) over Indian art has declined, and why numerous exceptional Indian artists of the 1980s have attempted to move in wider art circles.

J. J. Brody (1971) saw the heyday of the IAIA as the era in which Indian painting died and the Indian painter was born. Scholder was held up by Brody as the consummate example of this transition; and, of course, there was much truth—from the perspective of 1970—in Brody's observation. Scholder opened the door for modernist Indian art, and for about ten years he was the only artist to find acceptance in the mainstream art world. But, from the vantage of the 1980s, it is now sadly clear that Scholder's impact was far less than we had anticipated. Lavish advertisements announcing his various exhibitions spread across page upon page of the best national art publications, but few serious in-depth critiques of his work have appeared, in comparison with the number published about non-Indian artists of his standing. In the insular and Indianist Southwest, and in the trend-oriented galleries of Los Angeles and San Francisco, even in some of the showplaces of Chicago, Atlanta, Washington, D.C., New York City, and Paris, Scholder's work has received recognition. But as Scholder himself fully admits, the East Coast museums have very largely ignored his achievements. And today Scholder (along with most sophisticated Indian artists who identify with Indian subject matter) fully realizes that the potential for true international success of Indian art is very limited and problematical. Most of the Indian artists who have had some degree of public recognition as producers of Indian art are now trying, like Scholder himself, to get out of the field as quickly and quietly as possible. And most of the artists of Indian heritage who have been accepted in the international world of art (Leon Polk Smith, James Havard, George Morrison, and others) pursue their careers with little or no public emphasis upon their ethnicity (figs. 135, 240, 243).

In 1985, it is apparent to anyone who works as an art critic in New York City that Indian art has almost no chance of making an impact on the booming cosmopolitan art market; that it is very unlikely that anything called "Indian art" will soon be exhibited by the reigning international entrepreneurs of contemporary art; or that at this moment in time the Indian artist has any hope of altering the emphatic indifference of the powerful East Coast clique of contemporary art promoters, critics, and exhibitors. I must report with a great sense of disappointment that Indian art has received almost no serious attention from critics or writers, museum and gallery administrators, or collectors in the major eastern art centers.[4] There is, for instance, not a single fine arts museum of significance in Boston, Los Angeles, San Francisco, New York City, Chicago, or Washington, D.C., that currently has a single painting or sculpture by an American Indian on permanent exhibition. In talking to urbane writers, I have found that there is real doubt in their minds that any Indian has yet produced art of the first rank.[5]

It is significant that both Leon Polk Smith and James Havard (who are supportive of Indians and proud of their Indian lineage in private) have repeatedly declined to be associated with shows of Indian art—simply and, I think, justifiably because, as Leon Polk Smith has said, "I do not make any art but my own art, and I wouldn't want to be lined up with other painters simply on the basis of race any more than I would agree, if I were female, to be exhibited with other female artists" (Highwater 1978).

It is precisely this reaction which Brody (1971:206) could not anticipate in 1970, when he saw the "death of Indian painting . . . accompanied by the birth of Indian painters." What we are seeing today is the death of the Indian painter and the birth of the painter who happens to be an Indian. The ethnicity of the early decades of Indian art is no longer a viable basis for producing painting and sculpture. As T. C. Cannon observed almost a decade ago: "I have something to say about experience that comes out of being an Indian but it is also a lot bigger than just my race. It's got to do with my own mythology, the one I make up myself. That's what I want to express in my painting" (Highwater 1976:178).

Speaking about Fritz Scholder's work and the period of its ascendancy, George Longfish has said, "At its initial emergence, it was a new and exciting painting style; it has since evolved into a stereotyped *reaction* to traditional Indian paintings, i.e., the market seemed to open only to this single deviation" (Longfish and Randall 1982:25). In other words, the Scholder mannerism became a new stereotype, despite Scholder's continual efforts to avoid just that result. His example was duplicated by so many young painters and his works marketed in such a classical manner that soon he had unintentionally produced another "traditional art" that brought about yet another wave of disapproval and heretical experimentation. This time, however, the source of the reaction was not an institution, or the artists of an insulated regionalism, but painters and sculptors scattered widely throughout North America, most of whom had received their training as artists in academies that had no interest in ethnicity. Currently, "a vital aspect of the Contemporary Native American art movement is one which has little connection with the Institute" (Longfish and Randall 1982:25). In the sculpture of Bob Haozous (figs. 211, 226) and Richard Glazer Danay (figs. 30, 246), and in the paintings of George Longfish (fig. 228), George Morrison (fig. 243), and Neil Parsons we see the advent of artists who choose nontraditional subject matter as well as modern techniques and media. Longfish has observed:

> Characteristic of these artists is their emergence from the larger context of art as solitary artists in search of others with whom they might share their sensibilities and from whom they might learn. It was through the conventional lines of communication in the art world that they made contact, i.e., through exposure in art magazines, through shows at galleries and museums, and art conferences (Longfish and Randall 1982:27).

The upheaval at the Institute of American Indian Art and its subsequent removal to a secondary facility are complex political and aesthetic phenomena (with a number of disturbing aspects both within and outside the Indian world). I personally lament its problems. But at the same time, there is a positive aspect to the widening of the sphere of artists who are Indian. They are heralding a transition from facile identification with a moribund Indian nationalism to the aesthetic self-reliance that has always been the crucible of individuated art.

THE FUTURE OF THE CONTROVERSY IN INDIAN ART

Given this depiction of Indian individualists as rebels and heretics, let us recall that none of these artists is repudiating the validity of the Indian world or attempting to escape from it into some other world. To the contrary, as their statements and works often declare, they are highly traditional people, and their work focuses upon vital aspects of Indian culture. They often consider the inspiration for their paintings and sculpture to be visions, revelations, and the cumulative heritage of their people. They are among the most outspoken critics of the unthinking public display and commercialization of Indian ceremonial objects. They are among those Native Americans who are becoming increasingly vocal and resistant to the desecration of Indian religious life. In short, many of the new generation of artists are animated by a sense of spirituality and a deep involvement in their cultures, histories, religions, and symbols of power. Through this cultural involvement, their confidence has grown, and they have begun to interpret their legacies within the context of the modern world in which they live. Unlike the craftspeople of the past, today's artists insist upon presenting their own personal visions of reality—and they do so with or without tribal consent—because the very core of their unprecedented motivation is the desire to assert themselves as individuals who are Indian in highly personal, controversial, and idiosyncratic images and forms.

In a recent letter, sculptor Richard Glazer Danay summarized much of what we have discussed about the controversial aspects of Indian art, while at the same time pointing toward the future of the art created by Native Americans:

> Tradition Is The Enemy of Progress—I once saw this emblem carved over the door of a [Bureau of Indian Affairs] school. As applied by the BIA agents it has an obvious message, but as applied by Indians to other Indians it can be used to crush individual growth. There is a point at which history, environment, cultural patterns, and traditionalism recede, and art takes over. I think many people forget that something of the old is always in whatever is created new (Danay: personal communication, 1983).

For the first time, American Indians are producing a large population of intellectuals, scientists, and artists who selectively profit from, and effectively cope with, non-Indian mentality. During our decade, artists who are Indians have helped to create new definitions of what it will mean to be Indian in the twenty-first century and beyond. In their current controversial art, we clearly see Native Americans re-creating themselves as Indian individuals.

Notes

1. It should be mentioned that there has been a highly productive exchange of aesthetic ideas between mainstream art and the art of primal peoples such as American Indians (see Highwater 1981:47–49, 120).

2. This incident concerning Velino Herrera is the subject of much debate. Even if the event is legendary, it ideally serves as an apocryphal tale, exemplifying the stress between traditionalism and modernization among the Puebloan peoples. The conflict between Herrera and his village is reported by several sources as fact (see Snodgrass 1968:73). According to Arthur Silberman, of the Native American Painting Reference Library, Oklahoma City, however, there is no evidence that Herrera provided such drawings to officials. Likewise, inquiry into the cause of the rift between Herrera and his people has focused upon evidence from Case Number 1297, U.S. District Court for the District of New Mexico: namely, that Herrera and a group of citizens of Zia left the pueblo sometime in 1932 or 1933, in the aftermath of a bitter dispute involving a religious schism. Litigation concerning the expulsion and confiscation of property extended through the 1940s and into the 1950s. It is clear, however, that whatever the basis of the expulsion and confiscation of

Herrera's property, the case strongly reinforces the point that individuality in regard to traditional religious matters caused strong negative tribal reaction.

3. The plates of Katcina drawings were printed in the study with no signatures, and the list of illustrations bears no attributions; but at the beginning of his article, Fewkes (1903:13) does credit Kutcahonauû (or White Bear) as the artist he commissioned to make the drawings.

4. Having promoted Indian art for a decade, I am constantly amazed by the antagonism native painting arouses in urban critics. I am thinking, for instance, of the 1979 Heye Foundation exhibition *The Ancestors* at the New York Customs House, which art editor John Perreault of the *Soho News* defamed as "boy scout art."

5. Though almost a decade has passed since I made the following observation, I think it still applies to some degree: "Very few Contemporary Indian painters have achieved much, in comparison to non-Indian painters of the same idiom, probably because the idiom is new to them" (Highwater 1976:194).

Straddling the Cultural Fence:
The Conflict for Ethnic Artists within Pueblo Societies

EDWIN L. WADE

The market for American Indian arts and crafts has had a serious psychological effect on native artists and on their families and fellow community members. The participating artist introduces an alien, disruptive force into his native community in the form of Westernized beliefs, ideas, and values. His influence has radically changed the very nature of native art and has redefined the role and importance of the native artist in his community. The transition has been difficult. Community backlash against such artists can best be characterized as violent and unrelenting. Many have been the object of vicious gossip, witchcraft accusations, and social ostracism. Some have even been banned from their native villages or threatened with loss of life. The source of the controversy lies in the fundamental differences between mainstream and Native American world views. Two Southwestern Indian attitudes that cause particularly bitter conflict when challenged are man's relation to the supernatural, and what constitutes "a good man" within an egalitarian society.

MERCHANDISING THE GODS

A continual source of conflict between traditional Southwestern Indian ethos and the commercial art market has been the painting of ceremonial dances and the sale and display of sacred ceremonial items outside the native community. To understand why this conflict has been so intense, one must look to the Navajo and Pueblo conceptions of man's role in the universe.

For these Southwestern Indians, the universe is a place where all beings—men and supernaturals alike—are mutually dependent for survival. Man relies on the benign intentions of supernaturals, who determine whether his crops will grow and his people remain free from disease. At best, the supernaturals are seen as indifferent to man's plight; at worst they are vengeful. The Navajo feel that the balance could shift at any moment, and indifference become malevolence. Man must supplicate the spiritual beings through prayer and ritual, in order to persuade them to bring harmony to the earth. At the same time, spiritual beings such as the Yeis among the Navajo and the Pueblo Katcinas are equally dependent upon man. These beings have an overpowering need to be praised and worshiped. Bunzel (1932:489) noted that "the great divinity, the sun, and all the lesser divinities, the Katcinas, the rain-makers, the beast gods, the war gods, and the ancients, must be reminded that man is dependent upon their generosity; and that they, in turn, derive sustenance and joy from man's companionship."

The Puebloans, and especially the Hopi, believe that one man alone cannot fulfill the needs of the supernaturals. Performing the elaborate seasonal ceremonies—the Shalako, Niman, Summer Corn Dance, Mixed Animal Dance, and Buffalo Dance—requires the cooperation of an entire village. These ceremonies express communal gratitude for past favors while they petition for future abundance and the general well-being of the community.

At the root of Pueblo religion, then, is an intense belief that cosmic and earthly disharmony is caused by a failure of man's collective efforts to appease the supernaturals. Every villager, child or adult, observer or dancer, is expected to focus positive thoughts upon the ritual performances and to banish negative thoughts from consciousness. In light of this all-encompassing injunction, a failure of the collective can only result from the failure of an individual. In the marginal existence of the small-scale Pueblo farmer, there are inevitable dry years, untimely frosts, and other natural disasters. Rather than question the effectiveness of their religion, the Puebloans view such misfortunes as a consequence of antisocial behavior.

For Puebloans, one extremely offensive antisocial act has been the use of ceremonial dances in Indian paintings meant for sale to non-Indians. Though the artist may not have intended insult, such paintings have frequently been interpreted by traditionalists as an affront to the supernaturals. The commercial exploitation of sacred Pueblo rituals was the one negative thought, the selfish individualistic act, that could destroy the sanctity of the ritual.

Accusations have been harsh. The Hopi painters who illustrated J. Walter Fewkes's 1903 volume on Hopi Katcinas, for example, were labeled witches, and their paintings were considered instruments of sorcery. At Hopi and Zuñi, a witch is a "two-heart," a parasitic creature who preys upon the life force of others. A witch is a chaotic element that upsets the balance of all natural phenomena, and consequently disrupts the sacred dance ceremonials. An accusation of witchcraft is no minor charge; in Pueblo society, it is one of the few offenses that can invoke the death penalty.

Extremely bitter conflict arose over the painting of Katcina performances and the sale of Katcina masks and dance costumes. The explanation for this hostile reaction lies again in the communal nature of Puebloan religion. An individual does not own a ceremony or any of the paraphernalia used in its production. The seasonal dances, initiation rites, curing rituals, and other secret kiva ceremonies belong to the lineage groups, cults, or medicine societies whose members may inherit the

213. *Four Yei masks. Navajo. Ca. 1900, painted hide, hair, gourd, shell, 32 × 12 inches; painted hide, hair, shell, 16 × 15 inches; painted hide, hair, 13 × 10 inches; painted hide, hair, shell, fabric, 16 × 10½ inches. Philbrook Art Center, Tulsa, anonymous loan.*

Masks like these have been integral to universal world culture from the beginnings of the Stone Age to the present. The original role of the mask was not decorative, though

Western civilizations have reduced it to this, but was instead a vehicle for transfiguration. Donning the face of a god invested the mortal wearer with that being's persona. Various Native American peoples still maintain that masks possess this power and that, though they are not gods in themselves, they possess a spiritual potential which can be either beneficial or destructive, depending on human attitudes and actions.

214. Jar. Lois Gutierrez (1948–), Santa Clara. 1981, polychrome pottery, 6³⁄₈ × 7¹⁄₂ inches. Philbrook Art Center, Tulsa, 81.6.3.

This recent work by Lois Gutierrez imitates the form and some of the designs common to the sacred kiva jars of the Tewa Puebloans. By the 1920s, Maria Martinez had begun imitating sacred forms such as corncribs and stepped-terrace bowls. Though the imitation of sacred forms and designs has been practiced over the last sixty years of Pueblo pottery-making, traditional religious practitioners of the pueblos still feel an uneasiness when confronted with such vessels made for commercial purposes.

215. Ceremonial bowl. Zuñi. Ca. 1939, polychrome pottery, 5¹⁄₂ × 12 inches in diameter. Philbrook Art Center, Tulsa, Clark Field Collection, PO 216.

In the late nineteenth century, stepped-terrace prayer meal bowls became common throughout Pueblo ceremonialism. Cornmeal mixed with turquoise was placed in the center of the bowl, whose interior and exterior were decorated with fertility symbols such as tadpoles, horned toads, dragonflies, lightning bolts, rain marks, sacred serpents, mountain lions, and snow. These sacred objects excited the interest of white collectors and an illicit market for contraband vessels developed. By the 1920s, the Zuñi theocracy realized their inability to control this market, so they elected to allow commercial potters to produce inexact, unconsecrated facsimiles of medicine bowls for sale.

right to care for a mask and to wear it in a ceremony. As Ruth Benedict (1934:71) notes, Katcina masks "are owned and cared for . . . by family lines in the same houses that have cared for them . . . since the beginning of the world." Sacred art is never privately owned in the non-Indian sense of that phrase. An individual has no right to sell it, dispose of it, or even to show it indiscriminately.

More than for their importance as religious heirlooms, Katcina masks, god images, and fetishes are valued for their intrinsic spiritual life force, an extension of the supernatural being represented by the object.

> The use of masks is surrounded by special taboos. One must never try on a mask when not participating in a ceremony, else one will die. . . . If one is incontinent during a katcina ceremony the mask will choke him or stick to his face (Bunzel 1965:443).

Respect for the life force of the Katcina mask is in fact so strong that a priest is required to feed the mask. Cornmeal is placed around its mouth, or a bowl of food placed before it; the being within then consumes the spirit of the food. The priest also grooms the mask, repainting it if the earth paints show wear, and replacing feathers that are ragged or missing. If the mask can no longer be renewed, it must be ceremonially retired in a ritual that sends the Katcina spirit home with many blessings and expressions of gratitude.

Beginning in the 1890s, a number of Katcina masks and other sacred objects were sold or traded to museums and private collectors. The spirits that dwell in these objects have not, in most cases, been "sent home." The Puebloans feel that these spirits are being starved and abused, that they are prisoners, and that all the benefits they might have brought to the community are locked up with them. This abridgment of ethical responsibility toward the sacred by museums and collectors is an extremely serious problem and will continue as a source of controversy until Native American religious sensitivities are acknowledged.

The demand for the clandestine acquisition of sacred art objects has been so great, and the objects so hard to obtain, that many Indian artists have produced facsimiles and inexact, crude replicas. Commercial Katcina dolls are derived from the semisacred *tihu*; the Zuñi prayer-meal bowls that are offered for sale are commonly miniaturized, less elaborate versions of kiva step bowls (figs. 214, 215). Cardboard ice-cream cartons have been used as the foundations for fake Katcina masks. The commercial sale of these objects has only been accepted to a limited degree by the Puebloans. Objects reproduced with inexact fidelity are more likely to be allowed to be sold. The Katcina mask, however, is held in such reverence that even the ice-cream-carton replicas are considered profanities. Hopi and Zuñi, the only two pueblos that have actively produced nonsacred Katcina dolls, have been the most lenient in interpreting what can be commercialized. The depiction of Katcinas, Katcina performances, or kiva rituals is strictly forbidden among the Rio Grande pueblos; consequently, their commercial artists interpret minor ceremonial themes involving the public dances. Never are masked beings portrayed.

Acceptance of the commercialization of Navajo and Pueblo sacred arts is coming slowly, but only after much dissent and violence and the passing of generations of Southwestern Indians.

SERVING TWO MASTERS

The question of acceptable imagery is not the only source of friction between a contemporary Indian artist and his tribal group. An equally bitter, if more subtle, conflict is set up by his assumption of the role of "Indian artist" in a world dominated by non-Indians. The superstar image of a celebrated Native American artist conflicts with the Southwestern Indian definition of a good man in several ways.

The issue partly revolves around success. Success in mainstream American society is measured in terms of money, publicity, and prestige—precisely the commodities that arouse suspicion and distrust in the artist's home community when accorded him by the commercial Indian-art market. By obtaining the non-Indian earmarks of success, a Pueblo artist jeopardizes his ability to succeed as a tribal member, a "good man," in the context of his own group. The question is whether a man can succeed simultaneously in two worlds that define goodness and success differently.

Since the end of the 1970s, increasing numbers of Indians of all tribal extractions have attempted to assimilate into mainstream American culture. A common pattern has been to pursue a new urban life for a year or so, then for various reasons to return to the reservation and its values and customs. The Indian artist can thereby maintain a home on the reservation while also earning money and recognition from the public. In so doing, he remains under the close scrutiny of his neighbors and must conform to the image of a good man prescribed by his society, while at the same time playing the role of a sophisticated, Westernized art-market participant.

Residents of the pueblos have a clear conception of what constitutes appropriate and inappropriate behavior. The Zuñi image of a good man is typical:

> The ceremonious Zuñi place a high value on inoffensiveness and sobriety. They deplore an authoritative manner and strongly disapprove of aggressiveness and qualities of leadership. A man who manifests such traits is suspect as a witch ... and would formerly have been hung up from the ceiling by his wrists or thumbs until he confessed. ...
>
> Individualistic qualities are held in low esteem in the collectivized culture of Zuñi, where the maintenance of oneness with the universe is believed to depend on the subordination of individual ambition for the benefit of the group, lest the supernatural powers look with disfavor upon Zuñi and withhold their blessing (Spencer and Jennings 1965:318).

The Indian artist who gains notoriety, who might be interviewed on television, appear at gallery openings in white buckskin and turquoise, and have droves of Anglo patrons parked outside his house, is seen by his fellows as having all the qualities a good man does not possess. Although a good Puebloan should not be boastful, Margaret Gutierrez, a Santa Clara potter, says, "today our pottery is the finest and most beautifully worked pottery in the world, and it is known the world over" (Maxwell 1974:44). A good Puebloan holds individualistic qualities in low esteem, but Dextra Q. Nampeyo, from Hopi, says, "I want to keep my pottery unique" (Maxwell 1974:36). A good Puebloan is unselfish, cooperative, and kind to his fellow community members (Aberle 1951:16); nevertheless, one of Nampeyo's granddaughters says that the designs she and the other Nampeyo descendants use are theirs, and not free to be used by others. They have established a kind of copyright by publishing in papers that these designs are theirs (Collins 1974).

The conflict is intensified by success, in the non-Indian meaning of the term. The average craftsman is generally viewed by his community as humble and modest. As long as he remains faceless and nameless, his behavior will not be contradictory to the Puebloan image of a good man. But for some artists such anonymity is neither possible nor desirable. Their patrons know them by name and favor them over other craftsmen in the pueblo. To remain so favored, these artists must assert themselves and promote their work.

In traditional Puebloan society, the role of artist has carried little prestige. A woman shaping a well-formed pot, with pleasing designs, could at most expect the praise of her neighbors. Another potter might admire her wares, or discuss their designs with her. Decoration of utilitarian pottery during the historic Pueblo period was not critical to the welfare or survival of the society. Although men's production of sacred arts was crucial to the spiritual survival of the community, the demand for these arts was never great enough to warrant a class of professional artists.

One pursuit, however, was critical to survival: to be a successful farmer. Farming was the only legitimate full-time undertaking. Politics, the priesthood, art, war-making: all were part-time pursuits. Moreover, an individual could not aspire to leadership until proving to his community that he was a good man, a contributor to the general welfare. He had to be a good farmer. His own vitality was caught up inextricably with the vitality of his fields. Tall cornstalks and bright yellow, trumpet-shaped squash blossoms symbolized his right to be recognized as a productive Puebloan. Although today's agriculture only supplements the Pueblo economy, farming remains an important obligation every man must meet.

A Pueblo artist still must tend his fields. Even in the 1970s, an Indian artist who decided to straddle the cultural fence had to convince his elders that he had not "sold out" to the non-Indian

216. At left, Julian Martinez (Pho ka neh; 1897–1943) of San Ildefonso Pueblo, standing with Velino (Shije) Herrera (Ma Pe Wi; 1902–1973), middle, of Zia Pueblo, and Alfonso Roybal (Awa Tsireh; 1895–1955) of San Ildefonso.

217. Crescencio Martinez (Ta'e; 1879–1918) and his wife, Anna Montoya Martinez (1885–196?), at San Ildefonso Pueblo with Charles Wakefield Cadman, a musician and composer, ca. 1915.

world. He had to make his crops grow—close to a full-time job in summer—and yet find time to make and market his art.

Methods for coping with this problem were devised as early as the 1930s by several prominent commercial artists of San Ildefonso. When painters like Awa Tsireh (Alfonso Roybal), Julian Martinez, Wo Peen, and Oqwa Pi were absent from the pueblo for long periods of time, they hired Spanish American laborers to tend their fields (Soil Conservation Service 1935:51–52). When sales slumped, the hired labor was laid off and artists resumed traditional economic roles. One observer noted in 1935, "the bottom has dropped out of painting. The three principal painters [of San Ildefonso] are cultivating their fields this year" (Soil Conservation Service 1935:52). Women artists encountering similar problems developed similar solutions. A Pueblo woman's first calling is to be a conscientious housekeeper, wife, and mother. With the increasing need for cash income, however, women began to spend more time digging clay, and shaping, painting, and firing their pots. But Maria Martinez's career as a potter soared while her reputation as a good housekeeper remained unblemished; she employed Spanish American women to perform her household duties.

The Puebloans are in many ways frightened of change; and the commercial artist who succeeds in the Anglo world instigates social change, even if he or she juggles both the old and the new with exceeding agility. The extent to which Indian artists are capable of instituting radical—and even permanent—change in their communities is clearly illustrated in the events that occurred at San Ildefonso between 1900 and the late 1930s.

The story begins in the 1880s, when the first tourist pottery (San Ildefonso polychrome) was manufactured. By 1900 there was a husband-and-wife team specializing in pottery for the tourist market. Florentino Montoya painted the pots and his wife, Martina, shaped, polished, and fired them.

The success of this couple inspired other such alliances. Ten years later, the name of Crescencio Martinez was well known to Indian art collectors. He decorated the pottery made by his mother, wife, and sister. Among other famous husband-and-wife teams were Julian and Maria Martinez, and Juan Cruz Roybal and Tonita Martinez Roybal (figs. 107, 218; Chapman and Harlow 1970:25–27).

Pottery-making emerged as the most profitable profession for a San Ildefonso woman. Between 1910 and 1915 many more women joined the profession (fig. 219). A number of men who had worked with their wives in the manufacture of pottery turned to painting on paper to supplement their incomes, but it always ran a poor second to their wives' occupation. In the 1920s, when black-on-black ware had replaced the older polychrome and black-on-red traditions, there was not enough pottery to meet the demand. The team effort concept cut down at least some of the time required to finish a piece, and importation of Cochiti slip made a further contribution to the volume of pots turned out. Even the perfection of black-on-black tourist ware was a step in this direction, since it used less elaborate designs on smaller pieces.

These innovations changed San Ildefonso pottery to such an extent that the 1920s end product bore almost no resemblance to its progenitor of the 1880s. But if there were any cries of illegitimacy,

218. Juan Cruz (1887–?) and Tonita Roybal (1892–1945)
at San Ildefonso Pueblo, around 1935.

they came from outsiders and not from the pueblo. Changes in a secular art tradition, no matter how drastic, do not seem to distress Puebloans. What did distress them was that ambition and the lure of the dollar were urging their potters toward increasingly unorthodox behavior.

Maria Martinez stands out from this group of potters as the most forceful and inventive. Her boldness led her to buy her neighbors' unfinished pots, complete them, and sell them under her own name (Whitman 1947:105). She polished slip so meticulously that it became a black mirror, and her pleasing pots sold much more dearly than did the work of other potters. Resentment toward Maria grew quickly. She had challenged the egalitarian nature of Pueblo society; she could make more money because she was more skilled. Other San Ildefonsans began to realize that a pot or painting signed by a "better" artist brought more money:

> Adam Martinez (the son of Maria and Julian) makes naïve paintings for his parents' shop
> that are signed "Julian." On being asked why Adam did not sign his own paintings,
> Santana, Adam's wife, said: "Because they would not sell" (Soil Conservation Service
> 1935:51–52).

Meanwhile, the profit motive spawned even greater inventiveness. By the end of the 1920s, Maria had employed several relatives to assist in stages of pottery-making. The economic advantages of mass production became evident, and as the 1930s began, the experiment expanded into a full-scale cottage industry.

At Maria's and in other houses in the pueblo, specialized workers have been developed

219. San Ildefonso women making pottery on the lawn of the Palace of Governors in Santa Fe, around 1919. From left to right: Maria Martinez, Anna, unidentified, and Romona.

who regularly "slip" and polish the pots and, in some cases, mould them. Sometimes, as at Maria's, the group is a family group: a daughter-in-law, a husband's niece, a dependent sister, or others. These workers, if paid, Maria says receive $1.00 per day . . . with other employers, less successful, they are paid with wheat or corn. Where family dependents are not available, the poor regularly work for the rich in San Ildefonso potterymaking (Soil Conservation Service 1935:68).

At the height of the factory system, certain employees were responsible even for signing the artist's name on the bottom of the vessel: "The signature of the pot, made by the woman who applies the slip, is nevertheless 'Maria and Julian.' Dionicia, a young relative, was observed making these signatures as she worked. On inquiry Maria said: 'The pot is mine. . . . I moulded this pot' " (Soil Conservation Service 1935:68).

The overwhelming financial success of the major San Ildefonso artists introduced much more than just new production techniques. Two revolutionary changes in the structure of the society occurred. First, the buying and selling of labor became a permanent part of the pueblo's internal economy. Second, as the hiring of poorer community members became common, two economic classes grew out of a formerly egalitarian system.

As San Ildefonsan pottery production increased, the next step was marketing. The Fred Harvey bus tours inadvertently provided the new method of distribution by faithfully stopping at the doors of Maria, Antonita, and other prominent potters, so that tourists could meet these celebrated Indians in person. This steady, dependable flow of buyers soon led to the creation of small home retail shops. Porches and living rooms were stocked with baskets from the Jicarilla Apache, White Mountain Apache, and Ute, and with silverwork and textiles from the Navajo and Hopi (Soil Conservation Service 1935:57; Burton 1936:69).

Other Indian groups were anxious to deal with the San Ildefonsans, since they offered cash, rather than goods, in trade. No other Indian group in the United States had developed such entrepreneurial skills. A comparison with Tesuque Pueblo illustrates this point. Like most other Puebloans in the 1930s, the Tesuque poorly understood the concept of wholesaling, assuming it meant merely selling their materials to a trader. While San Ildefonsans usually required wholesale buyers to purchase fifteen to twenty pieces, Tesuque potters sold any quantity the trader would buy. Furthermore, they exchanged their pottery for groceries instead of cash. When a potter became desperate for food, she lowered her prices, allowing a trader to fill all his needs to the exclusion of the rest of the village. This meant, in effect, that if one woman had groceries for the week, her competitors went hungry (Soil Conservation Service 1935:55).

In a small community, where everyone is a relative or friend, nothing could be worse than competition for food. Tesuque's farmlands had been essentially depleted; there was almost no wage work available. Selling pottery meant survival, but it also meant turning on one's neighbor. The Tesuque were acting against the Pueblo concept of a good community member: instead of promoting the common good, they were ruthlessly undercutting each other. Resentment and hostility riddled the pueblo.

Although by contrast the San Ildefonsans applied Western economic principles to salvage a dying economy, no amount of financial security could change the fact that they too were experiencing serious social problems. The artist's stampede to claim a corner of the market was trampling traditional values and attitudes. "The pot now symbolized not the connection of the potter with the deep spring of Indian life, but her connection with the white life" (Soil Conservation Service 1935:105–106) and all the Pandora's box of troubles that entailed.

220. Rose Gonzales selling pottery, ca. 1935.

The most predictable outcome of this newfound surplus was jealousy and rivalry among potters. As one observer commented:

> Feelings have grown to such a pitch that women will not visit one another lest they be suspect of trying to spy on the number of pots their rivals may have or be accused of stealing designs. And women say jealously of one another, "She works night and day on her pottery" (Whitman 1947:106).

This competitiveness became generalized as an intense rivalry between the two halves of San Ildefonso Pueblo, the North and South plazas, which deepened as the economic gap between the two widened. Non-Indian patrons began to take sides. Friends of the South Plaza, such as Ina Cassidy, accused the North Plaza supporters of discriminating against the other half of the pueblo. They felt Rose Gonzales and Susannah Aguilar were being slighted by leaders of the Santa Fe Indian Fair. The South Plaza patrons were equally vocal, accusing Maria Martinez and Antonita Roybal of an unfair monopoly of the fair (Soil Conservation Service 1935:81).

What the North Plaza women won in wealth and prestige, the men lost in morale. Women potters became the heads of households, bought the family groceries, and paid the bills. Although a number of men helped their wives or other female relatives to design and paint pottery, it was the women's names that were associated with the work. With the exception of Julian Martinez, none co-signed pots they painted. This reversal of roles resulted in feelings of worthlessness and failure on the part of the men. Some sold their own paintings for extra cash, but this income was never substantial. Up until 1937, painters could expect to earn a maximum of nine hundred dollars in a good year, whereas the better potters made close to two thousand dollars a year as early as the 1920s (Brody 1971:88).

The incidence of alcoholism among men of the North Plaza rose markedly during this period (Soil Conservation Service 1935:85). By 1930 the level of alcoholism in the pueblo had seriously handicapped the smooth internal workings of the society, and women became the heads of households in an even truer sense.

This was evident on San Antonio Day—a day on which the returned school children are supposed to be brought into the spirit of the ceremonies. In a charming bower on the plaza, Maria and her sisters sat in beauteous raiment, watching with inner pain and devastation the debacle of the men. According to a reliable informant, the two male dancers and the entire chorus save one man (Romando Vigil) were drunk by evening and "lying in the ditch" (Soil Conservation Service 1935:85).

A pueblo can function only in a limited way without male authority figures. Religious and political leadership traditionally belonged to men; a woman could not be governor, *cacique*, or priest. Men had little chance in the 1930s to regain their roles as economic providers, but it was feasible for them to recapture their political and religious standing. Some women, such as Maria Martinez, began to push their husbands into sobriety and encourage them to take more interest in community affairs. Along with moral support, these women could provide the money needed to sponsor events such as weddings, dance ceremonies, and initiations. Taking on the costly responsibility of providing feasts for up to a hundred people, and financing wedding garments and dance costumes, brought great admiration and respect to the donor. Drawing on his wife's ample income, Julian Martinez was able to support community events generously. This show of goodwill enabled him to overcome his unfavorable reputation as a problem drinker. In fact, by 1940, he had so thoroughly regained the respect of the pueblo that he was elected governor.

221. Julian Martinez firing pottery, around 1940.

Julian's ascension is a case in point, illustrating further the social changes wrought directly or indirectly by the flourishing art of San Ildefonso pottery-making. His recovery of standing in the community would never have occurred even one generation earlier. In traditional San Ildefonso society, once a man brought shame upon his house, he could never qualify for a position of leadership, whatever his change of heart. However, by the time Julian was named governor, this had changed (Marriott 1948:267). The San Ildefonso coup d'état of 1925 was instrumental in establishing many new ground rules for the attainment of political power and leadership. The North Plaza faction, dominated by wealthy women artists and their families, had seized control of the pueblo from the poor farmers of the South Plaza, whose legitimate rule no longer had economic support. As the pueblo's future was dependent on the continued monetary support of the wealthy arts-and-crafts-producing families, the South Plaza had no choice but to capitulate to the new regime, which has remained unchallenged to the present.

The power struggle at San Ildefonso was facilitated by the commercial artists' close association with Anglo patrons and dealers. Through this association they gained financial independence from the rest of the village. As their economic reliance on fellow community members diminished, they began to make their own decisions and run their own affairs. When the non-art-producing families came to rely on the artists for the financial support of the pueblo, the artists' dictates inevitably were accepted. After the coup, it became important for political leaders, especially the governor of the pueblo, to have a good rapport with the white society. One of the governor's main functions was to act as a liaison between his community and the outside world. There could be no more logical candidate for this role than a commercial artist. When the North Plaza took over, they placed artists or members of art-producing families in key political positions: The new governor, Sotero Montoya, appointed as his assistants Julian Martinez and Juan Cruz Roybal, a pottery decorator. Richard Martinez became War Chief and Alfonso Roybal and Romando Vigil assisted him in his duties. All three were painters. Julian Martinez then became governor in 1940 and his son, Popovi Da, a potter, was elected to the office a decade later.

With the defeat of the South Plaza leadership, most of the North Plaza men abandoned their careers as painters and devoted their time to politics. Their wives continued to make pottery, pay the bills, and buy the groceries. But the men had a sense of purpose in their lives now; they had a reason for devoutly taking part in the religious ceremonies—and for remaining sober.

The role of the Indian artist has been totally redefined by the commercial Indian art market. Once the artist produced exclusively for the needs of his own community, but today he is almost solely concerned with the demands of white patrons. Commercial artists have to be striving, competitive, individualistic, and self-motivating. Unfortunately, these are exactly the qualities discouraged in many traditional Southwest Indian societies. Resistance to the acculturative influence of the commercial artist has followed a uniform pattern. Native community members resent the artist's newly acquired social mobility and wealth. As soon as the artist's superiority in marketing his personal talent and outstripping others financially has been proven, they view him as a threat to the egalitarian nature of their society.

Initially, native communities, and especially the Puebloans, used threats and physical coercion to suppress the commercial artist. Yet realizing that the extinction of their traditional economies is inevitable, they have slowly relaxed this pressure and have reluctantly begun to accept the ethnic-art market, with all its threatening influences, as their new source of subsistence.

VII

THE FUTURE

Frames of Reference: Native American Art in the Context of Modern and Postmodern Art

GERHARD HOFFMAN

INDIAN ART, THE CONCEPT OF THE FOURTH WORLD, AND THE MODERN PERSPECTIVE

When speaking of Indian art, one must take into account the concept of a Fourth World, which in cultural anthropology has gained acceptance as "the collective name for all aboriginal or native peoples whose lands fall within the national boundaries and techno-bureaucratic administrations of the countries of the First, Second, and Third Worlds" (Graburn 1976:1)[1]. These are people without countries of their own and without the power to control their own personal and collective lives. They are no longer "primitive" people, but live in continuous contact with the dominant culture; therefore, the two most important aspects of their art are integration and differentiation. Such "primal" societies (a term that has come more and more to replace the pejorative "primitive") are no longer isolated or autonomous, and their art is often produced neither for their own people nor according to their own unmodified tastes. Because of this, "the study of the arts of the Fourth World," as Graburn (1976:9) has stated, "is different from the study of 'primitive' art, . . . for it must take into account more than one symbolic and aesthetic system, and the fact that the arts may be produced by one group for consumption by another. The study of Fourth Worlds arts is, par excellence, the study of *changing* arts—of emerging ethnicities, modifying identities, and commercial and colonial stimuli and repressive actions."

The First World in which Indian culture is placed is Euro-America, the civilization that has dominated the movements and developments of modern art. In spite of its internal differences—for example, those existing between European and American traditions—Euro-American culture has a spiritual unity. An overarching term like "Western art" does not so much refer to geography as it does to particular attitudes, beliefs, and a cultural mentality, and these form a clearly definable whole, which we call Euro-American civilization.

When Indian art is viewed from a modern perspective, two major issues are raised. First is the relation of Indian art to the modernist art movements that originated in Europe, and to the sophisticated and elitist sensibility these movements fostered there and in the United States. Second is the place and function of Indian art in our fragmented, pluralistic, postmodern world. In this culture, the notion of identity—so central for the individualistically oriented West—is undergoing radical change, as are the concepts of reality versus fiction, truth versus cliché, and high art versus popular art. Even the existence of art itself as an autonomous entity has been challenged.[2]

222. Peyote Road Man. *Carl Sweezy (1881–1953), Arapaho. Ca. 1930, oil on paper, 21 × 12 inches. Private collection.*

As with his Shawnee compatriot Earnest Spybuck, Sweezy was a meticulous chronicler of the ceremonies of the Native American Church in Oklahoma. His carefully accurate ethnographic detail contrasts with the Expressionist use of color and symbolism in the Peyote paintings of the 1960s and 1970s, whose visual references to altered states were highly subjective. In this painting the Peyote Road Chief (ceremonial leader of a Peyote congregation) is a Christlike personage reminiscent of the central figures in the traditional *santos*, or saint, paintings of the Spanish colonial Southwest.

It has been argued by T. S. Eliot (1920:49) that each individual artist who wants to be genuinely innovative must acquire a historical sense, which "involves a perception, not only of the pastness of the past but of its presence" (see also Kramer 1974:13). For the Indian artist attempting to combine his Indian heritage with the traditions and methods of the Western art world, this means a continual striving to understand his own traditions, the myths and legends of his people, and the inner logic and evolution of modern art, all at the same time. As two of the greatest modern innovators, Matisse and Picasso, exemplify, perhaps it is even necessary to absorb the styles of the great masters of the past before one can fully participate in a cultural scene that has been formed by them. Intensifying the problem is the fact that, at this late stage, the various styles of modernism compose a simultaneous order, and have become both temporal and timeless.

Any analysis of Indian painting and sculpture, traditional or contemporary, has to take into account a number of perspectives, of which six are pertinent here: (1) the historical development of Indian art, its circumstances and conditions; (2) the traditions, legends, and myths of Indian culture, and their expression in Indian painting; (3) the adaptation of modern art styles by Indian artists and the reasons for their selections; (4) the expansion of the criticism of Indian art to include the concept of a Fourth World; (5) the effect of the majority cultural scene on minority art; and finally, (6) the concept of regionalism in an analysis of Indian art. This last is a concept that swings in two directions, both toward tourist art and nostalgic kitsch and toward what is perhaps a true alternative to empty, nationally interchangeable, and arbitrary art styles.

TRADITIONAL INDIAN ART AS PRIMAL ART

Indian painting today is pluralistic, and thus fits into the postmodern scene. It has the double problem of adjusting to an originally foreign artistic medium, easel painting, and at the same time preserving its Indianness (although the latter is not a goal of all contemporary Indian artists). The Indian artist must decide whether to adapt to mainstream Western art and lose his identity as an Indian artist (whatever that identity may mean, given the number of disparate Indian tribes and an ever-growing force of acculturation), or to try to preserve the images of his culture, recast in modern forms. The subjects of the twentieth-century traditional Indian painter are the well-known images of Indian Studio painting of the 1930s: scenes of daily domestic activities, weaving and pottery-making, the hunt, animals and nature, ceremonials and dance, war and conflict, peyote dreams, and other time-honored and time-worn themes cherished by white patrons as nostalgic tokens of a romanticized past.

Modernist times have been able to embrace traditional Indian art only by seeing it as genuine folk art. One difficulty, of course, has always been that Indian easel painting is not "genuine," in the sense of aboriginal. Paper and canvas were borrowed from the white man, who also instructed Indians in their use. This occurred, for example, at San Ildefonso Pueblo, in Oklahoma among the Kiowa, at Dorothy Dunn's Studio (founded in Santa Fe in 1932), and at the Institute of American Indian Art. Only if Indian art is seen as a changing art can one accept that it need not lose its genuineness when it adopts a foreign medium.

As the difficulty concerning the medium of easel painting in Indian art has been overcome, the two-dimensional, representational style of traditional Indian painting has profited from the revived appreciation of folk art. Folk and primitive art, with their stylization, directness, and timelessness, have served as sources of renewal for an overcivilized Western art audience dissatisfied with the cluttered scene of its own overpowering traditions. The result is a double perspective: traditional Indian art can be seen not only as naïve and picturesque folk art (in this case, the remnant of an ethnic tradition), but also as a primal art that embodies a true alternative system of aesthetic and epistemological values. One connection between traditional folk art, primal art, and modern art is their shared genuineness. In the case of traditional Indian art, this quality can be defined as primal and tribal, even though it was produced for outsiders. Through the insights of Sigmund Freud and Carl G. Jung, we have come to accept the primal sensibility not only as a historical phenomenon of the collective past but also as a permanent part of our unconscious, and thus a psychological fact. This, and our acceptance of culture as a multiplicity of different attitudes and values, have allowed us to perceive primal art as a valid expression of the human spirit.

THE PRIMAL ASPECT OF TRADITIONAL INDIAN ART

Cultures are differentiated by their image-making. Images portray "situations" placed in space and time, often peopled with characters who act and interact. The conception and depiction of space, time, and personal interaction are determined by one's specific historical conception of the outer and inner worlds. In the case of traditional Indian art, these elements of the image are stylized, often without linear perspective, resulting in a flat picture without background or foreground (fig. 197). The artistic process of selection, combination, and context-building seems to lack individuality and originality, in the Western sense of those words. On the other hand, the images that are formed are marked by wholeness, directness, and a kind of communal or universal spirit. The atmosphere of the paintings shows a close interrelationship between subjective feeling and the objective reality through which it is expressed. Subjectively, the painting conveys specific emotional content. Objectively, it presents the essence of nature and society, as seen through an archetypal image, such as an animal, a situation like hunting, or a social ceremony like dancing. The main factor is always the coherence of things and the ability of the human faculties to perceive and organize them. Dream and wakefulness, consciousness and the unconscious, body and spirit, all partake in the "feeling" of the picture. This is not achieved by the faithful representation of quantities of visible detail, but by their distortion, exaggeration, or abstraction according to the coherent emotional patterns of the painting.

Reality in these paintings is often mythical and ritualized. As Dufrenne (1973:119–120) has said: "For the primitive [person], truth does not lie in the insignificant appearances of the everyday world but in the great cosmic forces which course through this world, in the exemplary events recounted in myth and repeated ritual, and in all that gives meaning to appearances rather than receiving it from them."

This meaning, as Cassirer (1944:82) has stated, lies in the sympathetic view of nature, in the belief in "a fundamental and indelible *solidarity of life* that bridges over the multiplicity and variety of its single forms. [Man] does not ascribe to himself a unique and privileged place in the scale of nature."

This solidarity of life can be expressed in realistic terms such as scenes of everyday life, ceremonials, and dances, or in surrealistic ways, such as those often used to depict the visions of peyote dreams (fig. 222). In both kinds of painting, one finds the perception and conceptualization of an interaction of forces. The invisible is made visible. The expressive organ is the human body, which is not placed outside the context, as a spectator, but participates in, even creates the world through gesture, movement, and general expression.

Time in these traditional works of art is psychic (dream time) and cosmic, or eternal, not the mechanical time of the clock. It is the eternal now, not the linear time that underlies the concept of cause and effect and of progress. It speaks of cyclical repetition and variation, not of an isolation of movements. This psychic and cosmic time is sacred, and gives a mythical order to life. Time and

223. Number 1, 1948. Jackson Pollock (1912–1956), American. 1948, oil on canvas, 68 × 104 inches. Collection, The Museum of Modern Art, New York. Purchase.

motion are concretized into bodily action that is prior to and more essential than words and thoughts, just as things are made to participate in events. This time is part of space, and space participates in time.

Space, as Cassirer (1944:42) remarked, is the most fundamental dimension of the mythical world and of life in general. Wilhelm Worringer (1959:44), in his very influential book *Abstraction and Empathy*, argues that the "primal artistic impulse" (*Urkunsttrieb*) must be seen as a search for pure abstraction. This abstraction provides the artist's only "possibility of repose within the confusion and obscurity of the world-picture." Tortured by the "immense spiritual perception of space and by feelings of anxiety" (my translation), he is impelled to remove the particular thing that stimulates his interest from its unclear and confusing connection with the outer world, and make it independent "both of the ambient external world and of . . . the spectator—who desires to enjoy in it not the cognate-organic, but . . . necessity and regularity." Being himself bound to life, he can express these principles of life only through abstraction. This abstraction has, of course, various forms, and might appear not as pure abstraction but as stylization in traditional, realistic styles of representation in Western art. But whether through abstraction or through stylization (which differ only in degree), the spiritual and the material world unite. Therein lies the characteristic genuineness of primal and folk art, which can offer a truly alternative conception of the world, based not on individual taste, but on a communal and cosmic spirituality.

Action dynamizes space and concretizes time in motion. The buffalo hunt (Tahoma's *In the Days of Plenty*, fig. 175) and the dance motif (Kabotie's *Hopi Ceremonial Dance*, fig. 201) are outstanding examples of the aesthetic fusion of nature and man, space and time. Depending on the special traits of the tribal group, emphasis may be placed on the dynamics of the situation (as with the Plains Indians) or on the static quality of motion (as in the painted dances of the Pueblo Indians). We will see, however, that the particular dynamism or stasis of this fusion of time and space in motion is a phenomenon that is influenced by the development of Indian painting and the logic of that development.

The situation in a painting is unified through action and through the depiction of the human being, who appears as a participant in events. However, the overall integrating principle is not man, but proceedings that are larger than he is. They form the situation under which everything is subsumed and whose depiction aims at the essential, rather than the inclusive.

Ultimately, traditional Indian painting is characterized by the rhythm of line, color, and design. This concept of rhythm relates traditional Indian painting to modern painting, for instance, that of Matisse; the painters of German Expressionism; the Cubists Picasso, Braque, and Gris; the abstract painters Kandinsky and Mondrian; and the American Abstract Expressionists of the postwar scene.[3]

224. Puberty robe. Apache. Ca. 1870, hide and pigment, 43 × 32 inches. Philbrook Art Center, Tulsa, Elizabeth Cole Butler Collection, L82.1.95.

As with Navajo sand paintings, Apache hide paintings often have an exploding pattern in which elements radiate outward from a core point toward infinity. This design, seen on objects such as puberty robes (used in maturation ceremonies) or magician's capes, is related to the Navajo and Apache belief in the symbolic transference of power. Its focal point was thought of as an osmotic membrane through which power could be lured to activate the supernatural beings drawn on the ceremonial garment or sand painting. This belief in the properties of a powerful center that could conduct the curative and exorcise the demonic was attractive to Jackson Pollock, who often worked toward the center from the outer edges of his large paintings.

Indeed, Pollock was influenced in his action painting by Navajo sand paintings (figs. 223 and 224). This rhythm, despite differences of conception and technical means, also connects traditional with modern Indian painting.

TRADITIONAL INDIAN ART AND TOURIST ART

What we have so far presented is, of course, an ideal picture of traditional Indian art as primal art. It does not take into account the possibility of its trivialization into tourist art through the corrupting influence of the market, or, in other words, its transformation into kitsch. The question of where to draw the line between art and kitsch is most difficult to answer. To do so becomes more urgent the more one believes that a genuine traditional Indian art exists, which participates in the expression of the primal tribal spirit and embodies a valid alternative world view for Western society. But though traditional Indian painting has clearly been a primal expression, it has also been a business, catering to those with a taste for the old and for stereotyped romantic notions of the Indian as noble savage, bearer of powerful prescientific and non-Western wisdom.

How do we differentiate true, genuine traditional Indian art from its ready-made imitations? This question touches upon the more fundamental problem of separating kitsch from art. Its answer cannot be spelled out once and for all, but must be considered in the light of historical context. Obviously, one must look at the paintings themselves, not at the painters, their pedigrees, or their positive or negative associations with tribal life—all of which are relative. Primal art, whether considered as art or as folk art, is not exempt from the general rules of aesthetic judgment. The point at which genuine traditional Indian art is transformed into kitsch can only be determined by a comparison between the characteristics of the ready-made pieces of tourist art and the ideal qualities of primal art. The qualities of the truly expressive native piece are embodied, as we have said, in the concept and depiction of rhythmical unity.

Traditional Indian art does not negate, but confirms the coherence of the universe. Its characteristic is the balance of forms and movements. Therefore, the danger of its trivialization, heightened by the modern belief in ambiguity and multivalence, lies in a lack of tension. Since meaning can be constituted only dialectically, by contrasting a positive and a negative pole, harmony can only appear, or rather be concretized, in contrast to tension. This polar relation between tension and harmony is

225. Mesa. *Dan Namingha (1950–), Hopi. 1980, acrylic on canvas, 68 × 58 inches. The Gallery Wall, Santa Fe.*

Namingha captures the spirit of the land of his Hopi ancestors in his large, sunlit abstract canvases. What he has called the Cubist play of desert light and shadow is contrasted with the abstract forms of rocks, mesas, and buttes.

basic to all art—primal, folk, and elitist. Primal art, like folk art, may stress the harmony pole rather than that of tension. However, if tension disappears entirely, a gap between experience and expression opens up, resulting in art that is standardized and uninspired. When the artist takes a shortcut to harmony by omitting variation and complication, there is an overdose of feeling that is divorced from the concrete situation. The painting becomes sentimental formula art, void of the pleasures that lie in surprise and variety. It may become static, as do some examples of "Bambi" art, or it may express only a shadow of dynamism, as do some of the more sketchy hunting scenes. What is lost is the balance between feeling and the concrete situation that represents it.

THE VITALIZATION OF TRADITIONAL ART THROUGH TECHNIQUES OF MODERNISM

The development of Indian art toward the modern styles of Cubism, Futurism, Surrealism, and abstraction (see fig. 194) can be seen as an attempt on the part of the better and younger artists to escape the trivializations and formulas of their traditional art. They have tried to do this by heightening the expressive qualities of the picture through the dynamization of action (Quincy Tahoma, Allan Houser), atmospheric concentration (Swazo Hinds), abstraction and combination, for instance, of landscape features, figures, and masks (Dan Namingha), or collagelike arrangements of traditional figures and their stylized or abstracted backgrounds (Gilbert Atencio, Helen Hardin, Tony Da). The aim of all these approaches has been the same: to build up tension in the picture, not through the structure of the image alone, but also through pure color, shape, and line.

TRADITIONAL, ARCHETYPAL, AND REGIONAL INDIAN ART

Yet the most fundamental antinomy, one that constitutes the basic ambivalence of Native American arts, remains. Indian painting is both the true image of an alternative way of living, drawn from a historical context, and the romantic cliché of a dreamt-of freedom from the tensions of modern

226. Plaza Indian. *Bob Haozous (1943–), Chiricahua Apache/Navajo. 1983, bronze, 10¼ × 5½ × 5 inches. Private collection.*

Bob Haozous works within his own twentieth-century Indian world. The plaza figure in this bronze sculpture is a natural theme for Haozous, who lives in Santa Fe and is the son of another distinguished Indian sculptor, Allan Houser. As does his father, and as do many of the current generation of Indian artists, Haozous has great technical skill and his work shows a sophisticated use of the tools of the medium. Note the fine line, the deep patina, and the precise detail in this piece.

227. Seated Figure. *Henry Moore (1898–), British. 1930, alabaster, 18¼ inches. Art Gallery of Ontario, Toronto, Canada, purchase, 1976.*

civilization. In the case of traditional Indian art, we must ask whether and how the Indian image can truly fulfill the need of human beings, Indians and whites alike, to create visions of ideal harmony and dignity. Can the Indian image evolve from stereotype to archetype? Allan Houser has tried to work this alchemy by turning to sculpture and using the massive forms of stone and bronze (like Henry Moore, who influenced him), to extract the archetype from the cliché. Quincy Tahoma took the buffalo hunt, which the Kiowa artists of the 1920s probably still conceived of as the image of a lost freedom, and transformed it into the nostalgic symbol of a historical Age of Plenty. Purging motifs of sentimentality so that they may become symbols of the unconscious needs and drives of man has often been attempted in a new kind of regionalism. The danger that traditional Indian art will exhaust itself in stereotypes is both heightened and complicated by the dominance of a nostalgic regional style in the Southwest and by the development of Santa Fe, New Mexico, into a major art-market center of the United States.

In the Southwest (as evidenced in the pages of *Southwest Art* magazine), the lore of the Indian, the glamor of the cowboy, and the grandeur of the land are the paraphernalia of a regional art that has little to do with genuine Indian art. All the differentiations have become blurred, and Indianness

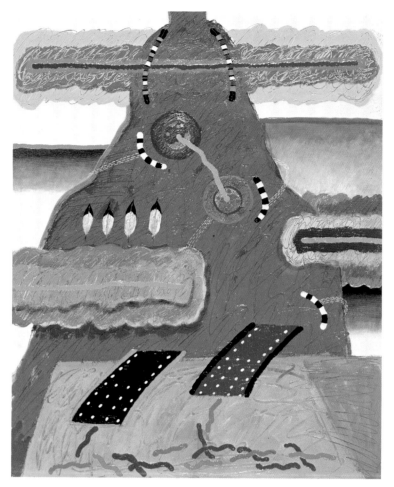

228. Spirit Guide/Healer. *George C. Longfish (1942–), Seneca/Tuscarora. 1983, acrylic and pencil on paper, 40 × 30 inches. Collection of the artist, Davis, California.*

Longfish's paintings are historically rooted, yet they suggest the perplexities of application of modern technology to universal human issues. In this work, as in *You Can't Rollerskate in a Buffalo Herd* (fig. 265), he experiments with abstract Indian symbols, fusing them with modern concepts of painting.

229. Revenge in Trade for a Wife. *Randy Lee White (1951–), Sioux. 1982, cast paper with acrylic pigment, 30 × 58 inches. Collection of the artist, New Mexico.*

230. Shoots the Soldier. *Randy Lee White, Sioux. 1982, cast paper with acrylic pigment, 30 × 58 inches. Collection of the artist, New Mexico.*

The aesthetic explorations of artists like Randy Lee White and G. Peter Jemison, especially their recent experiments with handmade paper sculpture, have taken them into the realm of the American craft-art movement. White's interest in the ironic fusion of historic Indian imagery with contemporary media is illustrated in his paper fabrications of traditional Ghost Dance shirts. These highly embellished shirts are associated with the earlier autobiographical war shirts and later with the Ghost Dance, which began in the early reservation period on the Plains. This movement was a messianic attempt to regenerate Indian consciousness through retrieval of traditional values and lifeways, in order to preserve Indian society from the white onslaught. Randy Lee White's resurrection of such images, executed for a mainstream market and translated into contemporary materials, results in beautiful and highly resonant works of art.

has come to serve a decorative function. Some Indian artists (George Longfish, for instance) have concluded that it is better to stay away from the Southwest. Longfish and others, like Jaune Quick-to-See Smith and Emmi Whitehorse (both of whom still live in the Southwest), have turned to an abstract style which still retains signs of their Indian heritage. Quick-to-See Smith, for example, uses pictographs and petroglyphs in her abstract paintings. Others have transformed the clichés of the Indian through irony (Fritz Scholder, T. C. Cannon; see figs. 212 and 181) or through a manipulation of traditional Indian painting, making reference, whimsical or ironic, to Indian or white stylistic traditions (Randy Lee White, Virginia Stroud, Jerry Ingram).

This is not to say that Indian painting in the Southwest is doomed to be second-class or merely tourist art if it does not infuse itself with the anxiety or irony of the modern experience. The crisis of postmodern art has resulted not only in cosmopolitan styles like Pop Art, or the parody of past movements, but also in a new kind of regionalism often combined with high modernism. In the United States, this regionalist movement often embraces the concept of ethnicity: for example, that

231. Crow. Kevin Red Star (1942–   ), Crow. 1976, mixed media on paper, 17½ × 23 inches. Private collection.

Red Star was among the first of the young Indian artists of the 1960s and 1970s to adopt assimilation images from the reservation period (such as reservation policemen and cowboys, and beaded leggings on pairs of Levi-Strauss blue jeans), converting them impressionistically into decorative collages of Euro-American and Indian imagery.

of Indians or Chicanos. The destruction not only of concepts of reality and aesthetic meaning, but also of the symbolic images of modern art has left behind a general lack of symbols and archetypes. This dearth has at least partly caused the boom in art photography and in Photorealist painting, not to mention the nostalgic return to nineteenth-century imagery, so obvious in the Southwestern revival of romantic cowboy-and-Indian painting. Although the use of modern styles could universalize the regional and ethnic image, the postmodern parodic attitude could, on the other hand, neutralize any excess of pastoral simplicity, emotion, and nostalgia. And that is exactly what some of the most successful Indian painters, Scholder, Cannon, Biss, Red Star, and Grey Cohoe, among others, have been doing. Their eclectic stylistic combinations of the expressive, the decorative, and the ironic have formed an ambivalent repertoire of recognizable but distorted images. Thus, at least an attempt is made to transform the stereotype into the archetype by its simultaneous acceptance and negation. An analysis of this development in Indian art might finally demonstrate that the artistic expression of minorities within majority cultures is based on a common structural principle. This principle includes (1) the combination of myth and history, (2) the attempt to purify the cliché, and (3) the search for art forms that concentrate, intensify, and generalize motifs, images, and rhythms, first in symbolic, then in ironic, and, perhaps, finally in playful popular modes.

The question of whether traditional Indian painting of the old school can escape becoming kitsch must be seen in still another context. For the differentiation between art and kitsch has become doubtful in a posthumanistic world that no longer has a fixed hierarchy of values and artistic standards. That the conflict between proponents of the traditional and champions of the modern/postmodern has abated lately appears to be less a sign of growing insight than of increasing helplessness in the face of ever more rapidly changing modes and styles of painting, the exhaustion of the cult of the new, and the extensive reconsiderations and reevaluations of art and culture.

MODERNISM IN WESTERN ART

Modernism was originally European, taking form through a dialogue among France, Germany, and Italy, with important contributions from the Scandinavian countries and England. After the Second World War, America led the way into postmodern forms of expression; New York replaced Paris as the creative and commercial hub of the art world.

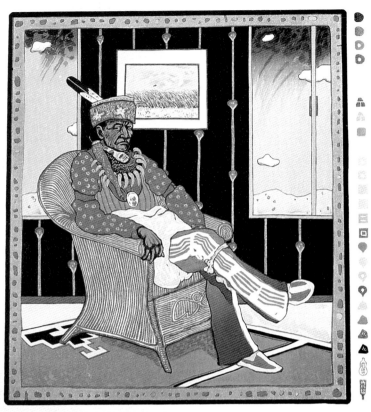

232. Collector #5 or Osage with Van Gogh. T. C. Cannon (1946–1978), Caddo. 1980, wood-block print on rice paper, 17¾ × 15 inches. The University of Tulsa.

This print by T. C. Cannon is among the most widely reproduced Indian works of the last decade. Cannon's tragic early death removed the most eloquent of the young Indian painters, but he was already famous for his wry and poignant portrayals of the resilience of Indian cultural and family life, and his work continues to influence the direction of Indian art. This image, which exists as a painting, poster, and woodcut, shows a finely dressed Osage sitting in his wicker chair between a Navajo rug and Vincent van Gogh's painting, *Wheatfield*, thus incorporating the worlds of mainstream and Indian art. Through the confident and smiling Osage, Cannon is saying that the modern Indian makes his own culture and his own art, drawing from both worlds. Paintings by Cannon were transferred by a traditional Japanese wood-block cutter onto as many as twenty-four blocks for printing by one of Japan's most distinguished printmakers.

The arrival of modernism in art initiated radical changes in at least three areas. First, it changed the concept and depiction of reality. The belief in an objective reality based on an obvious and unproblematic harmony between the outer and the inner realms gave way to the idea that reality exists somewhere in the relationship between subject and object, with the former becoming more and more the yardstick of true reality. Second, modernism existentialized both society's idea of the artist and the artist's idea of himself. He now stood at the center of the growing tensions between subject and object, individual and society, and between rational consciousness and the elemental impulses of the unconscious. These tensions caused an alienation of the artist from a realistically conceived outside world, from society, and even from the self, and led to the perception of the artist's life as tragic. Gauguin, Van Gogh, Edvard Munch, and Ernst Ludwig Kirchner stand as examples of this view. Third, new art forms developed, based on the need for a new kind of psychic and spiritual expressiveness, which could depict the "really real" beneath the outer surface. This process can lead, as with Cézanne and the Cubists, from the outer surface of reality to the aesthetic distillation of the spiritual form embedded in the material; or it can lead from the urges and the hallucinatory pictures of the innermost soul to their incorporation in external images, distorted in the process by psychic energy (Van Gogh, Munch, Emil Nolde). In both cases, however, the alienation of the subject from the world, from society, and from reason results in a new spiritual quest.

High modernism had been elaborated in its essential features by 1930. The unity of all these wildly contrasting directions of development was established by a common belief in the ability of art to represent modern experience, both as the artist lived it and as it had been developed and systematized in modern philosophy, psychology, sociology, and the natural sciences. The spiritual synthesis that the Middle Ages had found in metaphysical order, which from the Renaissance to the Enlightenment was transferred to human reason, and which the Romantic period assigned to the "deeper" region of feeling and imagination, was in modernism entrusted exclusively to the works of the creative imagination. Autonomous art as the objective correlative of an ambivalent and deeply disturbing subjective experience was the final synthesis of the modern mind. Autonomous art came to exist apart from empirical reality. It formed ambiguous aesthetic constructs that suggested simultaneously both unification and the ironic dissolution of unity. Modern art became a most serious and seminal force, both in individual works and in its logical and irreversible development from Impressionism to Symbolism, Expressionism, Fauvism, Cubism, Futurism, abstraction, and Surrealism, to mention only the most internationally influential directions it took.

FOUR MODERN STYLES AND INDIAN ART

In considering the influence of modernism on Indian art, it is not enough to mention certain parallels or influences, for example that of Cubism on painters like Oscar Howe or the group known as the Artist Hopid, especially Mike Kabotie and Millard Lomakema; of Art Nouveau and Matisse's decorative style on T. C. Cannon and Kevin Red Star; of Surrealism on Grey Cohoe; of Expressionism on Fritz Scholder (via Francis Bacon) and Frank Nieto; of Impressionism (combined with Expressionism) on Earl Biss; of Abstract Expressionism on George Morrison, George Longfish, Dan Namingha, Frank LaPena, and Jaune Quick-to-See Smith (with quite different results because of the eclecticism and individualism involved); of Pop art on Fritz Scholder, Harry Fonseca, and Richard Glazer Danay; or Photorealism on Ben Buffalo. Indian painting, a latecomer on the mainstream scene and not involved in the ideological conflicts and struggles that accompanied the birth of many new directions in art, has available for its expressive needs the whole spectrum of modern styles.

Four modern styles have suggested themselves especially to Indian artists.[4] First was the decorative style used by Gauguin and Matisse. For Gauguin, the decorative is a means to establish an aesthetic formula through pure line and color, and from that an artistic order, an integration and synthesis of the material without the illusion of an object. For Gauguin "the crass mistake [is] Greekness, beautiful as it is" (Haftmann 1962:39). One should not copy nature, but dream of it. These dreams aim at primeval states, the "ancient, sublime, religious" (Haftmann 1962:39); they direct attention to the primitive, to the exotic, and to folk art. Matisse's creative aim is the expression of a certain condition of the soul, influenced by surrounding things, but embodied in an autonomous aesthetic space, the *espace spirituel* of the picture. His formal means are the merging of foreground with background, surface with spatial depth, and object with decorative line, and the liberation of pure color and line. Matisse aims at canceling the tragic view of the world so as to establish a spiritual harmony through decorative pictorial means. Use of the decorative was already present in the pre-Columbian kiva wall paintings of the Hopi, and today it is seen in work by the Artist Hopid. In the paintings of Cohoe, Red Star, David Bradley, and G. Peter Jemison, however, it is a vehicle for expressing the schism in the existence and consciousness of the modern Indian.

The second modern style that influenced Indian art is Cubism, especially its later form, Synthetic Cubism. Liberation from linear perspective and from the need to transcribe the surface of an

233. Koshares with Cotton Candy. *Harry Fonseca, Maidu. 1982, acrylic on canvas, 24 × 30 inches. Collection of David and Marilee Clark, Tulsa.*

234. Koshares with Watermelons. *Harry Fonseca (1946 –), Maidu. 1983, acrylic on canvas, 30 × 20 inches. Philbrook Art Center, Tulsa, anonymous loan.*

Fonseca's Coyote appears in many wonderful guises: city Coyote, reservation Coyote, tourist Coyote, leather-jacketed Coyote, and mod Coyote. In recent years, Coyote has become more at home at the pueblo and in tribal ceremonies like the ones depicted here. As Fonseca creates more and more characters, and their personalities develop, a whole new mythology of modern Indian life unfolds. The old ways and old stories, in all their richness, once more provide a way to understand the new. The Fonseca Coyotes, consistent with traditional legends, are clever folk who both outsmart and are tricked by their environment.

235. Strawberry Dance, *Paper Bag series. G. Peter Jemison (1945–), Seneca. 1983, mixed media on handmade paper, 30½ × 22¼ inches. Collection of the artist, New York City.*

Both artistically and politically, Jemison has been among the leading forces advancing the right of Indian artists to experiment with imagery and materials, breaking from the supposed cultural tradition. The American Indian Community House Gallery in New York, which Jemison directs, was founded in part to provide a showcase where work by artists like George Longfish and Richard Glazer Danay could be assessed in the context of the contemporary American mainstream. Among Jemison's most strikingly original work is his *Paper Bag* series, handmade paper containers with colorful designs that are narrative, decorative, and vital. Like Matisse's arrangements of color, line, and form, these compositions convey a sense of a single moment taken from the sweep of an ongoing story and frozen in its visual perfection. The Strawberry Dance is a traditional June Iroquois dance.

236. Goldfish and Sculpture. *Henri Matisse (1869–1954), French. 1911, oil on canvas, 46 × 39⅝ inches. Collection, The Museum of Modern Art, New York. Gift of Mr. and Mrs. John Hay Whitney.*

In Matisse's arrangement of objects in space, foreground merges with background and line becomes lyrical as well as descriptive. Decorative vitality reminiscent of Matisse's work energizes the works of some contemporary Indian artists such as G. Peter Jemison and Grey Cohoe, though the messages conveyed by their works may be less harmonious than those of Matisse.

237. Untitled Hopi design. Millard Dawa Lomakema (1941–), Hopi. 1978, mixed media on board, 34 × 34 inches. Collection of the artist, Hopi, New Mexico.

The works of Millard Lomakema, one of a group known as the Artist Hopid, illustrate the antiquity of what critics call modernism in Indian art. Many of the themes familiar to the Hopi tribe for centuries are repeated in revival and modern art. This work, with its ceremonial dancer, stylized pottery designs, and supernatural figures rising from a storm cloud, uses ancient symbolic motifs evoking prehistoric kiva drawings.

object literally makes possible a precise handling of the world, effecting its aesthetic transformation through man's imagination. The object is analyzed by facets and recombined in simultaneous views that superimpose its imagined totality over the fragmentary details of its visible surface. Time becomes the fourth dimension of space (and, in Futurism, is further dynamized as movement, speed, and action). The painting is constructed according to its own logic and forms a hermetic and autonomous pictorial space in which nature is transformed into art. The Cubist can start with the object and transcend it into pure form, or he can start with an idea of form and translate that idea into an object. This gives Cubist painting great freedom and enormous potential to attain spiritual unity. The paintings become symbols of equilibrium; from the relationship between the object and its form there arises a third element, a spirituality in which the tension between man and the world attains a tenuous balance. Cubism and abstraction have exerted great influence on Indian painters, Howe, Kabotie, Lomakema, and Quick-to-See Smith, among others.

The third modern art style attractive to contemporary Indian painters is abstraction. In abstraction the tension between subject and object is avoided, or even negated, through the abolition of the outer world of things. Abstract painting is the dialogue of man with the inner world. In it the artist seeks the sympathetic unity of subject and object. Art is, in August Macke's words, the "expression of mysterious powers" (Haftmann 1962:180). In Kandinsky's book *Concerning the Spiritual in Art* (1947:67), he states that the "artist must train not only his eye but also his soul, so that it can weigh colors in its own scale and thus become a determinant in artistic creation." Kandinsky wrote in 1910 that he believed this inner necessity would lead to two future developments, both of which aim to express "the spiritual in art." The first, which Kandinsky himself founded with his first abstract watercolor that same year, is that of "Pure Abstraction," which seeks to transform material into energy through the use of pure color and line, to turn the universe into rhythm and kinetic structure, into visible music. The result is a dream world whose lyrical forms have been taken up, among the younger painters, by Emmi Whitehorse. For Kandinsky, Rousseau exemplified this development.

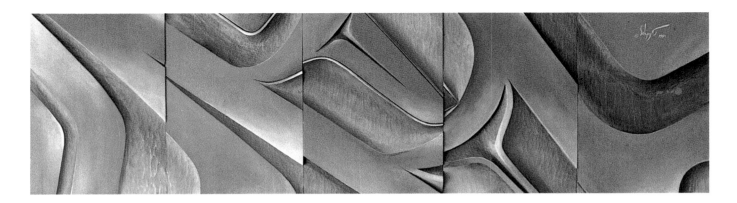

238. Stillwater #2. *James G. Schoppert (1947–   ), Tlin-git. 1984, carved and polychromed cedar, 16 × 54 inches. Collection of the artist, Seattle.*

239. Migrations. *James G. Schoppert, Tlingit. 1985, wood, walrus stomach, acrylic, string, feathers, 23½ × 34 × 5½ inches. Collection of the artist, Seattle.*

Schoppert's most recent wood sculptures have emphasized two fundamentally different approaches to contemporary Indian imagery. When exploring his own Tlingit design heritage, he draws on the rigid rules of the traditional formline system, dissecting and abstracting the elements in sculptures carved and painted on swelling and diminishing wooden surfaces, whose overall effect suggests the work of Louise Nevelson. However, when he is inspired by the southwestern Eskimo sculptors of the nineteenth century, his sensitive interpretations connect with and continue that remarkably Surrealist tradition.

Later inheritors of the spiritual-abstract approach included Klee, who spoke of his aim to "shift objects into the beyond" (Haftmann 1962:190) and used his fantastic figures for the depiction of the "irrepressible rhythm," which was playfully developed further by Miró and, among contemporary Indian artists, Jaune Quick-to-See Smith.

The fourth artistic method that lends itself to Indian painting is the unveiling of the magical dimension of objects. In the words of Haftmann, "it was discovered that the silent life of things possessed a special aura of strangeness, mystery, magic, which in the contemplating, reflective mind evoked a response expressing fear or irony, or a sense of deep kinship with things. The thing 'of hardest matter' became a component of human sensibility, and in it the unity of the outer and the

240. Eagle Egg. *James Havard (1937–), Choctaw/Chippewa. 1978, oil on canvas, 72 × 84 inches. The Williams Companies, Tulsa.*

Havard, a leading exponent of Abstract Illusionism, has earned an international reputation unrelated to his Indian heritage or to the world of traditional Indian art. His work, which creates an illusion of three-dimensionality on a flat plane through the use of flotation and shadows, stands at the opposite end of the Indian art continuum from the flat two-dimensionalism of the traditional studio painters. Although efforts to read Indian symbols into Havard's canvases may be misleading, it is hard to overlook the suggestion of medicine sticks, corn masks, and sand paintings native to the artist's heritage.

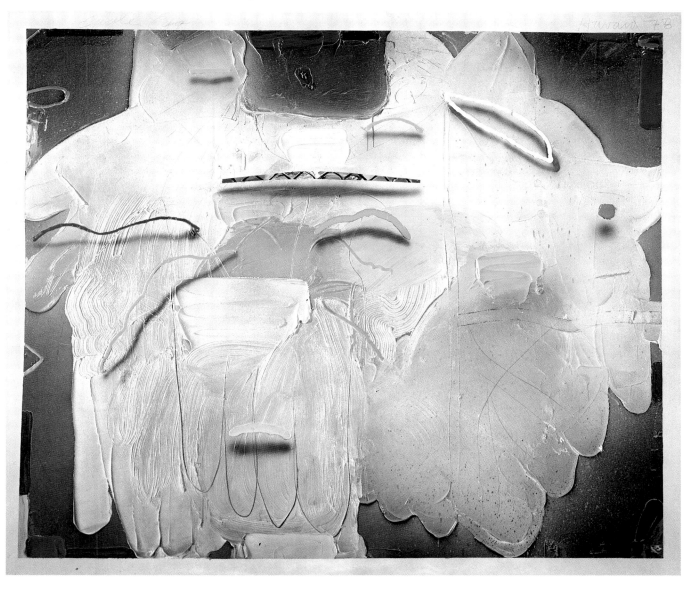

241. Black Lines. *Vasily Kandinsky (1866-1944), Russian. 1913, oil on canvas, 51 × 51⅝ inches. Solomon R. Guggenheim Museum, New York.*

242. *Landscape #2. Emmi Whitehorse (1956–   ), Navajo. 1981, watercolor, pastel, and pencil on paper, 22½ × 30 inches. The University of Tulsa.*

Whitehorse draws heavily on her native southwestern landscape for the inspiration of her colorful and precise abstract canvases. She is particularly influenced by traditional Navajo crafts, which she has reinterpreted in a series of homages to the older Navajo rug weavers, such as her grandmother.

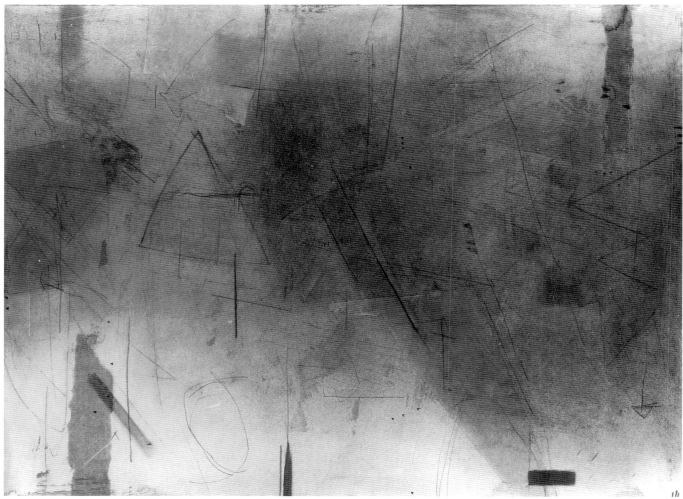

inner was once again achieved" (Haftmann 1962:126). Hopi painters Mike Kabotie, Millard Lomakema, and Dan Namingha are good examples of Indian artists using "the Magic Other," but so are the older Pueblo painters. Magical Realism is found also in the better pictures of traditional Indian painters.

THE INDIAN ARTIST BETWEEN MODERNISM AND POSTMODERNISM

It is not enough to point out a fundamental relationship between modern and primal art. Modern Indian art actually developed in the 1960s, when the syntheses of modernism were still unraveling. Post–World War II American Abstract Expressionism confirmed the tenets of modernism, but also presented the opportunity for an independent modern development in America. In the wake of Freud and Jung, and under the impact of the failure of social and artistic utopias and ideologies, the American Abstract Expressionists once more turned inward. They proceeded on the assumption that universal myths lived on in the collective unconscious and that the depiction of these myths represented an alternative to constructivistic modern art. Thus the Indian's and the white man's search for the mythic past intersected. In a much-quoted letter from Adolph Gottlieb and Mark Rothko (with Barnett Newman) to *The New York Times* in 1943, we read that they are concerned with "primitive myths and symbols that continue to have meaning today.... Only that subject matter is valid which is tragic and timeless. That is why we profess kinship with primitive and archaic art." Gottlieb's pictographs from the 1940s, with their cryptic images, schematic anatomic drawings of fishes, reptiles, birds, and animals, and abstract signs, recall the paintings of the Northwest Coast Indians, and are meant to call up man's prehistoric past. Rothko, Pollock, Clyfford Still, and Newman were concerned with the "Spirit of the Myth" (Janis 1944:118). Americans, unlike the European Surrealists who influenced them, gave up worn-out motifs and went in search of a new species of the sublime. Rothko, Still, and Newman developed color-field painting, which sought to avoid the juxtaposition of finite forms in favor of generous dimensions; from 1947 on, Pollock achieved the same effect of boundlessness in the furious, inexhaustible energy of his drip paintings, whose creation became a quasi-ritual act. Pollock had previously painted "mythic" pictures in close reference to Jung's writings and the examples he used of animal sexuality and night rites. Schapiro (1946:147) says of Pollock, Still, Rothko, and Newman that they sought "an absolute in which the receptive viewer can lose himself, [Pollock] in compulsive movement, the others in an all pervading ... sensation of dominant color."

As Clement Greenberg (1946:54) and others have noted, it was existentialism that determined the climate of the times for the action painters, albeit more atmospherically than philosophically.[5] To be mentioned here also are the representatives of "gesture painting," Robert Motherwell, Willem de Kooning, Hans Hofmann, Franz Kline, and Sam Francis. All were concerned with the true image, sought in combination with the unconscious and the mythic. The seductive potential of such myth-making (though private rather than communal) met the restless factions of Indian painting in the 1960s halfway. But Abstract Expressionism, which was existentially rooted in modernism, was called into question in the 1970s by another generation of artists, which included Robert Rauschenberg, Jasper Johns, and Allan Kaprow. Their mentor, John Cage, rejected existentialism as a basis for artistic expression, and pleaded instead, echoing Dada and Zen Buddhism, for a lighter, unsentimental, and playful intercourse with art, for the acceptance of "unsureness, accident, confusion, disunity" (Sandler 1974:449).

The whole modern and romantic concept of the artist was thus shaken. Cage reports a conversation with de Kooning in which the latter says, "We are different.... You don't want to be an artist, whereas I want to be a great artist." And Cage adds, "Now it was this aspect of wanting to be an artist... who has something to say, who wanted through his work to appear really great... which I could not accept" (Sandler 1974:453). He could not accept the grandeur of the work of art that is preserved, and instead propagated "impermanent art" whose purpose lay in defamiliarizing the viewer so as to make him see and hear with fresh senses, "just seeing what there was to see" (Sandler 1974:454). From the standpoint of defamiliarization and new combinations, any material is suitable, as Rauschenberg shows in his combine paintings. According to Cage, laughter was to replace the *ich-schmerz* (self-pain) of the Abstract Expressionists (Sandler 1974:449). Indian art, then, adapted the expressionist techniques of high and late modernism at a time when their very foundations were being shaken. The fundamental problems that resulted contributed to a constant tension between modern/postmodern art and Indian art.

Because Indian painting absorbed modernism late, after the new forms and ideologies had gained some acceptance, it could be more eclectic, more whimsical, more playful in its choices. This explains the succession of experimental modern art forms that appear both in Indian painting in general and in the works of individual Indian artists, for example those of Fritz Scholder (who was influenced not only by Francis Bacon, but also by postmodernist Pop Art). It also explains the juxtaposition of modern art and traditional styles in the works of painters like Mike Kabotie and Millard Lomakema, or Gilbert Atencio and Jerry Ingram. Dan Namingha says, "Experimentation helps create an artist's unique style." He is not concerned with "any particular style," saying, "If I would get stuck with one style, I don't know how I'd get out of it" (Highwater 1980:157). This experimentation permits, and perhaps even requires, numerous influences. Jaune Quick-to-See Smith, one of the most thoughtful spokesmen for her art, says, "I am the bridge-maker. Art and artists that are important to me are Oscar Howe, Paul Klee, Fritz Scholder, Robert Rauschenberg, Esteban Vicente, and [Richard] Diebenkorn, as well as the media of petroglyphs, pictographs, old skin robes, cave paintings, ledger art, and muslin painting" (Highwater 1980:180).

A second problem that results from the adoption of modern conceptions and forms by Indian artists lies in the difference between modernist and Indian motives. Modern art was originally the expression of an aesthetic and an epistemology deeply associated with the crisis of Western civilization. But in Indian art, modern art forms are used to express the alternative life experience of a minority culture. The spirituality of modern art, so obvious as an underlying current in later forms of Impressionism, and in Symbolism, Cubism, Expressionism, abstract art, and Surrealism, was a quest for the fulfillment and enhancement of the self. This quest could no longer be pursued in society, but only expressed (together with its tortures) in art. In Indian art, this kind of spirituality is communal and based on the land. Because of this, its expression can become "too easy," even in abstract art forms, thus negating the crisis both in the majority and minority cultures. On the other hand, compatibility of modernism with Indian painting makes it clear that modern art was ultimately more than an art of crisis. It was also an art of synthesis, and its integrating power remains, even after existential assumptions have changed. In fact, it could be argued that modern art forms became effective vehicles for Indian painting (as they would for any minority or Fourth World culture) only when they had been stripped of their ideological content. Conversely, the late forms of such styles can be revitalized by an infusion of new primal content springing from the ancient mythic vision of a holistic world, for example in Namingha's constructivistic landscapes and Katcina paintings, or in Jaune Quick-to-See Smith's combination of horses, buffalo, and pictographs with an Abstract Expressionist background.

243. American Landscape #3, *George Morrison (1919–   ),* *Chippewa. 1981, acrylic on canvas, 48 × 48 inches. Col-* *lection of the University of Tulsa.*

Morrison, a primary Indian exponent of Abstract Expressionism and a former professor of art at the University of Minnesota, was the first and most prominent Indian artist on the New York art scene in the dynamic years following World War II. *American Landscape #3,* with its brilliant colors, long lines, and haunting textures, suggests Morrison's search for order and his respect for nature's organizing whole. Because of his departure from Indian tradition, Morrison was until quite recently more widely known by mainstream critics and patrons than in the Indian art community.

244. *Untitled, Camus series. Jaune Quick-to-See Smith* *(1940–   ), Cree/Shoshone. 1980, pastel on paper, 19½ ×* *28 inches. Private collection.*

Jaune Quick-to-See Smith describes herself as a bridge-maker, influenced by European artists such as Paul Klee as well as by skin robes, ledger art, and the work of Oscar Howe. Her works combine elements of European mainstream modernism with archetypal evocations and identifiably Indian symbols, such as tipis and headdresses.

POSTMODERNISM AND INDIAN ART

The trends of the 1960s and 1970s have been described in such terms as "postindustrial," "postcultural," and "posthumanist," but also "postmodern" and "postabsurd," "postavant garde," or "postcontemporary." The terms themselves bespeak a number of new qualities in present-day society and culture which apparently can only be defined negatively and in contrast to what has been conceived of as modernism, at least in culture and the arts. If one seeks a common denominator for the uncertainty and discontinuity in private and public life, in sciences and in ethics, in economic, social, and cultural fields, one is struck by the situational orientation of all epistemological structures, which do not even attempt to arrive at a total view or a vision of the future. Following Foucault (1966:13), we may start from a particular set of assumptions. The first is that at the heart of the late-nineteenth- and early-twentieth-century experience is a persistent attempt to explore the invisible deep structure beneath the visible surface of things, for example, to discover the basic conditions of human existence through anthropology, psychology, and sociology. It follows that as the world has grown more complex, we have moved away from the concept of the human personality as a finite and definable entity, toward a perception of it as fragile and subjective. One can go a step further and see that the essence of postmodernism is a loss of even that fragile subjectivity as an integrating principle and its substitution by decentralized fields of experience, or "situations." Experience can no longer be controlled, dominated, and codified through depiction of a subject in the old way (Hoffman 1980).

This "post" quality of contemporary civilization is also the indication of a crisis in art, not only in traditional realistic or popular formula art, but also in the whole concept of "the modern," its existential foundation, its aesthetic sensibility, its artistic concepts, and its autonomous styles. The prefix "post-" signals doubt as to modernism's claim to be the sole legitimate expression of the world view and the general feeling of life in the twentieth century. However, as Cage's assertion that postmodern art ought to be more the expression of laughter than of self-pain suggests, this art also harbors opportunities. They lie in the breakup of a modern aesthetics already ossified into inflexible dogma, and in the reopening of the concept of art. Everything is possible; art is no longer separate from life, nor from the machine which is part of life, nor from the other communications media which, like art, supply man with fictions. Thus, Pop artist Roy Lichtenstein defines the aims of Pop art as "anti-contemplative, anti-nuance, anti-getting-away-from-the-tyranny-of-the-rectangle, anti-movement-and-light, anti-mystery, anti-paint-quality, anti-Zen, and anti all these brilliant ideas of preceding movements which everyone understands so thoroughly" (Tate Gallery 1974).

Finally, it is not only traditional Indian art that is in crisis, but also modern and even postmodern Indian art, insofar as the concept of art itself has come into question. It was the postmodern crisis of Western society and culture that first made the development of a modern Indian art possible. In the 1960s this crisis finally destroyed the belief in the central position of Western culture, which thus became receptive to other ways of looking at things. Pluralism became the mark of postmodernism, clearing the way for the cultural emancipation and the new self-consciousness of minorities. At the same time, postmodernism plunged Indian painting into a crisis even before it could completely come to terms with the complexity of the modern art labyrinth.

In this cultural vacuum it does not help to state, as Earl Biss does, "I'm an Indian and I paint Indians, but do I have to be classified as an Indian artist? I think that we Indians who are artists should be considered and referred to in the world sense" (Love 1978:12). First of all, the "world sense" of culture has become questionable, and secondly, Earl Biss, like Scholder, Red Star, Cohoe, and others, still paints Indians. That is the main point. Indeed, the advantage of the Indian artist is that he has not exhausted his images. They are still there; they have for him a genuine tradition in history and mythos, they mean something, and, as archetypal symbols with a treasure of rich connotations, they can be brought into the mainstream of art (see Berkhofer 1978). The work of A. R. Penck, who represented Germany at the 1984 Venice Biennale, recalls the motifs of prehistoric cave art; and a painting called *Attack* by the New York–based German painter Rainer Fetting is filled with Indian figures attacking the silhouette of New York. Both are leading representatives of a neo-Expressionist movement concentrating again on figurative content. Their work makes it clear that these images and their connotations are still important as material for mainstream Western painting.

The Indian artist can playfully remodel his images as quotations. Like T. C. Cannon, he can confirm them and make them ironic. Or he can distance himself from them and contemplate them

245. Cold Snap on the Prairie II. *Earl Biss (1948–), Crow. 1979, oil on canvas, 46 × 36 inches. Joan Cawley Collection, Wichita.*

The primary theme interpreted by Biss is that of a human emotional state conveyed through exaggeration or distortion of color or form, as in his depictions of compact processions of mounted horsemen almost absorbed by the frigid vacuum of a Plains winter landscape.

246. Kickapoos Have More Fun. *Richard Glazer Danay (1942–), Mohawk. 1982, ink on paper, 24 × 24 inches. Collection of the artist, Green Bay, Wisconsin.*

Richard Glazer Danay, a Mohawk construction worker turned college professor and artist, creates works that are jokes built upon jokes, words playing off words, and ironies layered upon ironies. Most famous for his painted hard hats and decorated buffalo, Danay often attacks Indian stereotypes through wry humor, as in these illustrated letters to "Dear Abby." In Danay's use of the ironic, the modern, the erotic, and the obscene, he boldly proclaims a sexuality only hinted at by traditional artists like Cecil Dick and Waldo Mootzka. His mixed-media "letters" refer to topics as varied as ancient Kickapoo love secrets and the mixed-blood Indian Burt Reynolds.

247. Georgia O'Keeffe. *David Bradley (1954–   ), Ojibwa. 1984, acrylic on canvas, 36 × 30 inches. Mr. and Mrs. Gary L. Wasserman, Birmingham, Michigan.*

Bradley's forte is visual satire. He uses a sometimes purposely naïve, almost folklike technique to convey his humorous social comments, in which the acculturated Indian looks back through the window of his past to a traditional tribal life. In this portrait of the New Mexico artist Georgia O'Keeffe as Whistler's Mother, Bradley takes wry note of the Southwest's links to European tradition.

from without, as Scholder often does. In any case, the cliché character of the romanticized Indian motifs, which lies in their fixedness, can be neutralized through irony. The postmodern parodistic stance is able to absorb any excess of pastoral or heroic simplicity, of emotion and nostalgia, and still keep the associative potential of the images intact. This is exactly what some of the most successful Indian painters—Scholder, Cannon, Biss, Red Star, Fonseca, Cohoe, Bradley—have done by means of their eclectic, expressive, decorative, and ironic styles. They present the viewer with an ambivalent whole, simultaneously recognizable and distorted. In the work of contemporary Indian artists, stereotyped situations can become ironically broken archetypes for today's world. Through a rich inventory of connotative images comes an articulation of the postmodern artistic credo of potentiality.

Is Indian art, like modern Western art, a final aesthetic attempt to regain the lost unity of life? Even the alternative—that traditionalism and modernism exist as regionalism (relegating Indian art to the status of a mental and artistic reservation within a mainstream culture)—is both real and unreal at the same time. Since cliché has become truth and truth cliché, the stylized compositions and modern constructions of a visionary Indian truth have gained a new, paradoxical value, but only as fictions of utopia.

OUTLOOK

Four fundamental conclusions can be drawn from what we have discussed. The first two have to do with the relationship of social reality to aesthetic form in Indian painting, the third with the relationship of Indian art to Western art in postmodernism, and the fourth with the concept of a Fourth World.

First, modern Indian art, insofar as it asserts the claim of modernism to represent an aesthetic totality as an artistic form, may be, like modern Western art before it, an attempt to represent the lost unity of life in art.

Second, if contemporary Indian painting adopts the aesthetic of postmodernism, with its emphasis on the uncertain, the unconnected, the merely superficial, and the transitory, then the artistic vision of life becomes a fiction, and can only be depicted as such. In the wake of the general uncertainty as to the nature of reality, identity, and art, or truth, genuineness, and beauty, differences pale. Under these circumstances, the differences between traditional and modern Indian painting blur too. The stylized, idyllic, and heroic compositions of traditional Indian painting and the designs of modern and postmodern Indian painting assume, at least epistemologically, the same status as mere fiction. Traditional pastoral images and the rhythmicized abstractions, color compositions, and ironically refracted clichés of contemporary Indian art all receive a new, paradoxical value, but only as constructive, playful, or ironic fictions of utopia. As such, they are part of the mainstream of Western painting. From this point of view, T. C. Cannon's observation on the relationship of traditional to modern Indian painting gains a postmodern justification (even if many contemporary Indian painters would not subscribe to it in quite this form): "Art is big, and there's room for everybody. I used to argue the old arguments about the traditional painters and the modern painters.... [But now I think] there's room for every kind of painter" (Wade and Strickland 1981:v).

Third, it is obvious that the postmodern world, with its breakdown of ideologies and social utopias, of dogmatic nationalism and aestheticism, is again on the path to the irrational and the imaginative, and that Indian art and postmodern art go hand in hand in trying to remain open to this potential. If in the course of detraditionalization and despiritualization we are not to lose the possibility of a diversity of relationships and meanings, then perhaps artistic fictions are necessary. In the realization of buried possibilities for experience and the imagination, Indian art and modern art run parallel. Epes Brown (1976:161) notes quite correctly: "The great hope for this search on the part of Indians and non-Indians consists in putting together a truthful and open dialogue in which no one tries to imitate the other, but instead everyone will rediscover and confirm the sacred dimensions." Here, perhaps, lies a common basis for a post-postmodern art, anchored in the collective unconscious.

Fourth, in addition to contributing to the cultural history of the Indian, an analysis of the development of Indian painting can enhance our understanding of the interaction of minorities and majorities in general. It can show that when Fourth World ethnic minorities adopt the art forms of cultural majorities, they develop according to a common structural principle, namely the combination of mythos and history. In the case of Indians and Euro-Americans, the mythical and archetypal experiences of the primal sensibility are cast into "alien" historical contexts. Since the minority is always seen only as "the Other," and as such is characterized by stereotyped features, the art of a minority leads first to representation, then to the cleansing of the clichéd concepts held by the majority (here, the noble savage and the evil savage). Associated with this is the search for art forms that concentrate, intensify, and generalize the traditional motifs, forms, and rhythms. In the process, the motifs appear first in symbolic forms, then, with increasing intellectual emancipation, in ironic, and perhaps finally in playful ways. At the same time, however, they assume a utopian character insofar as they retain the possibility of a primal form of experience. Thus the artistic striving of the minority coincides with the majority culture's entrance into the late phase of decentralization and pluralization.

Notes

1. See also Deloria 1974 and further references listed in Graburn 1976:8.

2. For the concept of the postmodern and its difference from modernism see Hoffman, Hornung, and Kunow 1977.

3. For a more detailed analysis of this aspect of modern art see Haftmann 1962.

4. Here I follow the lucid argument of Haftmann (1962)—who has written the best history of modern art up to the Second World War—although the conclusions about Indian art are, of course, mine.

5. As early as 1946 Clement Greenberg wrote: "What we have to do with here is an historical mood that has simply seized upon Existentialism to formulate and justify itself, but which had been gathering strength long before most of the people concerned had ever read Heidegger or Kierkegaard.... Whatever the affectations and the philosophical sketchiness of Existentialism, it is aesthetically appropriate to our age.... What we have to do with here, I repeat, is not so much a philosophy as mood" (1946:54).

Tall Visitor at the Indian Gallery; or, The Future of Native American Art

RENNARD STRICKLAND

SETTING. The opening of an exhibition of American Indian art at an unidentified museum in a western city. Perhaps it is Santa Fe, Taos, or Scottsdale, but it could be Tulsa or Denver or Seattle. All the objects in the show are real works of art, but installed in an imaginary gallery setting.

TIME. The present. It is 10:30 in the evening, and only a few members of the select preview audience remain. They have finished a catered cocktail repast of paté, fruits, cheeses, guacamole with chips, and miniature stuffed fry bread, and are about to exhaust the Scotch, bourbon, and vodka, having already disposed of the white wine and Perrier.

CHARACTERS. The characters in this dialogue are as real as anyone involved in the art world can ever be. None is intended to represent an actual person, but their dialogue is based on three decades of real conversation with real people at real openings of real Indian art shows. The narrator is the author, and the views expressed by the narrator represent the conclusions of the author. All other statements are composites.

The group standing around waiting to adjourn to another setting includes, besides the narrator, the following:

Lorenzo Canyon. Lorenzo is an elderly trader who inherited a trading post on the Navajo reservation from his grandfather and continues to promote Indian arts and crafts there. He markets rugs, jewelry, and pottery to tourists, serious collectors, and other dealers.

Ward L. Fox. Ward is an anthropologist and Indian art historian who holds a Ph.D. in archaeology and did field work in Africa, where he wrote a monograph on dance masks in primitive societies. He has also done field work among the "over-privileged" in the resort communities of Carmel and Santa Fe.

Harry Golightley. Harry is a middle-aged painter and sculptor. He is a full-blooded Indian from the Southwest who has lived in San Francisco for almost thirty years and maintains a home in Paris as well as a condominium in Maine. He is noted for his striking and colorful abstract oils on both Indian and non-Indian themes.

James J. Gradgrind. James is a "go-getter" dealer who operates several Indian galleries and who has organized an Indian-prints tax-shelter scheme that has funded innovative work by young Indian artists.

Jane Livingston Hemingway. Jane is a New York–based freelance art critic whose reviews, articles, and essays appear in slick and trendy art and decorator magazines. She produces glossy coffee-table books about Indian art.

Bentin Lookout. Bentin, a student at the Santa Fe Studio in the 1930s, has been widely honored as a leader among traditional painters. He paints in the so-called Studio style but has continued to be an original and dynamic painter using the two-dimensional style.

Joan Redbird. Joan is an Indian who has been both a student and an instructor at the Institute for

248. *Bag. Nez Percé. Ca. 1900, beadwork, fabric, hide, 10 × 8¾ inches. Private collection.*

249. Rose and the Res Sisters. *Harry Fonseca, Maidu. 1982, lithograph, 30 × 22½ inches. Private collection.*

The most popular and widely known of Fonseca's work is his series on Coyote characters, of which Rose is the heroine. Fonseca has been strongly influenced by the mainstream funk image and has used it to unite the Indian and the modern white world. Coyote grins, snickers, sings, dances, and cavorts in a world made suddenly absurd by his presence. In Indian mythology, Coyote is the universal trickster, armed with the cutting tongue of a fool, who becomes the mirror reflecting the world's follies.

American Indian Art at Santa Fe. She now devotes herself to her own career as a painter, but spends a good deal of time lecturing on Indian art and teaching printmaking.

Fannie Mitchell Youngwoman. Fannie is the granddaughter of an acclaimed Pueblo potter, and herself a highly gifted and creative potter and sculptor who no longer lives at the pueblo but returns for dances, to dig clay, and to fire some of her work. She is married to a white man who operates a wholesale Indian art gallery.

THE CURTAIN RISES
The crowd at the gallery is viewing the Indian art show.

NARRATOR (to no one in particular and to everyone in general). I have been asked to write an essay on the future of Native American art, to accompany a major Indian art exhibition as it travels across the country. I am expected to comment on trends, objects of art, current developments, and what they mean, and to suggest what, indeed, is the future of American Indian art. I thought maybe I could steal some of your ideas and pass them off as mine. So, here goes: *What do you think is the future of American Indian art?*

WARD L. FOX. As an anthropologist, let me tell you that that is a stupid question. A Really Stupid Question! The future of Indian art, as what? That is the question: Indian art, as what?

JAMES J. GRADGRIND. God, you academics. You want to have the first and last say on everything. You analyze it to death. You take the beauty out and then you leave us with nothing but dull, dry, footnoted pap. The future is the future is the future. Like a rose is a rose is a rose. Indian art is art by an Indian and will last as long as there are Indians and there is art.

FOX. It ain't so simple as that.... I mean, we have to know for what purpose and in what context we are asking about the future. Look at your rose. There are real differences between a nineteenth-

250. *Bowl. Effie Garcia (1954–   ), Santa Clara. 1983, carved black ceramic, 2½ × 2¾ inches. Philbrook Art Center, Tulsa, gift of Friends of American Indian Art, 82.17.2.*

Effie Garcia has emerged recently as one of the most celebrated contemporary Indian potters from the Southwest. Her work has an immediate appeal to both ethnic-art collectors and collectors of mainstream American art. She has adapted the 1930s Santa Clara preference for deeply carved ceramic designs by introducing Art Deco–influenced geometrics in place of the earlier curvilinear and animal motifs. Her slip-paint outlining of the recessed designs creates an exaggerated sense of depth, which contrasts dramatically with the mirrorlike polished surface of the vessel.

251. *Bowl. Jody Folwell (1942–   ), San Ildefonso. 1982, clay and ashes, 9 × 17 inches. Private collection.*

Jody Folwell abandoned the refined styles of twentieth-century Pueblo pottery to explore her own vision, reinterpreting her ancient heritage through ceramics. The design of this bowl retains the traditional motif of the deer, but here it is stylized unconventionally and drawn in bold color.

century Nez Percé beaded bag with a rose design in the center and Harry Fonseca's lithograph, *Rose and the Res Sisters*. The old purse is utilitarian; it is decorative; it is historic; it is lots of things. And so is the Fonseca. It is exciting; it is commercial; it is didactic; it is decorative; and it is entertaining with a contemporary message. There are still those well-heeled, sentimental patrons of "our aboriginal Red Brother" who see Indian art as a single, static phenomenon, derived from the "timeless purity of the Red Spirit." But I think that there are many futures for Indian art, just as there are many futures for Indian people.

BENTIN LOOKOUT. Pardon me, but the future that most interests me is next month, when I hope to have sold enough paintings to pay my daughter's tuition at law school. I've got awards and citations and acclaim up to my neck, just about level with my debts. Let me paint my pictures about my people and let me sell them. I want to tell the story right and true and fair. That's all. That woman I'm married to keeps at me all the time. Paint more. Sell more. Go to more shows. I might have done more and painted better, but with five kids, a mother-in-law, and a brother in jail whose family I'm looking after too—well, it ain't easy.

GRADGRIND (with evangelical zeal and the lust to represent a new artist). What you need is a good gallery, a good dealer. I could double your prices. In five years we could triple, quadruple them. We can set up a show for you in Paris.

LORENZO CANYON. Exploitation by dealers, that's the problem. In the old days, with the trading posts, we didn't have that. You new hot-shot promoters are destroying Indian art. I think—

JANE LIVINGSTON HEMINGWAY (interrupting with a raised hand). Oh no, you traders are the ones who destroyed pure Indian art by telling Indians what to sell, creating tourist crafts, inventing Oriental designs for Navajo rugs. You destroyed whatever future there was for Indian art.

By now, all are speaking at the same time.

HARRY GOLIGHTLEY. Nobody is going to tell me what to paint and what not to paint. I'm an artist who happens to be Indian, but I am an artist first and last.

FANNIE MITCHELL YOUNGWOMAN. I'm not going to make pots exactly like my grandmother's. *She* didn't make them like her grandmother's. She couldn't even make lids.

NARRATOR. STOP! (Screaming above the four artists.) *Wait! Wait!* This is very un-Indian! Dr. Fox

says Indians have passive personalities and are gentle and quiet and abhor public disputes. Why are all of you yelling?

JOAN REDBIRD. Like hell we're passive! What do you expect a white anthro to say? They're only interested in men's art and in their own preconceptions of Indian art.

NARRATOR. Can we take this in order? I like Dr. Fox's question about "the future as what." It seems to me that there are lots of futures. Maybe we can just run through a few of these without getting so excited. Surely we all agree that there is a future role for Indian art as a utilitarian and spiritual force in religious and ceremonial functions. And in a decorative role among Indians themselves.

LOOKOUT. It is hard to make white-man divisions, since Indian society doesn't divide itself and its own art into religous, political, or artistic pigeonholes. In so many ways, Indian art remains vital and alive, just as it was a thousand years ago in our dances and our everyday life. Lots of Indians still make objects in the old ways, using the old styles. And don't forget that we Indian people are ourselves real consumers of our own art for our own decorative purposes. We may not still use our pots for cooking and storage—anyone with sense prefers Tupperware, Teflon, and the Cuisinart—but we have beautiful Indian pottery sitting on our coffee tables. Who do you think wears all those ribbon shirts and buys those exquisite peyote fans and fancy dance beadwork and feathers?

YOUNGWOMAN. Look at the pottery here in this gallery. This pottery tells you everything you need to know about the future of Indian art. What I mean is that if you look at the recent works of ceramics you will see change, but you will also see continued quality and a quality that builds

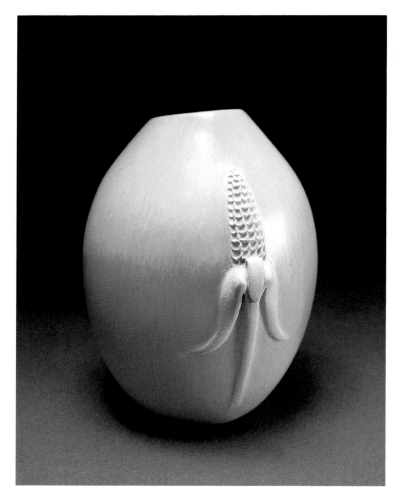

252. Jar. Iris Nampeyo, Hopi. 1983, ceramic, 3½ × 2¾ inches. Philbrook Art Center, Tulsa, gift of Friends of American Indian Art, 83.14.1.

At the forefront of innovative Hopi pottery-making are such artists as Helen Naha, Thomas Polacca, Dextra Quotskuyva, Al Colton, Joy Navasie, and Iris Nampeyo. Though relatively new to the art, Nampeyo has perfected the sculptural approach to ceramics first introduced by Elizabeth White and later developed by Al Colton. As important to the vessel's design as its meticulously polished surface is the delicately modeled appliqué cornstalk.

upon the best of the older tradition. For example, this Jody Folwell bowl is highly modern: the shape is different, but she decorates it with an old Zuñi heartline deer and other figures. She says she borrowed the motif of bullet holes in the animals from her friend Bob Haozous, and she has put ashes from the fire on which she made the pot inside, just like in the old fetish pots. Stella Huma and Effie Garcia are both contemporary Hopi potters, but their innovative designs are rooted in older Hopi concepts and forms, and their pottery is unique and individual. And look at the obvious pottery influence in the early painting of Dan Namingha, who may not even see how the Nampeyo heritage, through his mother and grandmother, lives on in his canvases. So they call pottery "craft" and painting "art." How are they different? Why is a Charles Loloma sculptured bracelet a craft item and not a sculpture? Look at this Inuit sculpture of a seal hunter. What do you call it? Art? Craft? Sculpture?

REDBIRD. I call them masterpieces of simplicity and elegance. They are art. And when we drive the academic nitpickers out of the museums, that will no longer be questioned. I look at those Haida and Kwakiutl bracelets and believe me, those are not crafts in the demeaning sense of the word. They represent fine design and eloquent craftsmanship and belong beside any other sculptural creation.

GOLIGHTLEY. Right on! Let's hear it for craftsmen, craftswomen, craftspersons, artists all—and for the glorious millennium, a future in Indian art (and all art) when a work stands or sits or hangs or dances on its own. What the hell difference does it make whether the design is on clay or silver or muslin or leather or ledger paper or canvas or wood or sand or wool or water? After all, Julian Martinez painted paintings as well as pots, and a lot of Indian painters have borrowed

253. Jar. Stella Huma (1917–   ), Hopi. 1983, polychrome pottery, 5¼ × 11 inches. Philbrook Art Center, Tulsa, gift of Friends of American Indian Art, 83.14.2.

Among the many pottery-producing Pueblo communities, Hopi has emerged as both one of the most innovative and conservative artistic centers. The potter Stella Huma has refined the early-twentieth-century ellipsoidal form of Hopi vessels, while retaining and mastering the historic design repertoire, and adapting it to accentuate the sculptural traits of her jars.

254. Seal Hunter. Inuit. Ca. 1960s, carved soapstone, 7½ inches in length. Philbrook Art Center, Tulsa, MI3240.

Eskimo sculpture illustrates the response of the artistic impulse to economic opportunity and clearly demonstrates that high levels of creativity can be retained while providing a reliable source of income for talented native artists. For at least a century, commercial carving has dominated Inuit, Northern Canadian, and Alaskan sculpture and still produces works of majesty and integrity. This mid-twentieth-century soapstone carving, made for sale to a white patron, portrays the historic life of the Inuit, a life which, paradoxically, has been largely displaced by the advent of Western customs, including the production of commercial art.

255. *Bracelet. Charles Loloma (1921–), Hopi. 1981, wood, coral, turquoise, ivory, 3 inches in diameter. Collection of the artist, Arizona.*

The jewelry of Charles Loloma fuses abstract contemporary forms with the ancient designs and principles derived from Hopi art and myth. When Loloma creates an object, even though it serves a function as a ring or bracelet, it is also an emotively generated sculpture. The visual strength and appeal of his work have helped to redefine the image of contemporary Indian art, and have had an impact on the larger domain of mainstream sculpture and design.

256. *Bracelet. Lloyd Wadhams, Haida. After 1962, silver, 2 × 2⁵⁄₈ inches. Philbrook Art Center, Elizabeth Cole Butler Collection, L82.1.85.*

The revival of Northwest Coast carving and design is among the most important achievements of contemporary Native American art. The hallmark of this revival has been an innovation and creativity that build upon the historic tenets of Northwest Coast sculpture, whether in wood, metal, or slate. Lloyd Wadhams' silver bracelet, like the jewelry of his fellow craftsmen Bill Reid and Charles Loloma, adapts and abstracts historic design elements into strongly sculptural jewelry that echoes the ancient beliefs and mythic images of ancestral times (see fig. 115).

or adapted from or been inspired by these works. And more recent painters, such as Helen Hardin and Dan Namingha, have been inspired by such designs. This kind of (pardon the expression) cross-fertilization is something we can expect more and more of in the future, and it is something that we artists are doing ourselves, without much help from the so-called experts.

CANYON. Did you know that Julian Martinez once painted an old black Ford (or was it a Chevrolet?) all over with black pottery designs, and then drove around in it? Back then, nobody thought much of it. I bet you could get a lot of money for that today. The Fred Harvey Company thought of the great revivalist Hopi potter Nampeyo as an employee whose pots they sold to tourists. They had only a piece or two of her work in their collection—probably things they couldn't sell. They weren't interested in contemporary curios; they had to have historic or prehistoric pots. You never know a Golden Age when you're in it.

YOUNGWOMAN. That's my point. Indian art collectors are looking to yesterday and thinking that what is a hundred or a thousand years old is true Indian, but what is today is not. Today is Indian, too. We may be in another Golden Age and not even know it.

NARRATOR. As an Indian historian, let me say that almost since the arrival of the white man there has been that illusive quest for the magic moment of "real Indianness," before Indian life and culture were tainted by things foreign. Well, Indian culture has never been, never was static or unchanging. Even before white contact, Indian life was evolving. Look at prehistoric pottery and sculpture from the same cultural area and see how they differ as time passes. Remember that the buffalo hunt on horseback came to the Indian only after the whites arrived with the domesticated horse.

LOOKOUT. This change and rebirth is not true only of pottery. Think of the beautiful engraved shells

257. The Shaman Restores a Dead Soul to Life. *Lyle Wilson (1955–), Haisla/Kwakiutl. 1980, pencil on paper, 14 × 19½ inches. Collection of the artist, Vancouver.*

Lyle Wilson clothes ancient Northwest Indian themes in innovative forms. In this drawing the ancient carved box is reinterpreted as a symbol of transformation and resurrection. In it, as in many old "symmetrical" designs, there are subtle and intriguing differences between details of the left and right sides.

258. Sculptural hat. Lelooska (1934–), Cherokee. Ca. 1979, carved and painted cedar with abalone-shell inlay, 10½ × 15¼ inches. Philbrook Art Center, Tulsa, Elizabeth Cole Butler Collection, 83.19.2.

Among the most popular of the storytellers and carvers of the Northwest Coast is a Cherokee Indian who has taken the name Lelooska. Although the classification of a Southeastern Indian artist who chooses to work in Northwestern traditions may cause problems for some, there is no question about the purity of Lelooska's sculptural vision and the integrity of his workmanship. This sculptural hat is true to the basic principles and designs of Northwest Coast carving.

from the Spiro Mounds. Today Knokovtee Scott, a Creek Cherokee, is doing shell engraving with the old designs. He is looking backward and taking his art forward into the future. I see the same thing with contemporary Eskimo carving and sculpture. It is beautiful and it is new, but the roots are old. Just to copy is bad, but I don't think it's bad to seek inspiration and to find your understanding from the old things. I love contemporary graphics, the prints, the blocks, the drawings of the Northwest Coast that are modern, that are done today, but they hearken back to the time of their ancestors. Is it not ironic that one of the most famous of the contemporary Northwest carvers is Lelooska, a Cherokee brother? I mean, the Cherokee are from the Southeast! That is a change, too. So much of the art is pan-Indian. We borrow from other tribes and combine styles. So many of us are Indians with a heritage in several tribes. We see what we like and we take it for our own.

HEMINGWAY. If that's so, how do we distinguish between Indian art made by a person who is Indian by blood, and art with an Indian theme, made in a traditional Indian style, using a traditional Indian method, but done by a white man?

REDBIRD. How can you ask that question when you could walk into a New York department store and buy a piece of jewelry made by a Cherokee using "Indian" designs which their Swedish buyer created based on her European image of the Navajo adaptation of an old Moorish pattern? But the store would have one hell of a time trying to sell genuine works of German-style silver, in the old traditional floral motifs of the Cherokee, because they don't look like Navajo squash blossoms assembled in a shop from precast shop findings bought in Albuquerque. You talk about the future. What kind of future is that?

NARRATOR. Let me interrupt. What is traditional isn't necessarily traditional by all definitions. I

259. Design. Julian Martinez (1897–1943), San Ildefonso. Ca. 1929, ink and watercolor on paper, 20½ × 25½ inches. Thomas Gilcrease Institute of American History and Art, Tulsa, 0236.257.

Although Julian Martinez is best known for the designs he painted on the pottery made by his wife, Maria, his paintings on paper and canvas are important examples of early Pueblo easel art. They illustrate the link between the older, utilitarian arts and the newer arts for public consumption. At their best, the intricately drawn pottery symbols stand successfully as works on their own, freed from the confining form of the vessel.

remember giving a lecture on the revival of traditional Cherokee red pottery by students at the Sequoyah Indian school. After the speech a Sioux woman in the audience informed me that she had been the teacher at Sequoyah and that she had made up the clay formula, mixed the glaze, and designed the styles. So a Sioux created a new style of traditional Cherokee pottery.

LOOKOUT. As a traditional painter, I can tell you just how traditional all this is. It is not what most people think. Indian painting of the last hundred years has changed, changed a lot. But that doesn't mean it isn't all still Indian. Look at these three works. The Acee Blue Eagle painting *The Deer Spirit* comes from just after World War II and it is a powerful—what we call traditional —painting in the two-dimensional style. The next one is Frank LaPena's *Deer Rattle/Deer Dancer*, from 1980. Finally, the latest is Fritz Scholder's recent *Deer at Laguna*, a monotype that seems to reach out and seize the spirit of its viewers, drawing them into the painter's world. I can feel the spirit in each of these. Each of them is in a different medium and in a different style, but each of them has something in common with the old hide shields that were painted

260. The Deer Spirit. *Acee Blue Eagle (1907–1959), Creek/Pawnee. Ca. 1949, watercolor on mat board, 21½ × 18¼ inches. Private collection.*

Acee Blue Eagle conveys a sense of the power of the supernatural through the small deer ghost figure which dominates this painting. Although executed within the strict tenets of the flat, unmodeled, backgroundless school of traditional Indian painting, the painting obtains depth and drama through the use of color and composition to draw the viewer toward the deer spirit. Blue Eagle was among the most prolific of the "Bambi" painters and author/illustrator of the popular children's book *Ecogee, The Little Blue Deer.*

261. Deer Rattle/Deer Dancer. *Frank LaPena (1937–), Wintu. 1980, acrylic on canvas, 48 × 34 inches. Private collection.*

This work by LaPena demonstrates the great continuity within Indian painting traditions despite changes in medium and style. With the dancer image he conjures mystery and intrigue to convey a sense of the magical essence of things Indian, and their relationship to things universal. Color and form express tranquility, but the death imagery and the inhuman passivity of the figure are ominous. The eyes in the ghostlike skull dominate the canvas to create a mystical apparition.

262. Deer at Laguna. *Fritz Scholder (1937–), Mission (Luiseno). 1981, monotype, 40½ × 31½ inches. Private collection.*

During the 1960s, Fritz Scholder, the most widely known and controversial of contemporary Indian artists, changed the form and direction of Native American painting with his bold, colorful canvases. Early in his career, Scholder challenged the artistic dominance of the "blue deer" or

"Bambi" style. In this work he shows that the treatment of the deer icon need not be a cliché. Scholder uses the monotype, a medium favored by an increasing number of Indian artists, to produce images as fresh and different from his earlier oils as those canvases were from the old "Bambi" style of painting.

with deer emblems. The old shields, with their spirits, had power and could help and protect. The design might come in a vision. All these works are concerned with power and with the spirit. I think that is part of it. There is a spirituality about Indian art. It speaks of power.

CANYON. Garbage! Garbage! Garbage! I am so tired of hearing this threadbare cliché about spirituality. Spirit, my foot! I'm an old-time Indian trader and I think it's time someone debunked the ambiguous, fraudulent idea that it is spirituality that makes a piece of art "Indian." Let's get a spirituality counter, like a Geiger counter. Then we can measure how Indian a thing is by how much spirituality it has.

GOLIGHTLEY. Not all Indians who are artists seek to identify with Indian art. Some of us are painting for the mainstream, not just for curio hunters and frustrated do-gooder rich women.

CANYON. More garbage. More garbage piled higher and deeper. Although some of you professionally trained modern artists would like to be accepted simply as artists rather than as Indian artists, you keep that old Indian label because it just might come in handy, give you the edge. You can exhibit in racially biased shows that are open only to Indians and that show only Indian artists. You get more exposure, get into more publications, and you don't have to compete in the real world. You try to have it both ways. You want to be a part of the mainstream while you sit in your safe little backwater.

HEMINGWAY. As a New York critic, I think that is unfair, although I must admit that no Indian artist matters very much where it counts, in New York, in Paris, or even in San Francisco. Oh, there is Fritz Scholder; he sells well. And James Havard, who was even in *Architectural Digest*. True, George Morrison was a part of the New York scene in the glorious fifties, before he went back to Minnesota. And they like Allan Houser and Joan Hill and T. C. Cannon in Paris, but mainstream—I hardly think so. There is not a single painting by an Indian artist on permanent display at the National Gallery, the Museum of Modern Art, or the Metropolitan, not to mention the Louvre.

GOLIGHTLEY. What you may not know is that for a long time there was an attempt to stop the future in Indian art, to hold off any change. Patrons and friends tried to turn Indian paintings into museum pieces and Indian painters into red mouthpieces for white perceptions of Indians. More damned Indians have frozen to death in painted trails of tears than the white man ever killed. Those of us who as artists were different were attacked as traitors to our Indian heritage, when we were being true to our native tradition of change. A great example of early ledger-style painting, such as the Cheyenne Buffalo Meat's *Indian Prisoners in Costume*, is a portrayal of his life and his experience on paper, a foreign medium given him by his white captors. The Cheyenne Arapaho Carl Sweezy described his Indian style of painting as the "Mooney Style," because the anthropologist James Mooney had shown him how to paint. That is why I get so mad when whites tell me how to paint and what to paint. I shall flee the next Indian art show where the grand prize goes to an Indian painter whose only idea of Indian art is a picture of someone transformed into an eagle. To whites, *that* is Indian art! It's kinda funny to think of white men standing over modern Indian nonrepresentational paintings, looking for tipis and buffalo and war bonnets in an abstract design, and declaring it Indian on the basis of the number of triangles that might be taken for tipis. That's why I like the work of Richard Glazer Danay so much, and Bob Haozous, too. What could be more Indian, and poke more fun, than Danay's *Mohawk Headdress* or Haozous's *Taos Lady*? They give it to the buffalo spotters and thunderbird counters right in their academic and critical hats, and with a good-natured kick to the proper portion of their anatomy as well.

263. Taos Lady. *Bob Haozous, Chiricahua/Apache/Navajo. 1977, pen and ink on paper, 19½ × 24½ inches. Private collection.*

The ironic side of the Southwest Indian art market is the subject of Bob Haozous's stylized depiction of a New Mexico art gallery cocktail party. His tableau includes patrons and artists who are identifiable as idealized types. Central to the social ritual in which they are engaged is the white society patroness surrounded by an admiring entourage of art aficionados. The cat is often a witch symbol in Southwestern tribal mythology.

264. Sensuous Cowgirl. *Bob Haozous, Chiricahua Apache/Navajo. 1981, painted limestone, 17 inches. Private collection.*

The idealized image of the Indian maiden has been replaced in the sculpture of Bob Haozous with a realistic modern woman who faces a fast-paced, insecure, and paradoxical life. *Sensuous Cowgirl* makes a social comment that is at once humorous, complex, provocative, and aesthetically satisfying.

HEMINGWAY. I think you're being unfair to patrons and critics. There have always been a few of us who have spoken out for Indian art. There was the prewar show at the Museum of Modern Art in New York, and in the 1950s they sponsored a one-man show for Joe Herrera. Why have Indian art if it doesn't represent the strengths of the red man—doesn't speak of his pulsating courage, and dramatic vistas?

REDBIRD. There's a certain type of New York critic who can't see past the East River, but she lusts after the art of the virile barbarian, not to speak of the virile barbarian himself. Corruption rears its ugly head even in the pure world of Indian art. You know some critics take gifts. Don't look so shocked. Some prehistoric and even historic pieces of Native American art bring more than a hundred thousand dollars at auction. There are major collections that are full of forgeries and fakes. And didn't the IRS and New York State go after a lot of celebrities who'd been trading museum art back and forth from their collections? And academics are as bad as anyone else; they're just cheaper. Why don't you talk about the future of Indian art as growth industry, as tax shelter, as investment, as occupation for scholars, as popular decorator item, and as symbol of bleeding-heart dedication to the downtrodden-lo'-the-poor-savage-and-vanishing-red-man? That's where the future is!

GRADGRIND. Dollars are important, and anyone who doesn't think so is crazy. More than one Indian community has been kept alive by the art market. Dat So La Lee wouldn't have been as productive without help from the art market. Maria herself created an industry that revolutionized her pueblo.

FOX (assuming center stage). But that's the bind, the so-called double-bind that presents tourist-taste airport curios as the model or the ideal for the community. The lowest common denominator dictates, and you end up with poster-paint rain gods and plaster-of-paris Katcinas. It wouldn't be so bad, except that the alternative economic opportunities for Indian people are so restricted. They are stuck.

REDBIRD. And even worse than that is the old-boy Indian patron network that says a painting isn't acceptable in the marketplace unless it is in a white-dictated style and on a predetermined topic. They prefer work by men, and the traditional women's arts they dismiss as crafts. Do you know that in Oklahoma there is an annual show which used to limit paintings to the theme of "The Trail of Tears"? That's like having all British artists required to paint about the Battle of Hastings or the Wars of the Roses, or having all blacks paint the slave ships coming from Africa, and limiting Jews to Holocaust art.

GRADGRIND. Some dealers do promote excellence and work with their artists to reach higher and higher levels of achievement.

CANYON. Bigger and bigger commissions. And more and more money for themselves.

GRADGRIND. Which means more recognition and more income for the ast. What artist—Indian or white—can complain about more money?

REDBIRD. Let me remind you that there is a hell of a lot more to Indian art than just dollars to put bread on the table, or new carpets in the condominium.

LOOKOUT. But you gotta pay the law-school tuition.

REDBIRD. In your list of futures, I'd like to talk about Indian art as polemic, Indian art as social conscience, Indian art as a unifying force, and Indian art as a statement of Indian values. Indian art decries the supremacy of white technological values and of a mass-man's (or mass-woman's, I guess) indifference to fellow human beings. That, to me, is the most important future of Indian art. It is a future which I believe is here now.

265. You Can't Rollerskate in a Buffalo Herd Even if You Have All the Medicine. *George C. Longfish, Seneca/Tuscarora. 1979–1980, acrylic on cloth, 86 × 96 inches. Private collection.*

George Longfish, a Northeast Woodlands Indian trained at the Art Institute of Chicago, has a remarkable ability to combine European technique with Indian images and themes. He opens a visionary door through symbol in his large, unframed canvases, which hang loosely from the wall, suggesting the freedom and flexibility of the ancient muslin tipi liners.

HEMINGWAY. As a New York critic, I say that all the time. The comfort, the relaxation of a library with a Navajo rug, a Gorman painting, Katcinas on the shelves, and a Maria pot here and there. America is finding the comfort and the serenity of her native peoples.

GOLIGHTLEY. Why should Indian art always make you comfortable? "The purpose of art," Braque wrote, "is to disturb." And good modern Indian art is disturbing, even frightening at times. My friend George Longfish says Indian art doesn't have to disturb, but he hasn't watched the reactions to his own wonderful canvases. Look at how people respond to the central figure in *Spirit Guide/Healer*. And how about titles like *You Can't Rollerskate in a Buffalo Herd Even if You Have All the Medicine*? It disturbs me, and I hope it disturbs others, particularly other

266. Indian document protesting railroads. Osage. 1889, scratchboard illustration, 5¾ × 9½ inches. The University of Tulsa, Shleppey Collection, McFarlin Library.

The use of art by Native Americans in political protest is not new. When the United States began to bring railroads through Indian Territory in the 1880s, a group of Osage lodged a formal protest, attaching this illustration to the document. The work is a particularly moving example of polemical art, but did not succeed in stopping the violation of treaty rights by the "no soul railroads." Note the Indian under the engine's wheels.

Indians—enough to make them think about what George and the rest of us are saying about Indian life in the now. Modern Indian art is also funny—funny because the tragedy is so great that our only salvation is in laughter, in our sense of humor. We have to see the irony in our lives; only then can we go on. Indian art has to be more than high-styled dens and game rooms filled with rugs, and more than socialites decked out in turquoise. Indian art must speak of Indian problems and potentials.

NARRATOR. Indian art has been filling that polemical role for a long time. This is not new. Do you know that wonderful Osage protest document submitted to Congress by the tribe, and published in 1879? It is one of the most eloquent Indian protests against the proposed federal policy of allotting Indian lands and selling the "surplus" to whites. There is a small black-and-white scratchboard picture on the last page. Drawn by an Osage, it shows a railroad train, with the name "No Soul" across the cab, running over an Indian figure lying on the railroad track, with an inscription something like "End of Indians" and "Theft of Millions of Acres." This protest, like others before and since, was ignored, even by the "friends of the Indian."

LOOKOUT. It's those damned "friends" we've got to worry about. Give me an enemy any day of the week.

FOX. Grey Cohoe goes to the heart of the Indian experience in *Tall Visitor at Tocito*, showing the white "Lady Bountiful" of the mission board or the arts and crafts commission in a pretty grim light. This painting is in the satiric tradition of Crumbo's *Land of Enchantment*, with its exaggerated New Mexico tourists, and Fred Kabotie's murals of drunken and dreaming whites at the Bright Angel Lodge at the Grand Canyon. Cohoe's colors and burlesqued anatomical proportions capture the wryest aspects of the ubiquitous "friends of the Indian." In *Tocito Waits for Boarding School Bus*, Cohoe addresses an experience that is uniquely Indian. Here we see a strong grandmother figure clutching a small boy. At first glance, one is struck by the enormous vitality of the color and the scene appears homely and accessible. But upon a closer look, you can see that the hands of the grandmother figure are like claws and that something suggestively red trickles down the boy's chest. A malignant shadow falls behind the grandmother and in it sits a cat—a witch in Navajo mythology—with a twinkling eye. Here are expressed all the uncertainty and apprehension of the Indian child who is sent unprepared into a white world. The painting becomes a metaphor for the clashing of two worlds. Paintings such as *Tocito Waits for Boarding School Bus* and *Tall Visitor at Tocito* are highly autobiographical. They speak to the whole Indian experience of education as a colonial reforming exercise designed, as even proponents acknowledge, to "destroy the Indian and preserve the man," to make red children white in thought and deed. You are right, Lookout, when you say that the friends have often been the real enemies. It is so too with the white-dictated definition of Indian art, and if those friends continue to have their way, the future of Indian art, like much of the past, will be a colonial artistic experience.

LOOKOUT. It sure takes you white boys a long time to say something. Some new things are bad. Some old things are good.

NARRATOR. It is possible to have terrible, trite traditional painting, just as it is easy to have mediocre modern art. The labeling itself is part of what is wrong. Another problem is the isolation of Indian art from the art community. Why do anthropologists and Indian specialists, and not art historians and critics, write about Indian art? Indian art must break the isolation and move out of the back room at the traders' shops.

GRADGRIND. There are some of us who try to show Indian works as real works of art and not just ethnographic curiosities. And we are having real success at it, too.

REDBIRD. I think another important development is the expanding role of the Indian artistic community itself. There is more formal and informal interaction among Indian artists. Museums are

267. Tocito Waits for Boarding School Bus. *Grey Cohoe (1944–   ), Navajo. 1981, oil and acrylic on canvas, 50 × 39 inches. Private collection.*

This highly autobiographical painting speaks to the whole Indian experience of education as a colonial and reforming exercise. In the synthesis of friendly color and hostile imagery is all the anxiety of the Indian child confronting white society. Cohoe's painting is a metaphor for the clashing of two worlds.

268. Tall Visitor at Tocito. *Grey Cohoe, Navajo. 1981, oil and acrylic on canvas, 60 × 48 inches. Private collection.*

Grey Cohoe counterposes a traditional Navajo woman with a bejeweled white authority figure, the "tall visitor" in this wry indictment of the white "Ladies Bountiful" who style themselves "friends of the Indian." Cohoe's paintings are in the tradition of satiric Indian images of whites: Northwest Coast carved argillite sea captains, Cochiti pottery effigies of opera singers and traders (fig. 195), and traditional watercolors such as Woodrow Crumbo's *Land of Enchantment* (fig. 202) and Fred Kabotie's Bright Angel Lodge murals at the Grand Canyon.

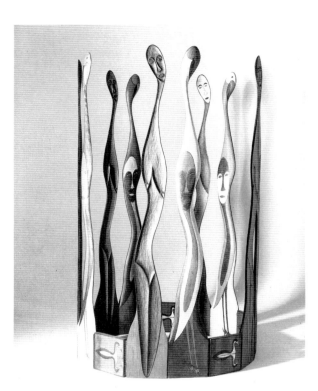

270. Ooger Ūk Inua (Walrus Spirit). *Larry Beck (1938–), Chnagmiut Eskimo. 1982, full-moon hubcaps, snow tire, anodized aluminum rivets, PVC plastic, chair legs, 18 × 20 × 10 inches. Collection of the artist, Seattle.*

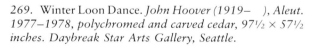

269. Winter Loon Dance. *John Hoover (1919–), Aleut. 1977–1978, polychromed and carved cedar, 97½ × 57½ inches. Daybreak Star Arts Gallery, Seattle.*

John Hoover believes that the tribal artist communicates with the spirit world as does the shaman and is thus more influenced by his cultural background than most non-Indian artists.

Students of historic artifacts know the ancient counterparts of Beck's pieces to have been constructed from randomly salvaged bits of ivory, wood, and skin. Beck constructs his masterful renderings of traditional Eskimo objects using found materials from the modern world —hubcaps, auto mirrors, kitchen utensils, and all the vast flotsam of man-made utilitarian objects. His work ranges from the monumental to the jewellike in scale.

taking serious notice of modern Indian art. The group of Hopi artists who came together in the 1960s to form the Artist Hopid are a good illustration of what Indians working together can produce.

FOX. You mustn't forget the increasing number of tribal arts and crafts groups and, of course, the Institute of American Indian Art in Santa Fe. The United States Indian Arts and Crafts Board continues to sponsor shows at places like the Southern Plains Indian Museum and Crafts Center. So there are a growing number of Indian-operated art markets and even a number of commercial galleries that are Indian-owned.

LOOKOUT. But most of them continue to have a Southwest bias. There is beautiful traditional and modern work being done in New York and North Carolina and Minnesota and Wisconsin and Washington and Oregon, not to mention the Canadian and Alaskan revivals. The tilt to the Southwest has been restrictive. I think some of the best things that are happening now are part of a conscious movement away from the Indian art of the Southwest.

HEMINGWAY. A couple of galleries in New York, Pittsburgh, and Boston now show Indian things, and the New York Indians still make masks and rattles and paintings. I think we are at a time when tribal distinctions are disappearing.

271. Wooden Pole Construction. *Truman Lowe (1944 –), Winnebago. 1983, wood and leather, 6 × 6 × 12 feet. Collection of the artist, Minneapolis.*

The Native American art movement has undergone fundamental change in the past decade. As younger artists continue to explore their individuality, often at the expense of their visual association with earlier Indian art, an aesthetic fusing of traditions and cultural styles has occurred. Lowe is one of these aesthetically restless spirits. His architectural constructs, evoking deserted villages, combine polemical issues with an approach also seen recently in work by Puerto Rican and black members of the craft art movement.

REDBIRD. Lady, you're crazy. Indians are creating out of their Indian experience and that experience is tribal, rooted in a specific place. Sure, lots of the experiences of Indians are the same, just as lots of Indian experiences are similar to those of whites and blacks. And a whole lot of us are urban Indians and our experiences are different from those of the reservation Indians.

GOLIGHTLEY. There you go again, assuming that all Indian art and all Indian artists are painting about Indians.

NARRATOR. I think we've talked generally about direction. Can I get some comments on specific trends and directions that suggest what the future will be like? For example, I see lots of new treatment of old themes. The Indian mask has served as inspiration not only for modern white painters, but also for modernism among Indian artists. There is the Choctaw artist James Havard's Abstract Illusionist *Corn Mask*, and some of the very earliest of Cheyenne Richard West's abstracts, such as *Apache Masked Dancer*. Larry Beck constructs masks out of automobile parts, kitchen implements, and other household forms. Karita Koffey has used the mask as inspiration for some of her finest ceramic pieces, as has Bill Glass. A particularly good illustration of this is found in John Hoover's wood carvings, which adopt and expand on earlier Northwest Coast wood-carving styles.

272. Car Scaffold Burial. *Ron Anderson (1944–), Comanche. 1984, Mercury Cougar with wood, cloth, glass, rawhide, feathers, mixed media. Collection of the artist, Lawton, Oklahoma.*

Although both the prehistoric and historic design of American Indian kivas, ceremonial sites, and village layouts were in a sense environmental sculpture, there are few Indian artists working at present who are known as environmental sculptors. A work such as Ron Anderson's *Car Scaffold Burial* is unique. The Mercury Cougar, wrapped in a funerary blanket and hoisted on a traditional Plains burial scaffold, was Anderson's private car; it was for years his transportation to his workplace, and his child was born in it. It was destroyed by a drunken driver whose insurance company refused to replace it. For Anderson, this was tantamount to stealing a man's horse and leaving him footbound out on the prairie. From this predicament came a piece of unprecedented protest art which is highly theatrical, and which at the same time makes a poignant statement about the necessity for mobility in both Indian and comtemporary white society. The scaffold stands on property belonging to Anderson, where it has been left to disintegrate among the elements of nature.

GOLIGHTLEY. He's right. Don't dismiss the old styles and techniques—they are very much a part of the future. We are seeing feather baskets still being made by superbly talented Pomo weavers, and the technique is being adopted by others, such as the Apache Moonwalker. And we are witnessing changes in weaving whereby new and more intricate styles with more vivid colors, like the so-called Burntwater, are winning prizes and outselling older patterns. I see a revival, certainly an homage, to the earlier Plains paintings in the works of such contemporary painters as Randy Lee White, Virginia Stroud, and Sharon Ahtone Harjo. It's fun to compare the old muslin *Exploits of Sun Boy* with Randy Lee White's painting, *Custer's Last Stand Revised*.

FOX. If you're going to compare influences, I'm prepared to predict that Indian painting of the future will be as much influenced by the non-Indian as by the Indian. The Indian artist or farmer lives in a world with TV and movies and white neighbors. How can you look at the work of T. C. Cannon, Joe Baker, Harry Fonseca, Ben Buffalo, Alvin Amason, Richard Danay, and Bob Haozous and not see that Indians live in the modern technological world? White influence is and was everywhere, and it has been for almost five hundred years. You see it from the argillite figures of ship captains carved by the Haida to the embroidery taught by French nuns in Canada, to the rug designs borrowed from Oriental carpet catalogues, to the baskets with patterns taken from Spanish coins.

HEMINGWAY. That is certainly true of paintings and painters. We all know that Art Deco borrowed from Indian designs and styles, but did you ever think that the Indian painters borrowed back? There is no question that the Mexican Surrealists influenced Gorman and Desjarlait. Fritz Scholder openly proclaims his debt to Francis Bacon. There are other sources, too, particularly the Orient and Abstract Expressionism, and now Funk art and Photorealism too. Jerry Ingram has elevated the idealized Indian of the frontier painters like Bodmer and Catlin into a contemporary idiom. And you can't say that the Cubism of Oscar Howe is the result of artistic isolation.

REDBIRD. The trouble is that those who tried to be different, like Joe Herrera, Ha So Deh, Patrick Desjarlait, Richard West, and Oscar Howe, were too often rejected by the Indian art establishment, despite their creativity and originality. Only now are they beginning to receive the recognition they have deserved all along. In the future, I see these early pioneer artists getting more and more honor, while the old "Bambi-style" painters are exposed for what they were.

LOOKOUT. Maybe I'm biased, but in the future I see a recognition of the classic early Indian painters. The gentle beauty and quiet simplicity, the intense coloring, and the depth of emotion will once again be appreciated. The works of the likes of Awa Tsireh, Fred Kabotie, the Kiowa Five, Ma Pe Wi, Carl Sweezy, and Waldo Mootzka will be in great museums. And they will be shown as examples of great art—not just Indian art but world art. In the future, many Indian artists will rediscover what was pure and fine and real. I've thought a lot about this. Some of these Indian

273. Nahookoos Fetish Pot. *Conrad House (1956–   ), Navajo. 1983, paint, quartz crystals, feathers, clay, metallic glaze, beads, 9 × 10 inches in diameter. Collection of the artist, Seattle.*

Among Conrad House's most enigmatic yet aesthetically satisfying works are the objects he refers to as his "sacred toys." This contemporary version of the ancient Puebloan fetish pot incorporates House's obsession with the dualities of life, and is in many ways reminiscent of the early historic Puebloan cosmic mobile (see fig. 14). Here, House has fused the sacred iconography of the past, including animal fetishes, the band of the winter Milky Way, the rainbow, and medicine plumes, to create an innovative sacred vessel for the future.

274. The Four Worlds. *Joe Herrera (1923–), Cochiti. Ca. 1954, casein on board, 16¾ × 12¾ inches. Private collection.*

The ancient Pueblo world provided the theme for many of Herrera's most innovative and dramatic paintings. Trained at the Sante Fe Studio and recognized as an important traditional painter, Herrera undertook the task of abstracting Pueblo symbolism in a style influenced by modern mainstream art theory and practice. In the early 1950s he became the first modernist American Indian painter to exhibit at the Museum of Modern Art, which before World War II had staged highly successful showings of traditional Indian arts.

paintings, like Blackbear Bosin's *Prairie Fire*, Fred Beaver's *Seminole Baby Naming*, Jerome Tiger's *The Four Moons*, and Carl Sweezy's *Peyote Road Man*, are true masterpieces. I have said enough. Sometimes we Indians can talk too long, too.

REDBIRD. I didn't mean to say that your generation—the earlier Indian artists—was not good, but only that it would not be good if we did not grow. Blackbear's *Prairie Fire* is a change from the Kiowa ledger paintings. It is dramatic and fluid and extends the old two-dimensional flat style. I think the future can be more of that refinement and extension, as well as dramatic departures. Most of us younger Indian artists respect, admire, even envy your generation and our father and mother artists, who have shown us the way.

FOX. In Japanese and Chinese art we have centuries of refinement and development of tradition. I see some of that sort of extended continuity in American Indian art. The risks are great because we are still so early in the process, and already there is the danger that the art will degenerate into clichés that are simply copies of copies of copies. But if we could develop a system of masters who inspire and instruct in ways that build and open up the tradition, then we might avoid stagnation.

HEMINGWAY. You aren't saying that this is all that Indian art should be, are you? You are aware that the name of the game has changed to multi-image originals, aren't you? And Indian artists are in the middle of all this, with lithos and posters, and video, computer, and laser art and photography.

GRADGRIND. We're back to my economics, you know. The Indian art market, like the whole of the art market, has changed dramatically in the last two decades.

CANYON. I disagree.

GOLIGHTLEY. I think what we are seeing is clear. The interest in Indian wall art is growing so fast that artists are responding in ways that maximize their artistic output. So we are witnessing the explosion of the graphics market in lithographs, silkscreens, etchings, woodcuts, engravings, posters, monotypes, pressed-paper sculptures, and four-color prints. I've also noticed more interest in pen-and-ink drawings and pencil sketches. The level of sophistication and craftsmanship of the Indian artists working in these areas is remarkable. This is particularly true with Northwest Coast and Eskimo graphics.

FOX. Let me suggest a couple of ways to look at the future of Indian art. You might look at it according to the divisions suggested in the *Magic Images* show[1]: historic expressionism, traditionalism, modernism, and individualism. These categories suggest the many directions of the future; as I have written many, many times, there are many mansions in Indian art. To understand the future of Indian art you have to see objects in categories as well: it helps to trace pottery, textiles, paintings, and jewelry as distinct arts. And it helps to look across a broad time frame. I think it is sometimes important to see the art from a tribal perspective, and other times by cultural area. For example, look at Southeastern Woodlands or Northern Plains art over four hundred years, and you get a sense of perspective.

NARRATOR (interrupting). You also have to have an understanding of the participants, their goals and viewpoints, as well as the broader issues that come from Indian society, and which transcend it.

CANYON. I hate to agree with Gradgrind, but isn't this a lot of garbage to go through to get an appreciation of beautiful works of art?

YOUNGWOMAN. You are back to treating us like specimens.

REDBIRD. Besides, I want real art critics and historians to look at us, not dingbat anthros and Boy Scout hobbyists.

HEMINGWAY. Listening to Fox, it sounds like you just want to ask questions. Reminds me of the story of Gertrude Stein on her deathbed. Someone asked her: "What is the answer?" She replied: "What is the question?" All you do is ask questions. I'll make a statement. In the future, Indian art will be recognized as an important art form, and will become a significant factor in world art.

CANYON. I'll take the other side of that. Indian art could so easily degenerate completely into tourist art, and the bad drive out the good. Think of the cost of making a Navajo textile. Who'll make blankets for 56¢ an hour, when you can make $3.60 clerking at the Safeway?

REDBIRD. For five hundred years, whites have been saying Indians and Indian art are disappearing. But we're still here, and we will be here for a long, long time, if you silly whites don't blow up the world.

NARRATOR. I don't think we'll ever come to a single conclusion. As far as I'm concerned, there are still a lot of questions to be answered, questions like: What is the current, viable Indian viewpoint? What is the nature of contemporary Indian society? Is that society producing artists? Are these artists Indian in viewpoint? Is an Indian artistic tradition being carried on? In what ways is Indian tradition changing? Is it possible to be both Indian and universal? Can an Indian be traditional and still work for a nontraditional market? Can work by an Indian artist be considered Indian if it is nontraditional in style or subject? When, if ever, does Indian art cease to be Indian?

I think all of you have made a number of important points. Indian art is very much alive and well. It is dynamic, independent, and evolving. We are witnessing in Indian art the classic drama of all living societies, that of continuity versus change. And that struggle can produce great art. Some of today's finest artistic achievements in this nation—indeed the world—are Indian. A thousand years from now, historians of the art of the twentieth and twenty-first centuries may look back upon our time and the coming decades as the great age, the mature flowering of a truly American art form. For we will see in the future not one Indian art tradition, but many. It will be like a thousand flowers in a single garden. We are now in the spring of that flowering. I cannot wait to see the garden in full bloom, to see those roses in all their variety. As we turn off the lights and leave this darkened gallery, let's remember that beautiful Chippewa verse:

As I gaze across the
prairie,
I feel the summer in
the spring.

THE CURTAIN FALLS

Note

1. *Magic Images* showed at Philbrook Art Center, Tulsa, in 1981. See Wade and Strickland 1981:4.

Glossary

ACCULTURATION.
The process of interaction between two societies in which the culture of the society in the subordinate position is drastically modified to conform to the culture of the dominant one.

ADENA.
A culture or mortuary complex that arose in southern Ohio around 500 B.C. and spread eastward as far as Delaware and New Jersey, blending with HOPEWELL culture around 100 B.C. Characteristic of the culture are platform tobacco pipes and lavish grave goods.

ARGILLITE.
A soft, carbonaceous shale quarried on the Queen Charlotte Islands in the Pacific Northwest that is easily carved with woodworking tools and takes a high polish when dried.

ARTIST HOPID.
A group of contemporary Hopi artists who utilize many of the techniques and artistic innovations of the twentieth century, as well as traditional symbols and stylistic conventions of ancient Hopi art, to express the aesthetic and cultural values of their people.

ATLATL.
A hand-held spear-thrower made of a rigid board or stick about twenty to twenty-five inches long, with a spur or pin at one end. The butt of a spear or dart rests against this spur, from which it is propelled in an overhand motion with great force. In function, the atlatl is an extension of the hunter's forearm.

BAMBI ART.
A term of derision applied to the Oklahoma and Sante Fe Studio schools of easel painting in the 1950s and 1960s by younger artists seeking to free themselves from the constraints of the established styles.

BANDOLIER BAG.
A general-purpose bag carried by men, called a Friendship Bag in Canada, with an attached shoulder strap or straps, worn like a bandolier. Usually made of wool, muslin, or buckskin, they were heavily decorated with beadwork, quillwork, or embroidery in styles of the Eastern Woodlands. The shoulder straps were sometimes finger-woven sashes.

BASKETMAKER PHASE.
A prehistoric culture period in what is currently called the "four corners region," encompassing parts of Colorado, Arizona, Utah, and New Mexico. It comprised the early stages of Anasazi culture, from about 200 B.C. to A.D. 700, antecedent to the Pueblo cultures.

BAYETA.
A commercial wool yarn raveled by the Navajo from woven goods obtained from the Spaniards, commonly used from 1788 to 1900, but especially from 1800 to 1880, when the "bayeta period" marked the high point of Navajo weaving. During this period, weavers blended native wool and bayeta yarn in a harmonious union.

BOOGER.
An Eastern Cherokee dance, and the masks worn by the dancers. The purpose of these is, in part, to ridicule strangers—Indian, white, and black—who are characterized by exaggerated facial expressions. The term also includes animal masks such as those of the buffalo, bear, and hornet, worn in dances for magico-religious purposes.

BUTTON BLANKET.
A wearing blanket of the historic period made by the tribes of the Northwest Coast by sewing buttons, usually old Chinese mother-of-pearl buttons, in an intricate animal design in the middle of a dark blue trade blanket, such as a Hudson Bay blanket. Red felt or broadcloth, sometimes decorated with buttons or shells, was sewn as a border around the blanket's perimeter.

CACIQUE.
The Carib word for "chief," often used to refer to the sacerdotal chief of an early historic Southeastern tribe, a Pueblo Indian tribe, or any Central or South American tribe.

CALUMET.
A Norman French word meaning "reed" or "cane," first applied to the stems of tobacco pipes and then also to their bowls. The large pipes were used in an intertribal ceremony east of the Missouri River in the 1600s to make peace and cement alliances for war. The pipe bowls were carved of stone, usually catlinite, and the stems were elaborately decorated with feathers. In English, these pipes are often called peace pipes.

CARAVACA CROSS.
A double-barred cross, with or without an Immaculate Heart at the stem, introduced to the American Southwest by Franciscan priests from the area of Caravaca in Spain. It was often equated with the dragonfly, which had special meaning to the Puebloans.

CATLINITE.
A soft red slate mined at Pipestone, Minnesota, for use in carving pipe bowls. It was named for the painter George Catlin, the first white American to see the quarries.

CHIEF'S BLANKET.
A type of blanket woven by the Navajo throughout the nineteenth century for their own use and that of members of other tribes, especially Plains tribes. The earliest, First Phase, were striped. The Second Phase saw a block design added to the stripes and in the Third Phase nine serrated triangles were arranged in groups of three along the outer edges and at the center of the blanket.

CLAN.
A social group whose members claim descent from a common ancestor, often a mythical figure. A clan is made up of lineages of kinsmen who share unilateral descent from a common known ancestor.

CLAN EMBLEM.
The representation or symbol of the being from which a kin group based on lineal descent derives its name, or under whose special patronage the group belongs; sometimes a totem.

COILED BASKETRY.
A basketry technique in which a spiraling foundation of rods or filaments is stitched together in any of several possible ways by means of a flexible weft, which usually creates the decorative effects.

CONTRARY WARRIOR.
A member of a Plains military society in which all are obligated to say the opposite of what is meant, do the opposite of what is demanded, and generally act contrary to common sense by performing spectacular feats, such as plunging their arms into boiling water.

COUNTING COUP.
The social practice among the Plains Indians of publicly reciting coups, or attested deeds of valor in warfare. This was the system whereby status and prestige were conferred for performing certain deeds, such as touching an enemy but not killing him.

CRADLEBOARD.
A carrying cradle for babies with a flat back made of wood, hard hide, basketry, wickerwork, or a sinew-laced elongated hoop. The baby was held in a buckskin or basketry pouch, often decorated, or tied on with buckskin or cloth straps. Eastern Woodland cradleboards were carved in relief and painted; the Plains style featured heavily beaded buckskin pouches on decoratively studded slats.

CREST.
A heraldic device; among Northwest Coast tribes the image of an animal or supernatural being that designates a noble family lineage.

CULTURE.
A set of learned ways of thinking and acting that characterizes a decision-making human group; in archaeology, a cluster of diagnostic features.

CULTURE AREA.
A geographical territory within which the cultures tend to be similar in some significant aspects. North American culture areas include the Eastern Woodlands (sometimes divided into the Northeast and Southeast), the Subarctic or Northern Woodlands, the Arctic, the Plains, the Southwest, California, the Great Basin, the Interior Plateau, and the Northwest Coast.

DANCE APRON.
A ceremonial garment commonly associated with the Northwest Coast, ornamented with crest designs and worn only in ceremonial dances.

DAWES ACT.
A General Allotment Act of 1887 which granted former reservation land to individuals, the amount of land per individual differing on different reservations. Reservation land not so allotted was usually sold by the government to non-Indian settlers, thus reducing drastically the amount of land reserved for Indians.

DEGIKUP.
A small-mouthed ceremonial basket of the Washoe. Between 1895 and 1935 the form was elaborated with finer technique and more complex designs. It was apparently chosen as the dominant basketry form made for sale because its expressive spheroidal shape allowed it to evolve both as a textile and as a sculpture.

DENTALIUM.
The shell of a gastropod which consists of a tubular cone open at both ends, so that it may be strung like a bead or sewn onto garments or objects as a decorative element.

DOG SOLDIER.
A member of a military organization among the Plains Indians who had an association with dogs (or horses) through visions or dreams.

EFFIGY PIPE.
A tobacco-pipe bowl of stone or pottery made in the shape of an animal, bird, or human, with the tobacco held in a hole in the animal's back or human's head.

EYE DAZZLER.
A type of Navajo blanket made during the 1890s using vividly dyed commercial yarns woven into colorful, jagged terrace patterns and zigzag designs.

FALSE EMBROIDERY.
In twined basketry (which uses two or more wefts), a decorative technique in which a third weft of contrasting color is wrapped around the two outer wefts and consequently remains invisible on the inside of the basket.

FALSE FACE DANCE.
A ritual performed by a member of an Iroquois medicine society while wearing a mask that imbued him with special powers to anticipate or cure disease.

FALSE FACE MASK.
The carved wood representation of a being seen in a dream or in the forest, worn by False Face Society members. A false face mask recalls the encounter of an Iroquois culture hero with a mask spirit; the mask itself has power and is treated with ritual respect.

FETISH BUNDLE.
A bag or wrapping containing one or more objects believed to possess consciousness, volition, immortal life, and the magic power to effect results mysteriously.

FIRST, SECOND, and THIRD MESAS.
Three geological outcroppings, or mesas, running north-south, on the Hopi Reservation in Arizona. Each has distinct or autonomous villages: Hano, Sichomovi, and Walpi on First Mesa, Shipaulovi and Shongopovi on Second Mesa, and Hotevilla and Old Oraibi on Third Mesa. In art, First Mesa is associated with pottery, Second Mesa with coiled baskets, and Third Mesa with wicker baskets.

FORMLINE SYSTEM.
The backbone of Northwest Coast two-dimensional design. Standardized units of decoration are executed using gently expanding and contracting lines that merge into a continuous outline of the subject. In painting, the primary formlines are usually black, and in relief carving they are the uncarved surface plane of the carved material.

FORT MARION.
The Castillo de San Marcos, at St. Augustine, Florida, the oldest masonry fort in the United States; used as a military prison for Indians from the Southern Plains from 1875 to 1878.

FRONTLET.
The central element in a Northwest Coast dance headdress, worn on the forehead. Usually carved of wood, painted, and decorated with abalone-shell inlays, copper, and sometimes mirrors, it represents an animal clan crest.

GERMAN SILVER.
An alloy of copper, nickel, and zinc used by Plains metalworkers to handcraft jewelry and accoutrements, using the same techniques as silversmiths.

GERMANTOWN.
Navajo blankets woven of tightly spun three- or four-ply commercial woolen yarn, dyed in brightly colored aniline and other synthetic dyes originally made in Germantown, Pennsylvania.

GHOST DANCE.
A religious movement that spread among the Indian groups of western North America during the latter part of the nineteenth century, based on visions of the Paiute Indian Wovoka, who foresaw the disappearance of the white man and the return of the buffalo.

GORGET.
A rectangular or circular tablet with perforations, worn hung around the neck. Mississippian gorgets were carved of shell with elaborate engravings and openwork designs.

HAMATSA RITUAL.
Also known as the Cannibal Dance. Part of a series of Northwest Coast dances, particularly among the Kwakiutl, known as the Winter Ceremonial, wherein young men are initiated as Hamatsa in the image of the Cannibal Spirit; a transfer of hereditary ceremonial property symbolizing rank and privilege, one of the highest in the aristocratic societies of the Northwest Coast.

HANDSOME LAKE.
An Iroquois League chief of the Seneca who had a series of visions in 1799, which led to the founding of the Longhouse Religion, a non-Christian alternative church that asserted Iroquois ethnic identity.

HEISHE.
Flat, uniform beads of shell, coral, turquoise, or other stone, made by rolling a string of drilled beads against an abrasive surface.

HOPEWELL.
A far-flung network of ceremonies and trade from about 100 B.C. to A.D. 700, which spread from Ontario to the area of present-day Kansas City, and from the Gulf of Mexico to Lake Huron. Traits include burial mounds and earthworks and widespread trade in exotic raw materials. The art style represents a high point in the artistic expression of the Northeast and indicates the presence of craft specialists and marked differences in wealth and status.

HOUSEPOST or HOUSE PILLAR.
A type of totem pole, carved to illustrate tribal mythologies and used on the Northwest Coast to support house rafters.

HUDSON'S BAY COMPANY.
A joint-stock organization originally chartered in London in 1670, which was granted sole trading rights in all the lands drained by the streams that flowed into Hudson's Bay, as it was then called. Stockholders grew enormously rich as agents made trading agreements with Indians to exchange European goods, especially beads and woolen cloth, for animal pelts.

IMBRICATION.
In coiled basketry, a technique in which a nonstructural filament is folded under each weft stitch on the outside of the basket to produce a looped or scaly texture, like that of roof tiles or the scales of a fish.

KATCINA.
A class of supernatural figures among the Pueblo Indians of the Southwest, benevolent anthropomorphic beings who live in mountains, lakes, and springs, and who personify natural phenomena such as plants and animals. Also, the doll or figure in Pueblo art that represents such a being.

KIOWA CALENDAR.
A calendar system used by the Kiowa, in which years are designated by names and glyphs for both winters and summers; the names are derived from some unusual event of each season.

KIOWA FIVE.
A designation given to the artists of the 1920s and thirties who were instrumental in forming the style or school of painting called the Kiowa School. The five are Spencer Asah, Stephen Mopope, Monroe Tsatoke, Jack Hokeah, and James Auchiah. The term is something of a misnomer, since other artists exerted significant influence.

KIVA.

A semisubterranean flat-roofed ceremonial chamber in a Southwest Indian pueblo. It is entered through a central threshold symbolizing the place where the first people emerged to inhabit the earth's surface. Masks and sacred objects are stored in the kiva and preparation for public ceremonies takes place there.

KOSHARE.

A Pueblo clown who personifies chaos, attempting to disrupt the sacred Katcina dance, amusing the audience during intervals in ceremonies, and disciplining the children.

LEDGER DRAWING.

A representational drawing of vignettes from the life of a nineteenth-century Plains Indian. Ledger drawings were so named because they were often drawn in blank ledger books obtained from white traders or soldiers.

LINEAGE. *See* CLAN.

LONGHOUSE.

A large, long building of the Eastern Woodlands. In early historic times, longhouses were usually made of arched saplings covered with bark, and housed several families. Chiefs' longhouses were also used for ceremonial purposes, and in later times longhouses of various materials were constructed solely for religious, tribal, or ceremonial use.

LONGHOUSE RELIGION. *See* HANDSOME LAKE.

MEDICINE BOWL.

A sacred ceramic vessel of the Southwest Pueblo, made to hold a purifying ceremonial drink or other magic substance referred to as medicine.

MEDICINE BUNDLE.

A collection of revered objects with assigned meanings and magical properties known to an individual or shared by a group, kept specially wrapped in hide or cloth, or in a specially constructed bag or pouch.

MÉTIS.

A Canadian term for people of mixed Indian and French (or sometimes Scottish or Irish) ancestry involved in the early fur trade.

MIDEWIWIN.

A religious, shamanistic society begun around 1700 among the Ojibwa peoples, particularly concerned with curing. It rapidly spread to all the Algonquian-speaking tribes of the Great Lakes/Illinois region and to the eastern Sioux.

MIDWINTER CEREMONY.

The longest Iroquois ceremonial in the calendrical cycle, beginning in January or February and lasting at least a week. In some longhouses it includes performance of the Four Sacred Rituals given by the Creator and confirmed by Handsome Lake: the Feather Dance, Thanksgiving Dance, Personal Chant, and Bowl Game; the Our Life Supporter Dances, a series of dances honoring corn, beans, and squash, may also be performed.

MIMBRES.

A region of the Southwest that in prehistoric times was part of the Mogollon subarea. It is famous for classic black-on-white pottery jars and bowls, decorated with highly complex geometric designs or lively painted portrayals of stylized frogs, rabbits, insects, birds, humans, and other life forms. Most date from around A.D. 1000–1300.

MISSISSIPPIAN.

Also called the Southern Cult. A cultural tradition developed in the central Mississippi and adjacent river valleys between A.D. 700 and 1000, with its greatest influence in the Southeast. It is characterized by maize agriculture, flat-topped temple mounds of enormous size, and a religious and artistic complex that reached a peak about A.D. 1300, and which represents a reworking of religious ideas from Mexico.

MONITOR PIPE.

A tobacco pipe characteristic of the Hopewellian and Mississippian eras that was made with a flat or slightly arched elongated base having an upright bowl, often in the shape of an animal, bird, human head, or other representational carving.

MOUNDS.

Prehistoric American earthworks found east of the Rocky Mountains. Effigy mounds were constructed in the form of birds, snakes, and other beings; conical mounds of the Hopewell era usually contained burials; and flat-topped temple mounds (terraced truncated pyramids) of the Mississippian era were as much as one hundred feet tall.

NATIVE AMERICAN.

A term pertaining to the various Indian tribes of the Americas, as well as the Inuit (Eskimo), Aleut, and, increasingly, Hawaiians, whose ancestors were aboriginal to America.

NATIVE AMERICAN CHURCH.

A church association incorporated in Oklahoma in the early 1900s to formalize a Christian-based ceremony known as the Peyote Cult or Mescal Cult, which now legally incorporates the ingestion of hallucinogenic buds of the peyote cactus in services.

OLLA.

A large-mouthed jar or pot of earthenware, used for holding water or grain.

OOLACHEN OIL.

Oil of the candlefish, an oily sea fish of the salmon family that frequents the northwestern shores of North America.

OPERCULUM.

The horny plate of one of many types of gastropod, serving to close the shell when the animal is retracted. The plates were used to decorate Northwest Coast bowls and other objects.

PAD SADDLE.

A saddle adapted from U.S. Cavalry riding gear by tribes of the Northern Plains and Plateau regions.

PAN-INDIANISM.

A modern style of music, dance, art, and philosophy that transcends tribal and regional styles. Its elements are drawn from many tribes and regions and from the non-Indian world. In some cases the style serves as a unifying basis for national Indian political action.

PEYOTE.

A variety of cactus found in Mexico and the southwestern United States, whose buttonlike tops are ingested to induce visions as part of a religious ritual.

PEYOTE FAN.

A fan or bundle of feathers used by a participant in a peyote ceremony to shield his or her eyes from the light of the fire and to wave purifying cedar smoke toward other participants.

PIPE-TOMAHAWK.

A tobacco pipe made by Europeans for trade to the Indians. It was made of metal with an eye to receive the handle and a sharp, hatchet-shaped blade for use in cutting wood or as a weapon. Many were etched and inlaid with silver or lead.

POLIKMANA.

The Butterfly Katcina Maiden, a potent fertility symbol of the Hopi in northeastern Arizona, distinguished by an elaborate TABLITA and radiating and triangular facial decorations.

PONY BEADS.

A type of glass bead larger than a seed bead, brought from Europe by traders early in the nineteenth century and used by Indians to replace quillwork. Originally only in black and white, pony beads were later made in a vast variety of colors.

POTLATCH.

Ceremonial feasting and gift giving, often competitive, among Indians of the Northwest Coast. The potlatch was part of an elaborate public display validating an initiate's rank, status, and privilege regarding the use of family designs, crests, songs, masks, and socially recognized names.

Powwow.

In modern times, an intertribal celebration incorporating music and dance, gifts, and a range of ceremonial elements from many tribes. A powwow is usually sponsored by a family, tribe, intertribal association, school, or other social or institutional group to honor individuals or groups, raise money, celebrate a special occasion, or simply promote intertribal fellowship.

Prestige item.

On the Northwest Coast, often an object of artistic excellence, made of rare materials, whose possession tended to be hereditary. Among the Plains and related cultures, such items could be trophies, personal medicine objects, or honorific standards that indicated the owner's personal valor or unique spiritual encounters.

Pueblo Revolt.

An uprising in August 1680, led by a native of San Juan Pueblo named Popé against the Spanish colonists and missionaries. The Pueblos remained independent of Spanish control for twelve years, until they were reconquered in 1692 by Diego de Vargas. During the revolt many Puebloans abandoned their settlements and took refuge in more defensible sites.

Quillworker society.

A society of Cheyenne women known as "the selected ones" who produced robes, containers, ornaments, and other objects, decorated with porcupine quills, for priests or tribal societies. The technical production of these objects was regulated by a carefully followed set of rituals, learned by the woman during a rigorous initiation period.

Rain god.

A kind of decorative figurine produced by Tesuque potters for sale to tourists, originally as part of a money-making scheme conceived by the trader Jake Gold in the late nineteenth century.

Reservation.

Land reserved by the U.S. government after 1876 for use by Indians. When a tribe ceded territory it had held by original occupancy to the government, a specified part was retained by the tribe. However, treaties expressly stated that the land was reserved by the government for the given Indians, thus recognizing the government as titleholder, not the tribe.

Roach *and* **roach spreader.**

A male Indian dancer's head ornament made of horsehair, deer hair, and/or porcupine hair, which stands up like a crest, running lengthwise across the head from the forehead to the nape of the neck. The spreader, a flat piece of bone, antler, or other material in the center of the headdress, may hold and support upright an eagle feather.

Saltillo.

The capital of the state of Coahuila, Mexico, noted for the fine serapes, or wool shawls, made there; also, any blanketlike shawl decorated with diamond and step-pyramid designs after the Mexican style.

Santa Fe Studio.

The studio at which painting lessons were given to Indian students at the Santa Fe Indian school, beginning in 1932; also, the style established by that school which, for the following forty years, was the major commercial painting tradition of the Southwest Indians.

Scrimshaw.

A method of decoration, in which shell, bone, or ivory is etched or carved and ink or dye is rubbed into the incised lines. Originally referring to such handiwork done by sailors on long voyages, the term is often applied to Inuit (Eskimo) decorations on walrus tusks, bone, and ivory.

Seed jar.

A ceramic vessel distinguished by a rounded base, high shoulder, and flat top with a small, rimless orifice at the center. The earliest examples of such forms come from the prehistoric Anasazi tradition of northeastern Arizona, where they were excavated and occasionally found to contain ancient seeds.

Serape.

A woolen blanket or shawl, often brightly colored with regionally varying designs, worn as an outer garment in Spanish-American countries. Navajo weavers adopted the designs of Mexican serapes for their own blankets in the mid-1800s.

Shaman.

A practitioner of magic or medicine who uses powers derived from direct contact with supernatural sources for curing and other beneficial rites; synonymous with medicine man, animal (or witch) doctor; called an *angakok* among the Inuit, a sorcerer or juggler in the Great Lakes area.

Shape shifter.

An individual or being possessed of the ability to transform its physical appearance. The trickster figures in North America often possess shape-shifter characteristics or abilities. *See* Trickster.

Shell hair pipe.

A hollow cylindrical shell bead, one and one-half inches or more in length, worn as a costume ornament. Prehistorically, these tubes were also made of bone, copper, or stone, and in historical times sometimes of glass, but most often from conch columella.

Sikyatki polychrome.

Matte-painted polychrome pottery of the late prehistoric and early historic period in the Hopi area, characterized by abstract motifs and curvilinear and asymmetric designs. Together with prehistoric Mimbres ceramics of southern New Mexico, Sikyatki ware was commonly held to be the superlative ceramic tradition of ancient North America.

Smithport style.

An undecorated tempered-clay earthenware produced in northwestern Louisiana and southwestern Arkansas between A.D. 500 and 1200. Bottles, bowls, and plates with smoothed but unpolished exteriors are found in gray to buff color, with some portions dark brown to black from differential firing.

Speaker's staff *or* **talking stick.**

Part of the ceremonial equipment of many Kwakiutl chiefs, used for emphasis when making a formal speech. Its carving represents family origins or myths, so that it is an iconic display of the power of a lineage as manifested through its chief or most prominent family member.

Spent indigo.

A diluted solution of the indigo dye commonly used by Navajo and Pueblo weavers in the nineteenth century. While they preferred the deep cobalt blue of clean indigo, they occasionally desired a powder blue or turquoise, which they achieved by dyeing the wool in a vat previously used for indigo, resulting in a weak or spent color.

Spiro Mounds.

A ceremonial center of the Mississippian period, south of the Arkansas River in present-day Oklahoma and Arkansas, which served as the trading gateway between the Southeast and the Plains. *See also* Mounds.

Strouding *or* **stroud cloth.**

An early woolen trade cloth from England, generally red or blue, sometimes with rainbow selvage.

Sucking doctor.

Among the Pomo and other California tribes, a medical practitioner who removed the source of an illness through the process of placing his mouth on the patient and sucking out the evil; the practice is generally associated with shamanism.

Sun Dance.

The annual ceremony of many Plains and Plateau tribes, characterized by a round arbor encircling a tall pole, upon which were hung ceremonial objects. Within the arbor various ceremonies, dances, and rites were carried out.

Tablita *or* **tableta.**

A flat wooden headdress of the Hopi, painted with various designs and often ornamented with feathers.

Tihu.

A very simple cottonwood plaque painted with a representation of a Katcina, given to children and used in other contexts by the Hopi; the origin of the Katcina doll.

Tipi.

A conical tent used by the Plains tribes, first made of hides, later of canvas stretched over poles.

Tipi liner.

A hide or canvas panel about three to six feet tall, hung around the inside of a tipi in winter to form an inner wall for warmth; sometimes painted with scenes of the exploits of the men of the family.

TLÁSULÁ.
A Kwakiutl ceremonial cycle, part of the initiation rites included in the Winter Ceremonies; the dance is motivated by a supernatural power. In English the cycle is known as the Weasel Dance or the Feather Dance. The dancer wears a carved frontlet and crownlike headdress from which eagle down is released during the dance and which has rows of white ermine (winter weasel) hanging from the back of the crown.

TOGGLE HARPOON.
The form of harpoon used on the Northwest Coast for killing whales and walruses; it has a pivoted cross blade instead of fixed barbs.

TOTEM POLE.
A tall, carved pole placed in front of a Northwest Coast house that depicted the guardian spirits of the family in the form of heraldic crest animals and birds.

TRADE BEAD.
A glass bead produced in Europe for trade to the Indians. Pony beads are larger and older, seed beads smaller and more recent.

TRICKSTER.
One of the great elders and an original force of creation, embodying the powers of both good and evil. He is a dualistic being, and his acts are not constrained by the laws of man. He is present in ancient North America in the guise of Coyote, Raven, and countless other manifestations.

TRINKET BASKET.
A small basket, usually lidded, made by the Inuit, Aleut, and Indians of the Northwest Coast, across the Great Lakes region, and in the Southeast.

TULAROSA.
A prehistoric site on the Upper Gila River in New Mexico from which come pottery pitchers, jars, dippers, and other ceramics, with black-and-white geometrical decoration both in solid color and hatched.

TWINED BASKETRY.
A technique in which two or more weft elements are twisted around the warps to create plain, three-element wicker, twill, or wrapped-twining weaves. Decorations based on color contrast are achieved through FALSE EMBROIDERY, wrapped twining, or overlay.

VISION QUEST.
The deliberate attempt to induce a visitation from a supernatural being, often in the form of an animal or bird, which could bestow power upon the human seeking the vision. The tradition is most prevalent among the Plains Indians.

VISION SHIELD.
A Plains war shield considered to be effective because of its painted magical designs, which represent a visionary encounter with the supernatural.

WAMPUM.
Any of several kinds of shell made into white and purple tubular beads, which were then woven into belts used in the Eastern Woodlands in early historic times as token of pledges made, and as money. Among the Iroquois, they acquired the character of a mnemonic device in which the designs, based on the contrast between the white and purple beads, were associated with conventionalized meanings. By the 1800s most other tribes of the Northeast were using wampum belts in all important ceremonial and political transactions, to accompany and give weight to the words spoken.

WAR BOOK.
A small book, originally of blank pages, such as a commercial ledger book or diary, obtained by warriors of the Plains tribes and filled with drawings of incidents and heroic deeds in their careers.

WEARING ROBE.
A buffalo, elk, or deerskin processed with the hair left on, often painted on the smooth side, and worn either with the hair side in, for warmth, or out.

WEDGEWEAVE.
A variation of Navajo tapestry weave with a characteristic zigzag pattern of diagonal stripes formed as the weft is inserted at an angle to the warp. Also known as a pulled-warp process, since the tension produced by this diagonally placed weft pulls the warp threads out of line as they are released, and creates a scalloped edge.

WINNOWING TRAY.
A flat basket used to separate chaff from grain by wind or a forced current of air.

WINTER COUNT.
A type of calendar kept by the Sioux in which each year is named by an event which occurred that year and a glyph symbolizing that event is drawn on a calendrical hide or paper. The counts of each winter, and thus each year, were arranged in a spiral from the edge of the calendar to the middle.

WINTER CEREMONIES. See TLÁSULÁ.

YEI.
A Navajo supernatural. Yeis, or Holy People, are impersonated by masked dancers in several God-Impersonator ceremonies, such as Nightway and Big Godway.

Bibliography

ABBASS, DONNA KATHLEEN.
1979 "Contemporary Oklahoma Ribbonwork: Styles and Economics." Ph.D. dissertation. Southern Illinois University, Carbondale.

ABERLE, DAVID F.
1951 *The Psychosocial Analysis of a Hopi Life-History*. Berkeley: University of California Press.

ADAM, LEONHARD.
1949 *Primitive Art*. Rev. ed. Harmondswoth, Middlesex: Penguin.

ALEXANDER, HARTLEY BURR.
1938 *Sioux Indian Painting. Part 1: Paintings of Sioux and Other Tribes of the Great Plains*. Nice: C. Szwedzicki. Portfolio with accompanying text.

ALSOP, JOSEPH.
1978 Art History and Art Collecting; Art Collecting: The Renaissance and Antiquity. *Times Literary Supplement*, no. 3982 (28 July 1978): 851–853; no. 3983 (4 August 1978): 891–893. London.
1982 *The Rare Art Traditions: The History of Art Collecting and Its Linked Phenomena Wherever These Have Appeared*. New York: Princeton University Press/Bollingen; Harper and Row.

AMERSON, L. PRICE JR.
AND ALLAN M. GORDON.
1981 *Confluences of Tradition and Change/ 24 American Indian Artists*. Davis, California: Richard L. Nelson Gallery and C. N. Gorman Museum.

ANTROPOVA, V. V.
1953 Sovremennaia chukotskaia i ėskimosskaia reznia kost [Contemporary Chukchee and Eskimo Bone Carvings]. *Sbornik Muzeia Antropologii i Etnografii, Akademiia Nauk SSSR* 15:5–96, 20 pls.

BARNETT, HOMER G., LEONARD BROOM, BERNARD J. SIEGEL, EVON Z. VOGT, AND JAMES B. WATSON.
1954 Acculturation: An Exploratory Framework. *American Anthropologist* 56: 973–1002.

BENEDICT, RUTH.
1934 *Patterns of Culture*. Boston and New York: Houghton Mifflin.

BENNETT, KATHY.
1981 Navajo Chief Blanket: A Trade Item among Non-Navajo Groups. *American Indian Art Magazine* 7(1):62–69.

BERKHOFER, ROBERT F.
1978 *The White Man's Indian. Images of the American Indian from Columbus to the Present*. New York: Knopf.

BLACKWOOD, BEATRICE.
1961 [Comment to Haselberger.] *Current Anthropology* 2(4):360.

BLAIR, WINK.
1976 Lelooska. *American Indian Art Magazine* 1(2):82–85.

BOAS, FRANZ.
1897 The Social Organization and the Secret Societies of the Kwakiutl Indians. Pp. 311–738 in *Report of the United States National Museum, 1895*. Washington, D.C.
1903 The Decorative Art of the North American Indians. *Popular Science Monthly* 63:481–498. Reprinted on pp. 546–563 of his *Race, Language and Culture*, New York: Macmillan, 1940.
1921 Ethnology of the Kwakiutl. *Thirty-fifth Annual Report of the Bureau of American Ethnology*. Washington, D.C.
1927 *Primitive Art*. Oslo: H. Aschehoug. Reprinted New York: Dover, 1955.

BOURNE, EDWARD GAYLORD, ED.
1922 *Narratives of the Career of Hernando de Soto in the Conquest of Florida as Told by a Knight of Elvas.... * New York: Allerton Book Co.

BRADBURY, ELLEN.
1976 *I Wear the Morning Star. An Exhibition of American Indian Ghost Dance Objects*. Minneapolis: The Minneapolis Institute of the Arts.

BRASSER, TED J.
1975 A Basketful of Indian Culture Change. *National Museum of Man Mercury Series, Canadian Ethnology Service Paper* 22. Ottawa.
1976 *"Bo'jou, Neejee!" Profiles of Canadian Indian Art*. Ottawa: National Museum of Man, National Museums of Canada.

BRODY, J. J.
1971 *Indian Painters & White Patrons*. Albuquerque: University of New Mexico Press.

BROWN, JOSEPH EPES.
1976 *Seeing with a Native Eye: Essays on Native American Religion*, Walter Holden, ed. New York: Harper and Row.

BROWN, THOMAS M.
1980 "Cultural Evolutionists, Boasians, and Anthropological Exhibits: A New Look at American Anthropology, 1887–1905." Master's thesis, History of Science. Baltimore, Johns Hopkins University.

BUNZEL, RUTH L.
1929 The Pueblo Potter: A Study of Creative Imagination in Primitive Art. *Columbia University Contributions to Anthropology* 8. New York.
1932 Introduction to Zuñi Ceremonialism. Pp. 467–544 in *Forty-Seventh Annual Report of the Bureau of American Ethnology, 1929–1930*. Washington, D.C.
1965 The Nature of Katcinas. Pp. 442–444 in *Reader in Comparative Religion. An Anthropological Approach*, William A. Lessa and Evon Z. Vogt, eds. New York, Evanston, and London: Harper and Row.

BURNETT, E. K.
1944 Inlaid Stone and Bone Artifacts from Southern California. *Contributions from the Museum of the American Indian* 13. New York: Museum of the American Indian, Heye Foundation.

BURTON, HENRIETTA K.
1936 *The Re-establishment of the Indians in Their Pueblo Life through the Revival of Their Traditional Crafts*. New York: Teachers College, Columbia University.

BYINGTON, CYRUS.
1915 A Dictionary of the Choctaw Language. *Bureau of American Ethnology Bulletin* 46. Washington, D.C.

CALDWELL, JOSEPH R.
1964 Interaction Spheres in Prehistory. In *Hopewellian Studies*, J. R. Caldwell and R. T. Hall, eds. *Illinois State Museum Scientific Papers* 12(16):133–143. Second printing 1970.

CALLANDER, LEE A. AND RUTH SLIVKA.
1984 *Shawnee Home Life: The Paintings of Earnest Spybuck*. New York: Museum of the American Indian, Heye Foundation.

CARPENTER, EDMUND.
1973 *Eskimo Realities*. New York: Holt, Rinehart and Winston.

CASSIRER, ERNST.
1944 *An Essay on Man: An Introduction to a Philosophy of Human Culture*. New Haven: Yale University Press.

CHAPMAN, KENNETH M.
AND FRANCIS H. HARLOW.
1970 *The Pottery of San Ildefonso Pueblo*. Albuquerque: University of New Mexico Press.

CHILD, IRVIN L. AND LEON SIROTO.
1971 Bakwele and American Aesthetic Evaluations Compared. Pp. 271–289 in *Art and Aesthetics in Primitive Societies*, Carol F. Jopling, ed. New York: Dutton.

CLARK, E. L.
1881a Letter to Col. P. B. Hunt, United States Indian Service, Kiowa, Comanche and Wichita Agency, Anadarko, Indian Territory, dated July 14, Camp, North Fork of the Red River. Manuscript, microfilm KA47, frame 853, Archives and Manuscripts Division, Oklahoma Historical Society, Oklahoma City.
1881b Letter to Col. P. B. Hunt dated July 20, Camp on the North Fork of the Red River. Manuscript, microfilm KA47, frame 880, Archives and Manuscripts Division, Oklahoma Historical Society, Oklahoma City.
1881c Letter to Col. P. B. Hunt dated July 26. Manuscript, microfilm KA47, frame 887, Archives and Manuscripts Division, Oklahoma Historical Society, Oklahoma City.

COE, RALPH T.
1976 *Sacred Circles: Two Thousand Years of North American Indian Art*. London: Arts Council of Great Britain.

COHODAS, MARVIN.
  1976 Dat so la lee's Basketry Design. *American Indian Art* 1(4):22–31.
  1976–1984 Research Notes, mss. in Cohodas's possession.
  1979a Lena Frank Dick: An Outstanding Washoe Basket Weaver. *American Indian Art* 4(4):32–41, 90.
  1979b *Degikup: Washoe Fancy Basketry 1895–1935.* Vancouver: Fine Arts Gallery, University of British Columbia.
  1979c The Washoe Florescence 1895–1935. *Vanguard* 8(5):6–10. Vancouver Art Gallery.
  1981 Sarah Mayo and Her Contemporaries. Representational Designs in Washoe Basketry. *American Indian Art* 6(4):52–59.
  1982 Dat so la lee and the Degikup. *Halcyon:* 119–40.
  1983 Washoe Basketry. *American Indian Basketry and Other Native Arts* 12:4–30.
  1984 The Breitholle Collection of Washoe Basketry. *American Indian Art* 9(4):38–40.
COLLIER, DONALD.
  1959 *Indian Art of the Americas.* Unpaginated. Chicago: Natural History Museum.
COLLINS, JOHN E.
  1974 *Nampeyo, Hopi Potter: Her Artistry and Her Legacy.* Flagstaff, Arizona: Northland Press.
CORNPLANTER, JESSE J.
  1938 *Legends of the Longhouse.* Philadelphia, New York, London, and Toronto: Lippincott.
CRM BOOKS.
  1971 *Society Today.* Del Mar, California: Communications Research Machines.
CURTIS, EDWARD S.
  1915 *The North American Indian,* vol. 10. Seattle: E. S. Curtis/Cambridge: The University Press.
  1926 *The North American Indian,* vol. 15. Seattle: E. S. Curtis/Cambridge: The University Press.
CUSICK, DAVID.
  1826 *Sketches of the Ancient History of the Six Nations.* Lewiston, Maine: Printed for the author.

D'AZEVEDO, WARREN
AND THOMAS KAVANAGH.
  1974 The Trail of the Missing Basket. *The Indian Historian* 7(3):12–13, 60, 64.
DELORIA, VINE, JR.
  1974 Foreword in *The Fourth World: An Indian Reality,* G. Manuel and K. Poslums, eds. New York: Free Press.
DIXON, GEORGE.
  1968 *A voyage round the world, in the years 1785, 1786, 1787, and 1788, performed in the King George, commanded by Captain Dixon/under the direction of the incorporated Society for the Advancement of the Fur Trade.* London: R. Randal, 1789. Reprinted as *A Voyage Around the World: But more particularly to the North-West Coast of America.* New York: Da Capo Press.
DOUGLAS, FREDERIC H.
  1934 Design Areas in Indian Art. *Denver Art Museum, Department of Indian Art, Leaflet 62.*

DOUGLAS, FREDERIC H.
AND RENÉ D'HARNONCOURT.
  1941 *Indian Art of the United States.* New York: The Museum of Modern Art.
DOUGLAS, FREDERIC H.
AND ALICE L. MARRIOTT.
  1942 Metal Jewelry of the Peyote Cult. *Denver Art Museum Material Culture Notes, Reports from the Ethnological Laboratory 17.*
DOWNS, JAMES F.
  1966 *The Two Worlds of the Washo.* New York: Holt, Rinehart and Winston.
DRUCKER, PHILIP.
  1940 Kwakiutl Dancing Societies. *Anthropological Records* 2(6). Berkeley and Los Angeles: University of California Press.
DUFRENNE, MIKEL.
  1973 *The Phenomenology of Aesthetic Experience.* Evanston, Illinois: Northwestern University Press.
DUNN, JOHN.
  1844 *History of the Oregon Territory and British North-American Fur Trade.* London: Edwards and Hughes.

EFIMOVA, ANTONINA KIRILLOVNA
AND EVGANIIA NIKDAEVNA KLITINA.
  1981 *Chukotskoe i èskimosskoe iskusstvo iz sobraniia Zagorskogo gosudarstvennogo istorikokhudozhestvennogo muzeia-zapovednika* [Chukchee and Eskimo Art in the Collection of the Zagorsk History and Art Museum]. Leningrad: Khudozhnik RSFSR.
EGGLESTON, M. C.
  1881 Letter to Col. P. B. Hunt dated July 19, Medicine Lodge Camp, North Fork, Red River. Manuscript, microfilm KA47, frame 867, Archives and Manuscripts Division, Oklahoma Historical Society, Oklahoma City.
ELIOT, THOMAS STEARNS.
  1920 Tradition and the Individual Talent. Pp. 47–59 in *The Sacred Wood. Essays on Poetry and Criticism.* London: Methuen.
EMMONS, GEORGE T.
  1907 The Chilkat Blanket. *Memoirs of the American Museum of Natural History* 3:329–401.
ERICKSON, JON T.
  1977 *Kachinas: An Evolving Hopi Art Form?* Phoenix: The Heard Museum.
ETTLINGER, LEOPOLD D.
  1971 Kunstgeschichte als Geschichte. *Jahrbuch der Hamburger Kunstsammlungen* 16:2–19.
EVANS, DAVID R.
  1977 Special Burials from the Lilbourn Site—1971. *Missouri Archeologist* 38:111–122.

EWERS, JOHN C.
  1939 *Plains Indian Painting.* Palo Alto, California: Stanford University Press.
  1955 The Horse in Blackfoot Indian Culture. *Bureau of American Ethnology Bulletin* 159. Washington, D.C.
  1967 Foreword. Pp. vii–x in *Two Leggings: The Making of a Crow Warrior* by Peter Nabokov. New York: Crowell.
  1978 Three Effigy Pipes by an Eastern Dakota Master Carver. *American Indian Art* 3(4)51–55, 74.
  1981 The Emergence of the Named Artist in the American West. *American Indian Art* 6(2):52–61, 77.
  1983 Plains Indian Artists and Anthropologists: A Fruitful Collaboration. *American Indian Art* 9(1):36–49.

FAGG, WILLIAM.
  1961 [Comment to Haselberger.] *Current Anthropology* 2(4): 365–367.
FARB, PETER.
  1968 *Man's Rise to Civilization as Shown by the Indians of North American from Primeval Times to the Coming of the Industrial State.* New York: Dutton.
FEDER, NORMAN.
  1980 Plains Pictographic Painting and Quilled Rosettes. A Clue to Tribal Identification. *American Indian Art* 5(2):54–62.
FEEST, CHRISTIAN F.
  1980 *Native Arts of North America.* London: Thames and Hudson/New York and Toronto: Oxford University Press.
FENTON, WILLIAM N.
  1978 Jesse Cornplanter, Seneca, 1889–1957. Pp. 177–195 in *American Indian Intellectuals,* Margot Liberty, ed. 1976 *Proceedings of the American Ethnological Society.*
FEWKES, J. WALTER.
  1903 Hopi Katcinas, Drawn by Native Artists. Pp. 3–126 in *Twenty-First Annual Report of the Bureau of American Ethnology.* Washington, D.C.
FOGELSON, RAYMOND D.
AND AMELIA B. WALKER.
  1980 Self and Other in Cherokee Booger Masks. *Journal of Cherokee Studies* 5(2):88–101.
FOUCAULT, MICHEL.
  1966 *Les mots et les choses: une archéologie des sciences humaines.* Paris: Gallimard.
FOWLER, DON F. AND CATHERINE S. FOWLER.
  1970 Stephen Powers' "The Life and Culture of the Washoe and Paiutes." *Ethnohistory* 17(3–4):117–149.
FRANK, LARRY AND FRANCIS H. HARLOW.
  1974 *Historic Pottery of the Pueblo Indians. 1660–1880.* Boston: New York Graphic Society.
FREILICH, MORRIS.
  1958 Cultural Persistence among the Modern Iroquois. *Anthropos* 53(3–4): 473–483.
  1977 Mohawk Heroes and Trinidadian Peasants. Pp. 151–216 in *Marginal Natives: Anthropologists at Work,* M. Freilich, ed. New York: Wiley.

GESSAIN, ROBERT.
1978 Masques Eskimo d'Ammassalik. *Le courrier du Musée de l'Homme* 3. Paris.
GILLILAND, MARION SPJUT.
1975 *The Material Culture of Key Marco Florida.* Gainesville: The University Presses of Florida.
GOLDWATER, ROBERT.
1973 Art History and Anthropology: Some Comparisons of Methodology. Pp. 1–10 in *Primitive Art and Society*, Anthony Forge, ed. London and New York: Oxford University Press.
GOTTLIEB, ADOLPH AND MARK ROTHKO WITH BARNETT NEWMAN.
1943 [Letter]. P. 9 in Letters to the Editor, *The New York Times*, June 13, section 2.
GRABURN, NELSON H. H.
1969 Art and Acculturative Processes. *International Social Science Journal* 21(3):457–468.
1976 *Ethnic and Tourist Arts. Cultural Expressions from the Fourth World.* Berkeley, Los Angeles, and London: University of California Press.
GREENBERG, CLEMENT.
1946 Art. *The Nation* 163(2):53–54.
GRIMMELSHAUSEN, JOHANN JAKOB CHRISTOFFEL VON.
1977 *Werke* 1. Berlin and Weimar: Aufbau-Verlag.
GRINNELL, GEORGE BIRD.
1923 *The Cheyenne Indians, Their History and Ways of Life.* New Haven, Yale University Press. Reprinted New York: Cooper Square, 1962.

HABERLAND, WOLFGANG.
1964 *The Art of North America.* New York: Crown.
1973 Die Oglala-Sammlung Weygold im Hamburgischen Museum für Völkerkunde (Teil 1). *Mitteilungen aus dem Museum für Völkerkunde Hamburg*, N.F. 3:79–106.
1981 Die Oglala-Sammlung Weygold im Hamburgischen Museum für Völkerkunde (Teil 7). *Mitteilungen aus dem Museum für Völkerkunde Hamburg*, N.F. 11:29–56.
HAFTMANN, WERNER.
1962 *Malerei im 20. Jahrhundert.* Munich: Prestel. Reprinted as *Painting in the Twentieth Century.* New York and Washington: Praeger, 1965.
HAIL, BARBARA A.
1980 Hau, Kola! *The Plains Indian Collection of the Haffenreffer Museum of Anthropology.* Providence: Haffenreffer Museum of Anthropology, Brown University.
HARLOW, FRANCIS H.
1977 *Modern Pueblo Pottery, 1880–1960.* Flagstaff, Arizona: Northland Press.
HASELBERGER, HERTA.
1961 Method of Studying Ethnological Art. *Current Anthropology* 2(4):341–343.
HAUPTMAN, LAWRENCE M.
1979 The Iroquois School of Art: Arthur C. Parker and the Seneca Arts Project, 1935–1941. *New York History* 60(3):282–312.

HAWTHORN, AUDREY.
1967 *Art of the Kwakiutl Indians and Other Northwest Coast Tribes.* Seattle: University of Washington Press.
HERSKOVITS, MELVILLE J.
1959 Art and Value. Pp. 41–68 in *Aspects of Primitive Art*, Robert Goldwater, ed. New York: The Museum of Primitive Art.
HIBBEN, FRANK C.
1975 *Kiva Art of the Anasazi at Pottery Mound.* Las Vegas: KC Publications.
HIGHWATER, JAMAKE.
1976 *Song from the Earth. American Indian Painting.* Boston: New York Graphic Society.
1978 Indian Dilemma. *Soho News*, January 5. New York.
1980 *The Sweet Grass Lives On. Fifty Contemporary North American Indian Artists.* New York: Lippincott and Crowell.
1981 *The Primal Mind. Vision and Reality in Indian America.* New York: Harper and Row. Reprinted New American Library, 1982.
HOFFMAN, GERHARD.
1980 The Foregrounded Situation: New Narrative Strategies in Postmodern American Fiction. Pp. 289–344 in *The American Identity: Fusion and Fragmentation*, Rob Kroes, ed. Amsterdam: Amerika Instituut, Universiteit van Amsterdam.
HOFFMAN, GERHARD, ALFRED HORNUNG, AND RÜDIGER KUNOW.
1977 "Modern," "Postmodern," and "Contemporary" as Criteria for the Analysis of Twentieth Century Literature. *Amerikastudien* 22:19–46. Munich.
HOLM, BILL.
1972a Heraldic Carving Styles of the Northwest Coast. Pp. 77–83 in *American Indian Art: Form and Tradition.* Minneapolis: Walker Art Center, Indian Art Association, and Minneapolis Institute of Art.
1972b *Crooked Beak of Heaven: Masks and Other Ceremonial Art of the Northwest Coast.* Index of Art in the Pacific Northwest, Number 3. Seattle and London: University of Washington Press.
1983 Form in Northwest Coast Art. Pp. 33–45 in *Indian Art Traditions of the Northwest Coast*, Roy Carlson, ed. Burnaby, British Columbia: Simon Fraser University.
HOLM, BILL AND BILL REID.
1976 *Indian Art of the Northwest Coast: A Dialogue on Craftsmanship and Aesthetics.* Houston: Institute for the Arts, Rice University.
HOULE, ROBERT.
1982 The Emergence of a New Aesthetic Tradition. Pp. 48–53 in *New Work by a New Generation.* Regina, Saskatchewan: Norman Mackenzie Art Gallery, University of Regina.
HOWARD, JAMES H.
1955 Pan-Indian Culture of Oklahoma. *The Scientific Monthly* 81(5):215–220.
1965 The Ponca Tribe. *Bureau of American Ethnology Bulletin* 195. Washington, D.C.

JACOBSEN, FILLIP.
1895 Sisauch-dansen. *Ymer* 15:2–23. Stockholm.
JAMES, GEORGE WHARTON.
1903 *Indian Basketry, and How to Make Indian and Other Baskets.* Pasadena: published privately by the author.
JANIS, SIDNEY.
1944 *Abstract and Surrealist Art in America.* New York: Reynal and Hitchcock.
JUDD, NEIL M.
1931 Indian Sculpture and Carving. Pp. 1–14 in *Introduction to American Indian Art*, Part II, John Sloan and Oliver Lafarge, eds. New York: The Exposition of Indian Tribal Arts, Inc.

KAALUND, BODIL.
[1979] *Grønlands Kunst: Skulptur, Brugskunst, Maleri.* Copenhagen: Politikens Forlag. Reprinted as *The Art of Greenland*, Kenneth Tindall, trans. Berkeley: University of California Press, 1983.)
KANDINSKY, WASSILY.
1947 *Concerning the Spiritual in Art and Painting in Particular.* New York: Wittenborn, Schultz.
KAUFMANN, CAROLE N.
1976 Functional Aspects of Haida Argillite Carvings. Pp. 56–69 in *Ethnic and Tourist Arts. Cultural Expressions from the Fourth World*, Nelson H. H. Graburn, ed. Berkeley, Los Angeles, and London: University of California Press.
KENT, KATE PECK.
1957 The Cultivation and Weaving of Cotton in the Prehistoric Southwestern United States. *Transactions of the American Philosophical Society* n.s. 47(3):457–732.
KING, JONATHAN C. H.
1977 *Smoking Pipes of the North American Indians.* London: British Museum Publications.
1979 *Portrait Masks from the Northwest Coast of America.* London: Thames and Hudson.
KIRK, RUTH E.
1952 Panamint Basketry—a Dying Art. *The Masterkey* 26(3):76–86.
KIRK, RUTH E. WITH RICHARD D. DAUGHERTY.
1974 *Hunters of the Whale.* New York: Morrow.
1978 *Exploring Washington Archeology.* Seattle and London: University of Washington Press.
KOSTICH, DRAGOS D.
1976 *George Morrison.* Minneapolis: Dillon.
KRAMER, HILTON.
1974 *The Age of the Avant-Garde: An Art Chronicle of 1956–1972.* London: Secker and Warburg.
KROEBER, ALFRED L.
1900 Symbolism of the Arapaho Indians. *Bulletin of the American Museum of Natural History* 13(7):69–86.
1902 Decorative Art. Pp. 36–150 in *The Arapaho. Bulletin of the American Museum of Natural History* 18:1–230, 279–454 (1902–1907).

LABELLE, MARIE-DOMINIQUE
AND SYLVIE THIVIERGE.
1981 Un peintre huron du XIXᵉ siècle: Zacharie Vincent. *Recherches amérindiennes au Québec* 11(4):325–333.

LONGFISH, GEORGE AND JOAN RANDALL.
1982 New Ways of Old Visions: The Evolution of Contemporary Native American Art. *Artspace* 6(3):24–27.

LOVE, MARIAN F.
1978 Earl Bliss, Artist. *The Santa Fean Magazine* 6(7):10–12.

LYFORD, CARRIE A.
1940 *Quill and Beadwork of the Western Sioux.* Lawrence, Kansas: Haskell Institute Press.

MACDONALD, GEORGE.
1983 Prehistoric Art of the Northwest Coast. *Indian Art Traditions of the Northwest Coast.* Roy Carlson, ed. Burnaby, British Columbia: Simon Fraser University.

MACNAIR, PETER, ALAN HOOVER,
AND KEVIN NEARY.
1980 *The Legacy: Continuing Traditions of Northwest Coast Indian Art.* Victoria: British Columbia Provincial Museum.

MALLERY, GARRICK.
1893 Picture-Writing of the American Indians. *Tenth Annual Report of the Bureau of Ethnology, 1888–1889.* Washington, D.C.

MARRIOTT, ALICE.
1948 *Maria: the Potter of San Ildefonso.* Norman: University of Oklahoma Press.
1956 The Trade Guild of the Southern Cheyenne Women. *Bulletin of the Oklahoma Anthropological Society* 4:19–27.

MASON, OTIS TUFTS.
1904 Aboriginal American Basketry. Studies in a Textile Art without Machinery. Pp. 185–548 in *Report of the U. S. National Museum,* 1902. Washington, D.C.

MAURER, EVAN M.
1977 *The Native American Heritage: A Survey of North American Indian Art.* Chicago: The Art Institute of Chicago.

MAXWELL MUSEUM OF ANTHROPOLOGY.
1974 *Seven Families in Pueblo Pottery.* Albuquerque: University of New Mexico Press.

MAYHALL, MILDRED P.
1962 *The Kiowas.* Norman: University of Oklahoma Press.

MCELWAIN, THOMAS.
1980 Methods in Mask Morphology: Iroquoian False Faces in the Ethnographical Museum, Stockholm. *Temenos* 16:68–83. Stockholm.

MCGUIRE, J. D.
1894 The Development of Sculpture. *American Anthropologist* old series 7:358–366.

MELDGAARD, JØRGEN.
1982 *Aron: en af de mærkværdigste Billedsamlinger i Verden/Silarsuarmi assilissat katersugaatit eqqumiinnersaasa ilaat* [Aron: One of the World's Most Remarkable Picture Collections]. Kalaallisut suliarinnittoq/Grønlandsk bearbejdelse: aaju. Copenhagen: Nationalmuseet.

MILLS, C. WRIGHT.
1959 *The Sociological Imagination.* London and New York: Oxford University Press.

MITCHELL, JOSEPH.
1960 The Mohawks in High Steel. Pp. 1–36 in *Apologies to the Iroquois* by Edmund Wilson. New York: Farrar, Straus and Cudahy.

MONTHAN, GUY AND DORIS MONTHAN.
1978 John Hoover: Aleut Sculptor. *American Indian Art* 4(1):50–55.

MOONEY, JAMES.
1896 The Ghost Dance Religion. *Fourteenth Annual Report of the Bureau of American Ethnology, 1892–1893.* Washington, D.C.
1898 Calendar History of the Kiowa Indians. Pp. 129–446 in *Seventeenth Annual Report of the Bureau of American Ethnology. 1895–1896.* Washington, D.C.

MORISSONNEAU, CHRISTIAN.
1978 Huron of Lorette. Pp. 389–393 in *Handbook of North American Indians* 15, *Northeast.* Bruce G. Trigger, ed., William C. Sturtevant, general ed. Washington, D.C.: Smithsonian Institution.

NEVERS, JO ANN.
1976 *Wa She Shu: A Washo Tribal History.* Reno: Intertribal Council of Nevada.

NEW, LLOYD KIVA.
1980 *American Indian Art in the 1980's.* Niagara Falls, New York: The Native American Center for the Living Arts.

NYE, WILBUR STURTEVANT.
1937 *Carbine and Lance: The Story of Old Fort Sill.* Norman: University of Oklahoma Press.

OKLAHOMA HISTORICAL SOCIETY. SEE CLARK AND EGGLESTON.

OLEMAN, MINNE.
1968 Lucy Lewis: Acoma's Versatile Potter. *El Palacio* 75(2):10–12.

OLSON, RONALD L.
1954 Social Life of the Owikeno Kwakiutl. *Anthropological Records* 14:3. Berkeley and Los Angeles: University of California Press.
1955 Notes on the Bella Bella Kwakiutl. *Anthropological Records* 14:5. Berkeley and Los Angeles: University of California Press.

PARKER, ARTHUR C.
1913 The Code of Handsome Lake, the Seneca Prophet. *New York State Museum Bulletin* 163.

PARSONS, ELSIE CLEWS.
1962 Isleta Paintings. *Bureau of American Ethnology Bulletin* 181. Washington, D.C.

PARSONS, TALCOTT.
1966 *Societies: Evolutionary and Comparative Perspectives.* Englewood Cliffs, New Jersey: Prentice-Hall.

PETERSEN, KAREN DANIELS.
1971 *Plains Indian Art from Fort Marion.* Norman: University of Oklahoma Press.

PETTER, REV. RODOLPHE C.
1915 *English Cheyenne Dictionary.* Kettle Falls, Washington. Privately printed.

PRICE, SALLY AND RICHARD PRICE.
1980 *Afro-American Arts of the Suriname Rain Forest.* Berkeley, Los Angeles, and London: University of California Press.

RAY, DOROTHY JEAN.
1982 Mortuary Art of the Alaskan Eskimos. *American Indian Art* 7(2):50–57.

RAY, DOROTHY JEAN AND ALFRED A. BLAKER.
1975 *Eskimo Masks: Art and Ceremony.* Seattle and London: University of Washington Press.

REDFIELD, ROBERT.
1959 Art and Icon. Pp. 11–40 in *Aspects of Primitive Art,* Robert Goldwater, ed. New York: Museum of Primitive Art.

REICHARD, GLADYS A.
1930 Form and Interpretation in American Art. *Proceedings of the Twenty-third International Congress of Americanists (N.Y., 1928):*459–462. New York.

RITZENTHALER, ROBERT E.
1969 *Iroquois False-Face Masks.* Publications in Primitive Art 3. Milwaukee: Milwaukee Public Museum.
1976 Woodland Sculpture: *American Indian Art* 4(1):34–41.

RODEE, MARIAN E.
1977 *Southwestern Weaving.* Albuquerque: University of New Mexico Press.
1981 *Old Navajo Rugs: Their Development from 1900 to 1940.* Albuquerque: University of New Mexico Press.

SANDLER, IRVING.
1974 1946–1960. Pp. 377–520 in *The Hirshhorn Museum and Sculpture Garden,* Abram Lerner, ed. New York: Harry N. Abrams.

SCHAPIRO, MEYER.
1946 The Younger American Painters of Today. *The Listener* (January 26, 1946):147. London.

SCHMALENBACH, WERNER.
1972 Grundsätzliches zur primitiven Kunst der Naturvölker. Pp. 428–432 in *Weltkulturen und Moderne Kunst,* Organisationskomitee für die Spiele der XX Olympiade, development and direction by Siegfried Wichman. Munich: Bruckmann.

SEARS, WILLIAM H.
1982 *Fort Center: An Archeological Site in the Lake Okeechobee Basin.* Gainesville: University Presses of Florida.

SHEEHAN, CAROL.
1981 *Pipes That Won't Smoke: Coal That Won't Burn: Haida Sculpture in Argillite.* Calgary, Alberta: Glenbow Museum.

SILBERMAN, ARTHUR.
1978 *100 Years of Native American Painting.* Oklahoma City: The Oklahoma Museum of Art.

SIOUI, ANNE-MARIE.
1981 Zacharie Vincent: Un œuvre engagé? *Recherches amérindiennes au Québec* 11(4):334–337.

SLOAN, JOHN AND OLIVER LA FARGE.
1931 *Introduction to American Indian Art*. New York: The Exposition of Indian Tribal Arts, Inc.

SMITH, J. G. E.
1980 *Arctic Art: Eskimo Ivory*. New York: Museum of the American Indian, Heye Foundation.

SNODGRASS, JEANNE O.
1968 *American Indian Painters. A Biographical Dictionary*. New York: Museum of the American Indian, Heye Foundation.

SOIL CONSERVATION SERVICE.
1935 *Tewa Basin Study: vol. 1: The Indian Pueblos*. Albuquerque: Soil Conservation Service.

SPECK, FRANK G.
1927 Symbolism in Penobscot Art. *American Museum of Natural History, Anthropological Papers* 29(2):25–80.

SPENCER, ROBERT F. AND JESSE D. JENNINGS.
1965 *The Native Americans*. New York: Harper and Row.

[STARR, FREDERICK, ED.]
[1903] *Iroquois Indian Games and Dances Drawn by Jesse Cornplanter, Seneca Indian Boy*. [No place, no publisher; pamphlet of 15 un-numbered leaves, copyright 1903 by Frederick Starr.]

STERN, NORTON B.
1893 Abram Cohn of Carson City, Nevada, Patron of Dat-So-La-Lee. *Western States Historical Quarterly* 15(4):291–297.

STEWARD, JULIAN H.
1941 Culture Element Distributions: XIII Nevada Shoshone. *University of California Publications in Anthropological Records* 4:201–359. Berkeley.

STRICKLAND, RENNARD.
1980 The Changing World of Indian Painting and Philbrook Art Center. Pp. 9–25 in *Native American Art at Philbrook*. Tulsa: Philbrook Art Center.

SWINTON, GEORGE.
1972 *Sculpture of the Eskimo*. Toronto: McClelland and Stewart.

TATE GALLERY.
1974 *Picasso to Lichtenstein*. London: Tate Gallery.

THOMAS, DAVIS AND KARIN RONNEFELDT.
1976 *People of the First Man*. New York: Dutton.

THOMPSON, MICHAEL.
1979 *Rubbish Theory. The Creation and Destruction of Value*. New York and Oxford: Oxford University Press.

TOLMIE, WILLIAM FRASER.
n.d. *Physician and Fur Trader*. Vancouver, British Columbia: Mitchell Press.

TRIGGER, BRUCE G., VOL. ED.
1978 *Handbook of North American Indians* 15, *Northeast*. William C. Sturtevant, general ed. Washington, D.C.: Smithsonian Institution.

VIVIAN, R. GWINN, DULCE DODGEN, AND GAYLE HARTMAN.
1978 Wooden Ritual Artifacts from Chaco Canyon, New Mexico. *Anthropological Papers of the University of Arizona* 32.

VOLLMAR, RAINER.
1981 *Indianische Karten Nordamerikas: Beiträge zur historischen Kartographie vom 16. bis zum 19. Jahrhundert*. Berlin: Dietrich Reimer.

WADE, EDWIN AND RENNARD STRICKLAND.
1981 *Magic Images. Contemporary Native American Art*. Norman: University of Oklahoma Press.

WALLACE, ANTHONY F. C.
1978 Origins of the Longhouse Religion. Pp. 442–448 in *Handbook of North American Indians* 15, *Northeast*. Bruce G. Trigger, ed., William C. Sturtevant, general ed. Washington, D.C.: Smithsonian Institution.

WARBURG, ABY.
1902 *Bildniskunst und florentinisches Bürgertum*, I. Leipzig: H. Seemann.

WARNER, JOHN ANSON.
1975 *The Life and Art of the North American Indian*. London: Hamlyn.

WEBSTER.
1959 *Webster's New Collegiate Dictionary*. 2nd ed. Springfield, Massachusetts: G. C. Merriam.

WHEAT, JOSEPH BEN.
1977 Patterns and Sources of Navajo Weaving. Pp. 11–14 in *Patterns and Sources of Navajo Weaving*, W. D. Harmsen, ed. Harmsen's Western Americana Collection.
1979 Weaving. P. 26 in *Enduring Visions*. Aspen, Colorado: Aspen Center for the Visual Arts.

WHITMAN, WILLIAM.
1947 *The Pueblo Indians of San Ildefonso*. New York: Columbia University Press.

WILLEY, GORDON R. AND JEREMY A. SABLOFF.
1974 *A History of American Archaeology*. San Francisco: W. H. Freeman.

WINGERT, PAUL S.
1950 Tsimshian Sculpture. Pp. 73–94 in *The Tsimshian, Their Arts and Music*, Viola E. Garfield, ed. New York: Augustine.

WINSHIP, GEORGE PARKER.
1896 The Coronado Expedition, 1540–1542. Pp. 339–614 in *Fourteenth Annual Report of the Bureau of Ethnology, 1892–1893*. Washington, D.C.

WOLFE, TOM.
1976 *The Painted Word*. New York: Farrar, Straus and Giroux.

WOLFF, JANET.
1981 *The Social Production of Art*. London: Macmillan.

WORRINGER, WILHELM.
1959 *Abstraktion und Einfühlung*. Rev. ed. Munich: Piper. Reprinted as *Abstraction and Empathy*, Michael Bullock, trans. New York: International Universities Press, 1959.

WRIGHT, MURIEL H.
1951 *A Guide to the Indian Tribes of Oklahoma*. Norman: University of Oklahoma Press.

WRIGHT, ROBIN K.
1980 Haida Argillite Pipes: The Influence of Clay Pipes. *American Indian Art* 5(4):42–47, 88.

Index

Page numbers in *italics* refer to illustrations

Aboriginal individualism, 172–75
Abstract art, *222*, 262, 264, 267, 272, *273–74*, 276, 301, 304
Abstract Expressionism, 18, 88, 200, 260, 268, 275, 276, *277*, 303
Abstract Illusionism, *273*, 301
Acoma pottery, 84, *85*, 126, 147, 186, 198
Adam, Leonard, 108
Adena culture, 72, 162, 307; effigy pipe, *163*
Aguilar, José Vincente, 194
Aguilar, Susannah, 252
Aleuts, 74, 158, 300
Algonquians, 55, 90, 165, 309
Alsop, Joseph, 27
Amason, Alvin, 303
American Landscape #3 (Morrison), *277*
American Museum of Natural History, New York, 29
Anasazi, 72, 307, 310
Anderson, Roy, protest sculpture by, *302*
Antelope Valley basket-weaving, 213–17
Antler carving, *136*
Apache, 237, 251, 261, 263, 295; basketry, *176*; hide bag, *139*; hide painting, *261*
Arapaho, 37, 46, 103, 174, 187, 188, 257, 294; pictographic painting, 59; shield, *37*
Arctic culture area, 29, 31, 40, 72, 74, 165–66; ivory carving, *88–91*, 165; masks, 166. *See also specific tribes and cultures*
Argillite carving, 69, 76, 84, 87, *137*, 166–67, 299, 307
Aristotle, 131*n*
Aron of Kangeq, 40
Arrowheads, 72
Art Deco, 303; in painting, 190, 192; in pottery decoration, 125, 183, 184, 186, 286
Artist Hopid, 268, 271, 300, 307
Art Nouveau, 268
Art of North America, The (Haberland), 174
Asah, Spencer, 190, 309
Astor, John Jacob, 190
Atencio, Gilbert, 262, 276
Athapaskans, 82
Atlatl, 74, 307
Auchiah, James, 190, 309
Austin, Mary, 191
Awa Tsireh. *See* Roybal, Alfonso
Axes, ceremonial, *24*, 124

Bacon, Francis, 268, 276, 303
Bacone College, 157, 195
Bad Heart Bull, Amos, 110, 227
Baker, Joe, 303
Bambi-style painters, 293, 303, 307
Bandolier, Adolf, 182
Bandolier bag, *81*, 307
Basketmaker Phase, 307; textiles, 151
Basketry, 69, 70, 76, 79, 150–52, *176–77*; Apache, *176*; coiled vs. twined, 86, 219, 220*n*, 307, 311; Maidu, *176*, 207; Miwok, 207, 212; Nootka, *86*, 87; of Northeast, 33, 82, 88; Northwest Coast, 29, *86*, 87; Paiute, *176*, 212, 214–15, 220*n*; Panamint Shoshone, 86, *86*; Pima, *176*; Pomo, *122*, 176, *177*, 207, 213, 302; of Southeast, 29; of Southwest, 31, 71; splint, 82; Washoe, 17, 151–52, *152*, 176, 203–4, *204–6*, 206–19, *213–15*, 218, 220*n*; Wikchumni, *71*
Beadwork, 33, *44*, 68, 70, 80–81, *81*, 82, 83, 88, 95–98, *116*, *117*, 139, 178, 215, *284*, 309; of Plains Indians, *34–35*, 37, 43, 66, 67, 77, 78, 81, 95, 96, 96–98, *121*, 128, *142*, 178–79
Bear's Heart (artist), 227
Beaver, Fred, 305
Beck, Larry, 301; sculpture, *300*
Begay, Harrison, 194; painting, *193*
Bella Bella, 134, 135, 136, 140*n*
Bella Coola, 133–36, *138*; headdress frontlets, *132*, 136; mask, *134*
Benedict, Ruth, 173, 245
Beothuk antler pendants, 74
Berninghaus, Oscar, 234
Billy, Mrs. Cruz I., baskets of, *177*
Biss, Earl, 201, 266, 268, 278, 281; painting, *279*
Blackbear Bosin. *See* Bosin, Blackbear
Blackfoot, 143, 174
Blackowl, Archie, 190, 228
Blankets, 100, 110–18, 122–23; button, *115*, 137, 307; Chilkat (Tlingit), 70, 113–14, *114*, 118, 137; Hopi, *112*; Navajo, 16, 33, 83, *106*, 110–13, *110–13*, 115–18, *119*, 122, 149–50, *150–51*, 308, 310; Northwest Coast, 16, *70*, 113–14, *114*, *115*; saddle, *78*, 79, 100, 110–11, *113*
Blind, The (Howe), *222*, 224
Blue Eagle, Acee, 195, 233, 292; painting, *293*
Boas, Franz, 29, 37, 108
Bodmer, Karl, 56, 57, 58, 174, 187, 303

Bone carvings, 136, 236
Booger masks, *130*, 164, 307
Bosin, Blackbear, 197, 305; painting, *196*
Bosque Redondo, 115, 117
Bowls, carved wood, 22, *135*, *149*
Bradley, David, 268, 281; painting, *280*
Braque, Georges, 260, 297
Breitholde, William, 216
Brody, J. J., 190, 202, 240, 241
Brown, Epes, 282
Bryant, Scees, 216
Buffalo, Ben, 18, 268, 303
Buffalo effigies, *26*
Buffalo Meat, 187, *188*, 294; paintings, *187*, 227
Bunzel, Ruth L., 37, 124–25, 127, 131, 143, 171–72, 184–85, 243
Button blankets, *115*, 137, 307
Buzzard (artist), 227

Caddo, 59, 201, 267; pottery, *156*, 158
Cadman, Charles Wakefield, 248
Cage, John, 275–76, 278
Cahokie Mound, 72
Caldwell, J. R., 67
Calendar glyphs, *58*, 58–59, 92, 308–9, 311
Calumets, 72, 307
Cannon, T. C., 18, 226, 239, 241, 264, 266, 268, 278, 281, 294, 303; woodblock prints, *201*, 267
Carson Valley basket-weaving, 203–4, 207, 210, 214, 216, 217
Carving, 68, 69, 70, 72–73, 79, 88, *88–91*, 124, *128–30*, 133–36, *134–37*, 147, 157, 158. *See also* Ivory carving; Shell carvings; Stone carving; Wood carving
Casas Grandes pottery, 144
Cassidy, Ina, 252
Catlin, George, 56, 57, 58, 59, 174, 187, 303, 307
Catlinite carving, 76, 82, 307
Cattaraugus Reservation, 42, 88
Cayuse, 14
Ceramics. *See* Clay figurines; Pottery
Cerno, B. J., seed jar by, *85*
Cézanne, Paul, 260
Chapman, Kenneth, 85, 182, 185
Cherokee, 94, 163, 291–92; masks, 128, *130*, 164
Cheyenne, 14, 46, 103, 174, 188; buffalo effigies, *26*; hide painting, *91*; necklace, 29; pictographic painting and ledger drawing, 55, *55*, 58, 59–60, 187, *187–89*, *195*, 227, 294; quillworker society, 144–45
Cheyenne Sun Dance (West), *195*
Chichester, Ella, 215, 220*n*

Chief's blanket, Navajo, 110, *110*, *112*, 115, 149, 307
Child Chief (Ponca chief), 97, 98
Chilkat: blankets, 70, 113–14, *114*, 118, 120, 137; shirts, 114; tunics, 120
Chino, Marie Z., 198
Chippewa, 94, 155, 233, 234, 273, 277; pipe bowl, 72
Chiricahua, 237, 263, 295
Choctaw, 94, 144, 273
Chumash stone carving, 160
Chunestudy, Don, 158
Clark, E. L., 46–47
Clay figurines, 160–61, 162, 182, 224, 299
Clothing, 29, 31, 33, 56, 69, 79, 81, 82, 91, 94, 97, 100, 107, 114–15, *116–17*, 120, 142, 174–75. *See also* Blankets; Hide clothing; Moccasins; Sashes
Clubs, ball-headed, 81, *164*, 165
Cochiti, 249, 304; clay figurines, 160–61, *224*, 299
Cohn, Abe, 203–4, *204*, 206–10, 211, 213–14, 215, 216, 218, 220*n*
Cohn, Amy, 204, 206–10, 220*n*
Cohn, Margaret, 206, 208
Cohoe, Grey, 18, 266, 268, 270, 278, 281, 298; paintings, *299*
Colbert, Gary, 195
Collins, John E., 184
Colorado River petroglyphs, *54*
Color-field painting, 275
Colton, Al, 288
Colton, Harold S., 182
Comanche, 14, 96, 174, 187, 197, 302; pictographic art, 55, *55*, 56, *56*, 59; shield, *101*
Contemporary art, 41–44, 197–202, 225–27, 234–42, 262–82, *284–93*, 301–4; painting, 18, 38, 41–42, *43*, 196, *197*, 200–201, *222*, 224–25, 229, *231–32*, 234, *234*, 235–39, *239*, 240–42, 262, *262*, 264, *264–66*, 266–68, *269–71*, *271–73*, *273–74*, 275–78, *277*, *279–80*, 281–82, 292, 293, 294, 297, 297–99, 299, 302–3, *304*; pottery, 154, 197–98, *286–89*, 288, 303; sculpture, 41–42, 155, *155*, 158, 237, 241, 263, *263*, 272, 295, *300*, 301
Copper work: Mississippian, *24*, 124; Tlingit dagger, *146*
Cornplanter, Jesse J., 40; painting, *42*
Coronado, Francisco Vásquez de, 56
Cradleboard, 96, 307
Cree, 179, 277; artifacts, 68, 83; pictographic images, 54, *55*

Creek, 31, 226, 231, 291, 293
Crow, 147, 174; fetishes, 27; mirror case, 66, 67; painting, 266, 279; pictographic painting, 55, 55, 59; riding gear artifacts, 77, 100, 121, 123; sword and case, 66, 67
Cruickshank, Robert, cross by, 80
Crumbo, Woodrow, 190, 195, 231, 233, 298, 299; painting, 231
Cubism, 18, 197, 222, 223, 224, 231, 260, 262, 267, 268, 271, 276, 303
Culture areas, 29–31, 308
Curtis, Edward, 206, 215, 216, 218
Cusick, David and Dennis, 40
Custer's Last Stand Revised (White), 228, 228, 302

Da, Popovi, 186, 199, 254; pottery, 186
Da, Tony, 197, 262; collage, 199
Dadaism, 275
Dakota, 163; painting, 39, 224, 225; pictograph, 58
Danay, Richard Glazer, 43, 241, 242, 268, 270, 294, 303; works of, 43, 279
Dance, 127–28, 129, 130, 137–38, 138, 243; apron, 116, 137, 308; ceremonial, controversy over depiction of, 229–30, 229–31, 243–46; sash and wands, 32. See also Ghost Dance; Sun Dance
Dat So La Lee. See Keyser, Louisa
Dawes Act (1887), 70, 308
Day, Roscoe, 216–17, 218–19
Decora, Angel, 40
Decorative style, 268, 270
Deer at Laguna (Scholder), 292, 293
Deer Rattle/Deer Dancer (LaPena), 292, 293
Deer Spirit, The (Blue Eagle), 292, 293
Degikup baskets, 151–52, 152, 204–5, 206, 207, 208, 212, 213, 214, 215, 217, 218, 218, 219, 220n, 308
de Kooning, Willem, 275–76
Delaware, 14, 94, 96, 164; bandolier bag, 81
DeMallie, R. J., 39
de Pue, Grace Blair, 213
Desjarlait, Patrick, 233, 234, 303; paintings, 232
De Soto, Hernando, 56
d'Harnoncourt, René, 107, 119
Dick, Cecil, 279
Dick, Lena Frank, 17, 203, 214, 216–17, 218, 218–19, 220n; basket by, 218
Dick, Minnie, 214–15

Dick, Tootsie, 17, 203, 213–14, 215–16, 217, 218, 220n; baskets by, 215
Diebenkorn, Richard, 276
Dluwúlakha ceremony, 136, 140n
Doanmoe, Etahdleuh, 60, 187, 190
Dogiagyaguat (tipi), 62
Dohasan III, 61–62
Douglas, Frederic H., 107, 119
Drawing, 38, 40, 88, 92, contemporary, 295; figurative, 45, 109, 187. See also Ledger drawings; Pictographic art
Dressler, Margaretta, 210–11, 213
Dunn, Dorothy, 194, 224–25, 235, 236, 238, 258

East: culture areas, 29; sculpture, 162–64. See also Northeast culture area; Southeast culture area; Woodlands Indians
Edenshaw, Charles, carving, 137
Eggleston, M. C., 46–47
Eliot, T. S., 258
Embroidery, 64–65, 68, 74, 79, 80, 82; bead, 33, 80–81, 81, 82, 83, 95–98, 116–17, 178; false (basketry), 74, 308. See also Beadwork; Quillwork
Emporium Company, 203–4, 205, 206–9, 214, 215–16
Entasis, in basketry, 152, 152
Eskimos, 38, 88–89, 165–66, 236, 272; ivory and walrus tusk carvings, 74, 88–91, 165, 236; petroglyphs, 54; sculpture, 165–66, 272, 289, 291, 300; throwing sticks, 74. See also Inuit
Ethnic art, 178–79, 187, 190
Etowah Mound, 72
Euro-American influences, 37–42, 76–92, 93–104, 155, 179–86, 197, 202, 223, 224, 233, 234, 236, 239, 266–77, 297, 303
Ewers, John C., 57, 174
Existentialism, 275, 282n
Exploits of Sun Boy, The (Silverhorn), 48, 49–50, 51, 60–61, 61, 62, 308
Exposition of Indian Tribal Arts (New York, 1931), 28, 157
Expressionism, 18, 257, 260, 268, 276. See also Abstract Expressionism
Eye Dazzler designs, 83, 94, 95, 111, 113, 115, 308

Fagg, William, 119–20
False-face mask, 164, 167, 308
Farb, Peter, 173
Fauvism, 268

Featherwork, 34–35, 99, 101, 101; Pomo baskets, 122, 176, 177, 213, 302
Feder, Norman, 58
Feest, Christian F., 178
Fenton, William N., 40
Fetting, Rainer, 278
Fewkes, J. Walter, 92, 182, 183, 230, 242n, 244
Fife, Phyllis, 198
Figurines. See Clay figurines
Folwell, Jody, 286, 288; ceramic bowl, 287
Fonseca, Harry, 18, 198, 268, 281, 303; Coyote character series, 269, 284, 285, 286
Fort Center, Florida, 71
Fort Marion, Florida, 59–61, 62, 187, 188, 227, 308
Four Bears. See Mato-tope
Francis, Josiah, 38
Francis, Sam, 275
Fred Harvey Company, 176, 180, 181, 183, 198, 251, 290
Freud, Sigmund, 259, 275
Frontlets, 132, 133, 136–37, 140, 308
Futurism, 262, 268, 271

Garcia, Effie, 288; ceramic bowl, 286
Garner, Ted, 158
Gauguin, Paul, 267, 268
George, Charley, Sr., 129
Ghost Dance, 37, 79, 80, 100, 103, 264, 308
Gila polychrome jar, 125, 127
Gitksan, 133
Glass, Bill, 158, 301
Gold, Jake, 224, 310
Gombrich, E. H., 108
Gonzales, Rose, 198, 252, 252
Gorgets, Mississippian, 36, 123, 308
Gorman, R. C., 297, 300
Gottlieb, Adolph, 275
Great Lakes tribes, 79, 81, 90, 155, 164, 309, 310; pipe implements, 73, 99
Greenberg, Clement, 275, 282n
Greenland, 38, 40, 74, 165–66
Grinnell, George Bird, 145
Gris, Juan, 260
Gropius, Walter, 124
Gros Ventre tribe, 58
Group aesthetics, 16, 17, 109
Gutierrez, Lela and Van, 198
Gutierrez, Lois, jar by, 245
Gutierrez, Margaret, 247

Haberland, Wolfgang, 174–75
Haftmann, Werner, 273

Haida, 76, 137; bracelets, 288, 290; carvings, 69, 76, 84, 87, 135, 137, 149, 166–68; headdress frontlets, 136; Kaigani blanket, 115
Handsome Lake religion, 90, 308. See also Longhouse religion
Hano (pueblo), 125, 182, 196, 198
Haozous, Bob, 158, 241, 288, 294, 303; drawing, 295; sculptures, 237, 263, 295
Happy Jack (scrimshaw artist), 236
Hardin, Helen, 262, 289
Hardy, Telge and Cordelia, 213–14, 215, 216–17, 220n
Harjo, Sharon Ahtone, 302
Harlow, Francis H., 173
Harpoons. See Toggle harpoon
Harrington, M. R., 39, 97
Ha So Deh, 303
Havard, James, 240, 294, 301; painting, 273
Headdresses, 101–2, 128, 132, 133–40
Henderson, Alice Corbin, 191
Herrera, Joe H., 194, 237, 296, 303, 304; painting, 304
Herrera, Velino (Shije, also Ma Pe Wi), 194, 229–30, 248, 303
Herskovits, Melville, 108
Hewitt, Edgar L., 182, 185, 230–31
Hide clothing, 31, 56, 69, 79, 91, 100, 103, 114, 117, 142, 174–75. See also Moccasins
Hide paintings, 30, 31, 37, 48, 51, 56–59, 74, 80, 91, 101, 103, 110, 114, 118, 131, 174–75, 187, 261, 276
Hill, Joan, 294
Hinds, Swazo, 262
History, pictorial recording of, 45–62, 174–75, 228; controversy regarding, 227–28; reading of, 51–53, 54–56, 58
Hofmann, Hans, 275
Hohokam culture, 160
Hokeach, Jack, 190, 309
Holm, Bill, 127, 128
Holmes, William Henry, 29
Hoover, John, 158, 301; sculpture, 300
Hopewell culture, 72, 162, 307, 308, 309; artifacts, 73, 123, 124, 157, 160

Hopi, 72, 82, 243–44, 246, 251, 300; blanket, *112*; bracelet, *290*; ceremonial shawl with weaver's mark, *170*; dance sash and wands, *32*; Katcinas, 92, *160*, 161–62, 170, 183, 230, 244–46, 309; painting, *192*, *230*, 231, *233*, *262*, 268, 271, 275; petroglyph, *54*; pottery, 84, 143, 147, 154, *154*, *180–83*, 182–84, 198, 247, 288, *288–89*, 310
Hopi Ceremonial Dance (Kabotie), 230, 260
Horse gear artifacts, Plains, *28*, 77, 78, 83, 100, *121*, 123, 128
Houle, Robert, 198
House, Conrad, fetish pot, *303*
Houser, Allan, 158, 262, 263, 294
Houston, James, 88–89, 166
Howe, Oscar, 18, 193, 194, 196, 223, 224–25, 231, 238, 268, 271, 276, 277, 303; paintings, *197*, *222*
Howling Wolf (artist), 187, 227
Hubbell, Lorenzo, Jr., 183
Hudson's Bay Company, 89, 93, 236, 308
Huma, Stella, 288; pottery jar, *289*
Hunt, P. B., 45–47
Hunter, Sarah, basket by, *86*
Huron: embroidery, 64–65, 82; painting, 40, *40*, *41*
Hyde, Douglas, 158

Imagery, 223, 259, 263, 278, 281; controversy of, 225–26
Impressionism, 234, 268, 276
Indian Art of the Americas (exhibition, Chicago, 1959), 169*n*
Indian Art of the United States (exhibition, New York, 1941), 28
Indian Arts and Crafts Board, Department of the Interior, 103, 300
Indian Prisoners in Costume (Buffalo Meat), 227, 294
Individuality: aboriginal, 172–75; conflicts and controversy in tribal society, 228–34, 246–54; modernist, 172, 197–202; reservation, 172, 175–97; of Washoe basket-weavers, 203–19
Ingram, Jerry, 264, 276, 303
Institute of American Indian Art (Santa Fe), 157, 158, 199, 201–2, 235–40, 241, 258, 300
In the Days of Plenty (Tahoma), *194*, 260
Inuit, 88–89; ivory and walrus-tusk artifacts, *88–91*, 310; painting, 38, 41, *236*; sculpture, 288, *289*. *See also* Eskimos

Iowa, 97
Iroquois, 31, 38, 88, 90, 308, 309, 311; beadwork hat, *44*; masks, 31, 88, 128, 130, 164, *167*, 308; painting, 40, *43*; pictographic images, 55, *55*
Isleta Pueblo, 230
Ivory carving, 74, *88–91*, 136, 165, 236

Jacobson, Oscar B., 190, 195
James, Lillie, 216–17, 220*n*
James, Maggie Mayo, 17, 203, 210, 212–13, *214*, 218; baskets of, *152*, *214*
Jefferson, Thomas, 56
Jemez pottery, 181
Jemison, G. Peter, 264, 268, 270; painting, *270*
Jewelry, 123; Cheyenne necklace, *29*; contemporary bracelets, 288, *290*; Plains, 90–91, 99, 101; Pueblo necklace, *79*; silver, 33, *79*, 88
Jim, Captain, 210–11
Johns, Jasper, 275
Jones, Ruthe, 195
Jung, Carl G., 259, 275

Kabotie, Fred, 193, 194, 231, 234, 260, 298, 299, 303; paintings, *230*, *233*
Kabotie, Mike, 268, 271, 275, 276
Kaigani Haida blanket, *115*
Kandinsky, Vasily, 239, 260, 271; painting, *274*
Kaprow, Allan, 275
Katcinas, 18, 92, 161–62, 183, 230, 243–46, 296, 308; dancers, *128*; masks, 244–46; Polikmana, *160*, 309; sashes, *32*, 170
Katsikodi, 103, 227; hide painting by, *103*
Kaw, 97
Key Marco, Florida, 71, 161, 164; wood carving, 71, *161*, 162
Keyser, Louisa (Dat So La Lee), 17, 151–52, 153, 203–4, *204*, 206–10, 212, 213, 216, 218, 219, 296; baskets of, *152*, *204–5*
Kickapoo, 100
Kicking Bear (artist), 227
Kidder, Alfred Vincent, 182
Kill Eagle, 58; hide painting by, *91*
Kills Two (Nupa Kte), 39, 227
Kincaid, Reese, 103
Kinetic art, 14, 127–28, *128–30*, 137–40, *138*

Kiowa, 45–53, 62, 174, 188, 197, 258; beadwork, *34*, 96, *96*; calendar, 58–59, 308–9; cradle, *96*; cross, *80*; Delaware influence, 96, *96*; fan, *34*; muslin painting, 15, 49–50, 51–53, 59, 60, 61, 61; pictographic and ledger art, 48, 49–50, 51–53, 55, *55*, 58, 58–62, 61, 187, 305; Sun Dance of 1881, 45–47
Kiowa Five, 92, 190, 195, 263, 303, 309
Kirchner, Ernst Ludwig, 267
Kiva, Pueblo, 14, 72, 309; step bowls, 245, 246; murals, 79, 111, 157, 190, 192, 268, 271
Klah, Hosteen, 84
Klee, Paul, 272, 276, 277
Kline, Franz, 275
Koba (artist), 60
Koffey, Karita, 301
Kollwitz, Käthe, 235
Kroeber, Alfred L., 34–35, 37
Kwakiutl, 76, 87, 134, 135–36, 137, 168, 288, 291, 308; dance apron, *116*; headdresses, 136–37; masks, *128–29*, 135–36, 147; *Tlásulá* ceremony, 129, 136, 137, 140*n*, 310

Lacy, Minnie, basket by, *176*
LaFitau, Father, 55
La Fontaine, Glen, 158
Lakota beadwork, 147
Land of Enchantment (Crumbo), 231, *231*, 298, 299
LaPena, Frank, 268, 292; painting, *293*
Ledger drawings, 38, 45, 51, 59, 60, 92, 103, 157, 187, *187–89*, 227, *227*, 276, 305, 309. *See also* Pictographic art
Leigh, William, 181
Lelooska, 158, 291; sculpture, *291*
Lesou (potter), 183
Lewis, Lucy Martin, 198; seed jar by, *85*
Lewis and Clark Expedition, 56, 57, 110, 174
Lichtenstein, Roy, 278
Loloma, Charles, 288, 290; bracelet, *290*
Lomakema, Millard Dawa, 268, 271, 275, 276; mixed-media work, *271*
Lonewolf, Joseph, 197
Long, Will West, 130
Longfish, George C., 18, 198, 238, 241, 264, 268, 270, 297–98; paintings, *264*, *297*
Longhouse religion, 38, *42*, 308, 309

Looking Elk, Albert, painting by, *234*
Lorette, Quebec, 40, *41*, 82
Loretto, Estella, 158
Lowe, Truman, construction by, *301*

McCartys polychrome, 84, *85*
Maces, ceremonial, *25*, 73
Macke, August, 271
MacKenzie, Sir Arthur, 134
Magical Realism, 273, 275
Mahier, Edith, 190
Maidu, 220*n*, 268, 284; basketry, 176, 207
Makah, 74; basketry, 87; wood carving, 71
Making Medicine, 60, 188; paintings, *188–89*
Mandan, 131; drawings, 38; pictographic painting, 54–55, *55*, 56, 57–58
Ma Pe Wi. *See* Herrera, Velino
Maps, 37–38
Marriott, Alice, 145
Martinez, Adam and Santana, 184, 250
Martinez, Anna Montoya, *248*
Martinez, Crescencio (Ta'e), 194, 229, 230–31, *248*, 249; painting, *229*
Martinez, Julian (Pho ka neh), 125, 184, 185, 186, 194, 198, *248*, *248*, 249, 251, 252–54, *253*, 288, 290; painting, *292*; pottery, *184*
Martinez, Maria, 18, 85, 125, 146, 154, 184, 185–87, 198, 199, 245, 248, 249, *250*, 250–51, 252, 253, 296; pottery, *184–86*
Martinez, Richard, 254
Masks, 301; Cherokee, 128, *130*, 164; Eskimo, 166; Iroquois, 31, 88, 128, 164, *167*, 308; Key Marco, *161*; Navajo Yei, *244*; Northwest Coast, 16, 127–28, *128–29*, 133–36, *134*, 147; Pueblo ceremonial, 71, 244–46
Mason, Otis T., 29
Materials, 68, 78, 80–81, 82, 83–84, 87, 178, 225
Matisse, Henri, 18, 239, 258, 260, 268, 270; painting, *270*
Mato-tope (Four Bears), 57, 131
Maximilian, Prince of Wied Neuwied, 57, 58, 97, 98, 146–47
Maxwell Museum of Anthropology, Albuquerque, 198
Mayo, Captain Pete, 210, 211, 212
Mayo, Sarah Jim, 17, 203, 210–12, *211*, 213, 215, 218; baskets, *211*, *213*

Medicine Flower, Grace, 197
Medina, Juan B., 194
Metalwork, *24*, 66, 67, 90, 124, *146*. *See also* Silversmithing
Mexican influences, 33, 59, 60, 83, 110, *111*, 163
Micmac pipe bowls, *73*, 76
Midewiwin cult, 79, 90, 309
Mills, C. Wright, 171
Mimbres pottery, 84, 85, 144, 309
Minetarce, 147
Mirabel, Vincente, 194
Miró, Joan, 272
Mississippian culture, 162, 309; ceramic vessel, *158*; shell gorgets, *36*, *123*, 308; stone artifacts, *24–25*, *36*, 72, *72–73*, 124, 162, *162*, 163
Mitchell, Stanley, 194
Miwok, 220*n*; basketry, 207, 212
Moccasins, 96–97, *97–98*, 103
Modernism, 18, 224–25, 234–42, 258, 262–76, 278, 281, 304; four styles of, and Indian art, 268–75; and individualism, 172, 197–202. *See also* Contemporary art
Mohawk: painting, *43*, 279; wood carving, *165*
Mohawk Headdress (Danay), *43*, 294
Moki blanket, *112*
Mondrian, Piet, 260
Monitor pipes, 73, *123*, 124, 309
Mono Lake Paiute, 212, 214–15
Montoya, Florentino and Martina, 248
Montoya, Sotero, 254
Mooney, James, 59, 60–62, 294
Moonwalker (artist), 302
Moore, Henry, sculpture, *263*
Moore, J. B., 83–84
Mootzka, Waldo, 233, 279, 303; painting, *192*
Mopope, Stephen, 190, 309
Morris, Earl, 182
Morrison, George, 155, 158, 240, 241, 268, 294; painting, *277*; sculpture, *155*
Moses, Kivetoruk, painting, *236*
Motherwell, Robert, 275
Mound Builders, 72, 162, 309. *See also* Adena culture; Hopewell culture; Mississippian culture
Mound City, Ohio, 72
Munch, Edvard, 235, 267
Museum of Modern Art, New York, 237, 296, 304
Museum of New Mexico, Santa Fe, 84
Music, 127, 137–39

Muskogee (Oklahoma) Public Library, 48, 51, 61
Muslin paintings, 15, *49*, 51–53, 59, 60, 61, *61*, 103, 227, 276, 297

Naha, Helen, 288
Nailor, Gerald, 194; painting, *193*
Nakwakhdakw tribe, 129
Namingha, Dan, 268, 275, 276, 288, 289; painting, *262*
Nampeyo (and family), 125, 143, 154, 180, 182–85, 196, 198, 247, 288, 290; pottery, *154*, *180–83*
Nampeyo, Anna, 182, *250*
Nampeyo, Dextra Quotskuyva, 247, 288
Nampeyo, Fannie, 125, 181, 183
Nampeyo, Iris, ceramic jar by, *288*
Naranjo, Michael, 158
Naskapi, 31
Native American Church, 33, 79, 80, 90–91, 100–101, 257, 309
Navajo, 13, 31, 33, 82–83, 139, 237, 243, 246, 251, 261, 263, 295, 303; painting, *193–94*, 194, 274, 298, 299; sand painting, 69, 84, 110, 261; textiles, 16, 33, 82–84, *106*, 107, *110–13*, 115–18, *119*, 122, 124, 149–50, *150–51*, 307, 308, 310; Yei masks, *244*; Yeis, 69, 84, 199, 243, 311
Navajo Woman Weaver (Tsinahjinnie), *194*
Navasie, Joy, 288
Neo-Expressionism, 278
Nevelson, Louise, 272
New, Lloyd Kiva, 199–201, 238
Newman, Barnett, 275
Nez Percé beadwork bag, *284*, 286
Nicholson, Grace, 206
Nieto, Frank, 268
Nolde, Emil, 235, 267
Nootka (Nuu-chah-nulth), 74, 135; basketry, *86*, 87; carving, *147*
Northeast culture area, 31, 33, 38, 79, 82. *See also* Woodlands Indians
Northwest Coast culture area, 29, 31, 33

Northwest Coast Indians, 14, 27, 31, 72, 74, 76, 79–80, 126–27, 133, 145, 146, 308; basketry, 29, *86*, 87 (*see also* Washoe); blankets, 16, *70*, 113–14, *114*, *115*, 307; carving, *31*, 69, 71, 76, 87, 124, *128–29*, *132*, 133–36, *134–37*, *147*, 149, 157, 158, 166–68, 290, 291, *291*, 299, 301; garments, 114, *116*, *120*; headdress and dance, *132*, 133–40; masks, 16, 127–28, *128–29*, 133–36, *134*, *147*; metalwork, 67, *146*, *290*; painting, 38, 41, 275; potlatch, 70, 309. *See aslo specific tribes and cultures*

Odawa, 40, 41
Oglala, 124
Ohettoint (artist), 60, 61–62
Ojibwa, 14, 40, 41, 163, 233, 280, 309; pictographic images, *54*; pipe bowl, *72*
O'Keeffe, Georgia, Bradley portrait of, *280*
Oklahoma Historical Society, Oklahoma City, 97
Oklahoma school of painting, 38, 41, 47, 92, 104, 157, 190–91, 195, *195*, 229, 258, 307
Okvik culture, 165
Omaha, 97; moccasins, 97, *97*
Oqwa Pi (painter), 248
Osage, 97; protest document, 298, *298*; roach and spreader, *101*; sashes, 94–95
Osage with Van Gogh (Cannon), 267
Oto, 14; club, *164*, 165; coat, *81*; pictographic images, *54*, *55*
Ozette, Washington, 71

Painting, 37, 38, *39–42*, 40–41, 88, 92, 109–10, 157–58, 187, 190–91, *190–97*, 194–96, *228–34*, 236, 248, 252, 256, *258–82*; hide, *30*, 31, *37*, 48, 51, *56–59*, 74, 80, *91*, *101*, *103*, 110, 114, 118, 131, 174–75, 187, *261*; kiva murals, 79, 111, 157, 190, 192, 268, 271; muslin, 15, *49*, 51–53, 59, 60, 61, *61*, 103, 227; sand, 69, 84, 110, 261; traditional, primal aspect of, 42–44, 259–62; on wood artifacts, *32*, 71, *128–29*, *134*, 135. *See also* Contemporary art, painting; Kiowa Five; Oklahoma school of painting; Pictographic art; Santa Fe Studio style of painting

Paiute, 208; basketry, *176*, 212, 214, 215, 220*n*
Panamint basketry, 86, *86*
Pan-Indianism, 29, 104, 291–92, 309
Panofsky, Erwin, 108
Parker, Arthur, 88
Parsons, Elsie Clews, 230
Parsons, Neil, 241
Patterns of Culture (Benedict), 173
Pawnee, 97, 293; pictographic painting, 55, *55*, 57
Peabody Museum, Harvard University, 56
Pena, Tonita (Quah Ah), 190; painting, *191*
Penck, A. R., 278
Penobscot, 37
Performing arts, 127–28, 137–40, *138*. *See also* Dance
Perreault, John, 242*n*
Peters, Susan, 190
Petroglyphs (rock art), 54, *54*, 147, 224, 264, 276
Peyote cult, 33, 90–91, 100–101, 257, 259, 309; fans, *35*, 101, 309
Peyote Road Man (Sweezy), *256*, 257, 305
Philbrook Art Center, Tulsa, 158, 195–96, 237
Photorealism, 18, 266, 268, 303
Picasso, Pablo, 239, 258, 260
Pictographic art, 45, 47, *49–50*, 51–62, *54–56*, 58, 61, 103, 109–10, 175, 224, 227–28, 228, 264, 275, 276. *See also* Ledger drawings
Picuris pottery, 147
Piegan Indians, 143
Pima basketry, *176*
Pipes and pipe bowls, *36*, 72–73, 73, 76, 87, *88–89*, 99, *123*, 124, 158, 160, *162–63*, 163, 308
Pipe-tomahawks, 81–82, 309
Plains culture area, 29, 31, 33

Plains Indians, 16, 17, 37, 45–48, 72, 124, 146–47, 173–75, 178, 228–29, 311; beadwork, *34–35*, 37, 43, 66, 67, 77, 78, *81*, 95, 96, *96–98*, *121*, 128, *142*, 178–79; cross, *80*; European influences on, 93–104; headdresses, *101–2*, 128; hide painting, *91*, 92, *103*, 109–10, 114, 118, 174–75, 187; jewelry, 90–91, 99, 101; ledger drawings, 38, 45, 92, 103, 157, 187, *187–89*, 227, *227*, 305, 309; main tribes, 174; muslin painting, 49, *51–53*, 59, 60, 61, *61*; painting, 38, 41, 92, 103, *190*, *190–91*, *195–97*, 225, 228, 229, 302, 305; pictography, 38, 48, *49–50*, *51–53*, 54, *55*, *55–62*, *61*, 103, 109–10, 175, 227; riding gear, *28*, 77, 78, *83*, 100, *121*, 123, 128; shields, 27, 37, 101, *101*, 311; textiles, *81*, 94, 100, 115. *See also specific tribes and cultures*
Plato, 131*n*
Polacca, Thomas, 288
Polelonema, Otis, 194
Polikmana Katcina, *160*, 309
Pollock, Jackson, 261, 275; painting, *260*
Pomo, 310; basketry, *122*, 176, *177*, 207, 213, 302
Ponca, 97; moccasins, 97, *97–98*
Ponca-Nez Percé Industrial School, 97, 98
Ponchos, 107, 114
Pop art, 18, 200, 264, 268, 276, 278
Pope, Mrs. George, 213
Postmodernism, 18, 264, 266, 275, 276, 277–78, 281
Potlatch, 70, 309
Potter, Evelyn Lake, basket by, *122*
Pottery, 43, 68, 145–46, 153–54; Acoma, 84, *85*, 126, 147, 186; Caddoan, *156*, 158; contemporary, 154, 197–98, *286–89*, 288, *303*; Hopi, 84, 143, 147, 154, *154*, *180–83*, 182–84, 247, 288, *288–89*, 310; Mimbres, 84, *85*, 144, 309; precontact Gila, 125, *127*; Pueblo, 17–18, 31, 84, *85*, 124, 125, *125*, 126, *127*, 147–48, 153–54, *153–54*, 171, 173, 175, *180–86*, 180–87, 197–98, *245*, 247, 248–52, *249–50*, 252–53, *286–89*, 303; Ramos, *144*; stepped-terrace, *245*, 246; Zia, 74, *75*, 125, *126*, 186; Zuñi, 37, 85, 126, 147–48, 186, *245*, 246. *See also* Clay figurines
Powwow, 309; costuming, 33, 103, 104

Prairie Fire (Bosin), *196*, 197, 305
Primal art, 258–62, 275, 276
Professionalism, artists', 123–24, 145, 157, 160
Prokopiof, Bill, 158
Pueblo Green Corn Dance (Kabotie), *233*
Pueblo Indians, 13, 27, 31, 38, 71, 72, 82, 128, 173, 178, 228, 307; Cosmic mobile, *30*; individualism in tribal society, 228–31, 246–54; kivas, 14, 72, 79, 245; necklace, *79*; painting, 157, 191, *191–94*, 194–95, 229–30, *233*, 248, 252, 262, 275; pottery, 17–18, 31, 84, *85*, 124, 125, *125*, 126, *127*, 147–48, 153–54, *153–54*, 171, 173, 175, *180–86*, 180–87, 197–98, *245*, 247, 248–52, *249–50*, 252–53, *286–89*, 303; tribal secrecy, 228–31, 243–46; weaving, 31, *32*, 33, 82, 111, 112, 170. *See also specific cultures*
Pueblo Potter, The (Bunzel), 143, 148, 171
Pueblo Revolt (1680), 82, 84, 111, 182, 310

Quick-to-See Smith, Jaune, 198, 264, 268, 271, 272, 276; painting, *277*
Quillwork, 37, 66, 67, 68, *68*, 69, 74, *78*, 80, 82, 88, 115, *117*, 128, 179; Cheyenne society, 144–45, 310
Quintana, Ben, 194
Quotskuyva, Dextra. *See* Nampeyo, Dextra Quotskuyva

Ramos effigy jar, *144*
Rauschenberg, Robert, 275, 276
Redfield, Robert, 107, 108
Red Horse (artist), 227
Red Star, Kevin, 201, 266, 268, 278, 281; painting, *266*
Red Totem (Morrison), *155*
Reichard, Gladys A., 37
Reid, Bill, 127, 158, 290
Reservation individualism, 172, 175–97
Riding gear. *See* Horse gear artifacts
Rio Grande Puebloans, 230, *233*, 246; artifacts, *30*, 31, *79*, 112
Rivera, Diego, 233
Roach and spreader, *101–2*, 310
Rochester (New York) Museum and Science Center, 88
Rose and the Res Sisters (Fonseca), 284, *285*, 286
Rothko, Mark, 275
Rousseau, Henri, 271

Roybal, Alfonso (Awa Tsireh), 194, 248, *248*, 254, 303
Roybal, Juan Cruz, 125, 186, 249, *249*, 254; pottery, *125*
Roybal, Tonita Martinez, 125, 186, 249, *249*, 251, 252; pottery, *125*
Rugs, Navajo, 83–84, 110, 117–18; pictorial, 115, *119*

Sacred art, 247; commercialization of, 243–46; in conflict with individualism, 228–31, 246
Saddle, Cree, *83*
Saddle bag, Apache, *139*
Saddle blankets, 78, 79, 100, 110–11, *113*
Sanchez, Abel, 194
Sand painting, Navajo, 69, 84, 110, 261
San Ildefonso Pueblo, 18, 199, *248–50*, 248–54, 258; painting, 190, 191, *191*, 194, 229, 230, 248, 252, 292; pottery, 85, 125, *125*, 126, 146, *184–86*, 185–87, 198, 248–52, *249–50*, 252–53, 286, 287
Santa Clara Pueblo: painting, *192*; pottery, 184, 198, *245*, 247, 286
Santa Fe, New Mexico, 239, 250, 252, 263; Institute of American Indian Art, 157, 158, 199, 201–2, 235–40, 241, 258; School of American Research, 185
Santa Fe Studio style of painting, 38, 41, 92, 191, *192–94*, 194–95, *196*, 197, 224, 229, *233*, 235, 258, 307, 310
Santee Sioux, 76; bonnet, *69*
Sashes: Hopi, *32*, 170; Osage, *94–95*
Saul, Chief Terry, 195
Scholder, Fritz, 18, 158, 200, 201, 224, 238–39, 240, 241, 264, 266, 268, 276, 278, 281, 292, 294, 303; monotype, *293*; painting, *239*
School of American Research (Santa Fe), 185
Schoppert, James G., sculpture by, *272*
Scott, General Hugh, 62
Scott, Knokovtee, 291
Scottsdale, Arizona, 202, 239
Scrimshaw, 236, 310

Sculpture, 157–68; Arctic, 165–66, 272, 288, *289*, 291; contemporary, 41–42, 155, *155*, 158, 237, 241, 263, *263*, 272, 295, *300*, 301; East, 162–63; Eastern Woodlands, 22, 68, 157, 163–64, *164–65*; Northwest Coast, *128–29*, 133, 146, *147*, 157, 158, 166–68, 290, 291, *291*. *See also* Clay figurines; Ivory carving; Masks; Stone carving; Totem poles; Wood carving
Seminole, 33, 94, 226
Seneca, 14, 88; mask, *167*; painting, *42*, *264*, 270, *297*
Seneca Arts Project, 88
Sequoyah Indian School, Tahlequah, Oklahoma, 292
Serapes, Navajo, 149–50, *150–51*, 310
Serpent Mound, Ohio, 72
Settelmeyer, Fred, 216–17, *219*, 220*n*
Seven Families in Pueblo Pottery (exhibition), 198
Shawnee painting, 39, 40
Shell carvings, Mississippian gorgets, *36*, 123, 308
Shell inlay, 132, 133, *135*, 146, *147*, *291*
Sherman, William Tecumseh, 48, 53
Shields, painted hide, 27, 37, 101, *101*, 311
Shinnecock wood bowl, 22
Shoshone, 277; hide painting, *103*; Panamint basketry, 86, *86*
Sikyatki ware, 84, 154, *182*, 182–83, 185, 310
Silberman, Arthur, 192, 242*n*
Silverhorn (Haungooah), 61–62; muslin painting, 15, 48, *49–50*, 51, *61*, 122, 302
Silversmithing, 33, 35, 79, 80, 88, 90, *290*
Sioux, 174, 178, 309, 311; beadwork, 78, 97, *142*, 178–79; buffalo effigies, 26; dress, *142*, 143, 178–79; painting, 39, 40, *197*, 222, 228, 264, *265*; pictographic painting, 58, *58–59*, *91*, 110; quillwork bonnet, *69*; saddle blankets, 78, 79, 100
Sloan, John, 191
Smith, Leon Polk, 240
Smithport ware, *156*, 310
Snodgrass, Jeanne, 237
Snooks, Tillie, 210, 216
Soapstone carving, 166, 289
Southeast culture area, 29, 31, 33, 38; wood carving, 71, *161*, 162
Southern Cult. *See* Mississippian culture

Southwest culture area, 31, 33, 71, 72, 126, 173, 263–64, 300; basketry, 31, 71; contemporary art centers of, 239–40; controversies of individualism in tribal society, 228–31, 246–54; painting, 38, 41, 92, 157, 190–91, *191–94*, 194–95, *229–30*, 264, 266, 268, *271*, *274*, *275*; pottery, 43, 84, *85*, 124, 125, *125*, 126, *127*, 144, 145–46, 147–48, *153–54*, 180–86, 197–98, *245*, 247, 248–52, *249–50*, *252–253*, 286–87; weaving, 31, *32*, 33, 55, 69, 82–84, *106*, *107*, 110–13, *110–13*, 115–18, *119*, 124, 149–50, *150–51*, *170*. *See also* Pueblo Indians; *specific tribes and cultures*

Speaker's staff, *31*, 310

Speck, Frank G., 37

Spirit Guide/Healer (Longfish), *264*, 297

Spiro Mounds, 291, 310; artifacts, *24–25*, *36*, 72, *123*, 124. *See also* Mississippian culture

Spybuck, Earnest, 40, 257; painting, *39*

Standing-Soldier, Andrew, 40; painting, *39*

Stanley, John Mix, 58

Steiner, G. A., 208

Still, Clyfford, 275

Stockbridge, 94

Stone, Willard, 158

Stone artifacts, 72–73; Mississippian (Spiro Mounds), *24–25*, *36*, 72, 124, *162*

Stone carving, *36*, 72–73, 76, 82, 84, 87, *123*, 124, *137*, *147*, 157, 160, 162, *162–63*, 166–67, *289*

Strickland, Rennard, 196

Stroud, Virginia, 264, 302

Subarctic, 31, 33, 74, 79, 82

Sun Boy (Kiowa Chief), *47*, 48, *49–50*, 51–53, 61, 62

Sun Dance, 45–47, 51–53, 61, 101, 103, 155, 173, 310

Surrealism, 18, 109, 262, 268, 272, 275, 276, 303

Sweezy, Carl, 257, 294, 303, 305; painting, *256*

Symbolism, 268, 276

Synthetic Cubism, 268

Tafoya, Serafina and Geronimo, 198

Tahoma, Quincy, 194, 231, 260, 262, 263; painting, *194*

Tall Visitor at Tocito (Cohoe), 298, 299

Taos Lady (Haozous), 294, *295*

Tattooing, 31

Taylor, Frank H., 227

Technology, 79–80, 82, 86–87

Telles, Lucy, 176

Tesuque pottery, 181–82, 251; figurines, 160, 182, *224*, 310

Tewa Puebloans, 182, 245

Textiles, 16, 71, 110–17, 139, 149–50; beaded, *44*, *81*, *95*, *116*, *117*, *121*; Hopi, *32*, *112*, *170*; marks of weavers, *170*; Navajo, 16, 33, 82–84, *106*, *107*, 110–13, *110–13*, 115–18, *119*, 149–50, *150–51*, 307, 308, 310; Northwest Coast, *70*, 113–14, *114*, *115*, *116*, 118, *120*; Osage sashes, *94–95*; painted, *15*, *31*. *See also* Blankets; Muslin paintings; Weaving

Throwing sticks, 74, 307

Tiger, Jerome, 226, 305

Tipi painting, 56, 59, 60, 62, 174, 310

Tlásulá ceremony, 129, 136, 137, 140*n*, 310

Tlingit, 74, 137; blankets, *70*, *114*; dagger, *146*; headdresses, 136, 137; leggings, *117*; tunic, *120*; wood carving, *31*, *135*, 167, 272

Tocito Waits for Boarding School Bus (Cohoe), 298, 299

Toggle harpoon, 74, 310

Toledo, José Rey, 194

Tom, Leanna, 176

Tonawanda Reservation, 88

Tonkeuh (artist), 60, 61

Totem poles, 69, 80, 88, 133, 155, 166, 168, 310–11

Traditional Indian art, 42–44, 65–92, 223, 224, 225; change in, 65–67, 258, 294; decline, 234–35; definitions, 67–68, 87–88, 92; and design, 68–69, 82–84, 86, 179, 181–83; meaning, 33–37, 68–69; as primal art, 258–61; reservation art, 178–96

Training in art, 124–27, 143

Trans-Mississippi and International Exposition (Omaha, 1898), 60

Tsadeltah (artist), 60

Tsatoka, Monroe, 190, 309

Tsimshian, 137, 167; amulet, *136*; headdresses, 136

Tsinahjinnie, Andrew, 194; painting, *194*

Tularosa ware, *153*, 153–54, 311

Tulsa, Oklahoma, 239. *See also* Philbrook Art Center

Tuscarora, 40, 264, 297

University of Arizona, Tucson, 201, 235

University of New Mexico, Albuquerque, 198

University of Oklahoma, Norman, 157, 190, 195

U.S. Department of Interior, Indian Arts and Crafts Board, 103, 300

U.S. National Museum, 29

Ute, 110, 251

Van Gogh, Vincent, 267

Velarde, Pablita, 194; painting, *192*

Vicente, Esteban, 276

Victory Dance (Howe), *194*, 197

Vigil, Romando (Tse-Ye-Mu), 190, 194, 253; painting, *191*

Vincent, Zacharie, 40; paintings, *40–41*

Vivas, Eliseo, 107

Wadhams, Lloyd, bracelet by, *290*

Wakashan, 76, 135

Walla Walla, 14

Walrus tusk carvings, *88–91*, 165

Wands: Hopi, *32*; Mississippian, *24*

Warburg, Aby, 108

Warhol, Andy, works by, *235*

Washakie, 103; hide painting, *103*

Washoe, 210, 219, 220*n*; basketry, 17, 151–52, *152*, 176, 203–4, *204–6*, 206–19, *213–15*, *218*, 220*n*, 308

Wa Wa Chaw, Princess, works by, *235*

Weaving, 33, 69; Navajo, 33, 82–84, *106*, *107*, 110–13, *110–13*, 115–18, *119*, 124, 149–50, *150–51*, 307, 308, 310; Northwest Coast, *70*, 113–14, *114*, *115*, 118, *120*; Pueblo, 31, *32*, 33, 82, 111, *112*, *170*; weaver's mark, *170*

Wedgeweave, 110, 111, *111*, 115, 311

West, Richard, 158, 195, 233, 301, 303; painting, *195*

Weygold, Samuel, 147

White, Randy Lee, 198, 228, 264, 302; paintings, *228*, *265*

White Bear (Kutcahonauû), 242*n*

Whitehorse, Emmi, 264, 271; painting, *274*

Wikchumni Yokuts basket, *71*

Wilson, Lyle, drawing by, *291*

Wilson (Woodrow) gift basket, 210–12, *211*, 218

Winnebago, 40, 301

Wolfe, Tom, 200

Wolff, Janet, 172

Wood carving, 71, 88, *132*, 133–35, *300*, 301; Arctic, 165–66; Cherokee booger masks, *130*, 164; Eastern Woodlands, 22, 68, 164, *164–65*; Hopi Katcinas, *160*, 161–62; Iroquois masks, 31, 88, 164, *167*; Makah, 71; Mound Builders, 162; Northwest Coast, *31*, 69, 71, *132*, 133–36, *134–35*, *149*, 167–68, *291*, *291*; Northwest Coast masks, *128–29*, *134*, *147*; Shinnecock bowl, *22*; Sioux or Cheyenne buffalo effigies, *26*; Southeast, 71, *161*; Southwest, 71; Tlingit, *31*, *135*, 167, *272*; totem poles, 69, 88, 133

Woodlands Indians, 22, 74, 82, 157, 305, 307, 309, 311; carving, *22*, 68, 157, 164, *164–65*; Southeastern, sash, *94*, *95*

Wo Peen (painter), 248

World's Columbian Exposition (Chicago, 1893), 29

Worringer, Wilhelm, 260

WPA (Works Projects Administration), 88, 190

Wright, Frank Lloyd, 124

Wyandot, 163

Wynne, Bruce, 158

Yanktonai Sioux, 197, 223

Yavapai Apache basket, *176*

Yeis, 18, 69, 84, 199, 243, 311; masks, *244*

Yellow Feather, 57

Yokuts, 71

You Can't Rollerskate in a Buffalo Herd (Longfish), *264*, 297, *297*

Zia, 229; pottery, 74, *75*, *125*, 126, 186

Zotom (artist), 60–61, 187, 227

Zuñi, 56, 112, 230, 247; Katcinas, 244, 246; pottery, 37, *85*, 126, 147–48, 186, *245*, 246; stone carving, 160

PHOTOGRAPHIC CREDITS

Figure 139 photograph by S. Autrum-Mulzer; 211 by Jeff Berry; 190 by Edward Curtis; 221 by Wyatt Davis; 69, 71, 259 by Mark Haines; 126 by Fritz Handl; diagram in figure 34 by Carol Haralson; 255 by Jerry Jacka; 241 by Robert E. Mates; 218, 220 by T. Harmon Parkhurst; 197, 204, 206–11, 250, 252, 253 by E. G. Schempf; 270 by Steven Young.

    Pictographic images in figures 35–41 redrawn by Gloria Young after Mallery 1890: 36f and 39, p. 206; 38, p. 576; after Mallery 1893: 35a and b, p. 704, 35c, pl. LII; 35d, p. 120; 35e, p. 757; after Ewers 1939: 36a–c, pl. 16; 36d, pl. 23; 36e, pl. 14b; 37a–c, pl. 15; 40, pls. 15, 16; after Mooney 1898: 41a, p. 284; 41b, p. 285.

ILLUSTRATION CREDITS

Figure 25 photograph courtesy of the Museum of the American Indian, Heye Foundation, New York; 27 courtesy of Musée du Québec; 29 courtesy of New York State Library, Albany, New York; 32 courtesy of U.S. Army Field Artillery and Fort Sill Museum, Fort Sill, Oklahoma; 59 courtesy of Denver Art Museum, Denver, Colorado; 80 courtesy of Linden-Stuttgart Museum, Stuttgart, West Germany; 121 (two photographs) courtesy of Museum für Völkerkunde, Hamburg, West Germany; 126 and 127 courtesy of Museum für Völkerkunde, Vienna, Austria; 138 courtesy of Museum für Völkerkunde, Munich, West Germany; 139 courtesy of the University Museum, University of Pennsylvania, Philadelphia; 162 courtesy of the State Museum, Oklahoma Historical Society, Oklahoma City; 182 courtesy of the Southwest Museum, Los Angeles, California; 183 courtesy of the Nevada State Museum, Carson City, Nevada; 184 by permission of the Huntington Library, San Marino, California, Grace Nicholson Collection; 185 courtesy of the Alpine County Historical Society, California; 186 courtesy of the University Museum, University of Pennsylvania, Philadelphia; 187 courtesy of Muriel Elges; 189 courtesy of the National Anthropological Archives, no. 79-4659, Smithsonian Institution, Washington, D.C.; 190 courtesy of the Vancouver Art Gallery; 191 courtesy of Margie Flores; 192 courtesy of California Department of State Parks and Recreation; 193 courtesy of Fred Settelmeyer; 199 courtesy of Elaine Horwich Gallery, Santa Fe, New Mexico; 212 courtesy of the Oklahoma Museum of Art, Oklahoma City; 216–21 courtesy of the Museum of New Mexico, Santa Fe (respective negative numbers 10289, 3742, 4032, 22957, 45979, 30932); 222 courtesy of the Native American Painting Reference Library, Oklahoma City; 223 courtesy of the Museum of Modern Art, New York; 227 courtesy of Art Gallery of Ontario, Toronto; 231 courtesy of the Native American Painting Reference Library, Oklahoma City; 236 courtesy of the Museum of Modern Art, New York; 238, 239 courtesy of Sacred Circles Gallery, Seattle, Washington; 241 courtesy of the Solomon R. Guggenheim Museum, New York; 245 courtesy of Joan Cawley; 272 courtesy of the Oklahoma Publishing Company, from the August 12, 1984 issue of *The Daily Oklahoman*, copyright 1984. All photographs reproduced by permission.